INFLATION AND WAGE BEHAVIOUR IN EUROPE

CONTENTS

Contributors

GIUSEPPE TULLIO, University of Brescia

ALFRED STEINHERR, European Investment Bank

HERBERT BUSCHER, Zentrum für Europäische Wirtschaftsforschung, Mannheim

PATRICK ARTUS, Caisse des Dépôts et Consignations, Paris

RAOUL SALOMON, Caisse des Dépôts et Consignations, Paris

MICHAEL J. ARTIS, University of Manchester, European University Institute, and CEPR

ZENON G. KONTOLEMIS, University of Manchester

S. MICOSSI, European Commission, Brussels

L. PAPI, European Monetary Fund, Washington, DC

IGNACIO MAULEÓN, Universidad de Alicante

JOSÉ LUIS RAYMOND BARA, Universidad Autońoma de Barcelona

HENK JAGER, University of Amsterdam

PAUL DE GRAUWE, University of Leuven

GIAN MARIA MILESI-FERRETTI, International Monetary Fund

PAUL ORMEROD, University of Manchester and Henley Centre, London

EELKE DE JONG, University of Nijmegen and Tinbergen Institute, Amsterdam

GERHARD KIRCHGÄSSNER, University of St. Gallen

JÜRGEN WOLTERS, Freie Universität Berlin

ERIC DE SOUZA, College of Europe, Bruges

PAOLA GIUCCA, Banca d'Italia

Introduction

In the Maastricht Treaty, convergence of inflation rates has been made one of the necessary conditions for the start of European Monetary Union (EMU) in Europe. It is therefore of great importance to understand the mechanism underlying the processes that lead to convergence or divergence in national inflation rates. The purpose of this study is to shed light on this issue.

This book contains twelve essays that study inflation and wage behaviour in the European Monetary System (EMS), their determinants, and their implications for the credibility and sustainability of the system's exchange rate arrangements (ERM). Direct evidence on wage and price formation and on expectations of selling prices is supplemented by indirect evidence on expectations from interest rate differentials. Issues of monetary control, notably as regards the stability of money demand in the ERM area, and the monetary policy of the pivot-country of the System, Germany, are also examined.

While these studies were being completed, the ERM broke down, in 1992–3, under the blow of real exogenous shocks (German unification) and growing policy conflict between member countries: however, the root causes of the breakdown seem to lie in price rigidities and divergent price levels and inflation rates. Thus, with hindsight, these studies take up added significance for the analyses and the insights they provided on the 'real' limitations of quasi-fixed exchange rates in ensuring price convergence.

Although the focus is on the EMS period, eleven out of twelve studies also cover the 1970s, mostly with the aim of verifying the existence of breaks in the estimated price and wage equations. These breaks, if they occur, are then associated either with the increased influence of Germany on other member countries and hence increased credibility of the then prevailing exchange rate parities, significant changes in domestic economic policies, or exogenous shocks like oil shocks.

One study also deals, among other topics, with foreign influences on expectations of German selling prices (De Jong, Chapter 10), and finds evidence in favour of the hypothesis that after 1984, forecasts based on the pre-1984 regressions systematically underpredict actual expectations of German selling prices, a sign that as the EMS became more credible, even Germany was not completely immune from other members' influences. Furthermore, several studies in this volume find that between 1982 and 1985 structural breaks (or significant changes in the coefficients of German variables) occurred in the equations determining inflation, expectations of inflation, wages and interest rates in France, Italy, and Belgium, suggesting that the exchange rate bands and hence the EMS acquired a significant degree of credibility only three to six years after its inception. For the Netherlands no major breaks were found by

Jager (Chapter 6) and Artis and Omerod (Chapter 9), because it was already a credible partner of Germany in the snake agreements.

Although the above-mentioned studies have been able to identify EMS effects on inflation and wage behaviour in at least some member countries, as long as national currencies issued by a national central bank continue to exist and the exchange rate can be changed, expectations of inflation and hence inflation itself will remain higher in countries where governments have had for a long time a tendency to engenier surprise inflation in order to stimulate economic activity. This 'reputational problem' and the fact that the private sector incorporates the probability of 'surprise inflation' into its inflation expectation formation lead to differences in inflation rates across member countries, even if governments do not abuse any more of their power to stimulate economic activity. This is the first cause identified by De Grauwe (Chapter 7) to explain why inflation differentials persisted across countries from January 1987 to September 1992, a period during which there was no general realignment in the system.

The second reason identified by De Grauwe to explain persistent inflation differentials is the differential productivity growth between traded and non-traded goods sectors in members countries (Balassa, 1964). More precisely the argument is that if productivity in the traded-goods sector of one country grows faster than productivity in the traded goods sector of another country (with productivity in the non-traded-goods sectors of the two countries assumed to grow at the same rate), then if wages are equalized across sectors, inflation in the high productivity growth country will be persistently higher and its real exchange rates will appreciate. The role of this factor is considered theoretically and empirically also by Mauleon and Raymond Bara on Spain (Chapter 5) and by Micossi and Milesi-Ferretti in 'Real Exchange Rates and the Prices on non-Tradable Goods' (Chapter 8). All three authors find that this explanation for persistent inflation differentials across member countries is empirically relevant but does not explain fully the persistence.

Two additional explanations are offered in this book of inflation differentials, and their importance is verified empirically. First, an exogenous 'wage push' is found to have played a significant role in Spain especially in the second half of the 1980s (Mauleon and Raymond Bara, Chapter 5), and expansionary fiscal policy is found to have influenced significantly the prices of non-traded goods in Italy. (Micossi and Papi, Chapter 4). In fact in Italy this factor alone explains virtually all of the increased inflation divergence with Germany between 1987 and 1991.

The same cause, namely expansionary fiscal policy, contributes to explain the acceleration of inflation in Germany after the German Economic and Monetary Union of 1 July 1990 (from about 2 per cent to almost 5 per cent). As argued by Tullio, Steinherr, and Buscher (Chapter 1) increased taxation to finance the reunification was shifted forward onto higher nominal wages to a degree which was about double that estimated for the period before the reunification. Increased government expenditures (and hence domestic aggregate demand) and the large expansion in the money supply of 1990 did the rest.

Finally, the domestic money stock is found to be a significant determinant of inflation in the 1980s, particularly in Germany and in the United Kingdom. In Germany, the anchor country of the EMS, while international reserve flows were not fully sterilized, the money supply nevertheless remained relatively exogenous, whereas in other member countries the money stock tended to became more and more endogenous, particularly after exchange rates became virtually fixed (January 1987) and capital controls were abolished. The United Kingdom joined the ERM only towards the end of the period under study and only with the large band; hence the money stock maintained a higher degree of exogeneity than, say, in Belgium and the Netherlands. In the United Kingdom the money supply is found to be a significant determinant of inflation only in its narrow definition (M0, Artis and Kontolemis, Chapter 3). Money is also influencing significantly with different lags (from two to five quarters) expectations of inflation in Germany, Belgium, France, and Italy (De Jong, Chapter 10).

In sum, the book identifies several causes of inflation and persistent inflation differentials in the EMS. Among the real causes particular attention is devoted to sectoral productivity shocks, but also import price shocks, exogenous wage pushes, taxes, and government expenditures are found to be important. To the extent that shocks of the above-mentioned type hit the various economies differently inflation differentials can persist for many years. The different reputation of governments and Central Banks and the fact that national monetary policies have not always been consistent with the long-run maintenance of fixed exchange rates, have also played a considerable role.

An interesting question is what factors have governed the speed of the decay of inflation differentials in the EMS in the 1980s. Several chapters suggest that the most important one may have been the timing and intensity of the shift in preferences of policy-makers, besides the initial inflation differential and the intensity of the 1979–80 oil shock. In addition the dynamism of the enterprise sector in increasing productivity (once it became clear that the exchange rate constraint was binding) and the degree to which wages in the traded and non-traded goods sectors are linked (Mauleón and Raymond Bara, Chapter 5) played an important role. Finally, the willingness of labour unions to de-index wages has played a role in France, Italy, and Belgium.

The question of the de-indexation of wages is important in the debate on whether the EMS really made a difference. Was de-indexation decided in a 'vacuum' or was the decision influenced by the exchange rate constraint? The latter is much more likely, although formal proofs about the endogeneity of de-indexation are not offered in this volume. The at least partial endogeneity of de-indexation of wages, the sharp constraints on monetary policy, especially after January 1987, the fact that the ERM forced sharp productivity gains on the industrial sectors of some countries, the increased autonomy of central banks which was part of the EMS–EMU process, the ERM constraints on governments' fiscal policies (much more in some countries than in others), all suggest that the ERM really made a difference. Many chapters in this volume contain evidence on the increased credibility of the system as the above-mentioned policies fell more into line.

The last two chapters are on interest rate convergence (Kirchgässner and Wolters, Chapter 11) and on the instability of national money demands (Tullio, De Souza, and Giucca, Chapter 12). They suggest that the need for fuller co-ordination of monetary policy across member countries has increased in the course of the 1980s, especially in the second half, as capital controls were relaxed and financial markets grew closer together. Under the pressure of increased capital mobility, central banks succeeded for a long time in counteracting with monetary policy the shocks to the stability of nominal exchange rates within the system. However, when shocks hit some countries more persistently than others, monetary policy alone was not able to guarantee the stability of nominal exchange rates in the long run. In this sense the failure of the EMS between September 1992 (with the exit of the British pound and the Italian lira) and August 1993 (with the enlargement of the fluctuation band from ± 2.25 per cent to ± 15 per cent) has to be attributed mostly to the fact that policies other than monetary policy did not fall into line (wage policies, fiscal policy, labour market policies), and to the impossibility of solving the reputational problem analysed by De Grauwe in Chapter 7.

In addition German reunification has at first postponed a necessary realignment by eliminating one of the main problems the system had—the large German current account surplus of the late 1980s—and by hiding the worsening competitiveness of several weak currency countries behind a strong foreign trade multiplier effect (Tullio, Steinherr, and Buscher, Chapter 1). However, after the initial aggregate demand stimulus originating in Germany subsided, it laid bare the underlying disequilibria and probably magnified the exchange rate crisis. The very restrictive monetary policy stance of the Bundesbank which continued well after the recession in Germany and Europe had started, and especially the discount rate increase of July 1992 certainly did not contribute to the stability of nominal exchange rate and the survival of the EMS.

German monetary policy in the years after the reunification is critically analysed in two chapters in this volume: the one by Tullio, Steinherr, and Buscher on wage and price behaviour in Germany (Chapter 1) and the one by Tullio, De Souza, and Giucca on the stability of the ERM-wide and German demand for money before and after the fall of the Berlin Wall (Chapter 12). The latter shows that while the ERM-wide demand for money is quite stable from 1979 to 1989 provided one takes into account currency substitution with the US dollar, the German demand for M3 (the official German monetary target) is not well behaved and becomes unstable after the fall of the Berlin Wall, even if one takes into account currency substitution with the US dollar and with other ERM member currencies. The authors conclude that this result erodes at its foundation the Bundesbank policy of monetary targeting (but not its policy of inflation targeting implicit in the monetary targeting), suggesting implicitly that an ERM-wide monetary aggregate may have become much more important in recent years to the control of inflation in Europe and in Germany itself.

Returning to the role of the Bundesbank in the September 1992 foreign exchange crisis and in particular to the previous very restrictive monetary stance, there are three interpretations of its behaviour. The first is that German monetary authorities believed in good faith in the stability of the demand for M3 and therefore had to increase interest rates (or keep them high) in order to fight inflation. The second is that they were really looking for an excuse to break up the ERM in order to stop the process towards European Monetary Union. In his latest book the former Chancellor Schmidt mentions that the majority of the members of the Bundesbank Council are against the idea of EMU and of a common currency. He also has some ideas about why this is so (*Handeln für Deutschland*, Rowohlt, Reineck bei Hamburg, 1994). The third is that it wants to exclude from EMU the weak members like Italy, Spain, and the UK.

Be that as it may, increased financial market integration seems to be changing the world in which we live. Sooner or later all central banks, even those of the largest countries in Europe, will have to find a better way to co-ordinate their anti-inflation policies with their partners than has been the case since the fall of the Berlin Wall. This book suggests that the best way to do so is to form a monetary union (MU), which is considered the best institutional set-up to guarantee the fastest convergence of inflation and the lowest inflation to all members consistently with high economic growth and the most efficient allocation of resources in Europe.

As De Grauwe argues in his chapter, in a monetary union at least one major source of inflation differentials—reputational differences—disappears. He argues therefore in favour of a rapid move to MU and shows that full convergence of inflation is not a necessary prerequisite, as MU is equivalent to monetary reform and past inflation and inflationary expectations belong to the history of another regime. He concludes that the conditions laid down in the Maastricht Treaty on inflation differentials and interest rate differentials are much too strict. Even the rule on the budget deficit may be too strict, as a sharp reduction in inflationary expectations and in interest rates in higher-inflation countries, which is likely to follow from MU, would reduce the budget deficit in those countries. The Maastricht conditions are not only too strict; the Treaty requirement that only countries which have not experienced a realignment for two years qualify for MU, contributed to the severity of the crisis as it may have led to the anticipation of 'one last realignment' before 31 December 1994.

Many people in Germany are afraid of EMU; this fear is motivated by the fear that EMU will lead to more inflation. In Chapter 10 De Jong shows that expectations of German selling-prices were influenced by the EMS after 1984. In Chapter 12 Tullio, De Souza, and Giucca show that currency substitution in Germany has become increasingly important, which suggests that without co-ordination Germany may risk an increased instability of its real economy or higher inflation in the years to come.

It is difficult to believe that governments will be convinced by the above arguments and that they will water down the Maastricht conditions and move faster towards MU. The most likely outcome is a return to an ERM of the type we have known from 1983 to January 1987, that is an ERM with somewhat greater flexibility of exchange rates than we have had after January 1987. In the meantime, despite the 1992–3 exchange rate crisis and the uncertain future of MU, progress in many areas is being made: central bank autonomy is now much higher in most countries than some years back; some countries, notably Italy, may finally be learning from experience that fiscal adjustment is a prerequisite for stable exchange rates; the worst consequences for Europe of German reunification may be behind us; the internal market and progress in information technology lead to growing interrelationships of European goods, services, and financial markets and thus more and more constrain the behaviour of governments. On the other hand, inflation differentials are likely to widen again as soon as the 1992–3 exchange rate changes start exerting their delayed impact on inflation. This may be an obstacle both to a return to the ERM and to MU. Yet, fortunately most important decisions in history are most of the time not taken on the basis of the technical advice of prudent bureaucrats. There is therefore still hope that some far-sighted European governments may take the lead in making the big leap forward as Helmut Schmidt and Giscard d'Estaing did in 1978 when they created the EMS.

The essays contained in this book were written for the European Commission under a SPES project (contract CT91-0053), of which Giuseppe Tullio was the co-ordinator. This book is divided into two parts: the six chapters of Part I contain six studies on inflation and wage behaviour and the role of the EMS in individual member countries. Countries are ordered by size and Belgium and the Netherlands have been treated jointly in one paper. The six chapters of Part II analyse the behaviour of one or more variables jointly for all (or most) ERM member countries. Two chapters deal explicitly with the issue of why there was insufficient convergence, especially in the period from January 1987 to September 1992 (De Grauwe, Chapter 7 and Micossi and Milesi-Ferretti, Chapter 8); two chapters deal with EMS effects: one on wages (Artis and Omerod, Chapter 9) and the other on expectations of selling-prices (De Jong, Chapter 10); and the last two deal with the consequences of financial market integration: convergence and co-integration of interest rates (Kirchgässner and Wolters, Chapter 11) and the instability of national demand for money functions and the role of currency substitution (Tullio, De Souza, and Giucca, Chapter 12). Two meetings were held by the members of the group, one at the University of Leuven in January 1992 and one in Castel Gandolfo in October 1992 in order to co-ordinate the papers *ex ante* as much as possible and to avoid overlaps.

Brescia, November 1994

PART I

National Studies

1

German Wage and Price Inflation before and after Unification

GIUSEPPE TULLIO
ALFRED STEINHERR
HERBERT BUSCHER

INTRODUCTION

During 1991 and 1992 German monetary policy became increasingly restrictive,[1] after the massive injection of money which occurred in 1990 as a result of the German economic and monetary union (GEMU).[2] The Bundesbank justified the degree of restrictiveness of monetary policy with the argument that inflation in the West (former Federal Republic of Germany) of the country had reached unacceptable levels (close to 5 per cent in some quarters of 1991 and 1992 for consumer price inflation and over 10 per cent in 1991 for wage growth) and that interest rates had to be kept high and the DM strong to attract foreign capital to contribute to the financing of the reunification.

Understanding the causes of the acceleration of wage and price inflation in the West of Germany after the reunification is of great interest in itself and of crucial importance to be able to judge the appropriateness of German monetary policy in the years 1991–2 and beyond. If inflation is mainly caused by the overheating of the economy, linked in turn to past expansionary monetary and fiscal policy, monetary tightness is certainly more justifiable than in the case in which inflation is mainly caused by actual and expected tax increases which continue also when the recession is well under way. There exists a monetary policy tight enough to reduce inflation, say, from 5 to 2 per cent within a given time-span, but the costs in terms of lost output and unemployment are likely to be much higher if the main causes of inflation are actual and expected tax increases which continue well into the recessionary phase as in Germany in 1992–3.

This paper focuses on the consequences of GEMU for price and wage inflation in the West of Germany. We first discuss how GEMU has affected the German government's expenditures and revenues (Section 1). This discussion

We would like to thank Paul De Grauwe, Franco Spinelli, and Stefano Micossi for helpful suggestions on earlier drafts.

[1] See the chapter by Tullio, de Souza, and Giucca in this volume for a measure of the degree of restrictiveness of German monetary policy in 1991 and 1992.

[2] The Berlin Wall fell in November 1989 and GEMU entered into force on 1 July 1990.

is important to understand the size of the tax increases that occurred during 1990–2. In Section 2 we estimate wage and price equations for the period 1976–90, in which the tax variables play a prominent role. We than forecast wages and prices for the period after 1990 to check for structural breaks. Finally, in Section 3 we give a broader interpretation to our results.

1. AN OVERVIEW OF THE FIRST YEARS OF UNIFICATION

In this Section we present an overview of net transfers to the East (former German Democratic Republic) and of the tax increases necessary to finance them. Before doing so it is useful to discuss briefly the main economic developments, especially in the East, as the amount of the net transfers is closely related to the collapse of production and the rise in unemployment.

After the GEMU entered into effect, industrial production and GDP collapsed in the East, as the Eastern industry was suddenly exposed to Western competition after years of isolation. Part of the collapse occurred in the first half of 1990 in anticipation of the opening up of trade and the ensuing freedom of Eastern citizens to choose between Western and Eastern goods. The collapse was unprecedented both by comparison with developments in Central and Eastern Europe in the period 1989–92 and with the fall in German industrial production during the Great Depression of the 1930s. Industrial production in East Germany fell by 28 per cent in 1990 and a further 54 per cent in 1991 or a cumulated 67 per cent in the period 1989–91 (Table 1.1).

TABLE 1.1. *Industrial production in Central and Eastern Europe, 1989–1992* (percentage changes)

	1989	1990	1991	1992
Poland	–0.5	–24.2	–14.0	4.2
Czechoslovakia	0.8	–3.7	–23.1	–14.0
Hungary	–1.0	–9.6	–19.1	–9.8
Romania	–2.1	–19.0	–18.7	–21.8
Bulgaria	–1.1	–17.5	–27.8	–20.0
Eastern Germany	2.3	–28.1	–53.5	0.9

Sources: PlanEcon (1992) and Deutsche Bundesbank, Monthly Reports.

By comparison the fall in industrial production in Poland, Czechoslovakia, and Hungary during the same years was 'moderate' despite the fact that these countries suffered even more than East Germany from the loss of export markets in the former Soviet Union.[3] In Romania and Bulgaria industrial

[3] The fall in East German exports to the former Soviet Union was attenuated and delayed by export-financing guarantees provided for some time by the German government.

production fell in the three years from 1989 to 1991 by approximately a cumulated 40 per cent, but contraction continued in 1992 whilst it stopped in East Germany. Thus, more than anywhere else the collapse in East Germany was immediate and deep. For comparison, it is interesting to note that from its peak in 1927 to its trough in the first semester of 1932 industrial production fell in the whole of Germany by 43 per cent, substantially less than in East Germany. Furthermore the drop occurred then over a period of four and a half years rather than two years. Thus the post-unification depression in East Germany is probably unprecedented in peacetime history both as far as the size and the speed of the collapse of production is concerned.

In the course of 1991 the index of industrial production reached its trough which was maintained during 1992. Yet, unemployment continued to rise in 1992. Official unemployment rose from 10.5 per cent in 1991 to 16 per cent in 1992. These figures exclude, however, a large number of part-time workers, workers temporarily subsidized under government programmes (Arbeitsbeschaffungsmassnahmen or ABM), retraining schemes, and early retirements. Once these workers are taken into account, the rate of unemployment rose from 19.6 per cent of the labour force in the last quarter of 1990 to about 39 per cent in 1992 (Table 1.2). Thus while the official rate of unemployment may peak at about the same levels as during the Great Depression (see Table 1.2), the true unemployment rate will peak, at best, at about two and a half times the official level. Unemployment would have been still higher in the absence of a large net emigration to West Germany (110,000 in 1991 and 50,000 in 1992) and a large number of early retirements (530,000 in 1991 and 810,000 in 1992), emphasizing the unprecedented nature of the East German 1989–92 depression.[4]

Comparing the production and employment cut-backs in the ex-GDR after unification with those of any other historic period is, of course, to be qualified. The Great Depression was mainly caused by a collapse of demand whereas the problem in the ex-GDR is one of fundamental structural change. In this respect comparison with reconstruction after World War II is closer to the mark, but also not directly comparable (see below). After World War II the economy had to rebuild its capital stock but did not need to catch up with a technological gap of twenty to thirty years, and did not need to adapt to an entirely new institutional and motivational set-up. On the positive side, Marshall aid for West Germany (FRG) amounted to much less than current West German transfers to East Germany.

Because the problem in East Germany is one of complete restructuring of the economy, a crucial policy choice was about timing. It could be done rapidly or slowly. The rapid approach ('big-bang') is likely to cause more unemployment but will generate more rapidly a reformed structure. A complete welfare analysis will have to compare the amount of resources (and other welfare costs

[4] In addition the number of workers residing in East Germany but working in West Germany rose from 80,000 in 1990 to 290,000 in 1991 and 375,000 in 1992.

TABLE 1.2. *Unemployment rate in East and West Germany 1988–1992 and in Germany 1928–32* (annual averages)

	East Germany		West Germany	Germany 1928–32[b]
	Official unemployment	Total unemployment[a]		
1988	[n.a.]	[n.a.]	7.6	1928: 4.8
1989	[n.a.]	[n.a.]	6.8	1929: 5.8
1990	2.6	19.6[c]	6.2	1930: 9.7
1991	10.5	35.9	5.5	1931: 14.3
1992	16.0	39.9	6.0	1932: 17.6

[a] Includes short-time workers (appropriately weighted), workers temporarily subsidized by the Government (Arbeitsbeschaffungs-massnahmen), workers involved in retraining programmes, and early retirements.

[b] Sources: *Institut für Konjunkturforschung, Konjunkturstatistisches Handbuch* (1933), and Sommariva and Tullio (1987) p. 168.

[c] Unemployment during fourth quarter of the year.

Source: *Deutscher Bundestag* (1992).

such as the disutility from being unemployed) lost due to unemployment with the sustained inefficiencies over time of the slow approach. Although such a complete analysis is theoretically perfectly feasible, there is little hope for a meaningful empirical application. It remains therefore an open question whether a 'big-bang' approach is to be preferred in net welfare terms. At any rate, once GEMU was implemented competitive conditions changed overnight for the ex-GDR and a 'big-bang' approach became unavoidable.

In Germany several parties pleaded strongly for a 'big-bang' solution. West Germany was ready to back up this approach with its financial resources and to put the economy of the ex-GDR on the successful market-based West German model. Whilst other sovereign reforming nations had to design their new institutions, appropriate laws, a financial system, a currency—all these became available to the ex-GDR overnight. Of course, some of the institutional features of the FRG are characteristics of a mature, rich Western economy and totally inappropriate for the developing East. It is very unlikely that some Asian countries would have become tigers if they had adopted German labour laws and regulations and were operated by the German bureaucracy. In one respect, however, the approach already has paid off. In most former socialist countries restructuring and price liberalization has resulted in high inflationary bouts due to a lack of monetary control. This has not happened in Germany.

The unemployment rate in West Germany moved in the opposite direction to that of East Germany both in 1989 and 1991, despite the large increase in the West German labour force, mostly stemming from immigration from East Germany. Unemployment fell from 6.8 per cent in 1989 to 5.5 per cent in 1991

(Table 1.2), but rose again above 6 per cent in 1992.[5] The opposite development of the labour markets in the two parts of the country is even more pronounced when one looks at changes in employment. This is done in Table 1.3, which shows that employment fell in the East from 9.5 million in 1989 to an estimated 6.2 million in 1992, or by a cumulated 3.6 million in only three years. During the same period employment in the West increased from 27.6 million in 1989 to an estimated 29.5 million in 1992, or by a cumulated 2 million people (Table 1.3). The sharp rise in real wages in the East contributed significantly to the development in the Eastern labour market. Gross nominal wages in industry rose from 35 per cent of the West German level in July 1990 to about 70 per cent of the West German level by mid-1993.

TABLE 1.3. *Employment in East and West Germany 1989–1992* (thousands)

	East Germany	Change	West Germany	Change
1989	9,681	—	27,631	—
1990	8,868	–945	28,487	+856
1991	7,179	–1666	29,219	+732
1992	6,160	–1019	29,460	+241

Source: *Deutscher Bundestag* (1992).

Akerlof *et al.* (1991) calculate that immediately after the economic and monetary union only 14 conglomerates employing 8.2 per cent of the East German industrial labour force were viable. With a 50 per cent labour cost subsidy, 37 per cent of the industrial labour force would have remained employed (Table 9 in Akerlof *et al.* 1991). In order to understand the damaging and unfortunate development of real wages in the East for employment and industrial production, several factors ought to be kept in mind. First, in post-war West Germany the government generally had an attitude of no interference in wage bargaining which it largely considered to be a private matter between workers and representatives of firms.[6] This attitude of benign neglect on the part of the German government had very damaging consequences in the West of the country in 1991 and 1992, when the government did not prevent the very large nominal wage increases, especially in 1991. Secondly, wage negotiations in the East even after the fall of the wall are still not comparable to wage negotiations in a market economy, where the owners of the firms have an interest in defending profits and the value of the firm. Thirdly, labour unions from West Germany provided support to 'inexperienced' labour unions in the East and

[5] If hidden unemployment is taken into account, then West German unemployment rises to 7.6% in 1992.

[6] The Bundesbank has at times during post-war history indirectly influenced incomes policies by threatening interest rate increases if wage rounds would turn out unfavourably for inflation or by postponing interest rate reductions until after the outcome of the negotiations.

their representatives were also sitting in the board of the still state-owned enterprises. Thus they were 'bargaining' to some extent with themselves. Fourthly, labour unions in the West had and still have a vested interest in a rapid increase in wages in the East in order to protect real wages and employment in the West.

The same vested interest can be attributed to West German industry whose prime objective is and was the conquest of maximum market shares in East Germany. The Federal government's benign neglect in East German wage matters can in turn be explained by the political pressure for wage convergence in the East and its desire to protect the interests of West German industry. This attitude seems to us totally unjustified given the fact that the Federal government is formally the owner of the enterprises to be sold and thus should also be trying to keep its value as high as possible. And since no true wage bargaining could take place in a non-market economy, the government should have intervened directly in such circumstances. By announcing the goal of income convergence to be realized as soon as possible the government, in fact, raised expectations and provided strong signalling for convergence.

To be sure many in the government and outside thought that a high wage differential between the East and West of Germany would have caused a massive outflow of workers from the East. However, the survey conducted by Akerlof *et al.* (1991) suggests that unemployment is at least as important a factor causing emigration as a large wage-differential.[7] Furthermore it is not the actual wage differential which causes emigration, but rather the expected wage differential (over a number of years) corrected for the expected capital gains that workers in the East could have cashed in if a different privatization policy had been pursued. This different policy could have entailed some distribution of shares to all residents in the East; some, not all, because the control of privatized firms is better left to western enterprises with the necessary know-how. The free distribution or the sale at a low price of the stock of housing and land could also have induced large expected capital gains and nullified the effect on emigration of even very substantial wage differentials. These two criticisms of the policy pursued by the Federal Government in the East—too rapid wage increases and a privatization policy not favouring the formation of wealth on the part of the eastern residents—have been made by several authors.[8]

It is clear that the faster the adjustment of real wages in the East to those prevailing in the West of Germany, the larger is the total investment that is required to bring the productivity of labour of East German workers to the higher real wage. The criticism that wages were increased too fast in the East has to be judged against the planned official and private investment effort in the years to come. We shall see that the planned investment effort is substantial,

[7] This view is backed up by the empirical work of Pissarides and McMaster (1990), estimating migration as a function of wage differences or wage growth differences and unemployment.

[8] See e.g. Sinn and Sinn (1991) and Gros and Steinherr (1991). They proposed a participation of East Germans in firms to be privatized by the Treuhandanstalt to slow down wage increases.

so substantial that the chosen path of rapidly increasing wages–high investment may turn out to lead to a rapid adjustment of real GDP per capita in the East, despite its high short-run unemployment costs.

It is unlikely that high real-wage growth has major effects on private investment as convergence of real wages to western levels is at any rate expected in the medium run. By the time a new project is implemented convergence will already be substantial. If investments are motivated by low labour costs they will choose an Asian location not East Germany. The attraction of East Germany is totally different: availability of a disciplined and skilled labour force, a known and tested West German institutional framework (with all its faults), an experienced administration, and formation of a rich consumer market.

High real-wages generate high transfers through various channels. One is the increased losses of firms financed by the Treuhand; another channel is increasing unemployment that results from more firms being closed down or from increasing lay-offs; and, finally, as unemployment benefits are geared to wages, they increase automatically with wages. We look first at total transfers to East Germany made by all levels of government in 1991 and 1992, before trying to assess the volume of real investment, both public and private that has so far been flowing to the East. Then we compare the figures with net transfers and investment in the Italian Mezzogiorno, the *locus classicus* of transfer waste. Net official transfers from the West to the East of Germany amounted in 1991 to DM139 billion and in 1992 to DM180 billion. In relation to Eastern GDP these transfers represented 62 per cent in 1991 and about 65 per cent in 1992. Even taking into account that GDP in the East was depressed, these figures are astonishing. By way of comparison net official transfers from the Centre-North to the South of Italy excluding interest payment on the public debt amounted to about 31 per cent of Mezzogiorno GDP in 1988.[9] The largest part of the net transfers from the West to the East of Germany came from the Federal government.

For evaluation of the chances to raise the productivity of labour in the East to Western standards and the prospect for economic growth in the future, one should try to split the figures reported above into current transfers and investment expenditures. Government expenditures on infrastructure and subsidies to private investment amounted to DM45 billion in 1992 (about 20 per cent of Eastern GDP). The sum of subsidies and of infrastructure investment is a measure of the government's support of the investment process in the East. By way of comparison, public investment expenditures in the Italian Mezzogiorno were only 8 per cent of GDP in 1988 (this figure excludes, however, the large investments by government-controlled enterprises).

[9] However, the net imports of goods and services were substantially less: they averaged 20.8% of GDP in 1970–4 and 19% from 1975 to 1987. This means that the Mezzogiorno used part of the proceeds from government transfers to export capital to the Centre-North or to the rest of the world. In 1988 this export of capital from the proceeds of government transfers amounted to about 12% in Mezzogiorno GDP. The analysis below shows that this perverse effect is not likely to occur in East Germany.

Public and private investment in East Germany amounted to DM83 billion in 1991 (36.9 per cent of East German GDP) and DM109 billion in 1992 (39.6 per cent of GDP). In this connection it is important to note that tax breaks and investments subsidies reduced the cost of a private investment in the East by about 50 per cent. The total investment–GDP ratios in the East of Germany are higher than they have been in the Italian Mezzogiorno in the 1970s and 1980s, where they amounted to about 20 per cent towards the end of the 1980s. It is worth mentioning first that the ratio of gross fixed capital formation to GDP has been always higher in the South of Italy than in the Centre-North (but much lower than the one in the East of Germany) and second that despite the higher investment ratio in the South per capita GDP in the South has been falling behind since 1975 rather than catching up (from just over 60 per cent in 1975 to about 52 per cent in 1988). There is obviously a major problem with the quality of investment expenditures and investment done by government-controlled enterprises in the South (the non-decisiveness of economic criteria in project evaluation). Private investment is also distorted by too generous investment subsidies. In addition it may be that official investment figures contain a component which has nothing to do with real productive investment as they are blown up by payments to corrupt government and party officials and organized crime.

The Italian example is clearly not one to follow. We feel, however, that the much larger size of the investment effort which is planned for East Germany, the presence of a reliable administration, more attention to the economic rather than the political return on investment (as shown also by the different privatization policy pursued by the two countries), and little evidence in Germany of investment expenditures being used as a channel to finance parties and organized crime, allow us to look at the East German experiment with a relatively higher degree of confidence in its success.[10]

The privatization of Eastern firms by the Treuhandanstalt (THA) is ahead of schedule and it is planned that THA will end operations by 1994. In its selling policy THA has favoured job guarantees and investment commitments by the purchasers rather than selling to the highest bidder. THA has also favoured quick privatization to restructuring of the owned enterprises. Tables 1.4(a) and (b) summarize its achievements up to May 1993. THA inherited 270 conglomerates with 8,500 enterprises. These were broken up into 12,672 firms and recast as joint-stock companies owned by the THA. After two years of operation, the THA has fully privatized 4,680 of these and partly privatized 5,400; 2,350 have been liquidated; and 2,442 remain. The number of workers in THA

[10] Some other features of the 'Mezzogiorno syndrome' might only emerge at a later stage and invalidate such a rather positive assessment. In particular, the new Länder represent a formidable coalition of interest groups campaigning for redistribution. This is the prevalent cause of the Mezzogiorno problem: the more than proportional political weight of the South united in the claims for redistribution and controlling the political system and the administration. The transfer of the capital to Berlin in the heart of the former GDR may create the same problem as the transfer of the Italian capital from Turin to Rome (via Florence).

TABLE 1.4(a). *Firms privatized by the Treuhandanstalt*

No. of firms privatized	Jobs guaranteed	Investments commitments (bn DM)	No. of firms still to be privatized
Sept. 1991: 3788	719,763	55.2	10,537
Mid-June 1992: 7,613	1,170,000	138.5	4,637
Mid-May 1993: 10,080	1,500,000	173.0	2,442

TABLE 1.4(b). *Subdivision of firms purchased by foreigners by end May 1992*

	No. of firms purchased	Jobs guaranteed (thousands)	Investment commitments (bn DM)
UK	68	14.2	1.6
Switzerland	68	14.1	0.7
France	48	14.7	2.3
Austria	43	8.6	0.5
Netherlands	29	5.7	0.9
USA	20	4.8	1.5
Sweden	19	3.5	n.a.
Italy	17	4.6	0.4
Others	54	n.a.	n.a.
TOTAL	366		

Sources: Deutscher Bundestag (1991), 70, Table 11; *La Repubblica*, 20 June 1992; and *Il Sole 24 ore*, 24 June 1992.

firms has fallen from 4,2 million to 500,000. In addition, some 15,000 small retail outlets have been sold off, and 7,000 property units (including 1,085 enterprises) returned to their former owners. The THA has also produced a revenue of DM40.6 billion from sales of firms, DM173 billion of promised future investment, and guaranteed 1.5 million jobs.[11]

The THA is a technocratic agency enjoying the freedom of action of a private corporation, but with the comfort of knowing that its losses will be absorbed into the government budget deficit. With independent legal status, it is free from the political controls required of other quasi-governmental agencies in Germany. Decision-making by the THAs 4,400 employees is centralized and secretive–even exempt from review under administrative law. The THA may be challenged under civil law on grounds of discrimination or monopoly behaviour, but no such suits have yet come to court. It is thus in a unique position: it is accountable neither to the market, nor to political or legal authorities.

Up to June 1992, only 366 firms or less than 5 per cent had been sold to non-West German enterprises. The most active foreign countries have been the UK,

[11] The recent economic downturn has raised doubts about the enforceability of these investments and employment commitments. At times enforcement would simply bankrupt the promoter.

Switzerland, and France. The number of East German firms sold by the Treuhandanstalt by country of origin of the purchasing firm is reported in Table 1.4(b). In terms of jobs guaranteed and investment commitments the contribution of non-German firms is close to 5 per cent.

The investment figures reported above and the speed at which the privatization is proceeding induce us to see the future growth prospect of East Germany with some guarded optimism, provided infrastructure investment and privatization continue at the same speed for some more years and the Italian mistakes are avoided. This is despite the excessive rise in wages and the initial legal mistake to favour restitution to old owners rather than monetary compensation.[12]

Turning to the consequences of the financing effort on the West German economic situation, we look first at government finances. Table 1.5 shows the enlarged public sector deficit, including the borrowing by the special reunification funds (Fund 'Deutsche Einheit', 'Kreditabwicklungsfond', 'EPR—Sondervermögen', 'Lastenausgleichsfond'), the borrowing by the post offices,

TABLE 1.5. *The consequences of reunification on German government finances, 1989–1993* (billion DM)

	1989	1990	1991	1992
Financing requirements:				
1. German budget balance	–22.2	–91.1	–123.1	–120.0
of which				
Federal government	–15.0	–45.2	–53.2	–41.0
Western Länder	–7.6	–19.5	–19.0	–14.0
Eastern Länder	—	—	–10.8	–15.5
Western local communities	+1.7	–4.0	–5.5	–8.0
Eastern local communities	—	—	–1.4	–6.5
German Unification Fund	—	–20.0	–30.5	–24.0
Other	—	–1.3	–5.5	–11.0
2. Social security	13.5	16.5	13.0	–28.0
TOTAL (1) + (2)	–8.7	–74.6	–110.1	–148.0
3. Treuhand, Postal Services, Railways, Public Sector, Housing	—	—	–41.1	–66.5
TOTAL (1) + (2) + (3)	–8.7	–74.6	–152.2	–214.5
as a percentage of GNP	[0.4]	[3.1]	[5.8]	[7.9]
Public Debt				
Total (1) + (2)	928.9	1,053	1,170	1,318
as a percentage of GNP	[41.4]	[43.4]	[44.7]	[48.6]
TOTAL (1) + (2) + (3)	1,039.2	1,225	1,377	1,589
as a percentage of GNP	[46.2]	[50.2]	[52.3]	[58.8]

Sources: *DIW, OECD Economic Surveys, Bundesbank Monthly Reports.*

12 This error has been later partially corrected with the so-called 'Hemmnisbeseitigungsgesetz' (see Sinn and Sinn, 1991) of 15 March 1991.

railways and of the THA. The overall borrowing is DM152 billion for 1991 (5.8 per cent of GDP) and DM215 billion for 1992 (7.9 per cent). Thus the worsening in government finances is substantial with respect to 1989, when the West German general government budget deficit was less than 1 per cent of GDP. The 1991 borrowing needs of the German government were approximately equal in absolute value to the general government budget deficit of Italy. Undoubtedly, the high budget deficit to be sustained for the years to come and the Bundesbank's determination to control inflation have led to a substantial increase in real interest rates, particularly of short-term rates. This increase has probably crowded out private investments both in West and East Germany.

The direct contribution of East German demand to West German growth stemming first from DM endorsement of monetary reform and later from wage increases was very substantial especially in the second half of 1990 and the first half of 1991. However, the positive net contribution of East German demand was offset to a large extent by the negative rest of the world net contribution, as Germany was running down its huge current account surplus. Table 1.6 shows that Germany's closest neighbours have benefited from higher demand in East Germany as much as, or even more, than West Germany.

We turn now, in Section 2, to tax increases and wage and price inflation in the years 1990–2.

TABLE 1.6. *The direct benefit of German integration to the outside world: Additional exports to Germany due to unification and their contribution to GNP* (in percentages)

	% Total exports		Contribution to GNP growth of additional exports to Germany	
	1990	1991	1990	1991
Belgium-Luxembourg	3.4	7.8	1.6	4.4
Netherlands	2.9	6.8	1.2	3.3
Austria	3.1	6.4	0.6	1.6
Denmark	3.0	6.1	0.6	1.6
Italy	2.8	5.4	0.4	0.9
Spain	2.1	5.5	0.2	0.6
Portugal	1.5	4.3	0.3	1.1
Switzerland	2.0	4.0	0.5	1.1
Finland	2.0	4.0	0.3	0.8
France	1.5	3.4	0.2	0.6
Sweden	1.4	2.8	0.3	0.7
UK	1.0	2.1	0.2	0.4
Greece	1.0	n.a.	—	—
Ireland	0.8	n.a	—	—
Norway	0.0	0.0	0.0	0.0

Source: *American Express Bank Review* (1991)

2. WAGE AND PRICE DEVELOPMENTS IN THE WEST OF GERMANY

It is often argued that unification represented a major demand shock for Western Germany. This is not obvious a priori as increased demand in Eastern Germany did not fall like manna from heaven. It is the result of monetary reform and West German transfers as argued in Section 1 and hence the question whether it resulted in a positive demand shock depends on the magnitudes of several effects. First, to the extent that transfers were financed through taxes and inflation, *ceteris paribus*, disposable real income in Western Germany was reduced. Second, in the integrated markets of the Community higher East German demand should benefit all Community (and non-Community) countries. Table 1.6 in Section 1 showed indeed that the Benelux countries benefited from reunification possibly more than West German producers without carrying the burden of financing the transfers. Third, to the extent that transfers were financed by borrowing crowding out of private investment may have occurred.

Unification, if it had any effect on prices via increased demand, should have had as great an impact on Benelux inflation as on West German inflation. The increasing inflation differential moving Germany from the floor of the Community inflation league to the upper tier, must therefore be explained by other factors. Before we develop our thesis that increased inflation was caused by a structural change in wage behaviour, consisting in a significant upward shift of the degree of forward-shifting of income taxes on wages, we wish to put aside another potential candidate for explanation, namely the initial impact of the price reform in the East after unification. Table 1.7 shows that since 1989 producer prices in East German manufacturing have fallen by about one-third. Consumer prices have risen by about 20 per cent since 1990–91 mainly due to higher prices of imported goods in relation to domestic goods and due to the increase of non-traded-goods prices such as rents from their abnormal low levels. Not counting the adjustment of non-traded-goods prices, the contribution of East Germany's price freedom to overall German inflation, if anything, has been negative (barring any possible demand effects on West Germany). The latter remark concerns inflation in the whole of Germany. It is to be noted, however, that what is generally called 'the German inflation rate' is only the West German inflation rate,[13] which is the one we wish to explain (and the only one we can explain by means of regression analysis). Then, where does the increase in the West German inflation rate come from? We argue from the wage side.

A strong influence on wage inflation arose from a rather tight West German labour market (despite massive immigration from the East) and above all from

[13] e.g. see the statistical pages of *The Economist*. There the German inflation rate for the period May 1992 to May 1993 say, is indicated as 4.2 %.

TABLE 1.7. *Evolution of prices in East Germany*

	Consumer prices (1990(2)–1991(1) = 100)					Producer prices (1989 = 100)			
	Aggregate	Food	Rent	Appliances	Textiles	Aggregate	Basic materials and raw materials	Investment goods	Consumption goods
Weight	100	30	5.6	11.5	9.6	100	30.1	28.5	17.2
1990(3)	94.3	98.7	80.0	96.7	90.6	63.4	52.4	68.6	53.1
1991(3)	106.9	103.4	126.4	102.9	103.5	63.1	51.7	64.2	52.0
1992(3)	120.7	105.7	304.5	105.8	105.4	63.9	51.4	64.3	52.2

Source: *Deutscher Bundestag (1992)*, 99.

the attempt by workers and labour unions to benefit from the expected unification boom and to shift forward the increased income and excise taxes (including the ones announced to enter into effect at later dates) which had been passed through parliament in 1991 to help finance the cost of reunification. The increase in indirect taxes contributed in turn in a significant way to the acceleration of price inflation which fed on wage demands. Table 1.8 summarizes the main tax increases which hit dependent labour in one way or another and Table 1.9 computes the effect of the above tax increases on the after-tax real wage of workers. According to our calculations, in 1991, despite the large increase in nominal hourly wages of over 10 per cent, the real after-tax wage fell by 1.7 per cent and in 1992 by even more. The simple calculations of Table 1.9 show on the one hand that workers in the West strongly resisted the tax increases to pay for unification. On the other they show that the 'aggressive' policy of the labour unions in the West has certainly not succeeded in preventing a drop in the after-tax real wage of workers, as the degree of forward shifting of taxation was less than complete. We shall see below, when discussing our estimates of the wage equations for the West, that both findings will be confirmed by the more rigorous econometric analysis.

TABLE 1.8. *Main tax increases to finance the costs of unification falling fully or partly on wages*

1. On 10 Jan. 1991, unemployment insurance was increased, effective 1 April 1991, from 4.3% of wages to 6.8%; at the same time contributions to retirement insurance was reduced by 1 percentage point.
2. On 10 Jan. 1991, first steps were taken to reduce progressively income-tax relief for Berlin West and areas bordering former East Germany.
3. On 17 June 1991, an increase of value added tax was decided, from 14 to 15%, effective 1 Jan. 1993.
4. On 1 July 1991 a solidarity personal and corporate income-tax increase was implemented amounting to 7.5% of taxes normally due, limited to a one-year period from 1 July 1991 to 30 June 1992.
5. On 1 July 1991 excise taxes on gasoline, fuel oil, other sources of energy and tobacco were increased.
6. Increase in insurance tax from 7% to 10%, effective 1 July 1991.
7. Reduced benefits provided by Bundesanstalt für Arbeit, effective 1993.

It is interesting to note that German policy-makers were faced in 1991 with a major dilemma: by announcing large tax increases for 1992 and 1993 so much in advance they contributed to the stabilization of financial markets but significantly destabilized thereby labour markets. In order to gain more insight into the effects of taxes and social security contributions on wages and prices in Germany, we have estimated wage and price equations on quarterly data from 1977 to 1990.

TABLE 1.9. *Estimate of effects of direct and indirect tax increases on real purchasing power of workers in West Germany, 1991–1992*

Gross wage bill of dependent workers in West Germany[a] (1)	Percentage change (2)	Gross wage bill net of income tax[b] % change (3)	Col. (3) net of social security contribution and indirect taxes[c] % changes (4)	Col. (4) net of rationally anticipated 1993 VAT increase[d] (5)	Growth in dependent employment (6)	Consumer price inflation (7)	Real purchasing power per worker ASS.1 (4)–(6)–(7) (8)	Real purchasing power per worker ASS.2 (5)–(6)–(7) (9)
1990: 1313.9	7.5	—	—	—	—	—	—	—
1991: 1422.5	8.3	6.9	5.1	5.1	3.3	3.5	–1.7	–1.7
1992: 1502.5	5.6	3.7	3.2	2.6	1.1	4.5	–2.4	–3.0

[a] In bn DM at current prices; Source: Deutscher Bundestag (1991), 158, Table 43.
[b] Source: Deutscher Bundestag (1991), 137, Table 37 and own estimates.
[c] Based on November 1991 estimates by Deutscher Bundestag.
[d] The difference between columns (5) and (4) is due to the addition to indirect taxes raised in 1992 of anticipated VAT for 1993. See point 3 of Table 1.8.

2.1 Wage equations

Starting with the wage equation, the dependent variable chosen is the nominal gross hourly wage rate. In Table 1.10 we present the estimates of several variants of Phillips-curve equations, augmented by expected inflation or expected wage growth, by wage taxes, social security contributions, and by productivity growth. The unemployment rate or its inverse is at times replaced by nominal income growth. The sample period extends from 1977 (2) to 1990 (2). A description of the data and their sources is given in Appendix 1. We first estimated the long-run relationship and tested for co-integration by the two-step Engle–Granger procedure. This is the simplest approach to test for co-integration or long-term equilibrium. At a later stage we shall introduce short-term dynamics by estimating the augmented Phillips curve with the error-correction model. Expected inflation has been computed by using an ARMA (1,1) model and expected nominal wage growth by an AR(5) process. The fitted equations are also given in Appendix 1.

The fit of all versions of the augmented Phillips curves in Table 1.10 is very satisfactory. The coefficients of the variables all have the expected signs, are different from zero statistically, in particular the demand-pressure variable (nominal income growth), inflation, productivity of labour and the tax variables. Based on the ADF-statistic we find co-integration at the 1 per cent level for most regressions. We use five different measures of tax variables affecting workers' incomes. These are defined in Appendix 1. Social security contributions seem to be particularly important in determining wage behaviour with a degree of forward shifting of around 0.57. However, equation (4) in which we use social security separately from wage taxes turns out not to be co-integrated. For the broader definitions of tax revenues the degree of forward shifting ranges from 0.19 to 0.26, depending on the regression and the tax variable used. Thus a one per cent tax increase led on average from 1977 (2) to 1990 (2) to a reduction of the after-tax wage of between 0.74 and 0.81 per cent.

To check whether the estimated relationships are stable we extended the sample size by two years to 1992 (2) and re-estimated selected equations of Table 1.10. The results are reported in Table 1.11 and Table 1.12. A dummy variable is added to all equations of Table 1.11 to capture the unusually high wage increases that took place in 1991, when, as argued before, wage demands also reflected announced tax increases for 1992 and 1993 (see Table 1.9) and according to our hypothesis the degree of forward shifting of taxation increased substantially. From Table 1.13 it can be seen that during 1991 nominal hourly wages grew at an average rate of 10.7 per cent as compared with an average rate of 4.9 per cent for the period 1976(1) to 1990(2) or 5.2 per cent for the extended sample period. The coefficients of the dummy variable which assumes the value of 1 in the four quarters of 1991 and zero otherwise range from 5.6 to 6.3 which is close to the difference of the average growth rate of wages between the

TABLE 1.10. *OLS-estimates of the German wage equation: 1977(2)–1990(2). Dependent variable:* w (absolute t-values in parentheses)

	(1)	(2)	(3)	(4)	(5)	(6)	(7)	(8)	(9)
Constant	–0.872	–0.498	–0.582	–1.424	–0.227	0.073	0.169	–0.376	0.060
	(0.955)	(0.559)	(0.648)	(2.006)	(0.246)	(0.123)	(0.296)	(0.613)	(0.098)
$y^n(-5)$	0.425	0.408	0.377	0.194					
	(3.209)	(3.135)	(2.801)	(1.773)					
w^e	0.407	0.324	0.385	0.304	0.432				
	(2.035)	(1.601)	(1.941)	(1.972)	(1.929)				
$y^r(-5)$						0.196	0.216	0.256	0.210
						(2.490)	(2.907)	(3.368)	(2.599)
$1/U$					9.725				
					(1.998)				
Π						0.341	0.369	0.340	
						(3.229)	(3.689)	(3.321)	
Π^e									0.342
									(2.995)
λ						0.700	0.690	0.733	0.701
						(5.378)	(5.637)	(5.983)	(5.302)
$t1(-5)$	0.187				0.207			0.257	
	(2.313)				(2.434)			(4.159)	
$t2(-5)$		0.222					0.263		
		(2.793)					(4.463)		
$t3(-5)$			0.225			0.250			0.246
			(2.587)			(3.653)			(3.536)
$t^w(-5)$				0.070					
				(1.583)					
sc				0.568					
				(6.275)					
R2(adj)	0.449	0.472	0.462	0.672	0.383	0.604	0.642	0.627	0.594
DW	2.234	2.288	2.310	1.270	2.094	1.946	2.061	1.931	2.016
SEE	1.659	1.622	1.639	1.279	1.755	1.406	1.337	1.363	1.424
ADF	–6.12***	–6.52***	–6.56***	–3.19***	–5.71***	–4.55***	–5.12***	–4.69**	–4.70**

R2(adj) = coefficient of determination, adjusted for degrees of freedom; DW = Durbin-Watson statistics, SEE = standard error of regression, ADF = augmented Dickey-Fuller test value, ***(**)(*) = significant at the (1), (5), (10)-per cent level.

TABLE 1.11. *OLS-estimates of the German wage equation: 1977(2)–1992(2). Dependent variable:* w (absolute t-values in parentheses)

	(1)	(3)	(5)	(7)	(8)	(9)
Constant	–0.379	–0.083	–0.038	0.150	–0.012	0.239
	(0.450)	(0.103)	(0.044)	(0.256)	(0.019)	(0.390)
$y^n(-5)$	0.404	0.351				
	(3.158)	(2.739)				
w^e	0.302	0.279	0.388			
	(1.681)	(1.576)	(2.125)			
$y^r(-5)$				0.256	0.286	0.249
				(3.455)	(3.784)	(3.196)
Π				0.370	0.341	
				(3.580)	(3.229)	
Π^e						0.369
						(3.184)
λ				0.566	0.622	0.596
				(4.833)	(5.411)	(4.897)
$t1(-5)$	0.201		0.195		0.227	
	(2.820)		(2.612)		(3.732)	
$t2(-5)$				0.239		
				(4.004)		
$t3(-5)$		0.243				0.221
		(3.180)				(3.286)
Dummy	5.699	5.597	5.983	6.323	6.274	5.916
	(5.105)	(5.306)	(5.120)	(7.604)	(7.402)	(7.100)
$1/U$			10.310			
			(2.268)			
R2(adj)	0.625	0.612	0.567	0.706	0.696	0.687
DW	2.169	2.246	2.125	2.070	1.976	2.002
SEE	1.638	1.611	1.702	1.403	1.424	1.445
ADF	–6.05***	–6.61***	–5.96***	–5.72***	–5.33***	–5.36**

Numbering of columns/regressions as Table 1.10. The variable Dummy is equal to one for the four quarters of 1991 and zero otherwise.

whole sample period and that of the year 1991. For all equations reported in Table 1.11 we find co-integration at the 1 per cent level of significance. The estimated coefficients are close to those of Table 1.10 and the general fit of the regressions is significantly improved.

In Table 1.12 we test more rigorously our hypothesis that the degree of forward shifting of taxation has increased after 1990(2) by adding to the explanatory variables of regressions (7)–(9) of Table 1.10 the variable *ti* (for *i*=1,2,3) multiplied by *D2* where *D2* is a dummy variable which assumes the value of 1 from 1990(3) to 1992(2) and zero otherwise. The coefficient of this variable measures the increase of the degree of forward-shifting after 1990(2) and the sum of the coefficients of *ti* and *tiD2* measures the degree of forward-shifting after GEMU. We find that the degree of forward-shifting increased from the range 0.19–0.26 to the range 0.46–0.54. The other coefficients do not change much with respect to the corresponding regression of Table 1.10 and the

TABLE 1.12. *OLS-estimates of the German wage equation: 1977(2)–1992(2) (test of hypothesis of increased forward shifting after 1990(2)). Dependent variable:* w (absolute *t*-values in parentheses)

	(7)	(8)	(9)
Constant	0.22	0.29	0.39
	(0.34)	(0.41)	(0.56)
$y^r(-5)$	0.20	0.24	0.23
	(2.36)	(2.65)	(2.47)
Π	0.34	0.33	
	(2.92)	(2.71)	
Π^e			0.37
			(2.78)
λ	0.77	0.79	0.75
	(5.95)	(6.02)	(5.52)
$t1(-5)$		0.14	
		(2.03)	
$t1(-5)\cdot D2$		0.32	
		(5.14)	
$t2(-5)$	0.17		
	(2.68)		
$t2(-5)\cdot D2$	0.37		
	(5.76)		
$t3(-5)$			0.13
			(1.78)
$t3(-5)\cdot D2$			0.33
			(5.04)
R2(adj)	0.62	0.59	0.59
DW	1.72	1.64	1.63
SEE	1.59	1.65	1.66

Numbering of columns/regressions as Tables 1.10 and 1.11. The dummy variable D2 assumes the values of 0 from 1977(2) to 1990(2) and the value of 1 from 1990(3) to 1992(2).

TABLE 1.13. *Descriptive measures of German nominal wage growth*

Period	Average	Standard deviation	Maximum	Minimum
76.1–90.2	4.865	2.199	10.22	0.76
76.1–92.2	5.242	2.520	12.59	0.76
90.3–92.2	7.974	3.149	12.59	4.09
91.1–91.4	10.708	1.472	12.59	9.06

explanatory power of the regressions remains high. The more than doubling of the degree of forward-shifting of taxation after GEMU suggests a lack of solidarity with Eastern workers on the part of their Western collegues. However, the degree of forward-shifting remained substantially less than one leading to substantial reductions in the after-tax wage, despite the very large nominal wage increases of 1991.

We also analysed the short-run dynamics by estimating error-correction models (EC models) in one and two stages for the regressions of Table 1.10. Apart from the error-correction term we were, however, unable to find significant short-run effects to improve on the co-integrating equation (the results are not shown here due to lack of space).

2.2 The inflation rate

We estimate two models of the inflation rate (of consumer prices): the first is a cost-push model where prices depend on wages and import prices, the second is an inverted demand for money function (consistent with the quantity theory of money). In the first model we regress the inflation rate on all the determinants of wage growth which were found relevant in the previous section (see Table 1.10) rather than wages themselves, namely expected inflation, productivity growth, aggregate demand or unemployment, and taxes. Expected inflation can also be assumed to influence inflation via the mark-up.

In regressions (1) and (2) of Table 1.14 all variables have the expected signs and are statistically significant. In regression (2) the nominal interest rate is added as a proxy for capital costs. This is, however, a rather unsatisfactory approximation. Regression (3) is a partial adjustment version of the inverted demand for money function. The fit of this equation is excellent and so is the significance of the estimated parameters.

Again, we start by testing for co-integration before moving on to short-term dynamics. All equations are co-integrated at the 1 per cent level of significance and in none of the equations' residuals can one find significant serial correlation at the usual significance levels (see the Q-statistics). The error-correction representation of the mark-up equation gives somewhat better results than for the wage equation but is still unsatisfactory (the results are not shown here for lack of space).

In Table 1.15 the out-of-sample forecasts for the three regressions of Table 1.14 are presented for the period 1990(3) to 1992(2). On the basis of the RMSE regressions (1) and (2)—that is, the mark-up model—perform much better than regression (3), that is, the quantity theory. This supports our view that the decisive factor in explaining the acceleration of West German inflation was the wage dynamics, itself sharply influenced by the increase in taxes. Particularly for 1991 the mark-up regressions forecast much better than the quantity theory.

TABLE 1.14. *OLS-estimates of the German inflation equation: 1976(1)–1990(2). Dependent variable:* Π (absolute t-values in parentheses)

	(1)	(2)	(3)
Constant	1.581	0.616	0.163
	(3.837)	(1.060)	(0.605)
i		0.182	
		(2.343)	
Δi			0.017
			(4.472)
p^i	0.092	0.076	
	(5.630)	(4.422)	
λ	−0.162	−0.107	
	(2.892)	(2.435)	
Π^e	0.633	0.538	
	(10.04)	(7.190)	
u	−0.092	−0.119	
	(2.522)	(3.267)	
$t1$		0.057	
		(2.400)	
$t3$	0.066		
	(2.198)		
y^r			−0.166
			(4.008)
Π(−1)			0.755
			(14.03)
$m(-4)$			0.131
			(3.948)
R2(adj)	0.934	0.937	0.943
SEE	0.475	0.463	0.449
DW	1.905	1.897	1.853
Q(12)	8.79	12.97	15.20
ADF	−7.09***	−7.03***	−6.77***

TABLE 1.15. *Forecasts of the German inflation process*: 1990(3)–1992(2)*

Period	Actual	Equation (1)	Equation (2)	Equation (3)
1990.3	2.984	1.355	1.722	1.782
1990.4	3.065	2.630	2.963	1.557
1991.1	3.001	2.662	3.008	0.832
1991.2	3.499	3.338	3.534	2.276
1991.3	4.802	4.168	4.242	4.191
1991.4	4.102	5.051	4.940	5.670
1992.1	4.496	4.292	4.260	6.632
1992.2	4.797	4.391	4.331	5.754
RMSE		0.749	0.601	1.515

* Static I—period ahead forecasts.

3. CONCLUSION

This chapter has focused on the causes of the acceleration of wage and price inflation in Germany in the aftermath of the 1990 unification. We estimated in Section 2 tax-augmented Phillips curves for West Germany from the second quarter of 1977 to the second quarter of 1990, stopping just before GEMU which entered into force on 1 July. We found a co-integrated and well-behaved relationship in which the degree of forward shifting of taxation is significant and in the order of 0.20 to 0.25. By extending the sample period to the second quarter of 1992 we showed that a structural break in the degree of forward shifting occurred after GEMU as workers tried to shift forward a significantly higher fraction of tax increases and possibly also tried to take into account announced tax increases to be enacted in 1992 and 1993. We found that while the degree of forward shifting more than doubled it remained significantly less than one.

Thus our tests seem to confirm the hypothesis that the high wage growth in the West, especially in 1991, is a sign of at least a temporary breakdown of the social consensus which had been one of the pillars of post-World War II German economic policy.

We then estimated from 1976 to mid-1990 two types of inflation models: a cost-push model where prices are assumed to depend on wages, import prices, and indirect taxes and a quantity theory (inverted money-demand) equation in which taxes play no role. By performing out-of-sample forecasts up to the second quarter of 1992 we showed that the cost-push model tracks inflation much better, indicating that tax factors cannot be neglected in trying to explain the acceleration of West German inflation in 1990–2. That excess demand cannot explain alone the acceleration of inflation during the period is also witnessed by the fact that the acceleration of inflation was negligible in Belgium and the Netherlands, two countries which benefited greatly from German reunification.

The unprecedented increase in the tax burden necessary to finance the large net transfers to the East cannot be fully understood without at least a summary analysis of the major economic developments in East Germany after unification. These developments are among the causes of the economic problems of Europe in 1992–3 and of the breakdown of the EMS in 1992–3. In Section 1 therefore we discussed these developments and the size of net transfers to the East. The effort put in place by the German government is probably without precedent in history; however, as witnessed by wage developments in the West, especially in 1991, and by the structural break in the tax-augmented Phillips curve, West German wage-earners were largely unwilling to finance the government effort.

Was the 2 per cent decline in West German real GDP and the related increase in unemployment which occurred in 1993 sufficient to bend workers and labour unions and make them more willing to finance the reconstruction effort? Judging from the moderate wage demands of 1993 this seems to be the case. It remains to be seen, however, whether the resumption of growth in West Germany in 1994 and 1995 will not lead again to the kind of more aggressive wage demands which we have witnessed in 1991.

It seems to us that the breakdown of social consensus in West Germany, doubts about the final success of unification, and the acceleration of inflation may have led the Bundesbank in 1992 into an excessively restrictive stance of monetary policy. It may even have nurtured a vicious circle of low or negative economic growth, increased uncertainty about the final outcome of the experiment, high real interest rates to fight the increased uncertainty which in turn slows down further economic growth. The crux of the matter concerns the power of monetary policy to fight inflation. Monetary policy is largely impotent in fighting cost-tax push inflation, at least in the medium run; worse still, if monetary authorities attempt to fight this type of inflation, costs in terms of lost economic growth are extremely high, as shown by real economic developments in Germany in 1993 (–1.9 per cent). One has to avoid, however, blaming only the Bundesbank for the difficulties of the German situation and its consequences for the Exchange Rate Mechanism of the EMS. The initial underestimation of the costs of unification, the lack of an income policy in both parts of the country, the slow and insufficient cut in expenditures not related to unification (subsidies, social security, defence) on the part of the Federal government and the Länder, all played and still play an important role.

APPENDIX

The Data for the Wage and Price Equations

For estimation purposes we computed growth rates against the corresponding quarter of the previous year, except for the unemployment rate. By doing so, we avoid unnecessary seasonality problems which are usually present in most German time-series. The first quarter of 1975 was chosen as starting-point because from this time on the Deutsche Bundesbank changed its monetary policy from controlling free liquid bank reserves to the explicit control of central bank money. In 1989 this target was replaced by the broadly defined monetary aggregate M3. Prior to estimating the equations we constructed proxies for the unobservable variables:

w^e = expected nominal wage growth,

π^e = expected inflation rate, and

n = normal employment growth.

The latter variable, n, was computed by using a three-quarters moving average of the level of actual employment. The growth rates of this smoothed time-series was then used as data for n.

To obtain the expected inflation rate we used the fitted values of an ARMA (1,1)-model of the actual inflation rate:

$$\underset{(2.694)}{\pi^e = 2.452} + \underset{(22.76)}{0.916\pi(-1)} + \varepsilon + \underset{(2.778)}{0.356\varepsilon(-1)}$$

SEE = 0.552 DW = 2.02 Q(12) = 5.48.

(t-values in brackets; Q(12) = Box–Ljung statistics to test for serial correlation in the residuals using 12 lags)

where ε is a white-noise error term with the usual properties.

Expected nominal wage growth is represented by the fitted values of an AR(5)-process of gross nominal hourly wage growth:

$$w^e = \underset{(4.83)}{4.64} + \underset{(1.48)}{0.213w(-1)} + \underset{(1.29)}{0.188w(-2)} + \underset{(2.01)}{0.287w(-3)} - \underset{(1.53)}{0.221w(-4)} + \underset{(1.81)}{0.261w(-5)}$$

SEE = 1.90 DW = 1.91 Q(12) = 9.05

For the 'fiscal measure' or 'tax variable' as an explanatory variable different measurements were used. Clearly, in the wage equation it seems natural to use the wage tax, t^w, and the contributions to the social security system paid by employees or paid by both, employees and employers. If in addition indirect tax payments are taken into account, then an even wider tax base is obtained. Therefore, three closely related measures are used to capture the influence of tax and social security payments on wage behaviour and the inflation rate:

(1) the growth rates $t1$ of $T1 = T^w + SCL$ with T^w = wage tax and SCL = social security payments by employees;

(2) the growth rates $t2$ of $T2 = T^d + SC$ with T^d = direct taxes and SC = total payments to the social security system; and

(3) the growth rates $t3$ of $T3 = T + SC$ with T = total taxes.

In addition, we also experimented with the growth of indirect taxes (t-^{ind}), without achieving much. At a first glance (graphs not shown) all three 'fiscal variables' move closely together. With a few exceptions the growth rates of $T1$ exceed those of $T2$ and $T3$ which may partly be explained by the fact that the wage tax is the most important tax receipt of the government followed by the two indirect taxes on sales (VAT) and mineral oil. The average growth rate of $t1$ amount to 6.19 per cent p.a. whereas for $t2$ the average rate is 5.78 per cent p.a. and for $t3$ 5.64 per cent p.a.

The other variables used in Section 2 are listed below. With the exception of the unemployment rate or its inverse and the interest rate all variables are expressed in growth rates. All variables exhibit substantial serial correlation, being highest for the unemployment rate and lowest for money supply growth. None of the variables considered shows white noise behaviour.

The hypothesis of a unit root has to be rejected for direct and wage taxes at the 5 per cent level of significance whereas we do not find a unit root at the 10 per cent level of significance in the variables total taxes and social security payments and in the first of our constructed fiscal variable.

The Data (quarterly, period 1975(1)–1992(2))

Symbol	*Definition*	*Source*
U	unemployment rate	DtBb-MB
p^i	growth rates of the price index of imports (1985 = 100)	DIW-VGR
m	growth rate of the quantity of money defined as M3	DtBb-MB
n	number of employees	DIW-VGR
λ	growth rates of hourly labour productivity in DM, at constant prices (1985 = 100)	DIW-VGR
w	growth rates of hourly gross labour income, defined as gross labour income divided by (number of employees times working days in a quarter times hours worked per day)	DIW-VGR
w^e	expected nominal wage growth—see text for construction	
y^n	growth rates of nominal GNP	DIW-VGR
y^r	growth rates of real GNP at prices (1985 = 100)	DIW-VGR
i	long-term interest rate, Umlaufsrendite festverzinslicher, tarifbesteuerter Wertpapiere	DtBb-MB
π	inflation rate; growth rate of the price index of private consumption	DIW-VGR
π^e	expected inflation rate—see text for construction	
sc	growth rates of total social security payments	DIW-VGR
SCL	social security payments by employees	DIW-VGR
t^d	growth rates of direct taxes (per capita)	DIW-VGR
t^w	growth rates of wage taxes (per capita)	DIW-VGR

t^{ind}	growth rates of indirect taxes (per capita)	DIW-VGR
T	total taxes	DIW-VGR
$t1$	see text for construction	
$t2$	see text for construction	
$t3$	see text for construction	

DIW-VGR: Deutsches Institut für Wirtschaftsforschung, Berlin, Volkswirtschaftliche Gesamtrechnung (national accounting system); DtBb-MB: Deutsche Bundesbank, Monatsberichte (Monthly Reports)

REFERENCES

Abelshauser, W. (1983), *Wirtschaftsgeschichte der Bundesrepublik Deutschland* (1945–1989), Suhrkamp, Frankfurt am Main.

Akerlof, G. A., A. K. Rose, J. L. Yellen, and H. Hessenius (1991), 'East Germany in from the Cold: The Economic Aftermath of Currency Union', *Brookings Papers on Economic Activity*, 1, pp. 1–106.

American Express (1991), 'The Beneficiaries from Germany's Import Boom', *American Express Bank Review*, 1/8.

Artus, P., and M. Kaabi, (1993) 'La crédibilité des parités du SME est récente dans le cas du franc', Document d'Etude 1993–04/E, Caiśse de Dépôts et Consignations, Paris.

Barro, R. J., and X. Sala-i-Martin (1991), 'Convergence', *Journal of Political Economy*, 99 (April).

Borchardt, K. (1982), 'Die Bundesrepublik Deutschland in den sekulären Trends der wirtschaftlichen Entwicklung', in K. Borchardt: *Wachstum, Krisen; Handlungspielräume der Wirtschaftspolitik*, Studien zur Wirtschaftsgeschichte des 19. und 20. Jahrhunderts, Göttingen: 125–50.

—— (1985), 'Nach dem Wunder: über die wirtschaftliche Entwicklung der Bundesrepublik', *Merkur*, 1: 35–45.

Collins S. M., and D. Rodrik (1991), *Eastern Europe and the Soviet Union in the World Economy*, Washington, DC: Institut for International Economics.

Deutsche Bundesbank, *Monatsberichte*, various issues, Frankfurt am Main.

Deutscher Bundestag (1991, 1992), *Jahresgutachten des Sachverländigenrates* 1991–2 and 1992–3, Bonn.

Deutsches Institut für Wirtschaftsforschung, *Volkwirtschaftliche Gesamtrechnungen* (national accounting system), various issues, Berlin.

Dornbusch, R., and H. Wolf (1992), 'Economic Transition in Eastern Germany', *Brookings Papers on Economic Activity*, 1, pp. 235–72.

Eichengreen, B., and C. Wyplosz (1993), 'The Unstable EMS', *Brookings Papers on Economic Activity*, 1, pp. 51–144.

Galli, G., and M. Onado (1990), 'Dualismo territoriale e sistema finanziario', in G. Galli (ed.): *Il sistema finanziario del Mezzogiorno*, special issue of *Contributi all'analisi economica*, Banca d'Italia, Rome.

Gros, D., and A. Steinherr (1991), 'Einigkeit macht stark: the Deutsche Mark Also?', in R. O'Brien (ed.), *finance and the International Economy: American Express Review Prize Essays*, OUP.

Il Sole-24 Ore, 24 June 1992.

La Repubblica, 20 June 1992.

Micossi, S., and G. Tullio (1992), 'Squilibri di bilancio, distorsioni economiche e performance di lungo periodo dell'economia italiana', *Rivista di Politica Economica*, 82 (July), pp. 39–92.

Mondo Economico, 30 May 1992.

OECD, *Economic Surveys*, various issues, Paris.

Pissarides, C., and I. McMaster, (1990), 'Regional Migration, Wage and Unemployment: Empirical Evidence and Implications for Policy', *Oxford Economic Papers*, Octr.

PlanEcon Report (1992), *Review and Outlook*, 9 (Dec.), PlanEcon Inc., Washington D.C.

Russo, M., and G. Tullio (1988), 'Monetary Coordination within the European Monetary System: Is there a Rule', International Monetary Fund, Occasional Paper, 61, also published in F. Giavazzi, S. Micossi, and M. Miller (eds.), *The European Monetary System*, Cambridge University Press.

Sinn, G., and H.-W. Sinn (1991), *Kaltstart*, J. L. B., Mohr, Tübingen.

Sommariva, A., and G. Tullio (1987), *German Macroeconomic History, 1880–1979: A Study of the Effects of Economic Policy on Inflation, Currency Depreciation and Growth*, Macmillan, London.

Tullio, G., E. de Souza, and P. Giucca (1994), 'The Stability of the Demand for Money Function in Europe and in Germany before and after the Fall of the Berlin Wall', Ch. 12 in this volume.

2

The EMS, Credibility, and Disinflation: The French Case

PATRICK ARTUS
RAOUL SALOMON

I. SURVEY OF THEORETICAL AND EMPIRICAL RESULTS

Most of the theoretical papers dealing with the functioning of the EMS assume that it is highly asymmetrical, Germany defining independently its monetary policy and the other countries having to stabilize the exchange rate of their currency *vis-à-vis* the DM (Giavazzi and Pagano, 1988; Fratianni and Von Hagen, 1990*b*; Giovannini, 1989; Wyplosz 1988, 1989; Giavazzi and Giovannini 1986, 1987, 1989). The primary cause of the asymmetry is not precisely known; it may be the position of the currency in the fluctuation margins (Bini-Smaghi, 1992), or the size of foreign assets or debt (Artus, 1992). The asymmetrical functioning is generally assumed to have been the source of the gain in credibility of central banks. Because of the linkage to a strong currency (the DM) at least if fluctuation margins were not too wide (Lane and Rosas-Suagz, 1992), monetary authorities were constrained to intensify the fight against inflation (Rogoff, 1985; Egebo and Englander, 1992); this corresponded to a change in the attitude of households, who more and more preferred price stability to low unemployment, as is shown by the analysis of the European Community's survey of consumer opinion (Collins and Giavazzi, 1992). The gain in credibility was limited by the existence of backward-looking and not rational expectations, and by rigidities of the labour markets. However, for some authors, increasing credibility proved inefficient (disinflation can only be very slow in the EMS, whereas it can be quite sharp with flexible exchange rates permitting a sudden appreciation (De Grauwe, 1989; Giavazzi, 1989), dangerous (gaining credibility by stabilizing exchange rates implied a strong variability of interest rates, high real interest rates (Artus, 1992*a*), the imposition of capital controls because of the high degree of capital mobility (Wyplosz, 1986, 1987; Giavazzi and Giovannini, 1986, 1987b; Drifill, 1988; Kremers and Lane, 1990), or destabilizing (in the case of new members, credibility was gained whereas excessive inflation persisted, implying too low real interest rates in the countries where restrictive policies would have been required for the purpose of domestic stabilization (Giavazzi and Spaventa, 1990; Artus and Dupuy, 1990; Miller and Sutherland, 1990).

Empirical research addresses both the issues of the functionning of the

EMS and of its effectiveness in stabilizing inflation through improved credibility (see a survey of empirical results in Artis, 1990).

- There seems to be weak empirical evidence for asymmetrical functioning. Foreign exchange interventions are made only by European central banks other than the Bundesbank; the German central bank sterilizes the effects of those interventions (Mastropasqua *et al.*, 1988; Bini-Smaghi and Micossi, 1989); German prices depend only on German production and monetary policy (Herz and Roger, 1992). The level of foreign exchange reserves has an effect on interest rates in France and Italy, but not in Germany (Giovannini, 1988). However, there is a reciprocal (two-way) causality between money supply in Germany and in the other European countries (Cohen and Wyplosz, 1989; Fratianni and von Hagen, 1989, 1990*b*; Mastropasqua *et al.*, 1988; Von Hagen and Fratianni, 1990; De Grauwe, 1989*b*; Mac Donald and Taylor, 1990; Weber, 1990; Giavazzi and Giovannini, 1987, 1988*a*, 1989). In the beginning of the 1980s, German interest rates were found to cause French interest rates; this causality apparently weakens after 1987, and the reverse causality appears (Weber, 1990).
- Membership of the EMS undoubtedly contributed to reducing nominal or real exchange rate volatility (Artus, 1990; Mac Donald and Taylor, 1990; Von Hagen and Neumann, 1992), and to diminishing inflation thanks to real exchange rate appreciation (Ungerer *et al.*, 1986; Russo and Tullio, 1988; Giavazzi and Giovannini, 1988; Vinals, 1990).
- However, disinflation apparently stemmed mostly from the exchange rate policy and not from a significant change in credibility.

Econometric price equations (in the case of France and of other countries like Italy or Belgium) are most of the time found to be stable; no significant difference in parameters between equations obtained for the beginning of the 1980s and for the recent period can be exhibited (Giavazzi and Giovannini, 1988*b*; Meen, 1991; Collins, 1988; Weber, 1989, 1990, 1991*a*); the durability of the effects of inflationary shocks has not changed significantly in the case of France (Weber, 1992).

Evidence is more mixed in the case of wage equations. Egbo and Englander (1992) find no instability in those equations for France before and after 1987; the same is true for Barrell (1991) and Barrell *et al.* (1990). However, in some cases (for instance Poret, 1990), the signs of a change in the way wages are formed are obtained: German inflation is used as a predictor of inflation in other countries (Artis and Nachane, 1990; Artis and Ormerod, 1991); German inflation and wages cause wages elsewhere (Artis and Nachane, 1989), which seems to confirm that the public (trade unions) expects inflation to converge towards the German standard, and hence that credibility mechanisms are at work.

- The formation of exchange rate expectation and the perception of exchange rate risk clearly have changed during the 1980s; estimating an exchange rate band model, Weber (1991*b*) finds that the probability of realignment is close to zero after 1987; Cohen and Wyplosz (1989) show that the spread between French and German interest rates depends, in the late 1980s, on fiscal policies and not on inflation differentials. However, this disappearence of exchange rate risk between European currencies may result more from the evolution of their economic situation (decrease in inflation) than from a gain in credibility of the monetary authorities.

Artis (1992) shows that between 1979 and 1983, real interest rates and inflation were negatively correlated in EMS countries, whereas the correlation becomes positive for the 1984–9 period. The same is found for the ranking of inflation rates and real interest rates in the European countries. This seems to contradict the idea of a significant gain in credibility.

2. THE MAIN FEATURES OF THE ECONOMIC EVOLUTION IN FRANCE DURING THE 1980S

Let us start with exchange rates (Fig. 2.1). The nominal exchange rate was devalued *vis-à-vis* the DM several times in 1982–3, then again in 1986–7. During the last six years, no change in central rates has occurred, the franc has oscillated inside its fluctuation margins, being close to its upper limit (3.42 franc/DM) at the end of 1989 and 1990 and during the summer of 1992, near the central rate (3.35 franc/DM) during the summer of 1990 and in the first half of

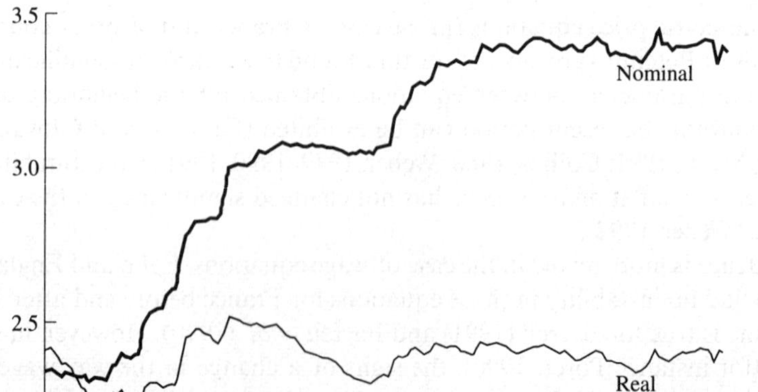

FIG. 2.1 Exchange rate franc/DM

Source: INSEE

1992. The real franc/DM exchange rate appreciated during the two first years of functioning of the EMS, then depreciated with the nominal rate in 1982–3. Between 1983 and 1985, it appreciated again, and after the change in central parity of 1986 it stabilized at a level quite close to the one observed at the beginning of 1980.

It is striking that no significant trend in the real exchange rate appears, which would indicate that the contribution of exchange rate policy to domestic disinflation was not so large.

Disinflation was, however, a key feature of the evolution. The inflation rate decreased from 13½ per cent in 1980 to 2.7 per cent in 1986 and 3.1 per cent in 1991. The inflation differential between France and Germany decreased by almost 10 p.p., from more than 7 p.p. in 1980–1 to –1½ percentage points in 1992 (Fig. 2.2). The similarity of the profiles of inflation and interest rate differentials (Fig. 2.3) is noteworthy. The interest rate spread between France and Germany reaches a maximum in 1982 (around 7 p.p.), like the inflation differential. It hits a first minimum in 1986 (slightly over 1 p.p. for short-term rates, 3 for long-term rates), then widens again in 1987; this corresponds to the last devaluation of the franc and also to a surge in inflation (see Fig. 2.2).

At the end of 1991, interest rate spreads had almost disappeared. Even if a slight positive differential remains, while inflation rates are now lower in France than in Germany, the parallelism between the evolution of prices and interest rates is clear. It is also clear that high nominal interest rates are observed during periods of turbulence on the exchange rate markets appearing like the one during the summer of 1992. Depreciating the franc implies higher rates for at least the following year.

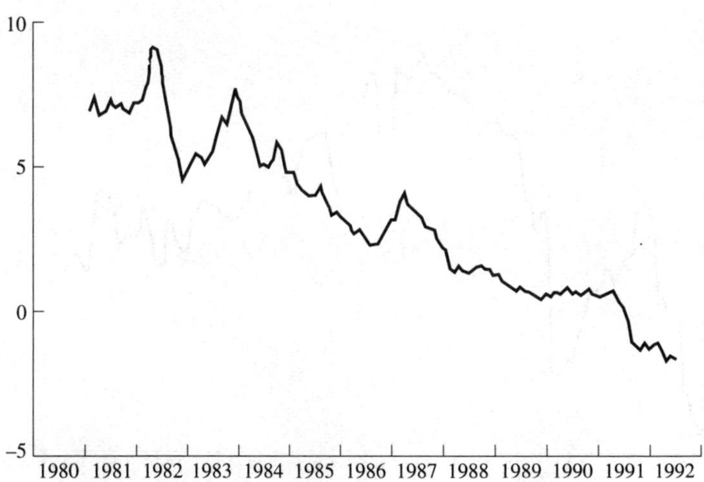

FIG. 2.2 Inflation differential between France and Germany (% year)
Sources: INSEE and DRI

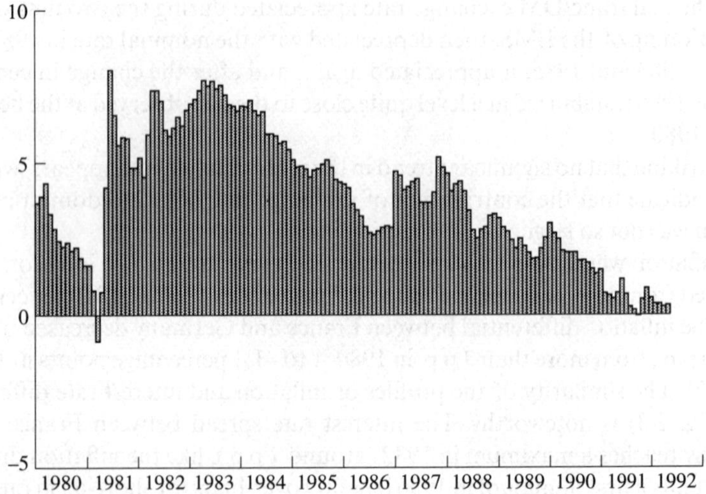

FIG. 2.3 Short-term interest rate differential between France and Germany (% year)
Sources: INSEE and DRI

A policy of exchange rate depreciation was pursued in two quite different circumstances. In 1982, a balance of payments crisis prevailed (Fig. 2.4): losses in official reserves between 1981 and 1982 exceeded 120 billion francs, and the first devaluations only strengthened the speculative movement against the franc. In 1986–7, no significant loss in official reserves occurred, with the exception of the period just before the elections. The devaluation decided by the right-wing government after the general election was aimed more at restoring

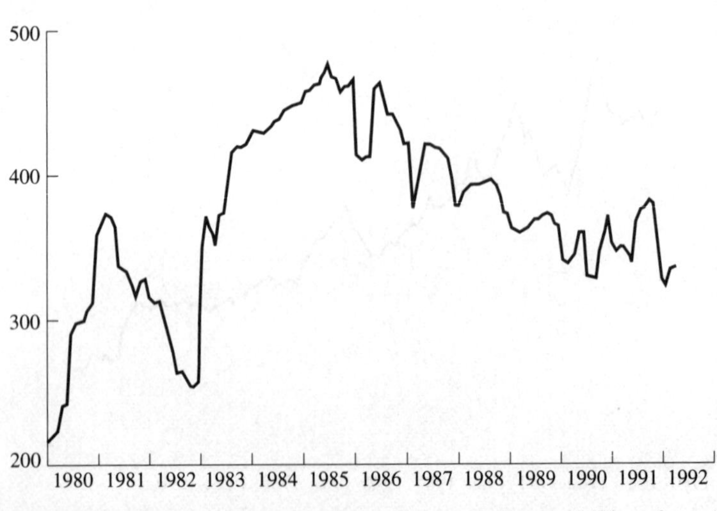

FIG. 2.4 Official foreign exchange reserves at Banque de France (billions francs)
Source: Banque de France

competitiveness, or at helping to decrease interest rates, which proved unsuccessful in the short run as seen above.

It seems unlikely that the changes in the franc–DM exchange rate had a significant influence on French inflation; the same is certainly not true for the evolution of the terms of trade. As far as the manufacturing sector is concerned, no sizeable change appears: export prices increase more than import prices from 1980 to 1985 (by about 1 per cent a year), then the terms of trade stabilize, which is certainly due mainly to disinflation. However, the picture is quite different when one considers the total of imports (Fig. 2.5): the relative price of imports drops by more than 20 per cent in one year between the second quarter of 1985 and the second quarter of 1986. The share of imports in GDP being at that time about 25 per cent, the decline in the relative import prices contributed (*ex ante*) by about 5 per cent to the reduction in domestic inflation, which was considerable. From 1986 onwards, the relative price of imports stayed almost stable. The causes of that evolution are known: between 1985 and 1987, the dollar depreciated by more than one-third *vis-à-vis* European currencies; the price of oil fell to half its previous level ($28.1 a barrel in 1985; $14.5 in 1986); and the reduction in the price of imported raw materials by France between 1985 and 1986 exceeded 20 per cent. It seems obvious that disinflation was considerably facilitated by this drastic change in the terms of trade, and it is not clear that membership of the EMS played a comparable role.

Wage policy also clearly contributed to disinflation. During the seven years (from 1983 to 1989), labour productivity grew continuously more than real wages (Fig. 2.6). That shift in the shares of labour and capital in the value added has more than offset the opposite evolution of 1981–2. During the two

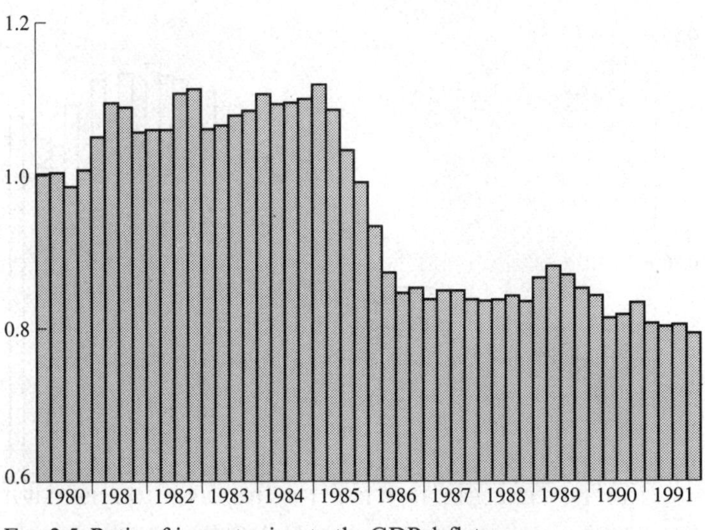

FIG. 2.5 Ratio of import prices to the GDP deflator
Source: INSEE, Quarterly National Accounts

last years (1990–1), slow growth implied a decline in productivity and the share of wages moved upwards. The tremendous improvement in the situation of firms during the 1980s appears clearly when one considers the profit ratio in the corporate sector (Fig. 2.7). Even after having slightly declined in 1990 and 1991, the ratio of gross operating surplus to value added was still at a very high level at the beginning of the 1990s. However, the profit rate showed a much sharper deterioration. This was due to the very quick increase in interest payments which started in 1989, when the decline in growth implied a surge in the borrowing requirements of the corporate sector.

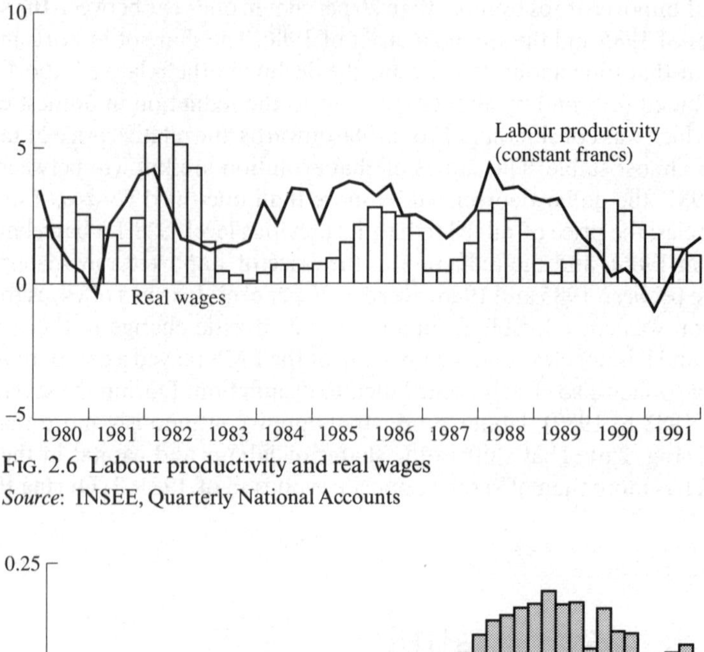

FIG. 2.6 Labour productivity and real wages
Source: INSEE, Quarterly National Accounts

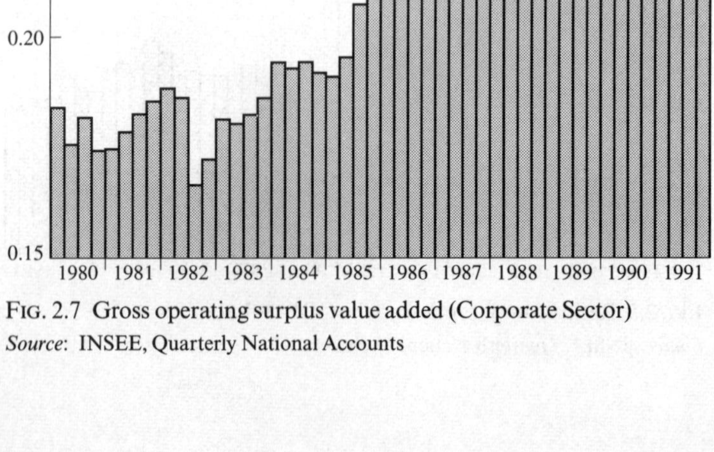

FIG. 2.7 Gross operating surplus value added (Corporate Sector)
Source: INSEE, Quarterly National Accounts

If the reduction in price increases is an important achievement of economic policies pursued in the 1980s, it is often argued that those policies had very unfavourable side-effects.

- Loss in competitiveness and insufficient investment: we have seen above that the real exchange rate (calculated with consumer prices) showed no significant long-term movement between 1980 and 1992; however, during the first half of the 1980s, export prices of industrial products increased steadily more than import prices, but by a relatively small amount (1 per cent a year). Non-price competitiveness is perhaps more important. The investment rate fell from 14 per cent in 1980 to 12 per cent in 1984, caught up steadily between 1984 and 1989 when in returned to the level of 1980, before reversing sharply during the 1990–1 recession. In fact, throughout the decade, the investment rate was such that the current balance remained almost in equilibrium (Fig. 2.8). The households' savings rate shows a very large decline (from 18 per cent in 1981 to 10 per cent in 1987 (Fig. 2.9)), partly offset by the slow increase in real wages which contributes to the progression of corporate profits after 1983 and therefore amortizes the reduction in total private savings. This decline leads to a parallel reduction in investment if current balance equilibrium has to be preserved since the public sector deficit did not change much during the 1980s. According to existing econometric evidence, the basic causes of the drop in the households' savings rate are the following: capital gains on stocks and on real estate; reduction in inflation rates; and repeated unexpected decreases in the growth rate of real income.

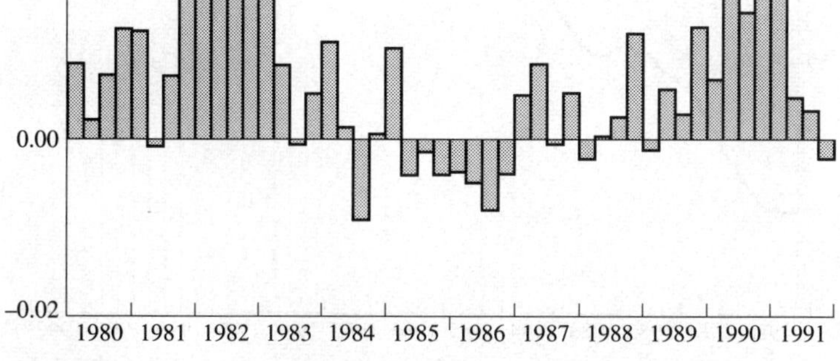

FIG. 2.8 Current account balance/GDP
Source: INSEE, Quarterly National Accounts

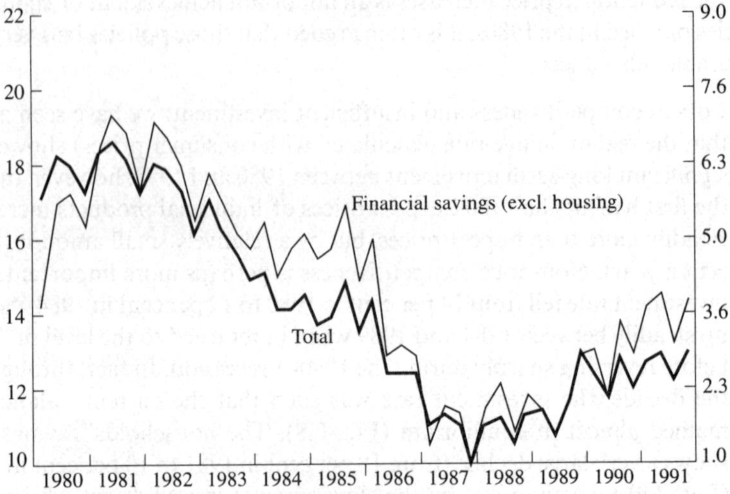

FIG. 2.9 Households' savings ratio (%)
Source: INSEE, Quarterly National Accounts

- Unemployment: registered unemployment more than doubled between 1980 and 1992 (Fig. 2.10); the average growth rate of labour productivity (2¼ per cent a year) was almost exactly equal to the average growth rate of GDP, whereas the labour force grew by more than 180,000 a year, mostly because of the increase in the participation rate of women.

To summarize, disinflation was a major achievement of economic policy in France. It certainly had external causes (depreciation of the dollar, low relative

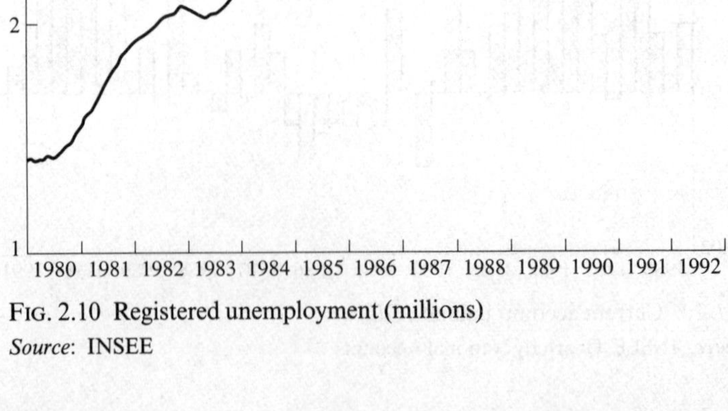

FIG. 2.10 Registered unemployment (millions)
Source: INSEE

prices for raw materials), but resulted also from a voluntary income policy. The role of the exchange rate policy is not clear. Different structural weaknesses are easily identified: a drop in the private sector savings rate; insufficient investment; and a low level of job creation. The permanently high level of real interest rate was certainly very harmful.

It is difficult, on the basis of this simple analysis of the data, to distinguish between the effects of membership of the EMS and those of traditional policies. Did improved credibility play a significant role in reducing wage inflation? Were real wages or prices in France influenced by competitiveness constraints, by exchange rate expectations; did the way interest rate spreads are formed change significantly because of EMS membership? Those various issues will be now addressed using econometric estimations for the major relevant variables.

3. PRICE, WAGE, AND INTEREST-RATE DETERMINATION IN FRANCE: AN ECONOMETRIC INVESTIGATION

Before turning to the final estimates, we briefly describe some preliminary statistical tests. We first ran unit root tests (see Table 2.1) in order to isolate non-stationary variables in each equation. We then ran co-integration tests on those variables, and checked that all the non-stationary variables appearing in each equation were actually co-integrated (Table 2.2).

The equations estimated are the following: GDP deflator, wage rate, CPI, and interest rate spread.

TABLE 2.1. *Dickey-Fuller tests* ($\Delta x = a_0 + a_1 x_{-1}$)

Dependent variable	Student *t* for coefficient a_1
Growth rate, GDP deflator	2.5
Growth rate, wage rate	1.5
Growth rate, labour productivity	8.2*
Growth rate, unit labour coast, Germany	6.5*
Growth rate, price of imported energy	4.7*
Growth rate, CPI	1.6
Growth rate, CPI, Germany	0.9
Growth rate, log of the ratio of real wages in France and Germany	2.6
Interest rate spread	1.6
Current account balance	3.5*
Inflation differential	0.8
Growth rate, FF/DM exchange rate	1.9
Short-term interest rate, Germany	0.8
EMS floor/actual exchange rate	4.2*

* hypothesis of unit root rejected.

TABLE 2.2. *Cointegration tests* ($\Delta\varepsilon = a_0 + a_1\varepsilon_{-1}$ where ε is the residual of the cointegration equation)

Variables appearing in the cointegration equation	Student t for coefficient a_1
Growth rates, GDP deflator and wage rate	4.9*
Growth rate, wage rate and CPI, France and Germany; log ratio of real wages	5.2*
Interest rate spread, inflation differential, short-term rate in Germany, growth rate exchange exchange rate	4.1*

* hypothesis of unit root rejected.

(a) Stability

We first analyse the stability of the determination of those variables by estimating simple equations in three sample periods: 1979–84 (first stage of the EMS); 1985–91 (last years of the EMS); and the full period 1979–91.

The growth rate of the GDP deflator is explained by the evolution of the wage rate and of labour productivity in France, of the unit labour cost in Germany, and of the price of imported energy (when that price increases, the GDP deflator decreases because of the slow adjustment of production prices) (Table 2.3).

The growth rate of the unit labour cost in Germany has an estimated negative coefficient, especially large for the first sample period (1979–84). This could represent the following mechanism: when labour costs increase more in France than in Germany, a depreciation of the franc is expected, which leads to an increase in producer prices. The significance of this variable disappears in recent years (1985–91), which could express the fact that firms do not expect any more in that period, that a loss in competitiveness will be compensated by a devaluation.

The equations estimated for the growth rate of the nominal wage rate (Table 2.4) are somewhat disappointing. Neither the unemployment rate in France nor the ratio of the wage in France to the wage in Germany prove to be significant. The F-test indicates that the hypothesis of stability of the coefficients in the two subperiods (1979–84 and 1985–91) is accepted. German inflation enters significantly, but its effect on wage formation in France did not apparently vary much during the 1980s. The speed of indexation has clearly changed. Wage indexation was almost instantaneous at the beginning the 1980s, but it is now lagged by at least two quarters. Domestic policy developments therefore seem to have proved more important in changing the mechanisms of wage formation in France than the evolution of the functionning of the EMS. If wage indexation on domestic inflation became partial and lagged, the spill-over effects of German inflation on wage levels seem to have remained approximately constant during the 1980s contradicting the hypothesis that increased credibility had an effect on the labour market.

TABLE 2.3. *GDP deflator (Dependent variable: quarterly growth rate of the GDP deflator (unit: %) (quarterly data))*

Sample period	Constant	Lagged dependent variable	Growth rate[a] nominal wage/head	Growth rate[a] labour productivity	Growth rate[a] unit labour costs Germany	Growth rate[a] price of imported energy	R^2	Dw	See
1979(1)–1991(3)	–0.16	0.16	0.86	–0.06	–0.20	–0.018	0.91	2.05	0.29
	(1.6)	(2.1)	(11.9)	(0.8)	(4.1)	(4.7)			
1979(1)–1984(4)	0.30	–0.03	0.98	–0.13	–0.36	–0.038	0.90	2.40	0.24
	(1.5)	(0.3)	(11.3)	(1.6)	(3.1)	(4.6)			
1985(1)–1991(3)	–0.01	0.22	0.60	–0.008	–0.10	–0.014	0.50	2.16	0.29
	(0.0)	(1.2)	(2.6)	(0.1)	(1.4)	(3.0)			

[a] unit: quarterly growth rate, %.
F-test for stability of coefficients (F6, 39): 2.39.

Table 2.4. *Wage rate (Dependent variable: nominal wage per head, quarterly growth rate, % (quarterly data))*

Sample period	Constant	Growth rate, CPI, France[a]			Growth rate[b] labour productivity (France)	Growth rate[b] CPI Germany	Relative wage[c]	Unemploy-ment rate	R^2	Dw	See
		t	*t*–1	*t*–2							
1979(1)–1991(3)	45.9	0.44	0.07	0.17	0.35	0.55	6.06	–0.02	0.90	1.14	0.35
	(1.9)	(3.9)	(0.6)	(1.7)	(9.1)	(2.7)	(1.8)	(0.2)			
1979(1)–1984(4)	47.3	0.62	0.09	0.16	0.38	0.63	6.36	0.009	0.82	2.02	0.37
	(0.9)	(3.1)	(0.4)	(0.9)	(1.5)	(1.3)	(0.9)	(0.1)			
1985(1)–1991(3)	–13.9	0.06	0.11	0.36	0.18	0.23	–1.97	–0.032	0.49	1.56	0.19
	(0.5)	(0.4)	(0.7)	(2.4)	(1.1)	(0.9)	(0.5)	(0.2)			
1979(1)–1991(3)	49.1	0.45	0.07	0.18	0.34	0.57	6.51	—	0.91	1.55	0.31
	(2.8)	(4.4)	(0.6)	(1.9)	(2.2)	(3.2)	(2.8)	—			
1979(1)–1984(4)	44.7	0.62	0.09	0.15	0.39	0.62	6.00	—	0.83	2.00	0.36
	(1.6)	(3.3)	(0.5)	(0.9)	(1.6)	(1.4)	(1.6)	—			
1985(1)–1991(3)	–14.7	0.06	0.10	0.35	0.17	0.26	–2.03	—	0.52	1.53	0.19
	(0.6)	(0.4)	(0.7)	(2.5)	(1.1)	(1.9)	(0.6)	—			
1979(1)–1991(3)	0.17	0.52	0.09	0.14	0.34	0.50	—	—	0.89	1.28	0.33
	(1.3)	(4.9)	(0.7)	(1.4)	(2.1)	(2.7)	—	—			
1979(1)–1984(4)	–0.79	0.77	0.15	0.23	0.40	0.35	—	—	0.81	1.91	0.38
	(1.8)	(4.6)	(0.8)	(1.4)	(1.6)	(0.8)	—	—			
1985(1)–1991(3)	0.54	0.07	0.09	0.39	0.16	0.29	—	—	0.53	1.55	0.73
	(3.8)	(0.5)	(0.6)	(3.3)	(1.1)	(2.1)	—	—			

[a] unit: quarterly growth rate, %.
[b] unit: average quarterly growth rate on last 4 quarters, %.
[c] ln ((nominal wage/head in Germany)/(nominal wage/head in France))
F-test for stability: equations with unemployment rate (F 8,43): 2.35; equations without unemployment rate (F 7,44): 2.32; equations without unemployment rate (F 6,45): 1, 56.

The growth rate of the consumption deflator is simply linked to the growth rate of the GDP deflator and to the growth rate of the price of total imports (Table 2.5). The estimation shows a decline in the second sub-sample period of the coefficient of import prices, probably due to the reduction in the price of oil and raw materials after 1985.

TABLE 2.5. *Growth rate of consumption deflator (%, quarterly data)*

Sample period	Constant	Growth rate GDP deflator	Growth rate import price	R^2	Dw	See
1979(1)–1991(3)	0.11	0.82	0.15	0.94	1.93	0.26
	(1.6)	(20.1)	(11.4)			
1979(1)–1984(4)	–0.04	0.87	0.17	0.84	2.17	0.28
	(0.2)	(10.5)	(10.5)			
1985(1)–1991(4)	0.34	0.55	0.11	0.39	1.72	0.24
	(2.5)	(3.7)	(4.1)			

Considering the two price equations (the producer price and the consumer price, see Tables 2.3 and 2.5), it appears clearly that the coefficient of domestic variables (the nominal wage in the first case, the GDP deflator in the second case) is smaller for the estimations done for the second subperiod (1985 to 1991) than for the first one (1979 to 1984).

This result is consistent with increased credibility of the exchange rate system (see for instance the discussion in the chapter by E. de Jong): domestic inflationary expectations, in a credible system, do not respond to an expectation of exchange rate depreciation when domestic causes of inflation increase, since the fixity of the exchange rate is credibly expected to be maintained. Credibility therefore leads to a reduction in the weight of domestic variables in the explanation of inflationary expectations and therefore of domestic prices.

The analysis of the determination of the three months interest rate spread between France and Germany shows interesting results (Table 2.6). While the effect of the current account on the interest rate differential is stable (a current account surplus by 1 per cent of GDP reduces the differential by 60 basis points), it is not the case for the effects of the other variables:

- The inflation differential has apparently a significant effect on the interest rate spread during the first years of the EMS, but not after 1985.
- A depreciation of the franc *vis-à-vis* the DM led, according to our results, to an increase in short-term interest rates in France during the first stage of the EMS but not in the more recent period; the same is true for the difference between the upper limit of the fluctuation margin and the actual franc/DM exchange rate; this difference represents the degree of tension on the parities in the EMS.
- The response of the French short-term interest rates to changes in German rates is much lower after 1985 (58 basic points for a 100 basic points increase in German rates) than before (93 basic points).

TABLE 2.6. *Interest rate differential (Dependent variable: 3 months interest rate, franc–3 months interest rate, Dmark[c] (quarterly data))*

Sample period	Constant	Current balance/ GDP (France)	Inflation[c] differential France-Germany[a]	Exchange rate f/DM	3 months interest rate[c] (Germany)	U–E[b]	R^2	Dw	See
1979(4)–1991(3)	–1.96	–63.45	0.80	2.32	–0.28	–16.23	0.58	0.99	1.16
	(0.3)	(3.2)	(4.4)	(1.5)	(1.6)	(2.4)			
1979(4)–1984(4)	–14.6	–56.57	0.94	6.65	0.07	–37.25	0.40	1.43	1.26
	(1.3)	(1.8)	(2.4)	(2.4)	(0.1)	(3.0)			
1985(1)–1991(3)	19.10	–62.69	0.12	–3.75	–0.42	–8.57			
	(3.3)	(2.7)	(0.7)	(2.4)	(3.2)	(1.6)	0.58	1.38	0.60

[a] last 12 months.
[b] U: upper limit of the exchange rate band of the EMS.
E: franc/Dmark actual exchange rate.
[c] unit: %, annual rate.
F–test for stability of coefficients (F 6,36): 4.85.

These results seem to indicate that French monetary policy became more independent in the second half of the 1980s (the link between French and German interest rates is less rigid) and that the credibility of the exchange rate policy increased considerably during the same period: more inflation or a depreciation of the franc inside the fluctuation margins did not imply an expected depreciation any more. The commitment of the French authorities to maintaining a stable parity of the franc became credible after 1985, which permitted a significant decrease in the size and volatility of exchange rate expectations.

The fact that the estimated response of short-term rates to German rates has decreased over time is somewhat puzzling, since capital mobility has increased and capital controls have been suppressed, which in theory should lead to a closer link between the interest rates in both countries. It is possible that in fact this result shows that between 1988 and 1992, the 'quality' of the German economy has deteriorated because of the effects of reunification, which permitted a decrease in the interest rate spread while the German interest rates were increasing steadily. We would therefore find the effect of a growing risk premium incorporated in German rates, and not of a growing independence of French financial markets.

The results presented above seem to indicate that (i) in the first half of the 1980s labour market equilibrium was mostly affected by domestic policies (wage increases, changes in the indexation mechanism) but not by the membership of the EMS; and (ii) effects of increased credibility appeared on the exchange rate market and in the way producer and consumer prices are determined after 1985. The expectations of depreciation of the franc respond less and less to inflation differentials or to the position of the franc in the EMS band. Price increases take less and less into account the evolution of competitiveness, signalling thus that a depreciation of the franc is no more expected to compensate for an excessive growth of production costs. The weight of domestic variables in the determination of producer or consumer prices is significantly smaller during the second sample period, indicating an increase in the credibility of the EMS and of the fixity of the exchange rate.

(b) *Changes in behaviour and in credibility: a measure using variable coefficients estimates*

We now try to confirm the results obtained above by estimating equations for the producer price, the wage rate, and the interest rate spread with variable coefficients.[1] We use a simple AR (1) representation for the coefficients which are allowed to fluctuate in time, i.e.:

$$c(t) = \alpha\, c(t-1) + c_0 + \varepsilon(t)$$

where $c(t)$ is the coefficient of a given variable of the behavioural equation at time t, α and c_0 are parameters, ε a white noise error term.

[1] For a survey of time-varying parameters technics see Avouyi-Dovi and Nicolai (1991).

To keep the estimation feasible, we limited to one the number of explanatory variables with a variable coefficient in each estimation.

(i) Producer price. Fig. 2.11 shows the evolution of the estimated coefficient of the spread of the growth rate of unit labour cost between France and Germany in the equation of the GDP deflator. As we found above, a widening of the spread of unit labour cost has a positive effect on the GDP deflator. The coefficient fluctuates widely but stays positive. After 1985, there is a breakdown in the evolution, the coefficient starts to fluctuate around zero, showing that the spread of growth rate of unit labour costs has no influence on the GDP deflator. We can easily interpret it as: since 1987 whatever the level of the spread, nobody excepts any devaluation to compensate a loss in competitiveness.

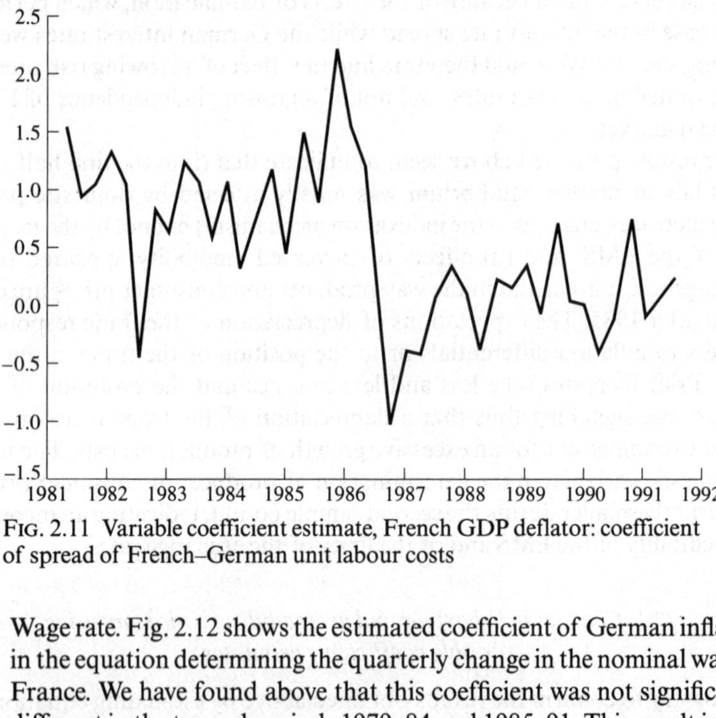

FIG. 2.11 Variable coefficient estimate, French GDP deflator: coefficient of spread of French–German unit labour costs

(ii) Wage rate. Fig. 2.12 shows the estimated coefficient of German inflation in the equation determining the quarterly change in the nominal wage in France. We have found above that this coefficient was not significantly different in the two subperiods 1979–84 and 1985–91. This result is confirmed by the variable coefficient estimation: the estimated coefficient fluctuates widely, but is on the average stable, around 0.3, no clear trend appearing.

The same is true for the coefficient of the relative level of wages in Germany and France (figure not shown). Wage formation seems therefore not to have been noticeably affected by the convergence of policies or by economic performance. No favourable effect of an increased credibility can apparently be

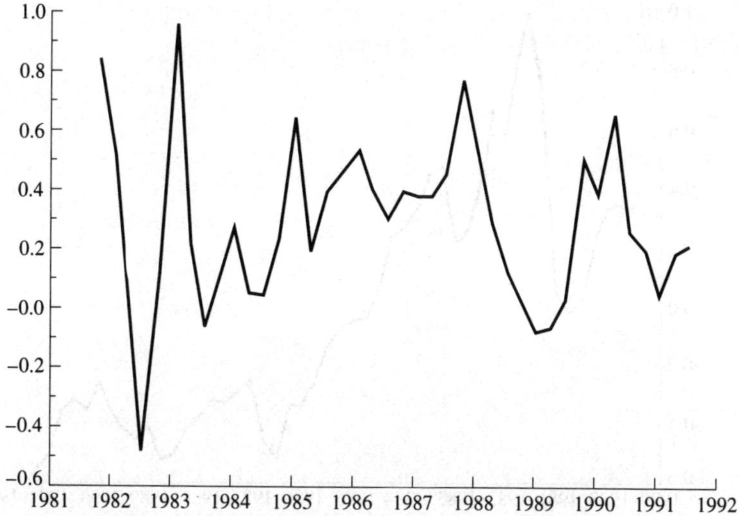

FIG. 2.12 Variable coefficient estimate, French wage equation: coefficient of German inflation

detected in the French labour market. However, the reduced influence of domestic variables after 1985 seems to point in the opposite direction.

(iii) Interest rate differential. The simple estimations performed above showed that the franc/DM exchange rate, the difference between the EMS band floor, and the actual exchange rate had significantly reduced effects on the three months' interest differential in the recent period (after 1985). This is clearly confirmed by the variable coefficient estimations.

Fig. 2.13 shows that the effect of the exchange rate on the interest rate spread is strong and positive between 1980 and 1983–4; that it disappears between 1985 and 1987 before becoming negative after 1988 (with the exception of 1990). This evolution can be easily interpreted. In the first period of functioning of the EMS, a depreciation of the franc led to an expected devaluation of the central rate, hence to a necessary increase in French interest rates. In the second period, a depreciation inside the fluctuation margins led to an expected appreciation, since the system became credible and no change in the central parity could be foreseen.

An exchange rate close to the lower limit of the fluctuation band leads indeed, if credibility is attained, to the expectation of an appreciation bringing the exchange rate back towards the central rate, hence a possible decrease in interest rates.

Fig. 2.14 shows, in a consistent manner, that the effect of the exchange rate coming close to the EMS band limit on the interest rate spread was very strong in 1980–2, and negligible afterwards. A clear effect of credibility gains on the reaction function of the central bank can therefore be detected.

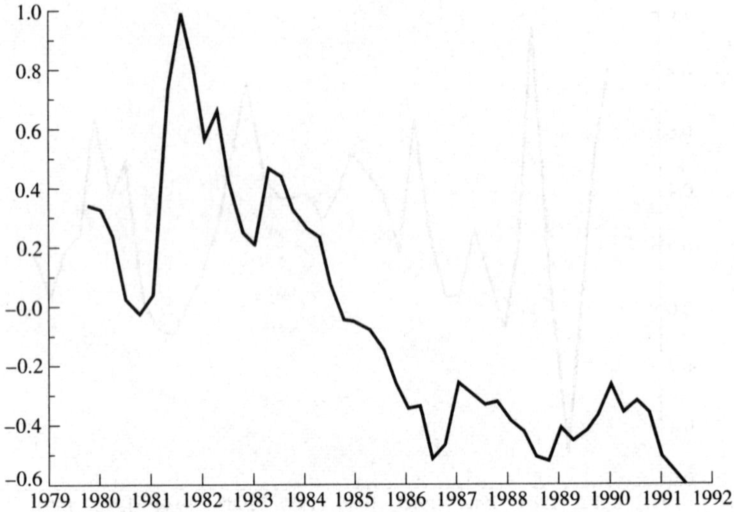

FIG. 2.13 Variable coefficient estimate, French–German interest rate spread: Coefficient of the franc/DM exchange rate

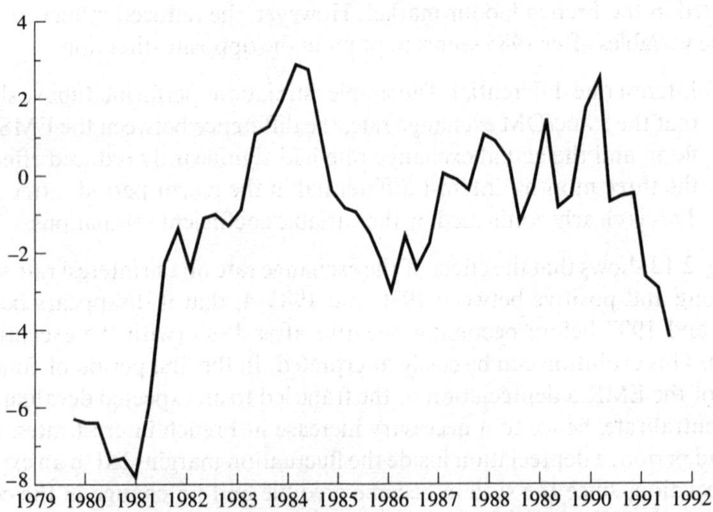

FIG. 2.14 Variable coefficient estimate, French–German interest rate spread: Coefficient of U–E (see table 2.6)

4. FOREIGN TRADE: THE ROLE OF PRICE AND NON-PRICE COMPETITIVENESS

We have seen above that the real exchange rate of the French franc did not move significantly between 1980 and 1992, whereas investment fell to a very low level during the first half of the 1980s, leading to a slow growth in potential output. The cost of disinflation and of becoming a member of the EMS might therefore stem more from losses in non-price competitiveness (insufficient supply) than from the real appreciation of the currency. To get some insight into the relative weights of price and non-price competitiveness, we have estimated equations for imports and exports of manufactures, including both price competitiveness variables and variables reflecting the degree of excess production capacity, i.e. the existence of exportable supply (Tables 2.7 and 2.8).

The results obtained show that whereas relative price effects play a large role (the elasticities of imports and exports with respect to competitiveness are 0.7 and 0.5), capacity utilization (alone or compared to its level in other countries) has a minor influence on imports and no influence at all on French exports. This seems to indicate that, at least during the 1980s, low investment had no major unfavourable effect on foreign trade, while gains in price competitiveness appearing after 1986 were of considerable benefit.

5. CREDIBILITY OF THE EXCHANGE RATE: A SIMPLE TEST BASED ON EXPECTATIONS

We have assessed above the improved credibility of the exchange rate system by examining the determinants of the interest rate spread between France and Germany. We here use the expectations implicit in the interest rate differential.

Assuming uncovered interest rate parity, we have:

ln (expected exchange rate) – ln (current exchange rate) = expected depreciation of the franc vis-à-vis the DM = interest rate differential (France Germany),

which allows us to build an estimate of the expected exchange rate corresponding to different time-horizons (depending on the maturity of the interest rates used in the above equation). Of course, this is a very simplified approach, since we ignore risk premia, irrational behaviour, and the effects of capital controls.

Figs. 2.15 to 2.17 show the evolution over time of the expected and actual exchange rates (Francs per DM), and of the EMS lower and upper limits. If the expected exchange rate stays above the EMS upper limit, it is clear that the fluctuation margins are not credible and that a depreciation of the central parity is expected. A non-zero probability of depreciation is obviously also consistent with an expected exchange rate inside the fluctuation margins.

The following points can be observed:

- The longer the expectation horizon, the larger the difference between the expected and the actual exchange rates, which is reasonable since a depreciation is more likely to occur in a long time-span.
- If one concentrates on the expectations built for 6 months or 12 months ahead, one observes that almost continuously between 1981 and 1989 the

TABLE 2.7. *Dependent variable: Log of imports of manufactures (real terms)*

Sample period	Constant	Weighted domestic demand	Moving average of log (import price/production price)	Time trend	Log of (degree of capacity utilization in France/in competing countries)	R^2	Dw	See
1980(1)–1991(3)	−7.08 (8.8)	1.28 (23.0)	−0.73 (4.1)	0.0035 (7.0)	−0.19 (2.4)	0.997	1.76	0.012

TABLE 2.8. *Dependent variable: Log of exports of manufactures–Log of foreign demand*

Sample period	Constant	Moving average of log (export prices/price of exports of competitors)	Time trend	R^2	Dw	See
1979(1)–1991(3)	6.47 (39.3)	–0.51 (5.2)	–0.0040 (10.0)	0.885	0.87	0.023

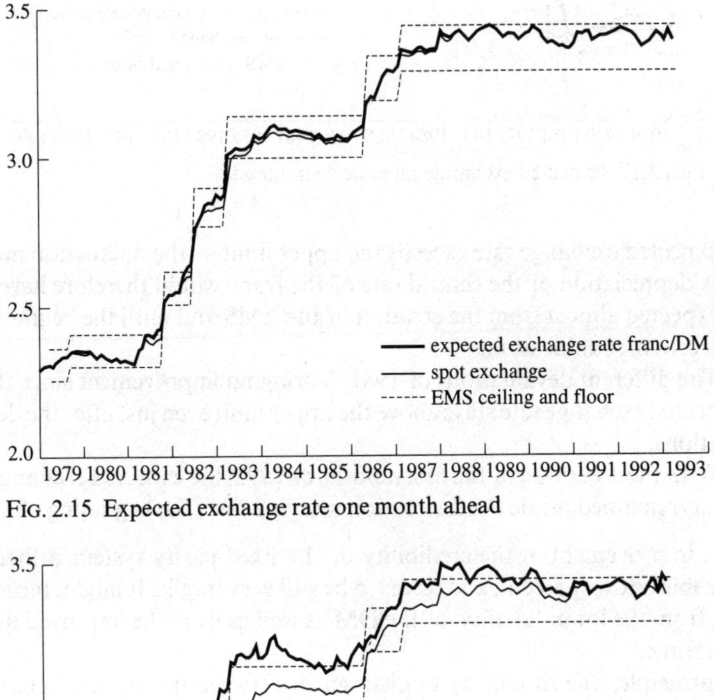

FIG. 2.15 Expected exchange rate one month ahead

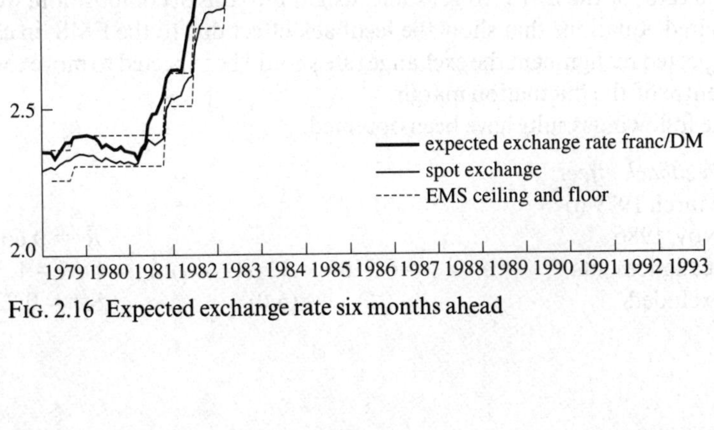

FIG. 2.16 Expected exchange rate six months ahead

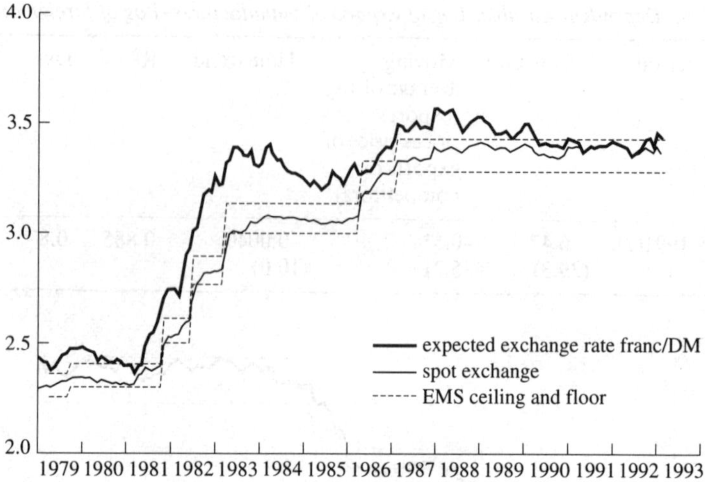

FIG. 2.17 Expected exchange rate one year ahead

expected exchange rate exceeds the upper limit of the fluctuation margin. A depreciation of the central rate of the franc would therefore have been expected almost from the creation of the EMS and until the beginning of German reunification.

- The different devaluations of 1981–3 bring no improvement since the expected exchange rate stays above the upper limit even just after the devaluations.
- With the exception of the first months of 1993, the expected exchange rate has remained inside the fluctuation margins since the beginning of 1990.

The improvement in the credibility of the fixed parity system is therefore noticeable but very recent, and seems to be still very fragile. It might, moreover, result from the lower 'quality' of the DM as well as from the improved quality of the franc.

In principle, one should try to distinguish between the expected change in the exchange rate for given fluctuation margins and the expected changes in the central rates of the EMS. To get some insight into this decomposition, we have estimated equations that show the feedback effect due to the EMS: in case of no expected realignment the exchange rate should be expected to move towards the centre of the fluctuation margin.

The following results have been obtained:

Feedback effect:
March 1979 to
Nov. 1986 $\bar{R}^2 = 0.66$
realignements $e - e_{-1} = 6.510^5 + .32\,(el - e_{-1})$ DM = 1.57
excluded (.1) (6.0) SEE = 0.22%

March 1987 to March 1993 $\quad e - e_{-1} = .002 + .20\,(el - e_{-1})$ $\quad \bar{R} = 0.11$
$\qquad\qquad\qquad (2.6) \quad (3.0)$ $\quad$ DM = 1.85
SEE = 0.39%

where *e*: ln (exchange rate franc/DM); *el*: ln (central EMS rate)

The existence of the feedback effect is confirmed, the exchange rate converging towards the central rate (with a lag of two to four months). It is, however, surprising to find a weaker feedback effect in the recent period (during which the exchange rate remained close to the upper limit for quite long time-periods). The presence of the effect makes the previous analysis still more convincing: when the expected exchange rate is above the fluctuation margin, a strong probability of depreciation exists since, normally, the exchange rate tends to move towards the centre of the fluctuation margin. The expected exchange rate (calculated as was pointed out at the beginning of this section) has a tendancy to show mean reversion towards the central rate; only in the case of a strongly expected depreciation of the central rate can it be outside the EMS fluctuation margins.

Finally, these results, even obtained with a very simple methodology, seem to indicate that indeed the credibility of the fixity of the franc/DM parity has increased, but that this improvement is quite recent and might still be quite reversible, as the most recent events have shown.

6. SUMMARY: THE CAUSES OF DISINFLATION IN FRANCE

To get an idea of the overall sources of disinflation in France between 1980 and 1991, we solve the group of equations discussed above and explain the GDP deflator, the wage rate, and the households' consumption deflator. Those equations can be written as follows:

$$\begin{cases} p^{C} = 0.824\,p^{Y} + 0.154\,p^{M} \\ p^{Y} = 1.019\,\mathrm{W} - 0.234\,ulc_{G} - 0.021\,p^{cn} - 0.65\,q \\ W = 0.691\,p^{c} + 0.569\,p^{c}_{G} + 0.339\,q + 6.51\,ln\left(\dfrac{W_G}{W}\right). \end{cases}$$

To get those expressions, we solve for the long-run relationship by adding up the coefficients of the lagged variables. This leads to the following long-run reduced form equation for the growth rate of the CPI.

$$p^{c} = .366\,p^{M} + 1.138\,p^{c}_{G} + .549q + 13.01\,\ln\left(\frac{W_G}{W}\right) - 0.234\,ulc_{G} - 0.021\,p^{cn}$$

(quarterly growth rates),

where p^{c}: growth rate of CPI
p^{Y}: growth rate of the GDP deflator

p^M: growth rate of import prices
W: growth rate of wage rate, France
ulc_G: growth rate of unit labour cost, Germany
p^{cn}: growth rate of price of imported energy
q: growth rate of labour productivity, France
W_G/W: ratio of wage rates in Germany and France.

The growth rate of the CPI in France increases more than proportionally with the CPI in Germany because of the large indexation of wages in France to prices in Germany; productivity growth increases inflation, since its positive effect on wages dominates its negative effect on producer prices. Unit labour costs in Germany have a negative effect on inflation in France, due to the implied change in exchange rate expectations.

We build three groups of effects on French inflation: effect of German prices and wages (p^c_G, ulc_G, W_G/W); effect of import prices (p^M, p^{cn}); the effect of labour productivity (q) (Table 2.9). Those three effects do not account for the whole of inflation because of the constants of the equations and of the unexplained residuals.

However, clear indications appear:

- Changes in labour productivity do not play a significant role, except in the last two years when the recession led to a decrease in the evolution of real wages.
- The slowdown in the growth of import prices explains about the half of the observed disinflation (1.0 to 1.2 per cent per quarter out of a total of 2 per cent).
- The evolution of prices and wages in Germany accounts for the second half of disinflation.

Inflation rates in France fell from 12 to 3 per cent a year between 1981 and 1986. This was caused, according to our estimation, both by the evolutions of world prices and of exchange rates (depreciation of the dollar mostly) and by the spill-over effects of low inflation in Germany on wage formation in France.

5. CONCLUSION

In this chapter, we have examined the main economic developments in France in the 1980s and focused on the effects of the EMS. It is commonly held that the EMS has had an influence on the French labour market, modifying the wage formation schema. We don't find in this chapter evidence of such a change. On the other hand, we have been able to show the breaking-up of the traditional relationship linking price, interest rate, and exchange rate. On the corporate sector side, firms don't expect any devaluation to compensate a loss in competitiveness. On the financial market side, the effect of the exchange rate

TABLE 2.9. *Causes of disinflation* (quarterly growth rates)

Year	Growth rate of inflation	Effect of German prices and wages	Effect of import prices	Effect of labour productivity
1979	2.8	0.8	1.2	0.4
1980	2.8	0.6	1.3	0.2
1981	3.2	1.1	1.0	0.6
1982	1.8	0.4	0.7	0.2
1983	1.9	0.4	0.9	0.2
1984	1.4	–0.2	0.6	0.5
1985	0.8	–0.6	–0.7	0.5
1986	0.6	–0.8	0.3	0.3
1987	0.5	0	0.3	0.4
1988	0.7	0.1	0.5	0.4
1989	0.7	0.4	–0.4	0.3
1990	0.7	–0.5	–0.2	0.1
1991	0.8	–0.4	0.1	0.1

on the interest rate spread decreases all through the period. In the end, nobody expects any change in the franc/DM parity even if the calculation of the expected exchange rate shows that this development is rather recent. Globally the credibility gain for the central bank seems to have had a significant role in French economic evolution.

On the whole, disinflation was made possible both by the spill-over effects of low inflation in Germany and by world disinflation and exchange rate movements. These direct effects of foreign prices on French prices played apparently a larger role than credibility gains in permitting disinflation in France.

Our result that wage formation was not significantly affected by EMS membership does not mean that credibility gains had no favourable effect on wage inflation. Credibility gains have limited the effects of cost increases on expected depreciation, and therefore on prices, which clearly helped to stabilize the price–wage spiral. The degree of nominal rigidity of the economy was therefore reduced, which contributed significantly to disinflation.

REFERENCES

M. Artis (1990), 'The European Monetary System: A Review of the Research Record', in G. Bird (ed.), *The International Financial Regime*, Academic Press, London.

—— (1992), 'Counter-inflationary Policy in the Framework of the EMS', *CEPR Discussion Paper*, 649, Mar.

—— and D. Nachane (1989), 'Wages and Prices in Europe: A Test of the German Leadership Thesis', *CEPR Discussion Paper*, 296 *Weltwirtschaftliches Archiv*, 126/1.

—— and P. Ormerod (1991): 'Is there an EMS Effect in European Labour Markets?', London School of Economics Workshop, 10 May 1991, London.

Artus, P. (1992*a*), 'Ecart de taux d'intérêt entre la France et l'Allemagne, asymétrie du SME et anticipations de change', Working Paper, 1992/15T, *Caisse des Dépôts et Consignations*, Paris.

—— (1992*b*), 'Politique salariale et taux d'intérêt en France dans les années 1980: peut-on envisager de poursuivre sur la lancée?', *Revue Economique* (May), 459–86.

—— and C. Dupuy (1990), 'Peut-il y avoir un nouveau SME?', Working Paper 1990/20T, *Caisse des Dépôts et consignations*.

Avouyi-Dovi, S., and J. P. Nicolai (1991), 'Coefficients stochastiques et séries temporelles: les modèles', Working Paper, 1991-06/T, *Caisse des Dépôts et Consignations*.

Barrell, R. (1991), 'Structural Change in European Wage and Price Systems: A Study of France and Italy', *London School of Economics Workshop*, 10 May, London.

—— J. Darby, and C. Donaldson (1990), 'Structural Stability in European Wage and Price Systems', *NIESR Discussion Paper*, 188.

Bini-Smaghi, L. (1992), 'Waiting for EMU: Living with Monetary Policy Asymmetries in the EMS', *Temi di discussioni del Servizio Studi*, Banca d'Italia, 168 (Apr.).

—— and S. Micossi (1989), 'Managing Exchange Markets in the EMS with Free Capital', Banca Nazionale del Lavoro, *Quarterly Review*, 171 (Dec.): 395–430.

D. Cohen and Ch. Wyplosz (1989), 'The European Monetary Union: An Agnostic Evaluation', *CEPR Discussion Paper*, 306.

S. Collins (1988), 'Inflation and the European Monetary System', in F. Giavazzi, S. Micossi, and M. Miller (eds.), *The European Monetary System*, Cambridge University Press.

—— F. Giavazzi (1992), 'Attitudes towards Inflation and the Viability of Fixed Exchange Rates: Evidence from the EMS', *NBER Working Paper*, 4057 (Apr.).

De Grauwe, P. (1989*a*), 'The Cost of Disinflation and the European Monetary System', *CEPR Discussion Paper*, 326 (July).

—— (1989*b*), 'Disinflation in the EMS and Non-EMS Countries. What Have We Learned?', *Empirica-Austrian Economic Papers*, 16/2.

—— (1989*c*), 'Is the European Monetary System a DM Zone?', *CEPR Discussion Paper*, 297 (Mar.).

Driffill, J. (1988), 'The Stability and Sustainability of the European Monetary System with Perfect Capital Markets', in F. Giavazzi, S. Micossi, and M. Miller (eds.), *The European Monetary System*, Cambridge University Press.

Egebo, T. and A. S. Englander (1992), 'Institutional Commitment and Policy Credibility: A Critical Survey and Empirical Evidence from the ERM', OECD Economic Studies, 18: 45–84.

Fratianni, M., and J. Von Hagen (1989), 'The European Monetary System Ten Years after', *Indiana University Discussion Paper*, 419 *and Carnegie-Rochester Conference Series on Public Policy*, 32 (Spring).

—— —— (1990*a*), 'Asymetries and Realignments in the EMS', in the European Monetary System in the 1990s, P. de Grauwe and L. Papademos (eds.), Longman, New York.

—— —— (1990*b*), 'German Dominance in the EMS: The Empirical Evidence', *Open Economics Review*, I.

Giavazzi, F. (1989): 'The Exchange Rate Question in Europe', *CEPR Discussion Paper*, 298 (Jan.)

—— and A. Giovannini (1986), 'The EMS and the Dollar', *Economic Policy*, 1 (Apr.).

Giavazzi, F. and A. Giovannini (1987*a*), 'Models of the EMS: Is Europe a Greater

Deutschmark Area?', in M. Bryant and R. Portes (eds.), *Global Macroeconomics: Policy Conflicts and Cooperation*, Macmillan, London.

—— —— (1987*b*), 'Capital Controls and the European Monetary System', *Euromobiliare Occasional Paper*, 1 (May).

—— —— (1988*a*), 'Can the European Monetary System be Copied outside Europe? Lessons from Ten Years of Monetary Policy Coordination in Europe', *NBER Working Paper*, 2786 (Dec.)

—— (1988*b*), 'The Role of the Exchange Rate Regime in a Disinflation: Empirical Evidence on the European Monetary System', in F. Giavazzi, S. Micossi, and M. Miller (eds.), *The European Monetary System*, Cambridge University Press.

—— (1989): 'Limiting Exchange Rate Flexibility: the European Monetary System', MIT Press, Cambridge, Mass.

—— and M. Pagano (1988), 'The Advantage of Tying One's Hands', *European Economic Review*, 24: 1055–82.

Giavazzi, F., and L. Spaventa (1990), 'The New EMS', *CEPR Discussion Paper*, 369 (Jan.).

Giovannini, A. (1988), 'How Do Fixed Exchange Rate Regimes Work: The Evidence from the Gold Standard, Bretton Woods and the EMS', *NBER Working Paper*, 2766 (Nov.).

Herz, B., and W. Roger (1992), 'The EMS Is a Greater Deutschland Area', *European Economic Review* (Oct.): 1413–25.

Kremers, J. J., and T. Lane (1990), 'Economic and Monetary Integration and the Aggregate Demand for Money in the EMS', *IMF Staff Papers* (Dec.): 777–805.

Lane, T., and L. Rosas-Suarez (1992), 'Credibility, Capital Controls and the EMS', *Journal of International Economics*, 32: 321–37.

MacDonald, R., and M. P. Taylor (1990), 'Exchange Rates, Policy Convergence and the European Monetary System', *CEPR Discussion Paper* 444 (Sept.).

Mastropasqua, C., S. Micossi, and R. Rinaldi (1988), 'Intervention, Sterilization and Monetary Policy in European Monetary System Countries 1979–87', in F. Giavazzi, S. Micossi, and M. Miller (eds.), *The European Monetary System*, Cambridge University Press.

Meen, G. (1991), 'Convergence, Divergence and Stability in the European Economies', SPES Conference, Paris (June).

Miller, M., and A. Sutherland (1990), 'The "Walter's Critique" of the EMS: A Case of Inconsistent Expectations', *CEPR Discussion Paper*, 480 (Nov.).

Poret, P. (1990), 'The Puzzle of Wage Moderation in the 1980s', Working Paper, 87 (Nov.), OECD.

Rogoff, K. (1985), 'The Optimal Degree of Commitent to an Intermediate Monetary Target', *Quarterly Journal of Economics*, 100/4: 1169–90.

Russo, M., and G. Tullio (1988), 'Monetary Policy Coordination within the EMS: Is There a Rule?', in F. Giavazzi, S. Micossi, and M. Miller (eds.), *The European Monetary System*, Cambridge University Press.

Ungerer, H., O. Evans, and P. Nyberg (1986), 'The European Monetary System: Recent Developments', *IMF Occasional Paper*, 48 (Dec.).

Vinals, J. (1990), 'The EMS, Spain and Macroeconomic Policy', *CEPR Discussion Paper* 389 (Mar.).

Von Hagen, J., and M. Fratianni (1990), 'German Dominance in the EMS: Evidence from Interest Rates', *Journal of International Money and Finance*, 9: 358–75.

—— and M. Neumann (1992), 'Real Exchange Rates within and between Currency Areas: How far away is EMU?' *CEPR Discussion Paper*, 660 (June).

—— (1990), 'EMU and Asymmetries and Adjustment Problems in the EMS: Some Empirical Evidence', *CEPR Discussion Paper*, 448 (Aug.).

Weber, A. (1989), 'The Role of Policy-Makers' Reputation in the EMS Disinflation: An Empirical Evaluation', *Center of Economic Research Discussion Paper*, 8803, Tilburg University.

—— (1991*a*), 'EMS Credibility', *Economic Policy*, 12 (Apr.).

—— (1991*b*), 'Stochastic Process Switching and Intervention in Exchange Rate Target Zones: Empirical Evidence from the EMS', *CEPR Discussion Paper*, 554 (July).

—— (1992), 'The Role of Policymakers' Reputation in the EMS Disinflations', *European Economic Review* (Oct.), 1473–92.

Wyplosz, C. (1986), 'Capital Controls and Balance of Payments Crises', *Journal of International Money and Finance* (June).

—— (1987), 'Capital Flows Liberalization and the EMS a French Perspective', mimeo, INSEAD.

—— (1988), 'The Swinging Dollar: Is Europe out of Step'? *CEPR Discussion Paper*, 241.

—— (1989), 'Asymmetry in the EMS: Intentional or Systemic', *European Economic Review*, 33: 310–20.

3

Inflation in the UK in the 1980s

MICHAEL J. ARTIS
ZENON G. KONTOLEMIS

INTRODUCTION

Inflationary experience in the UK, as elsewhere in the developed world, displayed a strong sensitivity to the rise in oil prices in the early 1970s. Over the course of that decade a variety of measures was introduced, including both incomes policies and restrictive fiscal and monetary policies, to bring inflation under control and a degree of success was eventually achieved, at the cost of a rise in unemployment. The UK was notably less successful, however, than most other developed countries in this battle, as Fig. 3.1(*a*) and 3.1(*b*) show. Nor was this poor performance redeemed by a notably better record in other respects. Productivity growth was low, even by UK standards, and a high cost was paid in unemployment for the control of inflation that was eventually achieved.

Although the policy performance of the 1970s looks much less woeful now, with the benefit of hindsight over the 1980s, than it did at the turn of the

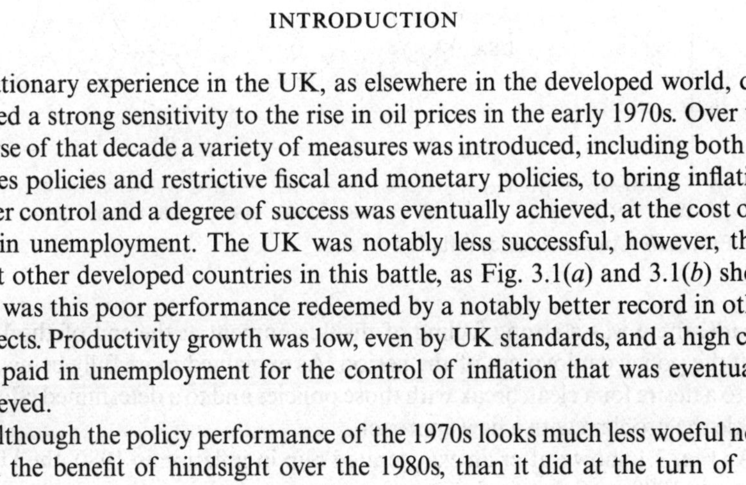

FIG. 3.1*a* Consumer price inflation: UK and G7 (percentage change)

The authors would like to acknowledge comments received from a SPES group seminar, especially those of Jurgen Wolters, which resulted in a considerable improvement to the chapter. They are also grateful to Robin Bladen-Hovell, Denise Osborn, and Wenda Zhang for useful comments.

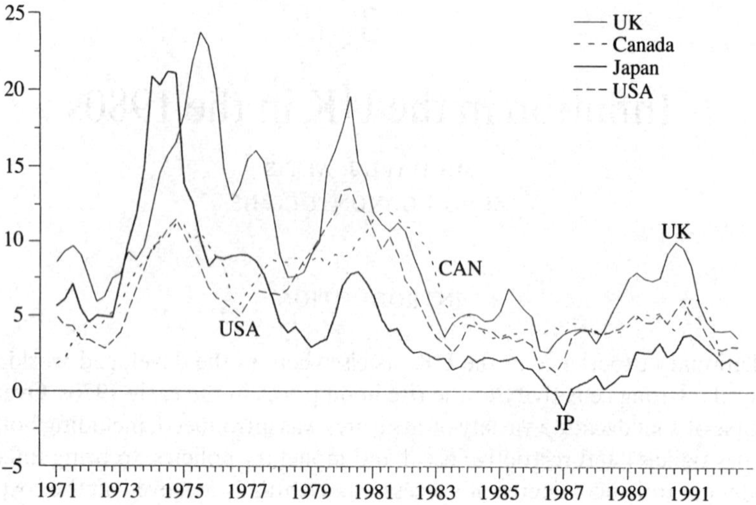

FIG. 3.1*b* Consumer price inflation

decade, there was a strong feeling of disillusionment at the end of the 1970s with the policy deployment of the period. As explained more fully below, this led to a desire for a clean break with those policies and to a determined effort to tackle the problem with a new approach.

As Fig. 3.1 shows, after an exaggerated blip in inflation in 1980, the UK in the early 1980s was then in the van of countries to reduce inflation in the wake of the second oil shock. Indeed, inflation fell very fast from early 1981 to 1983. The second important feature of the 1980s' inflation experience in the UK, however, is that from mid-1986 a tendency for the rate of price rise to increase sharply again became evident. From a low of 2.6 per cent in 1986, inflation recovered to a high of 9.9 per cent in 1990—a significant reversal of earlier counter-inflationary gains and a much more violent resumption of inflation than experienced elsewhere in the world. (The figures shown are for retail price inflation, which in the UK, though not elsewhere, includes the effect of sharply increased interest rates, a component of housing costs: but the difference remains even when this component is stripped out.) Then, late in the early 1990s, inflation was once more brought under control, falling quite heavily through 1990–2. The 'new' policies of the beginning of the new decade sought to control inflation by adherence to an internal standard (control of the money supply); by the end of the decade these policies had been abandoned. First, the authorities turned to an external standard—adherence through participation in the ERM to an exchange rate peg against the DM; then, after the *volte face* of 'Black Wednesday' (16 September 1992), sterling was floated and the authorities proclaimed an inflation target of 1–4 per cent. This time, intermediate targets, whether for the monetary growth rate or the exchange rate, were played down; instead an Antipodean style[1] 'direct targeting' of the inflation rate was preferred. The 1–4 per cent target was stipulated for RPIX inflation (that is, inflation in the RPI excluding mortgage interest payments). In public perceptions, at least, the prospect of rejoining the ERM became a rather distant target.

Aims of the chapter

This chapter provides a review of the UK's inflation experience in the 1980s. After a brief introduction, Section 1 provides a review of the policy record; as already indicated, the period is notable for an attempt to control inflation with new policies. It is important to review this claim with some care not only because of its intrinsic interest but also because a genuine policy innovation is more than likely to be associated with a structural break in the relationships discoverable by econometric methods of the type which we employ subsequently. Section 2 reviews the existing literature on the topic of the chapter, to which a number of distinguished contributions have been made. In Section 3 we introduce some original analysis of our own. The last section includes some concluding observations. Further results may be found in a discussion paper (No. 106) of the School of Economic Studies, University of Manchester, prepared by the present authors (Artis and Kontolemis, 1994).

1. THE POLICY DEPLOYMENT OF THE 1980S

The incoming Conservative Administration in 1979 set about constructing a framework for the control of inflation, which was formally unveiled under the title of the Medium-Term Financial Strategy (MTFS) in the budget of the following year. The centrepiece of the MTFS was a pre-announced four-year plan for the medium-term reduction of the growth rate of the money supply, on the £M3 definition (a broad definition). Alongside the medium-term trajectory for declining monetary growth was placed a plan for the steady reduction over the same period of the ratio of the PSBR to GDP (the PSBR being the sum of the budget deficit and the proceeds of 'nationalization'). The exchange rate was 'assumed to be determined by market forces' (*Financial Statement and Budget Report*, 1980). The description of the MTFS referred to the primacy of the money supply objective and also argued that the out-turn for unemployment would depend *inter alia* upon the expectations of those involved in the wage-bargaining process. It was hoped that the public commitment to the MTFS would influence those expectations. Inputs from both 'Friedmanian monetarism' and the 'New Classical Macroeconomics' can be recognized by

[1] Australia and New Zealand appear to have preceded other countries in turning away from intermediate target variable strategies for the control of inflation to strategies described in terms of the inflation target itself.

the ideologically sensitive economist in the statement of the MTFS. It was certainly new.

In the letter, the MTFS as originally projected, was to be a distinct and definite failure. That is, the monetary growth targets for £M3 were substantially and persistently overrun. In response, the strategy was reformulated; initially, both narrower (M1) and broader (PSL2) monetary aggregates were added to £M3 in the expression of four-year forward rates of decelerating monetary growth; in 1984 these were excluded and M0 was added. After 1987, £M3 was omitted altogether. Most important of all, the exchange rate was introduced as a conditioning factor in the response to an overrun of the monetary target.

This was made quite clear in the 1982 restatement of the MTFS: 'External or domestic developments that change the relationship between the domestic money supply and the exchange rate may . . . disturb the link between money and prices. Such changes cannot readily be taken into account in setting monetary targets. But they are a reason why the Government considers it appropriate to look at the exchange rate in monitoring domestic monetary conditions and in taking decisions about policy'. It is clear, too, that this practice, of conditionalizing the response to a target overrun on the exchange rate, preceded the formal acknowledgement of it. In other words, the inflexibility proclaimed as a virtue of the original MTFS ('there would be no question of departing from the money supply policy, which is essential to the success of any anti-inflationary strategy') gave way under the pressure of events, fairly quickly, to a more pragmatic policy.[2] Among the events in question, as detailed further below, was a large appreciation of the exchange rate, and a huge and very rapid increase in the numbers unemployed.

The unravelling of the MTFS into a more pragmatic policy in which the exchange rate figured prominently was associated with a shift of emphasis for all but some formal purposes (including the annual restatement of the MTFS) away from monetary aggregates towards interest rates. 'The' interest rate became identified as a monetary 'fine-tuner'; at the same time, the theme set for fiscal policy by the initial statement of the MTFS was maintained, so that with some exceptions the goals by which fiscal instruments were set continued to be medium-term in character. A popular characterization of this policy stance was that the Chancellor of the Exchequer was engaged in a game of 'one club golf'. With no constraints on the exchange rate, this one-target one-instrument policy can maintain inflation on target. Clearly, with a constraint on the exchange rate, this will no longer be possible; a situation of Tinbergian instrument deficiency ensues. The exchange rate objective creates the need for an

[2] Indeed, it was already evident to observers that the policy was compromised as early as the summer of 1980, when short-term interest rates were lowered despite an overrun of the monetary target. From his vantage point in the Bank of England, Fforde (1983) subsequently noted of this episode that 'it had to be judged that the performance of M3 required interpretation in the light of other indicators, including the exchange rate.'

additional instrument or else the abandonment, temporarily, of the inflation target.

This dilemma became obvious in the next policy phase to ensue, which was marked by Chancellor Lawson's decision to 'shadow the DM'. This policy was inaugurated in the wake of the Louvre Accord in 1987. Without ever being announced as official policy the authorities nevertheless allowed it to become clear that they were pursuing a policy of targeting the DM exchange rate with a ceiling of 3DM/£. This policy may have been an attempt to demonstrate that joining the ERM in a formal way would be an entirely feasible—even easy—matter, and may have seemed to be a natural progression from the pragmatic policy described above. Whatever the motivation for its introduction, it was abandoned after about twelve months. During the course of this policy phase it became clear that the interest rate was being held down by the exchange rate commitment to levels below those indicated as desirable on domestic grounds.

After this episode, monetary policy reverted for a time to its erstwhile more pragmatic stance, with the emphasis on interest rate increases to contain inflation. Then, in October 1990, the British government decided formally to participate in the Exchange Rate Mechanism of the European Monetary System. Perhaps reflecting experience in the 'shadowing' period, the 1991 restatement of the MTFS stated that 'There may be occasions when tensions arise between domestic conditions and ERM obligations, with domestic conditions pointing to interest rate levels either higher or lower than those indicated by ERM obligations . . .' but 'Any loss of discretion to respond to domestic monetary conditions is likely to be more than compensated for by the improved market confidence and reduced inflationary expectations that the ERM commitment is bringing about.'

Up to this point, then, it is possible to describe the decade as a whole as one in which there occurred a definite policy switch, away from an attempt to control inflation through adherence to an *internal* standard (afforded by money supply control) to an attempt to control inflation via adherence to an *external* standard (the rate of exchange of the pound sterling to the DM). This switch can be described as a decision to import the monetary policy of a country which has been markedly more successful than the UK in keeping inflation down. But, as it proved, it was not long before the British authorities reverted once again to an internal standard, this time not expressed in terms of a monetary target but in terms of a direct inflation target.[3] Following the events culminating in 'Black Wednesday' (16 September 1992), after which sterling was floated, the British government declared an objective of controlling inflation in the retail price index excluding mortgage interest payments (RPIX) within a range of 1–4 per cent. The Bank of England, unprecedently, was given powers to monitor the pursuit of this target in published reports.[4]

[3] Although, as during the period of adherence to the ERM, ranges for M0 continued to be announced these had long since been regarded as secondary to the main target.

[4] The first of these appeared in February 1993.

2. EXISTING STUDIES OF THE DISINFLATION PROCESS

There are several studies of the disinflation process in existence. They raise different issues for examination and deserve here a brief review. Later we collect up some of the ideas suggested in our own data analysis.

Data displays

First, however, we introduce Figs. 3.2–3.5 which provide data displays relevant to the account. Fig. 3.2 plots indicators of labour market conditions: the vacancy and unemployment rates (Fig. 3.2(*a*)) and output growth rates (Fig. 3.2(*b*)). The large rise in unemployment early in the 1980s stands out, as does the subsequent easing off and eventual fall in the late 1980s—giving way to renewed increases in the new decade. The vacancy figures tell a mirror-image story, but with a definite upward shift of unemployment against vacancies becoming evident during the decade. Finally, the output growth figures clearly mark out the severe recession of the early 1980s, the recovery, and then the boom and collapse of the late 1980s and early 1990s. Fig. 3.3 graphs the nominal and real exchange rates against the US dollar (Fig. 3.3*a*) and the DM (Fig. 3.3(*b*)). The real exchange rates are computed as the product of the nominal rate and relative producer prices. The exchange rate series record a sharp appreciation early in the period—then a depreciation from 1981 to the mid-1980s. Thereafter there is a tendency for the pound to appreciate against the dollar whilst continuing to depreciate against the DM. These movements were large. The real depreciation from the peak in 1981 to the trough in 1985, for example, afforded a gain in competitiveness of some 50 per cent against the dollar. There was a similar real depreciation against the DM, drawn out over a slightly longer period from 1981 to 1986–7. Fig. 3.4 contains a data display of monetary growth rates (M0 and M4)[5], inflation (prices), and the real interest rate.[6] The very different behaviour of M0 and M4 is discussed later in the chapter.

Finally, Fig. 3.5 plots indicators of fiscal policy: the ratio of the PSBR (excluding privatization receipts) to GDP, and the OECD's estimate of the cyclically adjusted or structural surplus as a proportion of (trend) GDP. The first of these indicators is chosen because the government's MTFS specified target ratios for the PSBR to GDP.[7] (In the event, the PSBR figures were heavily influenced by the receipts of the government's programme for the privatization

[5] £M3 was discontinued in 1987.

[6] Computed as the one-year interest rate, proxied by the sequence of four forward treasury bill rates, minus the annual forward rate of (RPI) inflation.

[7] Although Sargent (1981) attacked the MTFS on the grounds that monetary restraint was incredible in the absence of more fiscal discipline, his argument is not convincing in this instance (see Bean and Symons, 1989; Begg, 1987). However, note that in Matthews and Minford (1987), the reduction in the PSBR/GDP ratio is regarded as critical to the reduction in inflation between 1980 and 1984–5.

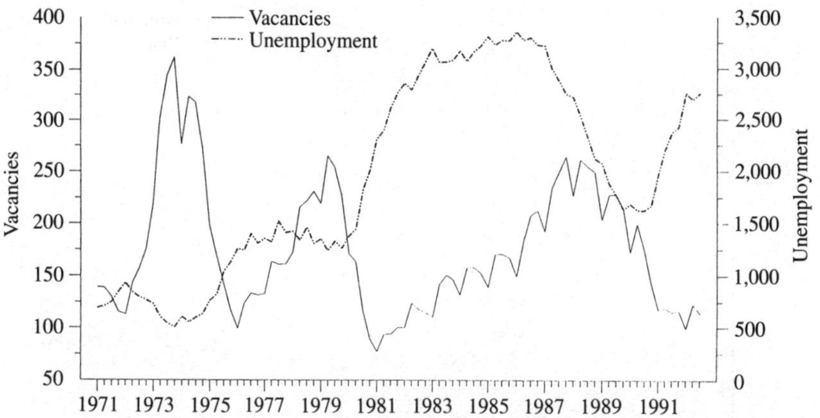

FIG. 3.2*a* Unemployment and vacancies (thousands, seasonally adjusted)

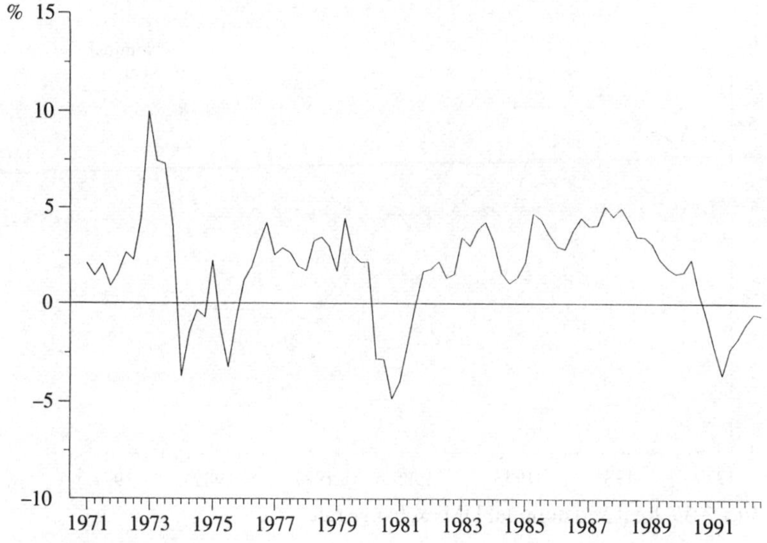

FIG. 3.2*b* Growth of GDP at constant prices (percentage annual change)

of state-owned assets, but as the counterpart of a sale of assets, privatization proceeds do not have the same economic significance as regular revenue receipts and it is more appropriate to use the data for the PSBR excluding privatization.) The OECD's measure of structural surplus corrects for cyclical influences. Measures like the OECD's have been criticized on a number of grounds; nevertheless, major movements in such measures probably do correctly indicate the 'thrust' of policy. On that basis, what can be seen is that there is a very strong fiscal contraction at the outset of the 1980s: between 1979 and 1982 the structural deficit ratio fell by 4.4 percentage points. This was followed

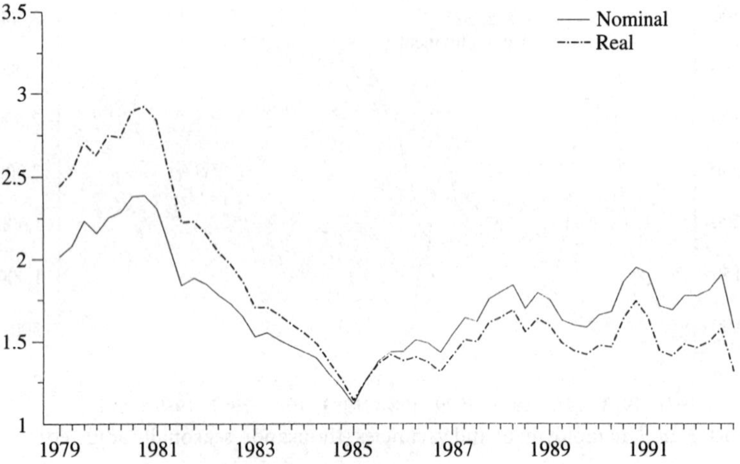

FIG. 3.3*a* Real and nominal dollar exchange rate

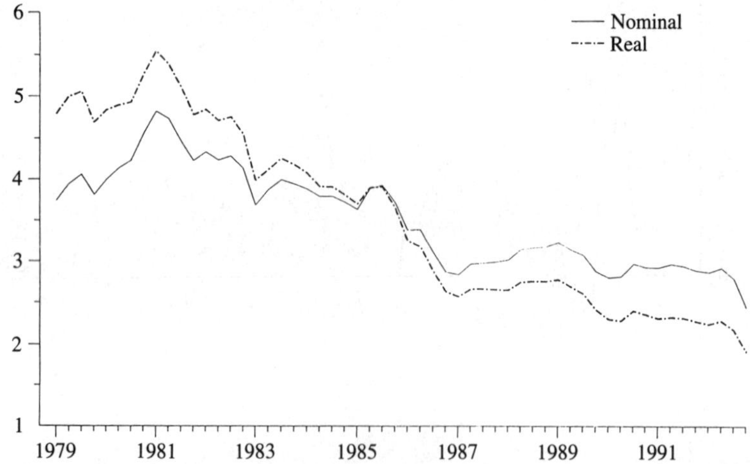

FIG. 3.3*b* Real and nominal DM exchange rate

by significant easing in 1983 and 1984 (a rise in the deficit ratio of 1.4 percentage points) with little further significant change until the tightening in 1988 and the subsequent rather drastic easing into the early 1990s; between 1988 and 1992, the deficit rose by over 3 percentage points.

The studies

Among the studies to be reviewed are those by Buiter and Miller (1981, 1983); Beckerman and Jenkinson (1986); Artis and Bladen-Hovell (1987); Artis *et al.* (1984); Rowlatt (1988, 1992); Bean and Symons (1989); Alogoskoufis and Spanos (1986); and Alogokoufis *et al.* (1992).

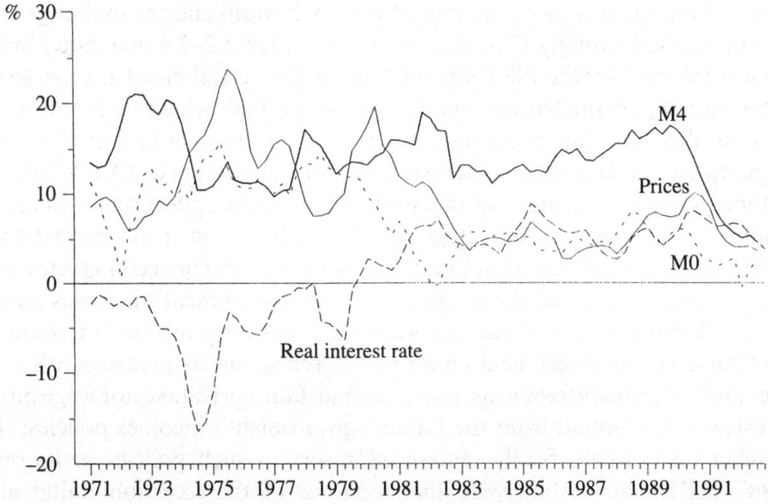

FIG. 3.4 Monetary indicators in the UK

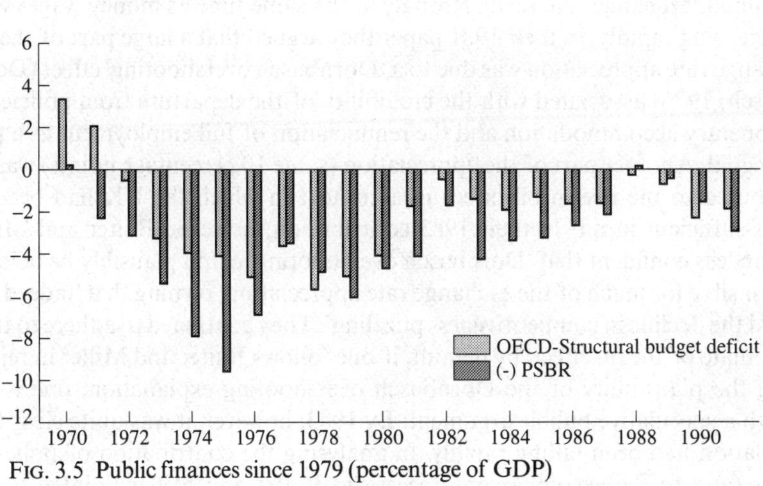

FIG. 3.5 Public finances since 1979 (percentage of GDP)

Buiter and Miller reported twice to the Brookings Panel on the progress of the 'Thatcher experiment'. On both occasions, indeed, they stressed that, at least in conception, the policies were 'new' and might on familiar 'Lucas' (Lucas, 1976) grounds be expected to lead to some disruption of existing measured relationships. However, they did not provide any extended econometric work to support this suggestion. At the time of preparation (1980–1) of the first of their contributions, the economic conjuncture in the UK provided a large number of puzzles to unravel. First, there had been a sharp rise in inflation in 1980, perhaps unexpected in view of the Thatcher government's dedication to beating inflation; the monetary targets had been overshot, leading to controversy as to whether or not monetary conditions were tight; but there was a large recession, verging on slump, in train and the exchange rate had appreciated strongly. (The data displays in Figs. 3.2–3.4 illustrate.) Inflation was falling after the 1980 blip, but had not yet consolidated at a low level. Buiter and Miller singled out two factors which had helped to produce the inflation blip: first, the incoming Conservative government had used its first budget to undertake a revenue-neutral shift from income tax to VAT. Whatever the longer-run consequences of this shift, the immediate effect was to raise the consumer price level by 4 percentage points, which showed up as a corresponding blip in the annual rate of inflation for another year. The second factor was a wage push; a legacy of the outgoing Labour government's incomes policy was a deferred package of sizeable wage increases for public sector workers. The Conservative government chose not to renege on its predecessor's promises and the public sector wage rise helped sustain a private sector wage push. All this was a rebound from the Labour government's incomes policies; the Thatcher government firmly renounced resort to such policies in its own counter-inflationary strategy. In their analysis of the recession Buiter and Miller emphasized the role of the drastic loss of competitiveness, with the nominal exchange rate rising strongly at the same time as money wages were increasing rapidly. In their 1981 paper they argued that a large part of the exchange rate appreciation was due to a 'Dornbusch overshooting' effect (Dornbusch, 1976) associated with the credibility of the departure from policies of monetary accommodation and the renunciation of full employment as a policy goal. Another part of the appreciation (some 10 percentage points) was attributed to the rise in oil prices in a context in which the UK had become self-sufficient in oil. In their 1983 contribution, however, Buiter and Miller were less confident that 'Dornbusch overshooting' could plausibly be held responsible for much of the exchange rate appreciation, owning that 'indeed, we find the decline in competitiveness puzzling'. They continued to adhere to their estimate of the oil effect; by default, if one follows Buiter and Miller in rejecting the plausibility of the Dornbusch overshooting explanation, one is left with a speculative bubble argument. By 1983, however, it was quite clear that inflation had been falling rapidly. In analysing the contribution of policy to this (and to the accompanying recession) Buiter and Miller pointed to the phase of tight fiscal policy which had ensued; whilst this was not obvious from unadjusted data, corrections for the effect of recession made it clear that policy had in fact been tight (as confirmed by the OECD structural surplus data shown in Fig. 3.5). Weak domestic demand and a low level of competitiveness were held primarily responsible for the disinflation.

Fforde's analysis of the pursuit of monetary targets (Fforde, 1983)—which ranged back over earlier periods—was extensively referenced by Buiter and Miller. Fforde argued that operating methods of monetary policy had not greatly changed and that monetary targeting as such was incidental to the main point of the 'new' policies—which was, simply, to drop the promise to maintain full employment in favour of the single-minded pursuit of low inflation. This was the 'downward management of demand'. This perspective enabled Fforde to point out that the overrun of the monetary targets need not imply a loss of credibility because a reduction of inflation had been achieved whilst the rise in unemployment was a demonstration that the full employment goal no longer had any purchase on policy. As he put it: 'as time went by it came to be realised that the strategy was more likely to be judged by its actual effect on the economy, and on the actual behaviour and expectations of the principal agents in it, than by the puzzling short-run behaviour of a particular monetary aggregate.' This did not mean that the monetary targeting was inessential, however; by switching attention to the minutiae of such controversies as which monetary aggregate to target, the policy-makers were relieved of the challenge of computing the unemployment cost of disinflation. Had such calculations been made, the policy departure might have been prevented, or watered down.

Alogoskoufis *et al.* (1992) constitutes the most recent attempt to search for a 'Thatcher effect', that is a credibility bonus. They set up a partisan model of inflation cycle, generalized to allow for unemployment persistence. The model predicts in general a marked difference in inflation expectations and actual wage inflation in election and non-election years. Under Mrs Thatcher's regime (to 1990), this difference disappears, which could be interpreted as a credibility effect.

Beckerman and Jenkinson (1986), however, were to argue that for a single OECD country like the UK a large unemployment cost would not be necessary to control inflation. Their argument was that the reduction in inflation in the OECD countries was essentially due to the fall in commodity prices that ensued through the 1980s. Whilst that fall itself might be due to the deflation of OECD demand (accompanied by rising unemployment), demand deflation or its unemployment proxy had no additional impact on the wage–price process. Their argument can be regarded as an econometric vindication of a Kaldor–Hicks style of model in which wages and value-added prices in the industrial countries are taken as fix-price whilst international commodity prices are flex-price. A fall in OECD demand reduces OECD prices through its impact on raw material input prices and hence via a cost–mark-up process on final prices. The argument denies the presence of demand effects in domestic wage-setting (i.e. no Phillips curve) and, as well, the presence of such effects in price mark-up processes. These restrictions have been found to be too strong by other investigators, though it is important to mention that a number of such investigators have concluded that the Phillips effect, in the UK, may be wholly or in part, a hysteresis effect (e.g. Andersen, 1992). That is to say, it appears to be changes in unemployment rather than its level that exert most leverage on the rate of wage inflation. A prominent finding of the LSE labour group (e.g. Layard and Nickell, 1986) has been that it is levels of the short-term unemployed, not of the long-term unemployed that count in the Phillips curve: it is as if the long-term unemployed had emigrated—they have no moderating influence on the rate of wage change. This is a finding in the spirit of the hysteresis argument, since we would expect a high correlation between the level of short-term unemployment and the change in total unemployment. As an alternative or possibly complementary argument, it should be pointed out that there is some evidence from shifts in the relationship between vacancies and unemployment (e.g. Fig. 3.2(*a*)) to the effect that the significance of unemployment as an excess demand indicator has changed (the NAIRU has increased): vacancy data are the preferred excess demand proxy in Kennedy (1992).

Alogoskoufis and Spanos (1986) adopt a hysteresis form of wage equation in their explanation of UK inflation. Their assumption about pricing is that a modified form of Scandinavian model holds, in which monetary imbalance influences the relative price of non-tradables. The exchange rate is treated as exogenous. The decomposition of inflation that their system leads to indicates that of the 12-point fall in the percentage rate of inflation between 1980 and 1984, some three-quarters is due to a fall in the rate of change of unit labour costs. Change in monetary growth on their account has little contribution to make to explaining the reduction in inflation over this period.

Whilst most of the work reviewed above has been centred on informal, single-equation, or at most small-system estimation, two studies are available which use whole-system model properties to comment on aspects of the disinflation in the early 1980s. These are the papers by Artis and Bladen-Hovell (1987) and by Artis *et al.* (1984). Both focus on the policy contribution to the disinflation by conducting counterfactual simulations on large models—in the first case, the National Institute model of the UK economy, in the second case, the models of HM Treasury and the National Institute.

The methodology employed in these whole-model exercises assumes away the Lucas critique and the results are in effect to be interpreted as conditional on the irrelevance of that critique. Whilst the main focus of the analysis is the movement of output, policy effects on inflation are a by-product. Both studies agree that fiscal policy was responsible for an *increase* in inflation in the early period, to the end of 1980, with both models suggesting that this effect was in the order of 4 percentage points. Thereafter, fiscal policy emerges as a substantial cause of the ensuing disinflation (confirming the informal Buiter–Miller analysis in that regard), through to the end of 1984: in each of the years 1982, 1983, and 1984, a reduction in inflation of 2–2½ per cent per annum is attributed to fiscal contraction. Monetary policy is attributed rather little effect; in the 1987 study a 'neutral' monetary policy is identified with a real interest rate of 1 per cent, and monetary policy activism with variations around this benchmark. By this criterion, monetary policy was not at all stringent in the period concerned. External influences (the world trade recession) equally have slight detectable impact. Policy effects on the exchange rate are computed to have been, on balance, in the direction of appreciation over the period as a whole: but for the first two to three years, the effect is in the direction of depreciation, reversing in favour of appreciation through the period. These studies thus imply that the major exchange rate movements in the period were not caused by policy but by non-policy influences.

Matthews and Minford (1987) present an alternative model-based analysis, using the Liverpool model. In this account, the major part of the reduction in inflation between 1980 and 1984–5 is due to a decline in *expected* inflation, in turn produced by a fall in the ratio of the PSBR to GDP, the long-run determinant of monetary growth and hence inflation in this model.

Rowlatt (1988) presents an ambitious and neatly executed attempt to unravel the wage–price spiral and so to provide a quantitative decomposition of inflation in the UK over the period from 1969 to 1985. Inflation is represented by producer price inflation and three equations are presented and estimated. The price equation is a mark-up over unit labour costs, import, costs and indirect input taxes, the mark-up depending on overseas competition and the economic cycle. Wages are determined in a 'real wage resistance' framework; past prices, the retention ratio, short-term unemployment, and profitability enter the equation along with competitors' prices and other variables (including dummies for periods of incomes policy). Dynamic and static homogeneity are imposed. The third equation is an equation for the exchange rate which depends, *inter alia*, on relative inflation, relative interest rates, and the value of North Sea oil. Endogenization of the exchange rate allows that part of exchange rate behaviour which reflects domestic inflation to be attributed to primary sources in the decomposition. The decomposition afforded does not permit attribution to fiscal policy or monetary policy *per se*; it turns essentially on an unravelling of the wage–price spiral, including therein the exchange rate part of the transmission mechanism. The final decomposition presented for the periods relevant to the current enquiry yields the followings:[8]

Contribution of:	1979–81	1981–5
World price inflation	5.6	4.8
Real commodity prices	4.4	1.9
Labour market influences	3.3	–0.9
Foreign exchange market	–2.7	1.0
Domestic goods market	1.2	–1.1
Total identified	11.8	5.7

Thus Rowlatt attributes the greater part of the reduction in inflation between the two periods to labour market influences, accompanied by a reduction in world inflation and an improvement in the terms of trade. These influences are indicated as more than sufficient to overcome an inflation-raising impulse from the foreign exchange market (reflecting the depreciation of sterling net of the contribution to that depreciation stemming from domestic inflation). In Rowlatt (1992), the analysis is extended to 1991, but results are expressed verbally and graphically rather than in tabular form. The chief contention is that

[8] The figures refer to the annualized percentage rise in price levels between the first quarters of the years shown.

the resumption of inflation in the second half of the 1980s is due to upward pressure on domestic goods and labour markets—adding 'about 4 per cent to domestic inflation rates during the years between 1987 and 1991'.

3. THE ANALYSIS OF INFLATION

In this section we present fresh evidence on the determinants of inflation in the UK. Whilst our chief interest is in the period from 1979 to the present (effectively, the end of 1991), the analysis uses data for the preceding decade.

First of all, we investigate the stability of some long-term relationships predicted by economic theory. These could form building blocks in a composite theory of inflation. Four relationships are of interest here: that between money and prices, that between foreign and domestic prices, that between wages and prices, and the 'mark-up' relationships between domestic prices, import costs, and wages.

The preferred econometric methodology is the Johansen Maximum Likelihood method and as a preliminary screening of the data we establish the order of integration of the data series that will be used in the investigation. The approach requires that the data series appearing in the first stage or long-run cointegrating relationship should be of the same order of integration.

Models of price formation

The dominant model of price formation in the UK through to the 1970s was the 'normal cost' hypothesis. According to this hypothesis prices (wholesale prices) are determined as a mark-up over normal costs (wage costs and import costs). The normalization of costs yielded steady prices through the cycle in the absence of supercyclical variations in wages and import prices. The price–normal cost margin was fixed—though on unadjusted costs the margin would be seen to vary. During the 1970s and still more the 1980s this model came to be challenged. The first challenge came from the application of the 'Law of One Price'—essentially the Scandinavian model in strong form; this was applied in a policy-relevant way in an influential article by Ball *et al.* in the *Economic Journal* (1977). The leading econometric models adapted their price formation equations to include a representation for foreign prices not just, as previously, raw material import prices, but finished goods prices. At the same time the evolution of a different cyclical experience in the UK forced the abandonment of cycle-normalizing procedures. The second major challenge stemmed from the monetarist assumptions of policy in the 1980s. Since this policy was based on an assumption that money causes prices, it seemed necessary to provide some empirical evidence for it.

In what follows we therefore look first at the exclusively monetary explanation of inflation. For the definition of money supply (£M3) that was adopted by the Thatcher regime, we find a clear and dramatic deterioration in relationships fitted to previous data. However, we find that for an alternative narrow measure of money (M0 or the extended monetary base), rather impressive in and out-of-sample properties for a money–prices relationship can be established. It is a belief that narrow money is the critical magnitude that has inspired the work of those economists whose monetarism is generally construed as being of the more radical variety and our findings appear to be consistent with their argument that the history of the 1980s disinflation in Britain would have been much smoother had the trajectory of M0 been smoother. (Although this statement begs a number of questions—among them how well M0 can be controlled and whether targeting of M0 would have invoked a Lucas critique on the relationship we are able to uncover.)

First, however, we consider the position for £M3, the monetary aggregate at the heart of the government's counter-inflationary strategy at the outset. Prior to the inauguration of the new policy regime, evidence for a robust relationship from £M3 to prices rested uncomfortably and informally on one data point—the 'two-year lag' between the monetary excess of 1970–1 and the inflation surge of 1973–4. Nevertheless, the primacy of £M3 and the 'two-year lag' between money and prices were elements in the new monetarist canon at the time. This was formalized in the government's response to the request of the House of Commons Committee on the Treasury and Civil Service to produce detailed evidence on the money–prices relationship. The Treasury was commissioned to provide the evidence. The resultant reduced-form relationship (HM Treasury, 1981) was replicated in Artis and Lewis (1991) who examined the effect of extending the sample period. Table 3.1 reproduces their results. As can be seen, the equation estimated over the period to the end of 1978, as the Treasury's was, has a high degree of explanatory power. Prices appear to be homogeneous in money and there is a lead of money over prices. The Treasury equation was estimated on data for £M3 which were adjusted for the effects of the 'corset' system of bank regulation (which was scrapped in 1980) and when Artis and Lewis also experimented with some rough adjustments for this they reported that their coefficient estimates moved closer to the original and were slightly more robust than the figures shown in the table. However, the basis for making such adjustments is far from certain and the parameter estimates shown are based on unadjusted data. What is striking is the way in which the parameter estimates change and the equation deteriorates as additional data are added. In each of the first two successive columns, moving to the right, four more quarters' data are added. The effect of adding the first additional year's data is dramatic, as the standard error rises by 50 per cent. The estimates in the final column are clearly greatly different from those in the original (first column). These results are not too surprising since we already know that inflation declined drastically even as rates of monetary growth (£M3 definition) consistently exceeded target. Data for £M3 ceased to be recorded after 1988, but as reported below the alternative broad money definition (M4) appears to be no better related to inflation.

TABLE 3.1. *Money to prices: A direct relationship*

	Estimation period			
	1966(3)–78(3)	1966(3)–79(4)	1966(3)–80(4)	1966(3)–88(4)
Dependent variable	Δlnp	Δlnp	Δlnp	Δlnp
ln M_{-1}	0.075	0.070	0.057	0.022
	(5.31)	(3.72)	(3.11)	(1.76)
ln M_{-14}	0.094	0.107	0.057	0.028
	(2.51)	(2.03)	(1.50)	(1.87)
dln M_{-12}	0.276	0.354	0.295	0.131
	(3.09)	(4.04)	(0.310)	(2.04)
ln P_1	–0.169	–0.166	–0.106	0.002
	(3.81)	(2.81)	(2.44)	(0.20)
dlnp_1	0.590	0.463	0.416	0.602
	(5.33)	(3.86)	(3.57)	(6.87)
$\bar{R}^2$	0.858	0.740	0.707	0.621
RSS	0.0017	0.0036	0.0044	0.0082
SE	0.0066	0.0090	0.0096	0.0102

Notes: Estimation is in natural logs; *p* is retail prices, M is M3. Constant terms and seasonals included in estimation but not reported. Figures in parentheses are *t*-statistics.
Source: Artis and Lewis (1991).

Properties of the data

Table 3.2 gives the conventional ADF-test statistics for the presence of a unit root in the levels (first column) or first differences (second column) of the series. The data are quarterly and seasonally adjusted. The gaps in the table of results indicate where the procedure has called a halt to further testing. The results indicate that most of the series can be treated as I(1); only two—*M4*, *CP*—appear to be I(0). We have also investigated the issue of stochastic seasonality in the series for the same period. The importance of testing for stochastic seasonality has been emphasized recently in a number of papers (see Barsky and Miron, 1989; Hylleberg *et al.*, 1990; Osborn *et al.*, 1988; Osborn, 1990, for example). For prices the presence of stochastic seasonality could well be of exceptional significance. Its presence would imply that inflation is more likely to take off in specific quarters of the year, for example. Artis *et al.* (1995) study the inflation cycle in the UK since the 1960s and they find that troughs in this cycle are usually associated with specific quarters, notably the fourth quarter of the year. Our investigation into seasonal unit roots (the results of which can be consulted in Artis and Kontolemis (1994)) produced mixed results and we proceed with the assumption that the hypothesis that there exist seasonal unit roots in any series can be rejected. We therefore use simple first-differences for our model.

TABLE 3.2. *Order of Integration in the data: ADF statistics (1970(1)–1991(4))*

Variable definition	Variable name	I(0)	N	I(1)	N
Retail prices	P	–0.98	5	–3.08	6
£/$ exchange rate	$er	–1.85	5	–3.97**	4
Unemployment	U	–1.68	5	–3.63**	4
£/DM exchange rate	DM	–2.99	1	–5.67**	1
Money supply M0	M0	–0.93	1	–4.65**	1
Money supply M4	M4	–4.43**	6		
Productivity	q	–1.76	5	–3.79**	4
Indirect taxes (index)	r	–3.29	5	–10.14**	1
Wage rates	W	–0.92	4	–3.76**	1
Import prices	PI	–1.68	6	–3.73**	1
Commodity prices	CP	–5.25*	1		
Output (GDP)	y	–2.10	5	–4.80**	1
Vacancies	VAC	–2.64	6	–3.62**	6
Treasury bill rate	i	–2.94	1	–6.16**	1
German prices	GP	–3.34	4	–5.10**	1

* Significant at the 90% level.
** Significant at the 95% level using MacKinnon (1991) values.
N indicates the number of lags of the dependent variable included in the ADF in order to eliminate autocorrelation from the error term.

Data definitions

P: Retail price index, CSO; M0: Narrow money, CSO; W: Weekly earnings in manufacturing; PI: Unit value of imports, IFS; r: indirect taxes; i: Treasury bill rate, CSO; GP: German prices in pounds, IFS; U: Unemployment rate, CSO; VAC: Vacancies reported at the job centres, seasonally unadjusted, CSO.

Testing for long-run relationships

The long-run relationships we test for in this section can all be argued to correspond to stylized policy suggestions for controlling the price level. Thus economic theory indicates that control can come through adherence to an internal or to an external standard. Internal standards may include a money supply target or a wages policy; the external standard suggests targeting the exchange rate against a low inflation currency. All these types of counter-inflationary policy have been used in recent British economic history. The full set of results for the long-run relationships investigated appears in Artis and Kontolemis (1994). Below we comment on excerpts from these results.

Money and prices

The first point to note is that, according to our earlier results (Table 3.2), prices and broad money (M4) are of different orders of integration, respectively I(1) and I(0) and thus no long-run co-integrating relationship exists between them. A different situation exists regarding narrow money and prices, which appear to be integrated of the same order and to form a satisfactory co-integrating equation. This interpretation, however, does depend on recognizing a blip in the co-integrating equation residual.

Table 3.3 summarizes the results of testing for co-integration between narrow money and prices. The top panel of the table reports the OLS regression result while the lower shows the maximum-likelihood estimates. The *CRADF* gives the value of the augmented Dickey–Fuller test for non-co-integration of the residuals from the estimated relationship. Similarly *CRDW* is the Durbin–Watson statistic for integration. If a variable is a random walk *CRDW* will be very small. If the variable is white noise then *CRDW* will be around 2. The *T*(*n*) statistic in the second panel is the trace statistic derived by Johansen (1988) with the associated 95 per cent critical value for the hypothesis that there exist *n* co-integrating vectors. The ADF test on the residuals of this equation fails the critical values given MacKinnon (1991), and thus does not reject the presence of a unit root. But it is as well to recall that these tests have low power and tend to overstate the order of integration, especially in the presence of innovations (see Perron, 1989; Hendry and Neale, 1991 for example). In this case it seems clear that the test is biased by a shock in 1979–80. This is revealed by the data display: Fig. 3.6 for example plots the recursive estimates of the ADF test. The 1979–80 blip is apparent.

TABLE 3.3: *Money (M0) and prices*

OLS: P = –7.78 + 1.29 M0
CRADF = –2.83, CRDW = 0.173
ML: P = 1.24 M0
T(0) = 17.71**(15.4)

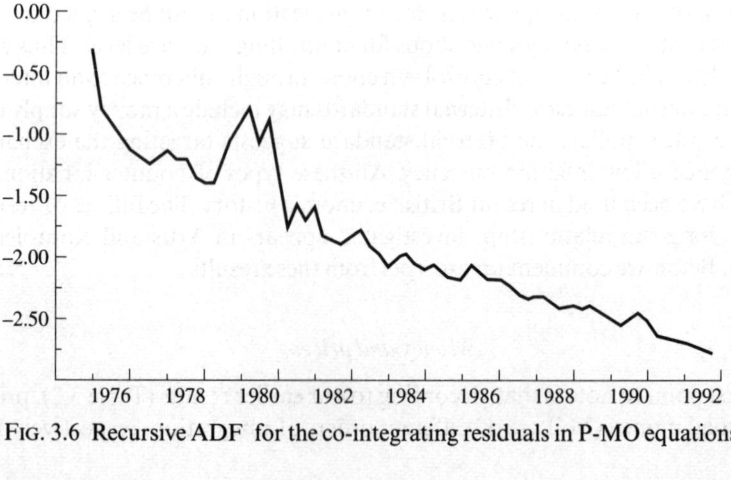

FIG. 3.6 Recursive ADF for the co-integrating residuals in P-MO equations

Confirmatory evidence of co-integration can be obtained from the Johansen Maximum Likelihood co-integration test (see Johansen, 1988; Johansen and Juselius, 1990). Johansen proposes a maximum likelihood (ML) method for estimating the long-run equations and derives likelihood ratio (LR) tests for co-integration in a Gaussian VAR model. His analysis depends crucially on whether a constant and/or trend are included in the VAR. Recently Cheung and Lai (1993) have shown that the LR tests are biased toward finding co-integration more often than Johansen's asymptotic theory suggests. This bias rises with the number of lags in the VAR. Additionally, they find that these tests are rather sensitive to the specification of the VAR, that is the number of lags in the system. One of the findings is that the ML tests are more sensitive to under- than to over-parameterization. Similarly the presence of MA dependence can lead to spurious co-integration results unless the number of lags is enough to eliminate such a problem. Finally, they recommend the trace statistic as being more robust to skewness and excess kurtosis in innovations.

According to the critical values we can conclude that in fact there exists one statistically significant relationship between prices and money—this is the one in Table 3.3. A constant has been included but it was concentrated out of the likelihood function. Following the comments of Cheung and Lai (1993) we estimated alternative specifications for $k = 2,4,6,8$ with or without a constant and trend, where k is the number of lags used in the VAR. Indeed the co-integrating vector is also quite robust to the alternative specifications. Furthermore, inspection of the plot of the co-integrating vector verifies the statistical evidence. Note that the ECM enters significantly only in the first (price) equation which is consistent with the weak exogeneity of money for the parameters of the price equation.[9] This further implies that the analysis can in fact proceed in terms of a single dynamic price equation conditional on M0.

WAGES AND PRICES

We next consider the labour market. The hypothesis is that prices and wages, or prices and wage costs are co-integrated, although the price–wage (cost) mark-up may vary with demand (unemployment).

Unemployment can affect prices through two distinct channels. First, it affects prices indirectly by influencing wage claims. Secondly, if unemployment is correlated with real output then it can be used as a proxy for a business cycle variable. Then in this case unemployment can capture the direct effect on pricing decisions of changes in demand. If unemployment is not perfectly correlated with real output then unemployment can be thought of as capturing the

[9] We do not perform a formal statistical test of the significance of the adjustment coefficients (a weak exogeneity test) as suggested by Johansen and Juselius (1990) for example. Our statement is merely based on casual observation of the standardized adjustment coefficient matrix.

first effect. Other variables such as capacity utilization, vacancies, or the growth of real output may be better candidates for evaluating the impact on prices of the second direct effect. In any case it may be difficult to identify correctly the two separate effects. Table 3.2 showed that the relevant data series—*P*, *W*, *q*, and *U*—all appeared to be integrated of the same order so that a valid co-integrating relationship among them might be found.

Table 3.4 shows a summary of the OLS and ML estimates of possible relationships. In the first two the unemployment term is suppressed. The coefficients of the productivity and wage variables are of opposite sign and close in magnitude. In both cases—that is with and without unemployment—we seem to obtain a statistically significant long-run equation. In fact, both the OLS and the ML estimates give extremely similar results. However, in the equations which include unemployment, the signs on the coefficient on unemployment are different as between the OLS and ML estimates although the other parameters are very similar. In the ML case both equations were obtained from VARs with a constant only and $k = 5$. Notice that the co-integrating vector enters significantly in the price, productivity, and unemployment equations and this further implies that the weak exogeneity of these variables with respect to the parameters of the long-run equation is rejected.

TABLE 3.4: *Wages and prices*

P =	2.96 + 0.998 W – 0.643 q
CRADF = –4.49, CRDW = 0.65	
P =	1.011 W – 0.761 q
T(0) = 36.30** (29.7)	
P =	2.87 + 0.979 W – 0.611 q + 0.0159 U
CRADF = –4.51, CRDW = 0.65	
P =	1.000 W – 0.709 q – 0.0093 U
T(0) = 47.60 **(47.2)	

The conventional pricing model in the UK is a mark-up model. Wages (wage costs) and import prices represent costs which are marked up into final prices. Where these are retail prices, indirect taxes need to be accounted for additionally in the last stage. The mark-up may be assumed to vary with the actual or expected state of demand in the goods market. For this reason we first run a regression of prices on wages productivity and capacity utilization. Central to this hypothesis is the proposition that at very high rates of capacity utilization firms push up their profit margins: when firms are faced with a capacity constraint they may take advantage of the opportunity to increase profits. The equation using capacity utilization is shown in the last row of Table 3.5. The same table shows the basic *P*, *W*, *q*, *U* equation augmented by money and import prices. In all three cases the LR co-integration tests reveal at least two statistically significant co-integrating vectors. Only the second (normalized vector) has an appealing economic interpretation. We therefore report these normalized for prices. Notice that the equation which includes M0 (second row) implies that unemployment has a positive effect on prices. In contrast, the equation with import prices has a 'correct' sign on unemployment and import prices although the effect of the latter is smaller compared to money. Adding both money and import prices does also produce an estimated equation with a 'funny' sign on money. In addition the weak exogeneity of productivity, wages, vacancies, and import prices for the parameters in the long-run equation is generally rejected.

TABLE 3.5: *The mark-up hypothesis*

P = 1.000 W – 0.709 q – 0.0093 U T(0) = 47.60 **(47.2)
P = 0.734 W – 0.469 q + 0.0099U + 0.3349 M0 T(1) = 53.15 **(47.2)
P = 0.964 W – 0.720 q – 0.0537 U + 0.0939 PI T(1) = 47.79 **(47.2)
P = 1.041 W – 0.826 q – 0.1461 U + 0.2937 PI – 0.2611 M0 T(2) = 50.44 **(47.2)
P = 0.980 W – 0.583 q + 0.074 CU T(0) = 58.66** (47.2)

Foreign and domestic price levels

Economic theory provides a presumption that domestic and foreign price levels will be linked through purchasing power parity if exchange rates are constant: or that exchange rates are determined by relative price levels. Bivariate co-integration tests, involving relative price levels and the exchange rate offer a simple way of testing for Purchasing Power Parity (PPP). Taylor (1988) is a classic example of this approach. More recent studies have tended to reject PPP for the short run (at least for post-WWII data), but to support it for the long run (e.g. Lothian and Taylor, 1992).

We test for PPP using both the £/DM and £/$ exchange rates for the period 1970–91. The formulation tested allows for both 'strong form' PPP and 'weak form' PPP depending as to whether the estimates support homogeneity in the relationship between relative prices and the exchange rate. When traded-goods prices for sufficiently well-defined categories of goods are used, the 'Law of One Price' might be expected to produce homogeneity. However, the data employed here pertain to retail prices so that a looser relationship might be more reasonably expected. Table 3.6 contains the key results; they may be interpreted as providing some support to the PPP hypothesis in its weak form, but not in the strong form; we discuss the latter first.

TABLE 3.6: *Purchasing power parity*

Dollar

(i) $P^{UK}/P^{US} = 0.372 - 0.843\ \$ER$
CRADF = –2.12, CRDW = 0.088
$P^{UK}/P^{US} = \quad -0.815\ \$ER$
T(0) = 7.45 (18.2)

(ii) $P^{UK} = -1.98 + 1.44\ P^{US} - 0.08\ \$ER$
CRADF = –1.77, CRDW = 0.08
$P^{UK} = \quad 2.25\ P^{US} + 8.52\ \$ER$
T(0) = 37.05** (34.6)

DM

(iii) $P^{UK}/P^{GE} = 1.31 - 1.08DM$
CRADF = –2.33, CRDW = 0.125
$P^{UK}/P^{GE} = \quad -0.33\ DM$
T(0) = 19.6** (18.2)

(iv) $P^{UK} = -6.32 + 2.45\ P^{GE} - 0.24\ DM$
CRADF = –2.05, CRDW = 0.15
$P^{UK} = \quad 1.24\ P^{GE} - 0.72\ DM$,
T(0) = 22.64 (24.3)

Although the evidence from the OLS co-integrating relationships does not appear to be supportive of the PPP hypothesis, the overall evidence seems to suggest that at the very least we should be cautious in rejecting it.

According to the critical values given in MacKinnon (1991) we cannot reject the unit root in the co-integrating residuals for any of the OLS equations.[10] Further investigation reveals however that there is some support for the PPP hypothesis. For example Fig. 3.7 shows the actual and fitted values for the UK prices from the weak PPP £/DM equation together with *ex ante* forecasts for forty quarters. The fitted and the forecast values do not systematically drift away from the actual values and one can imagine that the residuals from this equation should actually look stationary. We find similar evidence from the £/$ case.

Looking at the ML results for the PPP hypothesis, then, it is clear that in the case of the dollar we can find no evidence for a long-run relationship in its strong form but there is some evidence for the weak form. Table 3.6 shows a summary of the results. In this case the results are not so similar to those obtained from the OLS estimation. Furthermore, in the case of the dollar, the evidence from the first test, that is the strong PPP hypothesis, suggests that this long-run equation enters significantly only the second equation, consistent with the weak exogeneity of prices for the parameters of the exchange rate equation. The findings for the DM are similar but rather better in terms of expected signs and the sizes of the coefficients. However, the ML tests indicate a

10 The critical values for the co-integration tests vary according to the number of parameters that have to be estimated, See MacKinnon (1991) for example.

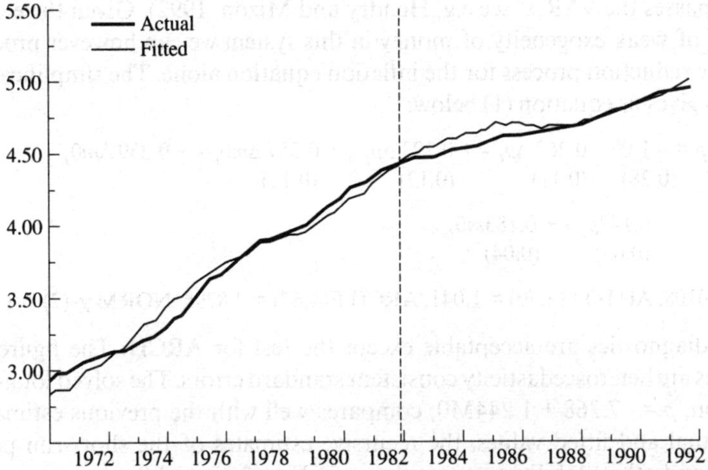

FIG. 3.7 Actual and fitted values and ex ante forecasts of prices from strong-form DM equations

co-integrating vector only for the strong-form equation as opposed to the dollar case.

From our results for the DM/£ exchange rate equation one can therefore conclude that the PPP hypothesis seems to hold for the period under investigation although the possibility of short-run deviations from it cannot be ruled out.

The dynamic equation

The next step is to look at the dynamic equations. We first investigate the dynamic forms of the long-run relationships we have looked at in the previous section. We then look at alternative dynamic equations by combining the competing theories. We begin with the P-M0 equation. The results from the earlier section have confirmed the existence of a co-integrating equation between prices and narrow money. Given the existence of co-integration we can rewrite the equations for P and M0 in their error-correction forms. It is striking that at a first glance we can notice the importance of money both in the short and long run in the inflation equation. In contrast, inflation is not at all significant in the growth of money equation. Without testing formally one can safely conclude that the causality runs from money to prices only. The 'statistical model' (see e.g. Spanos, 1986) represented by the simple P-M0 VAR, passes all the diagnostic tests and can therefore be treated as the starting-point of the search for a parsimonious 'econometric model' of inflation.

One can proceed with the simplification process within the VAR until a simple statistically acceptable model is found (absence of autocorrelation in such a reduced model implies that the 'econometric model' parsimoniously encompasses the VAR,[11] see e.g. Hendry and Mizon, 1992). Given the earlier finding of weak exogeneity of money in this system we can however proceed with the reduction process for the inflation equation alone. The simplification process gives us equation (1) below:

$$\underset{}{\Delta p} = -\underset{(0.28)}{1.07} - \underset{(0.11)}{0.263}\,\Delta p_{t-3} + \underset{(0.12)}{0.293}\,\Delta p_{t-4} + \underset{(0.11)}{0.357}\,\Delta m0_{t-2} + 0.259\,\Delta m0_{t-3} \qquad (1)$$

$$-\underset{(0.03)}{0.147}p_{t-5} + \underset{(0.04)}{0.183}m0_{t-5}$$

$\sigma = 0.0108$, AUTO $F(5,70) = 1.041$, ARCH $F(4,67) = 2.879^*$, NORM $\chi^2(2) = 1.76$

The diagnostics are acceptable except the test for ARCH. The figures in brackets are heteroscedasticity consistent standard errors. The solved long-run equation, $p = -7.268 + 1.244M0$, compares well with the previous estimates. The actual and fitted values, the recursive estimates of the short-run parameters, and other stability tests are shown in Figs. 3.8 and 3.9.

The reduced equation is stable and produces accurate forecasts. Fig. 3.8 displays the recursive estimates of the coefficients on lagged money and prices in first differences together with plus-or-minus twice their sequentially estimated standard errors, which provide an approximate 95 per cent confidence interval. Fig. 3.9 records the one–step residuals and corresponding standard errors. Additionally, we also include the one-step ahead Chow test and the sequences of break-point chow statistics. There is no evidence of instability in the simple

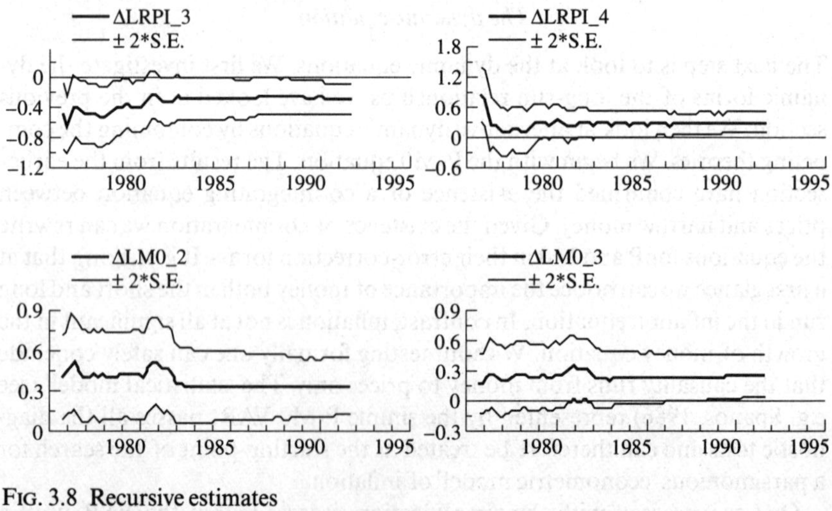

FIG. 3.8 Recursive estimates

[11] If a simple model is accounting for the results of a more general model within which it is nested then the simple model is said to parsimoniously encompass the VAR.

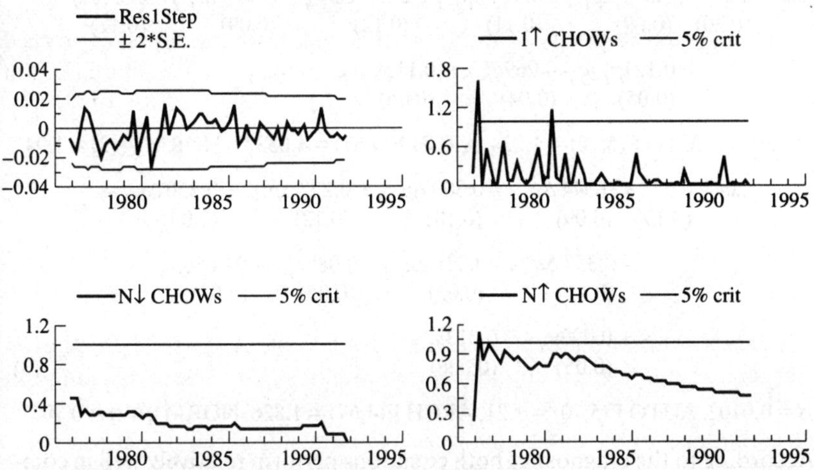

FIG. 3.9 Recursive stability tests

P-M0 dynamic equation. Fig. 3.10 displays 24 *ex ante* forecasts. The forecast statistics, $\chi^2(24)/24 = 0.283$, Chow $F(24,51) = 0.220$ [P = 0.990], indicate no stability problem. Although the estimated equation does not fit inflation perfectly, it picks up most of the turning-points, especially in the 1980s period.

One should not expect such a model to be able to forecast or fit well the oil shocks in the 1970s. In times of relatively unimportant exogenous influences as in the 1980s the model performs extremely well.

We now look at the equations involving prices, wages, productivity, and unemployment. The estimated simplified equations without and with unemployment are given below.

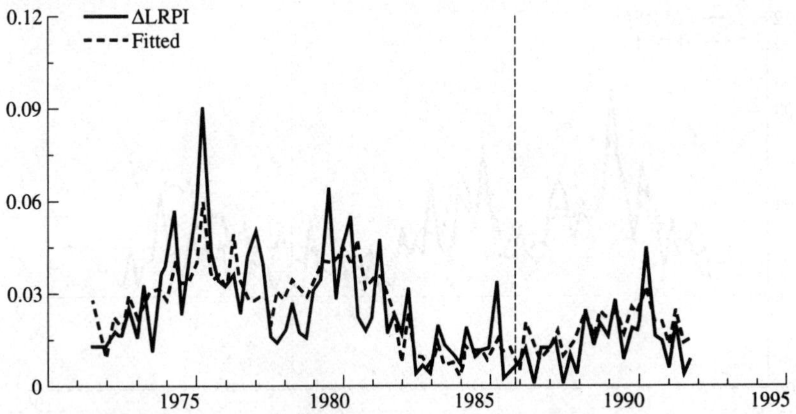

FIG. 3.10 Actual and forecast values

$$\Delta p = \underset{(0.20)}{0.351} + \underset{(0.09)}{0.371}\,\Delta p_{t-1} - \underset{(0.11)}{0.324}\,\Delta p_{t-3} + \underset{(0.12)}{0.217}\,\Delta p_{t-4} + \underset{(0.09)}{0.409}\Delta w_{t-2} - \underset{(0.12)}{0.323}\Delta q_{t-2}$$

$$- \underset{(0.05)}{0.121}p_{t-5} - \underset{(0.04)}{0.069}q_{t-5} + \underset{(0.05)}{0.115}w_{t-5} \qquad (2)$$

$\sigma = 0.0106$, AUTO $F(5,70) = 1.224$, ARCH $F(4,67) = 4.033^{**}$, NORM $\chi^2(2) = 1.94$

$$\Delta p = \underset{(0.19)}{0.377} + \underset{(0.09)}{0.344}\,\Delta p_{t-1} - \underset{(0.10)}{0.300}\,\Delta p_{t-3} + \underset{(0.12)}{0.227}\,\Delta p_{t-4} + \underset{(0.09)}{0.350}\,\Delta w_{t-2}$$

$$- \underset{(0.11)}{0.357}\,\Delta q_{t-2} - \underset{(0.02)}{0.071}\,\Delta u_{t-1} - \underset{(0.05)}{0.088}p_{t-5} - \underset{(0.04)}{0.085}q_{t-5}$$

$$+ \underset{(0.05)}{0.099}w_{t-5} - \underset{(0.006)}{0.013}u_{t-5} \qquad (3)$$

$\sigma = 0.0102$, AUTO $F(5,70) = 1.21$, ARCH $F(4,67) = 1.826$, NORM $\chi^2(2) = 0.70$

According to the diagnostics both equations perform relatively well in comparison with the simple price–money formulation. Yet both are relatively unstable, the forecast $\chi^2(24)/24 = 5.78$, for equation (3), while the Chow $F(24,47) = 0.6955$ [p = 0.83]. Fig. 3.11 shows the fitted values of the second equation together with 24 forecasts. It is clear that the model fails dramatically to forecast correctly the low-inflation period in the 1980s. One explanation for this may lie in the behaviour of unemployment; other studies (Layard and Nickell, 1986, for example) have noted that the steady rise in unemployment during the 1980s produced a huge increase in the numbers of long-term unemployed and it has been suggested that the long-term unemployed have little or no effect on the labour market. Adding other variables—money, import prices, or indirect taxes—did not serve to improve the *ex post* stability of the equation although, in-sample, there was an improvement. Another plausible explanation may be misspecification; a misspecified equation will in fact be highly unstable.

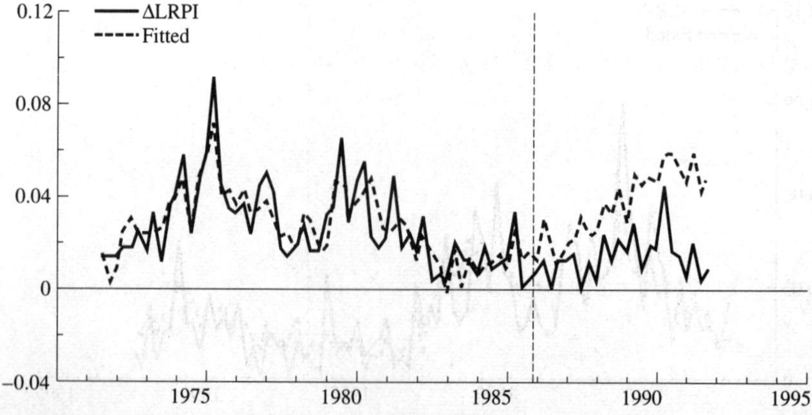

FIG. 3.11 Actual values and ex ante forecasts of equation (3)

Additionally, if we also add import prices in the VAR which includes P, W, q, and U, given the co-integration result from our earlier estimate of the error-correction model and simplify by dropping statistically insignificant variables, the estimated equation has a standard error equal to 0.0091 but still substantially overpredicts the actual inflation rate; the forecast $\chi^2(24)/24 = 7.31$ while the Chow $F(24{,}43) = 0.6285$ [p = 0.88].

In order to identify the source of the instability we can drop unemployment from the equation we estimated above which includes import prices. Dropping the dynamic unemployment term lowers the forecast $\chi^2(24)/24 = 0.74$ and Chow $F(24, 43) = 0.58$ [p = 0.92]. The estimated equation forecasts considerably better and the model does not overpredict inflation.

In the analysis that follows we therefore chose not to include unemployment in the error-correction terms or in the equation dynamics. For a demand proxy we use capacity utilization. Additionally, we use the information from the P-M0 co-integrating equation.

The preferred equation includes contemporaneous wage inflation, changes in indirect taxes, and productivity.

$$\underset{}{\Delta p_t} = \underset{(0.08)}{0.413\,\Delta w_t} - \underset{(0.008)}{0.015\,\Delta TBR_t} - \underset{(0.008)}{0.032\,\Delta TBR_{t-4}} + \underset{(0.039)}{0.158\,\Delta pm_t} + \underset{(0.04)}{0.140\,\Delta pm_{t-4}}$$

$$+ \underset{(0.01)}{0.030\,\Delta CU_{t-5}} + \underset{(0.15)}{0.520\,\Delta r_t} + \underset{(0.09)}{0.238\,\Delta m0_{t-3}} - \underset{(0.05)}{0.139\,\Delta\Delta q_t}$$

$$- \underset{(0.05)}{0.102\,(p - 1.29m0 + 7.78)_{t-4}}$$

$\sigma = 0.0095$, DW = 1.75, AUTO LM(1 to 5) = 1,30, ARCH F(4,67) = 1.86
NORM $\chi^2(2) = 0.610$, Sargan $\chi^2 = 2.80$

This is estimated using two-stage least squares given the endogeneity of wages. A simple comparison with an OLS equivalent indicates no big difference except for the estimate on wages. The model performs well and has a lower standard error than from the P-M0 equivalent. There are no problems with the diagnostics and the model rejects the inclusion of a lagged dependent variable. Furthermore the model is stable and forecasts accurately.

Table 3.7 shows the contribution of each variable in the previous equation to the explanation of inflation over the period. The explicand is the average quarterly rate of inflation in each year (shown in the last column of the table). The disinflation of the first part of the 1980s goes from 1980 to a trough of 1986. Over this period there is a fall of 2.75 percentage points in quarterly inflation. Most of this is accounted for, according to our estimates, by a decline in wage inflation, by a fall in (sterling) import price inflation, and by a reduction in the monetary pressure on prices, coming (in the table) through the ECM term, this last contribution being about as important as the other two combined. The resumption of inflation subsequently, from 1986 to 1990, is also due in large part to monetary expansion (via the ECM term) but this time rises in import prices

TABLE 3.7. *Contributions to quarterly inflation*

Year	Wages	ECM	Imp. pr Lag 4	Imp. pri	Cap. ut Lag 5	Cap. ut Lag 6	Ind. tax	Int. rate	Predict	Actual
1980	1.020	0.768	0.402	0.177	–0.166	–0.104	–0.046	0.827	2.878	3.543
1981	0.916	0.043	0.287	0.385	0.292	0.138	0.205	0.727	2.991	2.800
1982	0.642	–1.097	0.624	0.133	0.019	0.090	–0.006	1.027	1.432	1.507
1983	0.674	–0.876	0.216	0.237	–0.029	–0.036	–0.062	1.036	1.159	1.231
1984	0.594	–0.573	0.384	0.330	–0.082	–0.038	–0.101	0.707	1.220	1.173
1985	0.592	–0.490	0.535	–0.120	–0.158	–0.114	0.109	0.800	1.155	1.343
1986	0.568	–0.359	–0.195	0.076	–0.133	–0.051	0.071	0.579	0.556	0.849
1987	0.588	–0.075	0.124	–0.013	0.047	0.031	–0.025	0.845	1.523	1.005
1988	0.606	0.443	–0.020	0.025	–0.047	–0.086	–0.023	0.692	1.588	1.576
1989	0.570	0.457	0.041	0.255	–0.272	–0.243	–0.046	0.672	1.433	1.825
1990	0.672	0.277	0.414	–0.006	0.168	0.083	0.162	0.861	2.631	2.383
1991	0.546	–0.266	–0.009	0.085	0.167	0.149	0.138	0.894	1.703	1.015

(including a 'devaluation effect') are about equal in importance with a significant contribution coming also from excess demand. Wage inflation *per se* is not so marked. Interest rates are shown as contributing positively throughout reflecting the downward trend of interest rates over the period as a whole (and the fact that the effect is lagged by up to a year). As the explicand is the rate of inflation in the retail price index, which includes mortgage interest payments, the negative sign obtained on the interest rate terms reflects a balance of conventional (negatively signed) demand effects and an 'arithmetic' effect of positive sign, with the former effect dominating.

4. CONCLUSIONS

Inflation experience in the United Kingdom during the 1980s and 1990s embraces a wide variety of policy response, with a poor record of success. At the outset of the 1980s, the authorities implemented a programme of monetary disinflation based on the targeting of £M3, a broad monetary aggregate. The stability in the relationship of money to prices required by such a policy was not to be found for £M3, and in this sense the policy was a failure. Inflation did, however, fall even if the monetary targets themselves were overrun; but the fall in inflation took place against the background of growing excess capacity and rising unemployment. The next principal policy phase involved a switch from the internal £M3 target to a target for the exchange rate when the pound sterling was put into the ERM in 1990. This policy, too, was to prove a failure in the sense that the authorities were forced, in less than two years, to abandon their ERM commitments. In between these failed experiments, there was an episode of more eclectic policy in which there was a marked resumption in inflation, only brought to an end by a phase of severe disinflation based on high interest rates and reinforced by a period of membership of the ERM sought, and maintained for a while, at a high exchange rate. After the 1992 ERM crisis, which resulted in the floating of the sterling against the ERM currencies, policy became directed at expected prices. Intermediate variable targeting took a back seat in favour of this 'direct' targeting of inflation. It is too early to give any verdict on the success of this strategy; the low inflation experienced during the months following the withdrawal of sterling from the ERM through to the end of 1993 provided no test of the authorities' resolve.

The econometrics of inflation in the UK has traditionally been seen as an analysis of a mark-up process on wage and import costs. Monetary factors are not represented in such an approach, except indirectly. In our own analysis we endeavoured to start from a different angle, basing ourselves on some basic building blocks, using co-integration analysis to examine key relationships—those between money and prices, between domestic and foreign prices, and between wages, import costs, and prices. It proved unexpectedly difficult to find good evidence for the traditional mark-up view of inflation and unexpectedly easy to find evidence of a money–prices relationship—provided that money is defined as narrow money, M0, rather than broad money.

Neither of the present authors is associated with a monetarist position in general and no doubt with further work it would prove possible to give a better account of the mark-up approach. The money–prices finding may not be policy-exploitable either, for well-known ('Lucas critique') reasons. So we do not suggest that policy would certainly have been better had the authorities concentrated on M0 from the start. Nevertheless, it is worth nothing that our 'best' results were obtained by focusing on the money–prices relationship. In our analysis both the disinflation of the early mid-1980s and the subsequent resumption of inflation in the late 1980s and early 1990s have their most important explanation in the waning and waxing of monetary (M0) growth. Other factors were not unimportant but the influence attributed to money stands out.

REFERENCES

Alogoskoufis, G. S., and A. Spanos (1986), 'On the determinants of annual consumer price inflation in an open economy: the UK 1963–84', mimeo, Birbeck College.

—— B. Lockwood, B., and Philippopoulos, A. (1992), 'Wage Inflation, Electoral Uncertainty and the Exchange Rate Regime: Theory and Evidence', *Economic Journal*, 102/415.

Andersen, P. S. (1993), 'OECD Country Experiences with Disinflation', in (ed.) A. Blundell-Wignall, *Inflation, Disinflation and Monetary Policy*, Reserve Bank of Australia.

Artis, M. J., and R. Bladen-Hovell (1987), 'The UK Monetarist Experiment 1979–1984', *International Review of Applied Economics*, 1/1.

—— —— R. Karakitsos, E. and B. Dwolatzky (1984), 'The Effects of Economic Policy 1979–1982', *National Institute Economic Review*, May, 108.

—— —— D. Osborn, G. Smith, and W. Zhang (1995), 'Predicting Turning Points in the UK Inflation Cycle', *Economic Journal*, Sept. 105/432.

——and Z. G. Kontolemis (1994), 'Inflation in the UK in the 1980s', University of Manchester, Department of Economics Discussion Paper, 106.

—— and M. K. Lewis (1991), *Money in Britain*, Philip Allan.

Ball, R. J., T. Burns, and J. S. E. Laury (1977), 'The Role of Exchange Rate Changes in Balance of Payments Adjustments', 'Economic Journal', 87: 1–29.

Banerjee, A., J. J. Dolado, G. W. Galbraith, and D. F. Hendry (1993), *Equilibrium, Error Correction and Co-integration in Econometrics*, forthcoming, OUP.

—— —— D. F. Hendry, and G. W. Smith (1986), 'Exploring Equilibrium Relationships in Econometrics through Static Models: Some Monte Carlo Evidence', *Oxford Bulletin of Economics and Statistics*, 48: 253–77.

Barsky, R. B., and J. A. Miron, (1989), 'The Seasonal Cycle and the Business Cycle', *Journal of Political Economy*, 97: 503–34.

Bean, C., and J. Symons (1989), 'Ten Years of Mrs T', *CEPR Discussion Paper*, 316 (Apr.).

Beckerman, W., and T. Jenkinson (1986), 'What Stopped the Inflation: Unemployment or Commodity Prices?', *Economic Journal*, 96 (Mar.): 39–54.

Begg, D. (1987), 'Fiscal Policy', in R. Dornbusch and R. Layard (eds.), *The Performance of the British Economy*, Clarendon Press, Oxford.

Britton, A. J. C. (1991), *Macroeconomic Policy in Britain 1974–1987*. Cambridge University Press.

Buiter, W. H., and M. H. Miller (1981), 'The Thatcher Experiment: The First Two Years', *Brookings Papers in Economic Activity*, 2: 315–79.

—— —— (1983), 'Changing the Rules: Economic Consequences of the Thatcher Regime', *Brookings Papers in Economic Activity*, 2: 305–79.

Charemza, W. W., and D. F. Deadman (1992), *New Directions in Econometric Practice*, Edward Elgar, Cheltenham.

Cheung, Y-W, and K. S. Lai (1993), 'Finite-Sample Sizes of Johansen's Likelihood Ratio Tests for Cointegration', *Oxford Bulletin of Economic and Statistics*, 55(3): 313–28.

Dickey, D. A., D. P. Haza, and W. A. Fuller (1984), 'Testing for Unit Roots in Seasonal Time Series', *Journal of the American Statistical Association*, 79 (June): 355–67.

Doornik, J. A., and D. F. Hendry (1992), *PC-GIVE Version 7: An Interactive Econometric Modelling System*, Institute of Economics and Statistics, University of Oxford.

Dornbusch, R. (1976), 'Expectations and Exchange Rate Dynamics', *Journal of Political Economy*, 84: 1161–76.

Engle, R. F. and C. W. J. Granger (eds.) (1991), *Long-Run Economic Relationships*, OUP.

Fforde, J. S. (1983), 'Setting Monetary Objectives', *Bank of England Quarterly Bulletin*, 23: 200–8.

Fuller, W. A. (1976), *Introduction to Statistical Time Series*, John Wiley, New York.

Granger, C. W., and P. Newbold (1974), 'Spurious Regressions in Econometrics', *Journal of Econometrics*, 2: 111–20.

Hendry, D. F., and G. E. Mizon (1992), 'Evaluating Dynamic Models by Encompassing the VAR', in P. C. B. Phillips (ed.), *Models, Methods and Applications in Econometrics*, Blackwell, Oxford.

—— and A. J. Neale, (1991), 'A Monte Carlo Study of the Effects of Structural Breaks on Unit Root Tests', in P. Hackl and A. H. Westlund (eds.), *Economic Structural Change: Analysis and Forecasting*, Springer-Verlag, Vienna, 95–119.

H. M. Treasury (1981), 'Background to the Government's Economic Policy', *Report of the House of Commons Treasury and Civil Service Committee, Monetary Policy*, iii, Appendices, HMSO, London.

Hylleberg, S. (ed.) (1992), *Modelling Seasonality*, OUP.

—— R. F. Engle, C. W. J. Granger, and B. S. Yoo (1990), 'Seasonal Integration and Cointegration', *Journal of Econometrics*, 44: 215–238.

Johansen, S. (1988), 'Statistical Analysis of Cointegrating Vectors', *Journal of Economic Dynamics and Control*, 12: 231–54.

—— and Juselius, K. (1990), 'Maximum Likelihood Estimation and Inference on Cointegration—with applications to the Demand for Money', *Oxford Bulletin of Economic and Statistics*, 52: 169–210.

Kennedy, M. C. (1992), 'The Economy as a Whole', in M. J. Artis (ed.), *Prest & Coppock's The UK Economy*, 13th edn. Weidenfeld & Nicolson.

Layard, R., and S. Nickell, S. (1986), 'Unemployment in Britain', *Economica*, 53: S121–69.

—— —— and Jackman, R. (1991), *Unemployment: Macroeconomic Performance and the Labour Market*, OUP.

Lothian, J. R., and M. P. Taylor (1992), 'Real Exchange Rate Behaviour: The Recent Float from the Perspective of the Past Two Centuries', IMF (Oct.).

Lucas, R. E. (1976), 'Econometric Policy Evaluation:—A Critique', in K. Brunner and A. Meltzer (eds.), The Phillips Curve and Labour Markets, Supplement, *Journal of Monetary Economics*, 2: 19–46.

MacKinnon, J. G. (1991), 'Critical Values for Co-integration Tests', in R. F. Engle and C. W. J. Granger (eds.), *Long-Run Economic Relationships*, OUP: 267–76.

Matthews, K., and P. Minford (1987), 'Mrs Thatcher's Economic Policies 1979–87', *Economic Policy*, 5: 57–101.

Osborn, D. R. (1990), 'A Survey of Seasonality in UK Macroeconomic Variables', *International Journal of Forecasting*, 6: 327–36.

—— A. P. L. Chui, J. P. Smith, and C. R. Birchenhall (1988), 'Seasonality and the Order of Integration for Consumption', *Oxford Bulletin of Economics and Statistics*, 50: 361–78.

Perron, P. (1988), 'Trends and Random Walks in Macroeconomic Time Series', *Journal of Economic Dynamics and Control*, 12: 297–332.

—— (1989) 'The Great Crash, the Oil Shock and the Unit Root Hypothesis', *Econometrica*, 57: 1361–402.

Pierce, D. A. (1972), 'Residual Correlations and Diagnostic Checking in Dynamic-Disturbance Time Series Models', *Journal of the American Statistical Association*, 67: 339, 636–40.

Rowlatt, P. (1988), 'Analysis of the Recent Path of UK Inflation', *Oxford Bulletin of Economics and Statistics*, 50: 335–60.

—— (1992), *Inflation*, Chapman and Hall, London.

Sargent, T. (1981), 'Stopping Moderate Inflations: The Methods of Poincaré and Thatcher', repr. in T. Sargent (1986), *Rational Expectations and Inflation*, Harper & Row, New York.

Spanos, A. (1986), *Statistical Foundations of Economic Modelling*, Cambridge University Press.

Walters, A. A. (1986), *Britain's Economic Renaissance*, OUP.

4

Italy's Inflation Problem in the 1980s: The Role of the Public Sector

S. MICOSSI
L. PAPI

1. INTRODUCTION

After slowing down to around 6 per cent in the mid-1980s, Italian inflation failed to decline further in the second half of the decade: actually, over the period 1987–91 it increased (Fig. 4.1), despite sizeable declines in international prices and in the value of the dollar. The inflation differential relative to the best EMS performers stabilized at around 2.5–3 percentage points. Thus, increasing rigidity in the exchange rate policy, notably after Italy joined the ERM narrow band, led to a considerable real appreciation of the lira (of the order of 6–7 percentage points in 1989–92).

These developments have prompted renewed interest in the inflation problem. Since the aggregate monetary policy constraint, introduced by ERM participation, seems to have been only partially effective in bringing about inflation convergence, attention shifted to structural features of the economy, namely the role of the public sector and services. Certain inefficiencies in the labour market may also have fostered the resurgence of inflation.

In this chapter attention is drawn to the public sector's role in explaining Italy's inflation performance in the 1980s. The chapter is organized as follows. The main features of Italy's inflation problem are described in Section 2; Section 3 reviews the results of recent research on the effects of the public sector on inflation and presents the basic facts; Section 4 discusses a simple model for the analysis of the main (aggregate) demand and supply effects of the public sector; Section 5 reports the results of estimating price equations that include public sector variables among the regressors. The main findings are summarized in Section 6.

We thank Bill Branson, Paul De Grauwe, and Giuseppe Tullio for useful comments, Gabriella Briotti for guiding us into the intricacies of public sector accounts, Marco Malgarini for helping in the estimation and testing with Microfit, and Gianna Bargagli for excellent assistance in building our data bank. Financial support by the EC SPES program is gratefully aknowledged.

2. ITALY'S INFLATION PROBLEM

In the early 1980s, inflation slowed down markedly, after the high rates of the 1970s, but failed to converge fully to that of the EC's best performers. In 1987–91 it started to creep up again (Fig. 4.1).

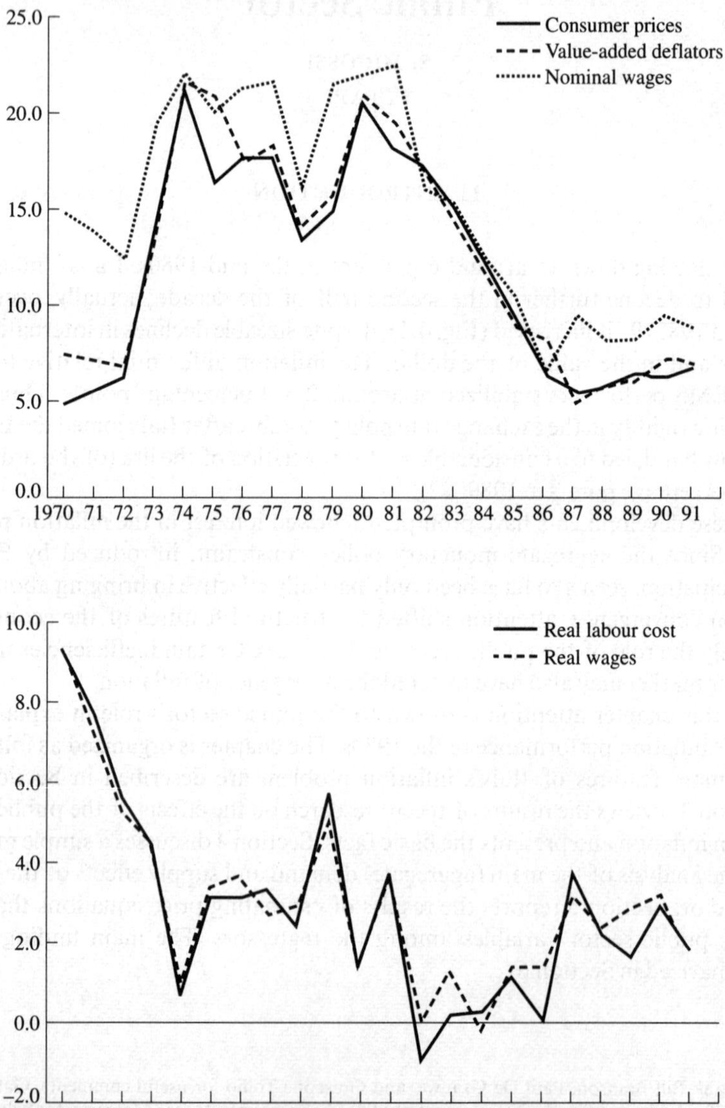

FIG. 4.1. Prices and wages (percentage changes)

The analysis of the determinants of inflation in the 1970s had stressed excess demand (due to excessive monetary creation and/or public sector deficits), wage push and distributional conflict, and rising costs of imported inputs. Indexation (the 'scala mobile') was seen as a key factor in amplifying external shocks, distorting the wage structure, and making aggregate demand management ineffective (for a survey of that debate see Guiso, 1985).

In 1979 Italy joined the exchange rate mechanism (ERM) of the EMS; real interest rates became positive and relative price differentials were less than fully accommodated by the exchange rate. After partially restoring profit margins and balance sheet positions, thank to inflation and exchange rate devaluation in the late 1970s, in the early 1980s industry underwent extensive restructuring, with large increases in productivity and efficiency. Agreements with the unions made it possible to weaken wage indexation, slow wage increases, and restore some flexibility in the labour market. Sizeable increases in taxation after the mid-1980s halted the expansion of the primary (non-interest) deficit of the public sector (Gressani *et al.*,–Guiso–Visco, 1987; Giavazzi and Spaventa, 1989; Micossi and Traù, 1989; Cipolletta and Heimler, 1989).

Thus, the recovery of inflation in 1987–91 remains puzzling, since many causes of inflation in the 1970s had been removed, monetary exchange-rate discipline had remained tight, and over time the public sector's contribution to demand appeared to decline.

As a result, some authors (Visco, 1992 and Barca-Visco, 1993) have stressed 'structural' components of inflation, namely labour market rigidities, the non-competitive nature of the service sector (where most of the wage and price pressures seem to have originated: see also OECD, 1991 and CER, 1991), and 'incomplete adjustment' in industry (where the return of profitability did not seem to lead to an acceleration of investment in new products and technologies comparable to that observed abroad). However, these explanations are not fully satisfactory. It is still necessary to explain how it was possible that workers, industry, and the entire service sector could remain unresponsive to market pressures and sustain wage and price developments that were inconsistent with the exchange rate constraint.

Several features of Italy's experience are worth stressing in this regard. First, the resurgence of inflation originated domestically.[1] Indeed, through the second half of the 1980s and in 1990–1 Italy experienced falling import prices (in lire), partly as a result of a steadily appreciating real exchange rate (Table 1) and falling dollar prices of raw materials in international markets.

A second feature worth stressing is that unemployment was steadily rising during disinflation and only slightly recovered in the ensuing period of rapid expansion of activity (Fig. 4.2). The increase in unemployment which was concentrated in the Mezzogiorno (the eight southern regions), did not put downward

[1] These results were obtained from simulations of the Centro Studi Confindustria econometric model, following the methodology used by Gressani *et al.* (1987).

TABLE 4.1. *Selected indicators of prices and wages* (average yearly percentage changes)

	1980–91	1980–5	1986–9	1990–1
Consumer price index	10.4	15.2	5.5	6.4
goods	9.7	14.5	4.7	5.9
services	12.0	17.0	7.1	7.4
admin. goods and serv.	10.8	16.2	5.2	6.3
tariffs	11.0	17.0	4.5	7.0
Contributions to CPI increases[a]				
tariffs			0.3	0.5
indirect taxation			0.6	0.4
Producer prices	6.1[b]	10.5[b]	3.1	3.7
Export prices	7.4	13.6	1.2	2.2
Import prices	6.6	14.6	–1.2	0.1
Terms of trade	0.7	–0.8	2.4	2.1
Real effective exchange rate	0.7	–0.1	0.8	3.1
Value added deflators				
total GDP	11.0	15.3	6.7	7.5
manufacturing	8.1	12.3	4.6	2.9
private services	11.8	16.4	7.1	8.0
public administration	13.8	17.4	9.2	12.3
Compensation per employee				
total economy	12.3	16.3	8.3	9.9
manufacturing	12.2	16.5	8.1	9.1
private services	11.5	15.2	7.7	8.5
public administration	13.6	17.1	9.2	12.3
Productivity				
total economy	1.9	1.8	2.7	0.9
manufacturing	4.3	4.9	4.5	2.0
private services	0.5	–0.5	2.2	–0.2
public administration	–0.1	–0.4	0.1	0.1
Unit labour cost				
total economy	10.4	14.4	5.6	8.9
manufacturing	7.9	11.1	3.6	7.0
public services	11.0	15.7	5.5	8.7
public administration	13.7	17.5	9.1	12.3

[a] Impact effect
[b] Starting year: 1981.
Source: ISTAT.

pressure on wages, and was accompanied by the virtual disappearance of internal migration (Dell'Aringa, 1993; Bodo and Sestito, 1991; Attanasio and Padoa Schioppa, 1990). Real wages declined only in one year (1982), then picked up with a distinct acceleration in the second half of the decade (Fig. 4.1 and Table 4.1). Formal econometric testing has failed to confirm any significant role of price expectations in helping disinflation or mitigating adjustment costs, in terms of lost output and employment (De Nardis and Micossi, 1991; Egebo and Englander, 1992).

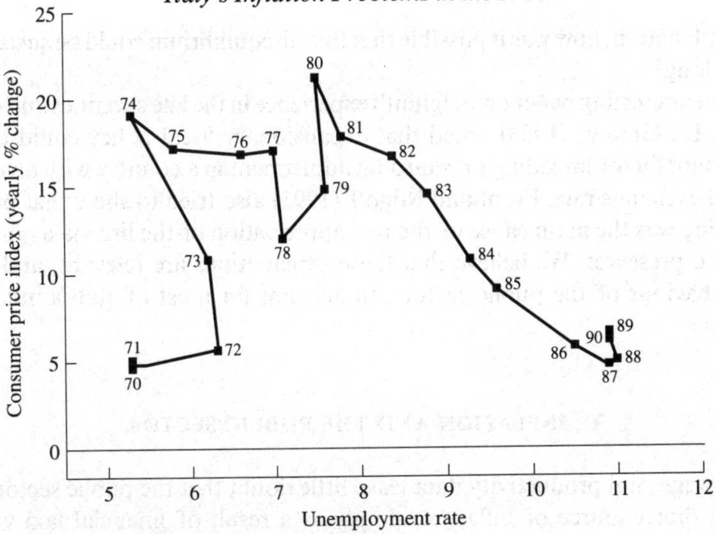

FIG. 4.2. Inflation and unemployment

Thirdly, exchange rate discipline mostly affected industry, where remarkable productivity increases were recorded, the rest of the economy much less. In the public sector, in the first half of the eighties, productivity declined, partly as a result of increased employment absorbing labour shed by industry; productivity increased modestly in most private services (Pellegrini, 1992). Through the 1980s, the price of services rose at rates well above those of manufactured goods (Table 1; CER, 1991 and Visco, 1992); the resulting increase in their relative prices outpaced that observed in other European countries (Visco, 1992 and centro Studi Confindustria). Since in private services wages were rising more or less in line with manufacturing, one suspects rising margins; some evidence to this effect is presented by Visco (1992).

These developments should be placed against the background of appreciating real exchange rate, widening current external deficit and—in the second half of the 1980s—below-average growth of Italy relative to its EC partners. Consumption always rose more rapidly than GDP, and more rapidly than in the rest of the EC. Exports and investment grew less than GDP and below the European average. Imports grew more than GDP (with a strong rise in import penetration), almost in line with the rest of Europe (Eurostat and ISTAT, National Accounts). The real appreciation of the lira contributed to shifting relative prices and resources towards domestic absorption, namely consumption (mainly services), and away from exports and investment in industry.

Now the question posed at the beginning of this Section stands out more clearly: how was it possible that consumer prices, notably the prices of services, and wages could continue to increase steadily above the European average despite non-accommodating monetary policy? And, since the persistent shortfall of domestic supply relative to domestic demand must be an important part of the explanation, how was it possible that this disequilibrium could be sustained for so long?

In an interesting paper on Belgium's experience in the late seventies and early 1980s, De Grauwe (1983) noted that expansionary fiscal policy could be an important factor impeding or retarding adjustment in a country with an over-valued exchange rate. Froot and Rogoff (1991) also tried to show that public spending was the main cause of the real appreciation of the lira via aggregate demand pressures. We believe that these explanations are relevant, and that the behaviour of the public sector can account for most of Italy's inflation problem.

3. INFLATION AND THE PUBLIC SECTOR

Price, wage, and productivity data leave little doubt that the public sector has been a direct source of inflation, simply as a result of financial laxity and inefficient management.

The non-sale service (public administration) deflator displayed an average yearly increase of 13.8 per cent in 1980–91, declining from 17.4 per cent in 1980–5 to 9.2 in 1986–9, and rising again to 12.3 per cent in 1990–1. The corresponding figures for manufacturing were 8.1 per cent in 1980–91, 12.3 in 1980–5, 4.6 per cent in 1986–9, 2.9 per cent in 1990–1 (Table 4.1). Thus, the public sector deflator increased at a rate that was a multiple of the private industry deflator and has been rising since 1986.

The public sector also had the highest wage increases and the lowest productivity gains in the 1980s. In 1990–1 unit wages increased by 12.2 per cent, after growing 8.4 per cent in 1986–9 (8 and 7.4 per cent respectively in manufacturing). As a result of higher growth over a decade, in 1991 the average compensation per employee (based on National Accounts data) was just above 49 million lire for the public administration, and around 40 million for the rest of the economy (41 for industry, 39 for services).[2]

Loose budget constraints, inefficiency, overmanning and generous wages also characterize much of public utilities, public entreprises, and the banking system (which is also largely publicly-owned). For instance, the Mediobanca (1992) survey of 1790 large companies shows average wages of 55 million lire for private companies and 58 for public companies in 1991. This number rises to 63 million lire for public utilities in the sample, and 71.5 million lire for transportation. Most public companies have accumulated large debts, often close to or above the value of their annual sales.

[2] Nominally, the public sector displays a higher share of high-quality jobs and higher-education employees, which has been used to argue that the average compensation should indeed be higher in the public sector: the fact is that very often upgrading of positions and employees has been used to grant wage increases, while in most cases only the worst graduates from high schools and universities would take jobs in the public sector.

Detailed studies on public utilities were conducted by Prosperetti (1992*a*, *b*; see also Centro Studi Confindustria 1992*b*): they show in general higher costs and lower quality of services, relative to the other industrial countries.[3]

As can be seen in Table 4.1, 1986–9 was the only period when public utility tariff increases were below those of the consumer price index; tariffs were clearly a factor slowing disinflation in 1980–5 and adding to resurgent price pressures in 1990–1. To a certain extent, the behaviour of 'administered' prices was similar, although these did not outpace the consumer price index in 1986–91. The significant increase of the second half of the 1980s in indirect taxation also had direct repercussions on prices. It can be gauged that tariffs and indirect taxation have added 'mechanically' almost 1 per cent to CPI growth every year since 1987 (Table 4.1).

A recent study prepared for the EC Commission (Ernst and Young, 1992) on public procurement has provided fresh evidence on the high costs paid by the public sector for services, supplies, and equipment. Important side-effects such as lowering technological standards and muting competitive pressure in suppliers' markets are also identified.

Extensive government intervention altered relative prices, income distribution, and the structure of production and employment systematically. Large increases in direct taxation and social security contributions that had led Italy, at the end of the 1980s, to an above-average tax pressure relative to the EC, added further to distortions.

Some basic facts are worth recalling in this regard. Italy's decision to become a member of the EMS, in 1979, coincided almost exactly with a sharp acceleration in public spending, leading to some 11 percentage points increase in the ratio of public spending to GDP over the ensuing decade (Table 4.2). Revenues were also growing rapidly as a share of GDP, less rapidly than spending until 1985, more rapidly afterwards. As a result, the public sector deficit continued to increase (to a peak of 13 per cent of GDP) until the middle of the decade, and declined afterwards; it remained above 10 per cent of GDP throughout the 1980s and early 1990s, leading to a sharp increase in the debt-to-GDP ratio (which in 1990 reached 100 per cent).

[3] Some peculiar features of tariff policies enhanced their adverse inflationary and efficiency effects: (i) Tariff policies were decided on a year-by-year basis to maximize political control over company management; this induced a very short-sighted attitude in corporate decisions, and made these decisions dependent on the vagaries of the political junctures. The adverse consequences of this on investment decisions and technological levels are difficult to quantify, but certainly important. (ii) Tariff increases were, at times, restrained or delayed to magnify the slow-down in the consumer price or cost-of-living indices, critical magnitudes for wage negotiations, and price expectations. However, this did not lead to any slow-down in costs or improved efficiency but resulted in higher deficits, later to be taken up by the Treasury; periods of restraint were usually followed by higher-than-average increases in subsequent periods. (iii) The structure of tariffs was distorted for redistributive purposes; on balance, a higher share of costs fell on manufacturing and commercial activities, while household services were generously subsidized. This helped mute even further the role of price signals for management and disconnect productivity from price developments.

TABLE 4.2. *Selected variables in public sector finances* (yearly percentage changes and percentage ratios to GDP)

	Percentage changes				Percentage ratios to GDP		
	Nominal 1980–91	Real 1980–91	Nominal 1987–91	Real 1987–91	1979	1986	1991
Total spending	16.1	5.1	10.9	4.5	41.2	51.0	53.9
net of interest	15.4	4.4	10.3	4.0	36.2	42.5	43.7
Current spending	16.3	5.2	11.3	4.9	37.1	45.9	49.4
Interest payments	20.5	9.0	13.7	7.2	5.0	8.5	10.2
Personnel	15.2	4.2	11.6	5.2	10.8	11.7	12.8
Pensions	16.0	5.0	12.0	5.5	9.6	11.2	12.4
Transfers to entreprises	11.6	1.0	3.2	−2.7	2.8	3.1	2.3
Total revenues	16.7	5.6	12.0	5.5	31.6	39.4	43.7
Tax revenues	17.9	6.6	13.2	6.7	16.5	21.9	25.7
direct	18.8	7.5	12.3	5.9	8.4	12.9	14.5
indirect	16.7	5.6	14.2	7.7	8.0	9.1	11.2
Social security contrib.	14.9	3.9	10.8	4.5	12.8	13.9	14.7
Total balance[a]	−10.9		−10.6		−9.6	−11.6	−10.2
net of interest[a]	−2.9		−1.6		−4.6	−3.1	−0.0
Current balance[a]	−6.3		−6.0		−5.6	−6.8	−6.1
Total debt					61.6	88.2	104.0
Per memoriam							
GDP	13.6	2.8	9.7	3.4			

[a] Percentage ratios to GDP.

Source: ISTAT, National Accounts.

The increase in spending was largely concentrated, by functional category, in interest payments, personnel, pensions and other welfare spending; by government level, in decentralized spending units (local governments and the health management bodies, USL: Franco, 1992). In the second half of the 1980s there was a distinct slow-down in transfers to enterprises (they declined in real terms) and capital spending, while payments to households accelerated in real terms (Table 4.2).

Revenues grew more rapidly than GDP throughout the decade, with indirect taxes and social security contributions picking up in 1987–91. The tax burden remained unevenly distributed, with agriculture, small handicraft, most small distribution and liberal professions, and the Mezzogiorno *de jure* or *de facto* subject to a very light burden. Distortions are magnified by the complexity of legislation, the large number of special cases, and poor administration. There is evidence that forward-shifting of taxation by wage-earners was significant and increasing over time (Tullio, 1986; Micossi and Tullio, 1991): of course, the outcome has been that increases in direct taxation have become more inflationary. The share of taxes collected from enterprises, the self-employed, and the regions of the Centre-North increased during the decade.

Therefore, on the whole, there was sizeable redistribution, through the budget, in favour of households in lower-income brackets and the Mezzogiorno, against households in middle-high-income brackets, enterprises, and the Centre-North. Moreover, since most revenues were collected centrally and an increasing share of spending was undertaken by decentralized spending units, administrators were encouraged to overlook the budget constraint, while the beneficiaries of spending programmes and citizens in general had limited perception of their costs.

Closer inspection of disaggregate data for households and enterprises can help to complete the picture. As for households, it was mentioned already that the increase in spending mainly took the form of direct job creation, pensions, and other benefits; there was a large increase both in the number of people receiving benefits and in the average payment (Franco, 1992). Fig. 4.3 shows that the increase in payments well outpaced that of revenues, so that net transfers to households rose. In the Mezzogiorno in 1988 the public sector's personnel and welfare spending reached 49 per cent of the area's GDP, some 70 per cent of disposable income (Micossi and Tullio, 1991).

In Table 4.3 we have decomposed increases in disposable income by source: the growing weight of payments from the public sector—interest payments, welfare, public sector wages—is striking. Public sector wages and pensions 'explain' 41 per cent of disposable income growth in 1980–91 (5.3 percentage points out of 12.9 total nominal growth), 46 per cent in 1987–91 (4 per cent out of 8.8); if interest payments on public debt are included these numbers become respectively 56 per cent in 1980–91 and 63 per cent in 1987–91. As a result, between 1980 and 1991 the weight of public salaries and welfare payments in households' disposable income grew from 29 per cent to 38 per cent and that of interest payments on public debt went from 5 per cent to 12 per cent; the weight

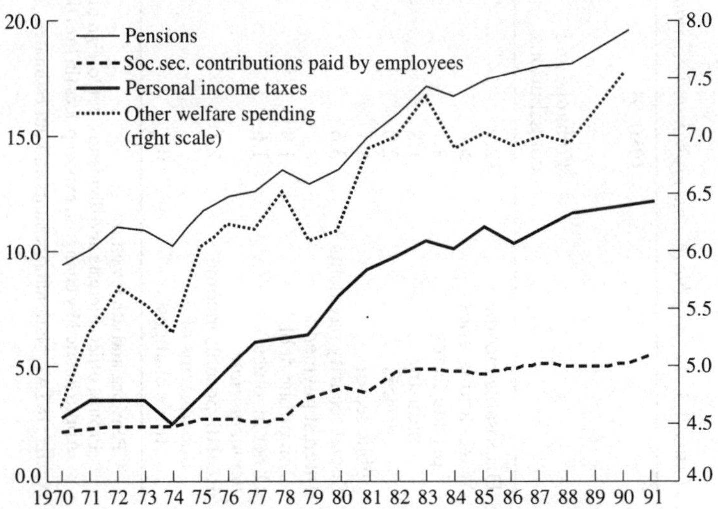

FIG. 4.3. Households: Pensions, other welfare spending, and personal income taxes (percentage ratios to disposable income)

TABLE 4.3. *Disposable income growth and its components* (yearly geometric averages)

	1980–91		1987–91		Share in disposable income level	
	% change and contributions	Share of total increase	% change and contributions	Share of total increase	1980	1991
Disposable income	12.9	100.0	8.8	100.0	100.0	100.0
Wages and salaries	5.8	45.0	4.2	47.7	46.2	45.4
private sector	4.1	31.8	2.9	33.0	35.7	32.8
industry	1.8	14.0	1.2	13.6	19.7	15.2
services	2.0	15.5	1.4	15.9	13.1	15.1
public sector	1.7	13.2	1.3	14.8	10.5	12.6
Social security payments [a]	3.6	27.9	2.7	30.7	18.6	25.8
Interest payments on public debt	1.9	14.7	1.5	17.0	4.7	12.3
Other incomes [b]	1.6	12.4	0.4	4.5	30.6	16.5
per memoriam						
Real disposable income	2.1	100.0	2.6	100.0		
due to terms of trade changes[c]	0.5	23.8	0.2	7.7		

[a] Pensions and other welfare.
[b] Profits, other interests and dividends, net foreign income and residual item.
[c] Approximated by change in export prices (in lire) times exports at constant prices minus.

Source: ISTAT, National Accounts and our estimates.

of manufacturing wages fell from 20 per cent to 15 per cent. Micossi and Tullio (1991) have shown that government transfers and redistributive expenditure were a major factor in raising private consumption and the aggregate propensity to consume: directly, because transfer recipients show a higher-than-average propensity to consume, and indirectly, via (positive) wealth effects of public debt and (positive) effects of the terms of trade gains stemming from the real appreciation of the lira.

Turning to enterprises, three aspects should be noted. First, during the 1980s there was a trend ('structural') increase in the tax wedge between labour cost and net pay: Italy's wedge ranks among the highest in the industrial world (Centro Studi Confindustria, 1990). Secondly, for the first part of the decade the trend increase was delayed, or hidden, by discretionary exemptions from part of statutory rates of social security contributions (Fig. 4.4). Cost-reduction effects were reinforced by a temporary unemployment compensation scheme (Cassa integrazione guadagni) that made it easier for firms to shed labour and reduced labour costs (see also Giavazzi and Spaventa, 1990). Thirdly, transfers to enterprises were used to foster the restructuring process but also worked to protect sectors hit by declining competitiveness: this shows in the high share of transfers that were utilized for 'defensive' purposes as well as by the small share that was reserved for manufacturing, exports, and R & D (Ford and Suyker, 1989; Centro Studi Confindustria, 1992*a*).

Large increases in personal transfers also had important consequences on the labour market. Despite unemployment being largely concentrated in the South and labour productivity differentials of the order of 20 per cent between the North and the South, wages were almost equalized, and migration from the

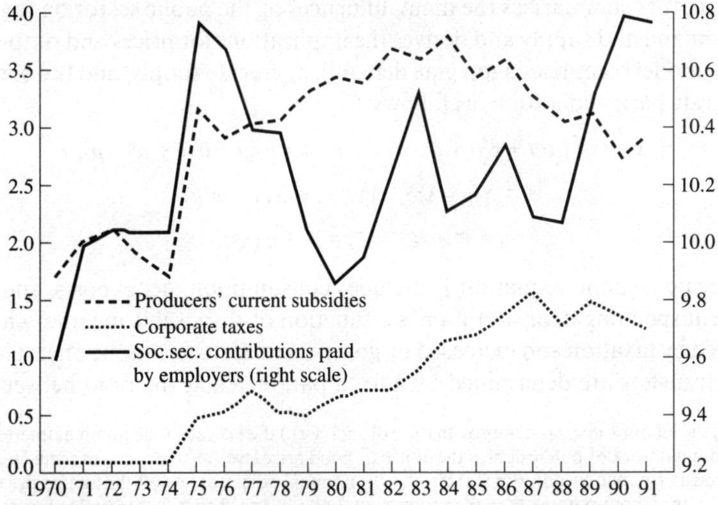

FIG. 4.4. Corporate sector: Social security contributions paid by employers, producers' current subsidies, and corporate taxes (percentage ratio to GDP)

South to the North came to a virtual halt in the 1980s. The difference in labour costs that would have resulted from equal wages with different productivity was offset by special exemptions from social security contributions in the South; not only was there no tendency for the productivity gap to close, but in the 1980s it widened again (Svimez, 1992).

Bodo and Sestito (1991) in their accurate analysis of Italy's labour market show that in recent years there was a significant increase in 'wait' unemployment in the South, where the increase in transfers was concentrated, and that this can contribute to explain the observed declining sensitivity of wages to unemployment. Micossi and Tullio (1991) present evidence that in the 1980s welfare spending in the South was 'leading', rather than following, unemployment. Attanasio and Padoa Schioppa (1990) confirm that the decline in internal migration flows has been a consequence of increased government transfers.

In general, real wage resistance must have been encouraged by ready availability of public support for workers displaced from industry during the phase of restructuring. Moreover, since workers tended to move to the 'protected' sector during cyclical downswings, but the reverse flow was weaker during upswings, the labour market in the 'exposed' sector tended to remain close to full employment, and wage pressures were ready to develop as soon as industry growth accelerated (De Nardis and Micossi, 1991; Bodo and Sestito, 1991).

4. THE MODEL

In this section we present a simple model, with one good and one factor of production, that summarizes the main influences of the public sector on (aggregate) demand and supply and derives the implications for prices and output.

The model comprises aggregate demand, aggregate supply, and the open interest rate parity condition, as follows:[4]

$$y^{d} = \alpha\bar{l} - \alpha t + \beta(i + d - p) - \gamma(i - \pi^{e}) + \xi g + \theta(\bar{e} + p^{*} - p), \tag{1}$$

$$y^{s} = \eta\,[p - \lambda p^{e}_{c} + \ln\nu - t + \omega_1 \bar{l} - \omega_2 k], \tag{2}$$

$$i = i^{*} + (e^{e}_{+1} - \bar{e}) = i^{*} + \phi(\pi^{e}). \tag{3}$$

Aggregate demand (equation 1) includes consumption, net exports, and government spending. Consumption is a function of disposable income, which is reduced by taxation and increased by government transfers to the unemployed; these transfers are determined by a fixed parameter, k, the ratio between the

[4] $\bar{l}$ is the labour force, t (an approximation of $\ln(1 + t)$) the tax rate, i the nominal interest rate, d the nominal stock of public debt, p the domestic good price level, $\pi^{e} = p^{e} - p_{-1}$ expected inflation (equation 8), g public spending in real terms, e the nominal exchange rate, p^{*} the foreign price level, $u = \bar{l} - l$, ν the labour parameter in the production function, specified as $y = \nu l$ (in log form), and k the ratio of the unemployment compensation payment to the wage. Lower case variables, except i, k, and t, are natural logarithms; all parameters are positive.

unemployment compensation and the current wage, and the number of unemployed workers. Consumption increases with interest payments on government debt (income effect) and the debt level (wealth effect: the propensity to consume out of interest payments and debt is assumed to be the same), and decreases with rising real interest rates. Net exports are a positive function of the real exchange rate,[5] and real government spending is exogenous.

Aggregate supply (equation 2) is derived from a simple labour market model:

$$w = p + (\nu - 1)\, l + \ln\nu - t. \tag{4}$$

$$w = \lambda p_c^e - \omega_1 u + \omega_2 k. \tag{5}$$

Equation (4) is the labour demand function (in log-form): the real labour cost equals the marginal productivity of labour, the real labour cost being real wage plus taxation. Taxation is specified as a mark-up over net wage: in this formulation taxation can be interpreted as anything that introduces a wedge between wage and labour cost. Similarly, any subsidy that reduces this wedge, such as a relief on social security contributions or other transfers to producers, can be treated as a (multiplicative) 'mark-down'.

In the labour supply function (equation 5), the wage demanded by workers is an increasing function of expected consumer prices, p_c^e, and of the unemployment-compensation-to-wage ratio (k: an increase in k raises the reservation wage), and a negative function of unemployment. While we have not allowed for this possibility in our formulation of equation (5), it is conceivable that in the real world a high value of k could correspond to a low value of ω_1: indeed, for $k = 1$, there is no reason why unemployment should have any effect on wages (since the same income would be earned regardless of whether one was working or not). It should also be noted that equations (4) and (5) entail full forward-shifting of taxation.

The Consumer Price Index (equation 7) is a weighted average (with weights δ and $1 - \delta$) of prices of domestically produced goods and imported goods:

$$p_c = \delta p + (1 - \delta)\,(p^* + \bar{e}). \tag{6}$$

The price of imported goods is known with certainty since foreign prices and the exchange rate are assumed to be fixed. Price expectations of home produced goods (that enter equation 5) are assumed to be determined as a function of past prices:

$$p^e = \rho p_{-1} \tag{7}$$

so that

$$\pi^e = (\rho - 1)\, p_{-1} \tag{8}$$

and

$$p_c^e = \delta p^e + (1 - \delta)\,(p^* + \bar{e}). \tag{9}$$

[5] A rising (nominal and real) exchange rate corresponds to depreciation.

Hence, the (short-run) aggregate supply (equation 2) depends positively on current domestic prices. The supply curve shifts 'leftwards' for higher past domestic prices (that determine current price expectations) and foreign prices (expressed in domestic currency), taxation (wider tax wedge), and k ratios; it shifts 'rightwards' for higher lnν (that reflects higher productivity) and labour force (that, *ceteris paribus*, would lead to downward pressure on wages).

In the long run the supply curve becomes vertical: with $\lambda = 1$ (full indexation of wages to consumer prices), $p = p^* + \bar{e}$ (goods market arbitrage works), and $p^e = p$, equation (2) becomes

$$y^s_{LR} = \eta\,[\ln\nu - t + \omega_1 \bar{l} - \omega_2 k] \tag{10}$$

The long-run level of output will always be lower than full-employment output (defined, from the production function, by $\bar{y} = \nu\bar{l}$) since $\eta\omega_1/\nu < 1$ and all the other terms inside the square brackets are negative; the gap is an increasing function of t and k.

Equation (3) is the interest arbitrage equation. We have assumed that the current exchange rate level (e) is a policy instrument, exogenously set, and that the expected exchange rate (at time $t + 1$) is an increasing function of expected inflation. The function ϕ incorporates any change in the risk premium for changing expected inflation. If $\phi' > 1$ or ϕ' and $\phi'' > 0$, an increase in expected inflation raises the real interest rate.

The model can be solved for income and prices (we have set $k = 1$ for simplicity). We obtain:

$$y = \mu_o\bar{l} - \mu_1 t + \mu_2 (i + d) - \mu_3 (i - \pi^e) + \mu_4 g + \mu_5 (p^* + \bar{e}) + \mu_6 \ln\nu - \mu_7 k - \mu_8 p_{-1} \tag{11}$$

$$p = \mu_9\bar{l} + \mu_{10} t + \mu_{11} (i + d) - \mu_{12} (i - \pi^e) + \mu_{13} g + \mu_{14} (p^* + \bar{e}) - \mu_{15} \ln\nu + \mu_{16} k + \mu_{17} p_{-1}, \tag{12}$$

where:

$$\mu_0 = \frac{\eta[\alpha + \omega_1(\beta + \theta)]}{(\beta + \theta + \eta)},\ \mu_1 = \frac{\eta(\alpha + \beta + \theta)}{(\beta + \theta + \eta)},\ \mu_2 = \frac{\eta\beta}{(\beta + \theta + \eta)},\ \mu_3 = \frac{\eta\gamma}{(\beta + \theta + \eta)},$$

$$\mu_4 = \frac{\eta\xi}{(\beta + \theta + \eta)},\ \mu_5 = \frac{\eta\,[\theta - \lambda(1 - \delta)(\beta + \theta)]}{(\beta + \theta + \eta)},\ \mu_6 = \frac{\eta\,(\beta + \theta)}{(\beta + \theta + \eta)},$$

$$\mu_7 = \frac{\eta\,(\beta + \theta)\,\omega_2}{(\beta + \theta + \eta)},\ \mu_8 = \frac{\eta\lambda\delta\rho}{(\beta + \theta + \eta)},\ \mu_9 = \frac{(\alpha - \omega_1\eta)}{(\beta + \theta + \eta)},$$

$$\mu_{10} = \frac{(\eta - \alpha)}{(\beta + \theta + \eta)},\ \mu_{11} = \frac{\beta}{(\beta + \theta + \eta)},\ \mu_{12} = \frac{\gamma}{(\beta + \theta + \eta)},\ \mu_{13} = \frac{\xi}{(\beta + \theta + \eta)},$$

$$\mu_{14} = \frac{[\theta + \eta\lambda(1 - \delta)]}{(\beta + \theta + \eta)},\ \mu_{15} = \frac{\eta}{(\beta + \theta + \eta)},\ \mu_{16} = \frac{\eta\omega_2}{(\beta + \theta + \eta)},\ \mu_{17} = \frac{\eta\lambda\delta\rho}{(\beta + \theta + \eta)}.$$

Government spending has the standard (initial) positive effects on income and prices, via aggregate demand. Income falls in response to higher taxation since aggregate demand and aggregate supply are both reduced. The effect of taxation on prices is ambiguous since prices are reduced via aggregate demand (that falls) but increased via aggregate supply (that falls too).

With elastic (short-run) aggregate supply (larger η), taxation is more inflationary and contractionary, and government spending is less inflationary and more expansionary. The positive effect of taxation on prices is larger than that of government spending if $\eta - \alpha > \chi$: this condition shows that the inflationary impact of taxation is stronger in countries with a high propensity to save (low α), such as Italy. Furthermore, the price and income effects of changes in government spending and taxation depend on the parameters θ (aggregate demand elasticity to real exchange rate changes) and β (the propensity to consume out of interest payments and wealth): higher values of these parameters reduce the positive effect of government spending on income and prices and the effect of taxation on prices, and increase the contractionary effect of taxation. It is a property of this model that the deficit reduction effects of a given increase in the tax rate are lower for higher initial level of the tax rate.

Raising k (ratio of unemployment compensation to current wage) always raises the price level; the effect on income is ambiguous since aggregate demand goes up and aggregate supply goes down. The effect on prices is stronger for higher ω_2 (impact of k on reservation wage) and η (supply elasticity).

In the long run, of course, quantity (output) effects of changes in aggregate demand tend to disappear, and price effects are magnified; higher taxation or subsidies reduce the long-run output level, again with adverse effects on prices.

When domestic prices rise, if the nominal exchange rate is held fixed, the real exchange rate q appreciates, the real exchange rate (competitiveness) being defined as follows:

$$q = \bar{e} + p^* - p. \tag{13}$$

The reduced form equation for q, from our model, is:

$$q = \bar{e} + p^* - \mu_9\bar{l} - \mu_{10}t - \mu_{11}(i + d) + \mu_{12}(i - \pi^e) - \mu_{13}g - \mu_{14}(p^* + \bar{e}) + \mu_{15}\ln v - \mu_{16}k - \mu_{17}p_{-1}. \tag{14}$$

Depending on the value of ρ and the functional form of ϕ it is possible that the real exchange rate appreciation goes hand in hand with an increase in real interest rates: this happens if the increase in prices leads to increased expected inflation (which happens with $\rho > 1$) and the risk premium rises more than expected inflation.

Any increases in government spending, including subsidies to unemployed workers, lead to the standard result of real exchange rate appreciation. The effects of taxation on q are not clear-cut: when taxation is inflationary (the adverse effect on supply is stronger than that on demand) rising taxes will reduce q, inducing real appreciation.

Over time, the appreciation of the real exchange rate should set in motion equilibrating changes in domestic wages that would eliminate the initial excess demand (since consumer prices are falling and output is falling in the export sector). However, if nominal wages are 'downwards sticky' and increased unemployment in the export sector is met with increased transfers from the government (rising k ratio), the real appreciation could persist and lead to a cumulative increase in unemployment and public spending for transfers. Increasing real interest rates could aggravate the picture and, to the extent that the debt to GDP ratio is large, also make the debt stability conditions more stringent.

It is interesting to examine what happens in our model if the tax rate is made endogenous so as to maintain a balanced budget at all times: this highlights the properties of a world where the government keeps on raising taxes to match ever-increasing welfare spending. Let us assume that the government debt and non-transfer public spending are equal to zero, and that transfers are financed by taxation. We add the balanced-budget constraint to our model:

$$tWL = kW(\bar{L} - L) \tag{15}$$

(W is net wage, L employment, and $\bar{L}$ the labour force, all current values); equation (15) determines the tax rate t. With $k = 1$, the tax rate t turns out to be equal to:[6]

$$t = \frac{(\bar{L} - L)}{L}. \tag{16}$$

Aggregate demand becomes:

$$y^d = -\gamma' (i - \pi^e) + \theta' (\bar{e} + p^* - p), \tag{17}$$

where the parameters γ' and θ' are smaller than γ and θ in equation (1): the aggregate demand schedule becomes flatter. Aggregate supply is:

$$y^s = \eta' \{p - \lambda\delta p^e - \lambda(1 - \delta)(p^* + e) + \ln v + (\omega_1 - 1)\bar{l} - \omega_2 k\}, \tag{18}$$

where η'. is negative.[7] Thus aggregate supply is negatively sloped; the system is stable when aggregate supply is steeper than aggregate demand. It is easy to see that in the stable case any aggregate demand shock (such as an increase in public spending) is at the same time contractionary and inflationary; fiscal policy has perverse effects.

5. PRICE EQUATIONS

The specification of the estimating equation for prices is only loosely related to the price equation obtained from the model. The long-run equation from the model, in implicit form, is as follows:

[6] This implies that $\ln(l + t) = u$; we substitute this expression for u in the labour demand function, and abandon the approximation made previously.

[7] With our assumptions, the demand for labour is upward-sloping; the reason for this is that when employment goes up the effect on productivity (which is decreasing) is more than offset by the reduction in the tax wedge, so that the net effect is positive. We then consider the case in which labour demand is steeper than labour supply, since this ensures stability of the labour market.

$$p = f(\bar{l}, t, i, d, i^*, g, (p^* + e), \text{lnv}, k). \quad (19)$$

The price level is directly related to foreign prices (in lire), public debt and public spending, workers' subsidies, possibly the tax rate (to be taken as the entire tax wedge: direct taxes plus social security contributions minus transfers to producers); inversely related to nominal and real interest rates, the labour force and lnv.

Three sets of equations were estimated, having as dependent variables respectively the total value-added deflator (*P*), the industry deflator (*IP*), and the service deflator (*SP*). Separate equations for prices in the industry and services were estimated to 'capture' possibly different effects of our public sector variables across sectors.

The foreign price variable (P^*) is a weighted average of the prices of Italy's trade partners in domestic currency. Productivity is defined as GDP per worker. The social security contributions variables (*TSC* for the total, *TSCW* for contributions paid by workers, *TSCE* for contributions paid by employers) and current producers' transfers (*PS*) are divided by full-employment total value-added: thus our rate of contribution, subsidy or transfer can be taken to represent the 'long-run' (structural) incidence of those components.

Government spending includes purchases of goods and services, deflated with their deflator, dependent labour income, pensions, and interest payments on public debt (deflated with the private consumption deflator).

We have adopted an error correction specification: the general form of the estimated equations is:

$$\Delta y - \beta \Delta \mathbf{x} + \alpha y_{-1} + \gamma \mathbf{x}_{-1}, \quad (20)$$

where y is the dependent variable and $\mathbf{x}$ is the vector of regressors. The parameters β are the impact coefficients; α is the adjustment coefficient and the expression $-\gamma/\alpha$ gives the long-run coefficients.

We were not able to identify any strong and stable effect of the real interest rate on inflation: possible reasons are simultaneity with the dependent variable and the inclusion of foreign prices among the regressors (in the past accelerations in imported inflation were associated with loose monetary policy, low interest rates, and depreciations, and the contrary was true when imported inflation was low). We tried to tackle the simultaneity problem with instrumental variables estimation, with little success. Therefore, the second explanation probably applies: in other words, the foreign price variable would seem to embody the exchange rate–monetary policy effect on domestic inflation.

Among the public sector variables, no significant effect was identified for the unemployment-benefit proxy variables (defined as in the wage equations); also, the debt stock appeared to contribute to the explanation of inflation only marginally when public spending was included among the regressors. The coefficient of direct taxation was never significant and sometimes showed a negative sign: indeed from our model the sign of taxation in the reduced-form equation for prices is ambiguous, due to the contemporaneous presence of demand and supply effects. The labour force variable showed no explanatory power.

Eventually, we estimated 'broad' equations (equations 2, 3, and 4 in Tables 4.4 to 4.6) that included among regressors foreign prices, productivity, and public sector variables: current public spending, social security contributions (in some cases with separate variables for payments by employers and employees), and transfers to producers, and compared their performance with that of equations where these variables were excluded (equation 1).

In Table 4.4, we report our estimates for the aggregate value-added deflator. In the basic equation (equation 1), foreign prices are very significant, both in the short and the long run, with a long-run coefficient not statistically different from 1, as one would expect. The impact effect of productivity on inflation is negative, whereas it becomes positive in the long run. While the explanation of the short-term coefficient is straightforward, a positive long-run coefficient is troublesome: in the long run labour productivity can conceivably contribute to lowering prices (less-than-unitary wage elasticity to productivity increases) or have no effects (unitary wage elasticity to productivity increases), but should not display a positive sign (which could only be the result of higher-than-unitary wage elasticity to productivity changes). This finding could reflect the high (upward) sensitivity of wages to cyclical upswings, due to the fact that the 'working' labour market operates most of the time close to full employment (see Section 3). It could also be the result of spurious correlation between the common cyclical components of prices and productivity. Indeed, when we include public spending (equation 4), lagged productivity becomes insignificant.

Equations 2 and 3 include social security contributions (*TSC*, and *TSCW* and *TSCE* separately for workers and enterprises) and producers' transfers (*PS*), but not public spending. Social security contributions add to inflation with an elasticity of 0.206, when introduced as a single variable (equation 2) and 0.105 and 0.087 respectively for contributions paid by employers and workers (equation 3). Transfers to producers are found to have contributed to reducing inflation: the coefficients are higher and more significant in equation 3 than in equation 2; the impact effect rises from –0.028 to –0.04, and from –0.151 to –0.182 in the long run. The variable-deletion tests for social security contributions (*TSC* in equation 2; *TSCE* and *TSCW* in equation 3) and producers' transfers, in differences and lagged values, reject the null hypothesis. Equations 2 and 3 perform distinctly better than equation 1, in terms of fit, notably in the last five years: the fitted values obtained from the equations containing public sector variables miss the 1991 observation, but they track well the resurgence of inflation in 1987 to 1990.

A distinct improvement in the estimates is obtained when the current spending variable (*RG*) is introduced: the impact elasticity is close to one-fourth, and the long-run coefficient is 0.41. This equation with public spending also displays the best out-of-sample performance, and indeed tracks very well the recovery of inflation after 1987.

TABLE 4.4. *Total economy value added deflator* (ΔP) (sample period: 1961–91 (annual data))

Independent variables	Equation 1		Equation 2		Equation 3		Equation 4	
	Coeff.	(t)	Coeff.	(t)	Coeff.	(t)	Coeff.	(t)
Δp^*	0.420	(7.087)	0.415	(7.893)	0.406	(8.090)	0.413	(8.478)
ΔPR	–0.574	(–3.271)	–0.352	(–1.715)	–0.258	(–1.227)	–0.309	(–1.756)
$\Delta TSCW$	—	—	—	—	0.105	(2.468)	0.098	(2.453)
$\Delta TSCE$	—	—	—	—	0.087	(1.114)	0.091	(1.323)
ΔTSC	—	—	–0.206	(2.428)	—	—	—	—
ΔPS	—	—	–0.028	(–0.926)	–0.040	(–1.343)	–0.049	(–1.853)
ΔRG	—	—	—	—	—	—	0.249	(2.216)
$P(-1)$	–0.232	(–4.945)	–0.409	(–5.731)	–0.455	(–5.775)	–0.557	(–5.999)
$P^*(-1)$	0.233	(5.122)	0.408	(5.617)	0.428	(5.884)	0.474	(6.424)
$PR(-1)$	0.103	(2.556)	0.147	(2.015)	0.207	(2.432)	—	—
$TSCW(-1)$	—	—	—	—	0.135	(2.892)	0.146	(3.425)
$TSCE(-1)$	—	—	—	—	0.241	(2.499)	0.208	(2.328)
$TSC(-1)$	—	—	0.352	(3.031)	—	—	—	—
$PS(-1)$	—	—	–0.062	(–1.571)	–0.083	(–2.086)	–0.101	(–2.812)
$RG(-1)$	—	—	—	—	—	—	0.229	(3.269)
$CONST$	–0.284	(–1.929)	0.066	(0.133)	0.076	(0.140)	–2.156	(–2.057)

TABLE 4.4. *(cont.)*

Independent variables	Equation 1		Equation 2		Equation 3		Equation 4	
	Coeff.	(*t*)	Coeff.	(*t*)	Coeff.	(*t*)	Coeff.	(*t*)
Estimation tests								
	$R^2 = 0.905$		$R^2 = 0.933$		$R^2 = 0.940$		$R^2 = 0.950$	
	DW = 1.525		DW = 1.987		DW = 2.114		DW = 2.080	
Serial correlation[a]	F(1,24) = 1.438		F(1,20) = 0.055		F(1,18) = 0.383		F(1,17) = 0.160	
Functional form[b]	F(1,24) = 0.619		F(1,20) = 0.282		F(1,18) = 0.005		F(1,17) = 0.019	
Normality[c]	$X^2(2) = 3.706$		$X^2(2) = 0.365$		$X^2(2) = 1.452$		$X^2(2) = 1.449$	
Heteroscedasticity[d]	F(1,29) = 0.285		F(1,29) = 0.191		F(1,29) = 0.003		F(1,29) = 0.739	
Variable deletion[e]	—		F(4,21) = 3.640		F(6,19) = 3.480		F(8,18) = 5.197	
Out-of-sample prediction tests								
Mean error	0.021		0.002		0.013		–0.003	
Abs. mean error	0.021		0.011		0.015		0.007	
Root mean sq. error	0.027		0.0136		0.021		0.009	
Predictive failure[f]	F(4,21) = 1.264		F(4,17) = 0.736		F(4,15) = 1.025		F(4,14) = 0.373	

[a] Godfrey's test.
[b] Ramsey's RESET test.
[c] Jarque-Bera's test.
[d] Anscombe's test.
[e] Test for the deletion of ΔTSC, $TSC(-1)$, ΔPS, $PS(-1)$ in equation 2; $\Delta TSCW$, $TSCW(-1)$, $\Delta TSCE$, $TSCE(-1)$, ΔPS, $PS(-1)$ in equation 3; ΔTSW, $TSW(-1)$, $\Delta TSCE$, $TSCE(-1)$, ΔPS, $PS(-1)$, ΔRG, $RG(-1)$ in equation 4.
[f] Chow's predictive failure test, predictions 1987–91.

Legenda (all variables in natural logarithms):
P = Value added deflator (1985 = 100); P^* = weighted average of foreign prices in domestic currency (in Italian Lira); PR = GDP per worker; TSC = social security contributions divided by full employment value added; PS = producers' transfers divided by full employment value added; $TSCW$ = social security contributions paid by workers divided by full employment value added; $TSCE$ = social security contributions paid by employers divided by full employment value added; RG = real current public spending (wages, pensions and interest payments deflated with the private consumption deflator, and current purchases deflated with their deflator).

Summarizing, equation 1 (without public sector variables) predicts a decline in inflation starting in 1988, while the increase in inflation, that lasted until 1990, is best explained by equation 4 and less well by equations 2 and 3. The 1991 slight decline is overestimated by all equations (i.e. there is underprediction of 1991 inflation), but equation 4 produces the smallest prediction error.

The estimates for the industry deflator are reported in Table 4.5. Foreign prices become even more significant, as one would expect: the impact coefficient is larger while the long-run coefficient remains statistically not different from 1. Productivity reduces inflation in the short run more than in the previous set of equations (with the exception of equation 1) and its statistical significance is improved. On the other hand, the lagged (level) variable has a negative coefficient in equations 2 and 3 and its significance falls to nil. Social security contributions are still an important and significant explanatory variable; the coefficient of total contributions equals the sum of the coefficients on contributions paid by workers and employers (equation 3). An important difference relative to the total-economy equation is that neither government expenditure nor producers' transfers contribute to explaining changes in the deflator; for this reason, the variable-deletion test on all public sector variables is below the critical value. However, when the test is repeated separately for social security contributions only, the null hypothesis is rejected.

The predictive performance of the equations with public sector variables (equations 2, 3, and 4) does not improve upon that of the equation without them (equation 1) when the estimate refers to the sample period 1961–87. There is always overprediction of inflation. However, if the sample period is extended to include also 1988, equations 2, 3, and 4 provide a better forecast and track the 1991 observation almost exactly. Finally, equations 2, 3, and 4 appear superior to equation 1 in terms of residuals diagnostics: equation 1 shows absence of normality in the residuals while this problem disappears in the estimates that include social security contributions.

The results for the value-added deflator of services are presented in Table 4.6. The impact coefficient of foreign prices is smaller than in the previous two equations and in one case (equation 2) the long-run parameter is statistically smaller than 1. Productivity has a negative coefficient in the short run, and is similar in size to that of the total deflator equation; the long-run coefficient is larger and highly significant. Note however, that the large size of this coefficient in the total deflator equation can reflect spurious (cyclical) correlations: indeed, lagged productivity becomes insignificant when public expenditure is included among the regressors (equation 4).

Comparison between the coefficients of government spending in the service deflator and the total deflator equations shows a stronger effect of public spending on service prices in the long run (0.457 in the service sector, 0.346 in the total economy when social security contributions are introduced as a single variable, and 0.41 when they are introduced as separate variables for workers and employers). This evidence confirms the hypothesis made in Section 2:

TABLE 4.5. *Industry value added deflator* (ΔIP) (sample period: 1961–91 (annual data))

Independent variables	Equation 1		Equation 2		Equation 3		Equation 4	
	Coeff.	(*t*)	Coeff.	(*t*)	Coeff.	(*t*)	Coeff.	(*t*)
ΔP^*	0.572	(9.732)	0.569	(12.013)	0.574	(11.568)	0.573	(9.961)
ΔPRI	–0.411	(–4.630)	–0.456	(–5.329)	–0.468	(–5.285)	–0.468	(–5.030)
$\Delta TSCW$	—	—	—	—	0.094	(2.132)	0.094	(1.991)
$\Delta TSCE$	—	—	—	—	0.172	(2.490)	0.167	(2.163)
ΔTSC	—	—	0.258	(3.636)	—	—	—	—
ΔRG	—	—	—	—	—	—	0.017	(0.142)
$IP(-1)$	–0.343	(–4.369)	–0.404	(–4.802)	–0.391	(–4.327)	–0.395	(–4.052)
$P^*(-1)$	0.337	(4.712)	0.392	(5.057)	0.371	(4.573)	0.372	(4.347)
$PRI(-1)$	0.035	(1.212)	—	—	—	—	—	—
$TSCW(-1)$	—	—	—	—	0.058	(1.344)	0.059	(1.286)
$TSCE(-1)$	—	—	—	—	0.145	(1.934)	0.133	(1.185)
$TSC(-1)$	—	—	0.196	(2.187)	—	—	—	—
$RG(-1)$	—	—	—	—	—	—	0.005	(0.150)
$CONST$	–0.061	(–0.549)	0.478	(2.576)	0.614	(2.293)	0.521	(0.758)
Estimation tests								
	$R^2 = 0.937$		$R^2 = 0.956$		$R^2 = 0.953$		$R^2 = 0.949$	
	DW = 2.132		DW = 2.124		DW = 2.116		DW = 2.091	
Serial correlation[a]	F(1,24) = 0.481		F(1,23) = 0.256		F(1,21) = 0.238		F(1,19) = 0.162	
Functional form[b]	F(1,24) = 0.323		F(1,23) = 0.069		F(1,21) = 0.002		F(1,19) = 0.003	
Normality[c]	$X^2(2) = 6.041$		$X^2(2) = 0.140$		$X^2(2) = 0.282$		$X^2(2) = 0.246$	
Heteroscedasticity[d]	F(1,29) = 0.133		F(1,29) = 0.220		F(1,29) = 0.056		F(1.29) = 0.051	
Variable deletion[e]	—		F(2,24) = 6.820		F(4,22) = 3.525		F(6,20) = 2.145	

Out-of-sample prediction tests				
Mean error	0.000	–0.012	–0.012	–0.014
Abs. mean error	0.006	0.012	0.012	0.014
Root mean sq. error	0.007	0.013	0.013	0.015
Predictive failure[F]	F(4,21) = 0.172	F(4,20) = 0.370	F(4,18) = 0.312	F(4,16) = 0.303

[a] Godfrey's test.
[b] Ramsey's RESET test.
[c] Jarque–Bera's test.
[d] Anscombe's test.
[e] Test for the deletion of ΔTSC, $TSC(-1)$, ΔPS, $PS(-1)$ in equation 2, $\Delta TSCW$, $TSCW(-1)$, $\Delta TSCE$, $TSCE(-1)$ in equation 3 and $\Delta TSCW$, $TSCW(-1)$, $\Delta TSCE$, $TSCE(-1)$, ΔRG. $RG(-1)$ in equation 4.
[f] Chow's predictive failure test, predictions 1987–91.

Legenda (all variables are in natural logarithms):
IP = industry value added deflator (1985 = 100); *P** = weighted average of foreign prices in domestic currency (in Italian Lira); *PRI* = product per worker in industry (industry V.A. per worker); *TSC* = social security contributions divided by full employment value added; *TSCW* = social security contributions paid by workers divided by full employment value added; *TSCE* = social security contributions paid by employers divided by full employment value added; *RLPAI* = current public spending (wages, pensions and interest payment deflated with the private consumption deflator, and current puchases deflated with their deflator).

TABLE 4.6. *Services value added deflator* (ΔSP) (sample period: 1961–91 (annual data))

Independent variables	Equation 1		Equation 2		Equation 3	
	Coeff.	(*t*)	Coeff.	(*t*)	Coeff.	(*t*)
ΔP^*	0.296	(4.557)	0.304	(5.703)	0.315	(5.843)
ΔPRS	–0.568	(–3.792)	–0.326	(–2.333)	–0.427	(–3.046)
ΔTSC	—	—	0.140	(1.717)	0.163	(2.067)
ΔPS	—	—	–0.044	(–1.511)	–0.043	(–1.528)
ΔRG	—	—	—	—	0.155	(1.317)
$SP(-1)$	–0.216	(–5.705)	–0.360	(–7.544)	–0.467	(–6.803)
$P^*(-1)$	0.228	(5.581)	0.399	(7.466)	0.435	(6.969)
$PRS(-1)$	0.147	(3.758)	0.253	(3.687)	—	—
$TSC(-1)$	—	—	0.227	(2.045)	0.255	(2.374)
$PS(-1)$	—	—	–0.116	(–3.043)	–0.109	(–3.090)
$RG(-1)$	—	—	—	—	0.214	(3.844)
CONST	–0.460	(–3.121)	–0.793	(–1.538)	–2.446	(–2.727)
Estimation tests						
	R2 = 0.905		R2 = 0.944		R2 = 0.964	
	DW = 1.784		DW = 2.351		DW = 2.307	
Serial correlation[a]	F(1,24) = 0.001		F(1,20) = 1.489		F(1,19) = 1.022	
Functional form[b]	F(1,24) = 1.886		F(1,20) = 0.357		F(1,19) = 0.805	
Normality[c]	X2(2) = 0.491		X2(2) = 0.455		X2(2) = 0.103	
Heteroscedasticity[d]	F(1,29) = 0.030		F(1,29) = 0.217		F(1,29) = 1.586	
Variable deletion[e]	—		F(4,21) = 5.360		F(6,20) = 8.006	

Out-of-sample prediction tests			
Mean error	0.026	–0.000	–0.003
Abs. mean error	0.026	0.010	0.009
Root mean sq. error	0.031	0.012	0.009
Predictive failure[f]	$F(4,21) = 1.461$	$F(4,17) = 0.733$	$F(4,16) = 0.399$

[a] Godfrey's test.
[b] Ramsey's RESET test.
[c] Jarque-Bera's test.
[d] Anscombe's test.
[e] Test for the deletion of ΔTSC, $TSC(-1)$, ΔPS, $PS(-1)$ in equation 2 and ΔTSC, $TSC(-1)$, ΔPS, $PS(-1)$, ΔRG, $RG(-1)$ in equation 3.
[f] Chow's predictive failure test, predictions 1987–91.

Legenda (all variables in natural logarithms):
SP = services value added deflator (1985 = 100); *P** = weighted average of foreign prices in domestic currency (in Italian Lira); *PRS* = product per worker in the service sector (services V.A. per worker); *TSC* = social security contributions divided by full employment value added; *PS* = producers' subsidies divided by full employment value added; *TSCW* = social security contributions paid by workers divided by full employment value added; *TSCE* = social security contributions paid by employers divided by full employment value added; *RG* = real current public spending (wages, pensions and interest payment deflated with the private consumption deflator, and current purchases deflated with their deflator).

service prices could not have continued to increase as they did without nourishment from current public spending.

Social security contributions perform better when in aggregate form, and the estimated coefficients are smaller than in the previous price equations (the impact coefficient is 0.14 and the long-run coefficient is 0.63). At variance with the findings for industry, producers' transfers are relevant in reducing service inflation, especially in the long run (with a coefficient of –0.322 in equation 2 and –0.232 in equation 3). This result is reasonable since most producers' transfers went to services, in particular transportation companies (two-thirds of the total).

Once again, comparison between the equations with and without public sector variables definitely favours the former: the variable-deletion tests, largely beyond the critical value, the equation fit, and the out-of-sample prediction statistics offer unambiguous evidence of a distinct improvement in explaining the behaviour of the service deflator. Equation 1 underpredicts inflation in all years 1988–91, with increasing forecasting errors in absolute terms. Equation 3, which is the best performer, underpredicts only in 1991. This error could be due to the increase in administered prices that occurred in 1991, well beyond the average inflation rate, and perhaps to increasing margins. This could also be the reason for underprediction in the total deflator equations that was noted above.

6. CONCLUSION

We have argued that one cannot understand Italy's inflation problem in the 1980s—failure of inflation to converge to the low rates of Europe's best performers, and the recovery of inflation in 1987–91—without taking into account the role played by government policies and the public sector.

The following government influences on inflation were identified:

(i) Lax wage, purchasing, and management policies maintained continuous direct pressure on the economy's average costs and the consumer price index.

(ii) Extensive intervention to provide income support or tax relief to individuals, groups, regions, and industries distorted relative prices, greatly muted competitive stimuli, and hampered adjustment in response to the exchange rate discipline. This seems to be the main reason for the malfunctioning of the labour market and the fact that somehow expectations seem to have played a limited role in fostering adjustment.

(iii) The increase in public spending and the redistributive implications of the budget account for most of the explanation of rapid consumption growth and strong domestic demand during a protracted period of exchange rate appreciation.

In the course of the 1980s, there was a large trend increase in government size and tax pressure; its inflationary consequences were hidden, during the first half of the decade, by increasing net transfers to enterprises and households, but surfaced fully once the need to halt debt growth forced the government to become a net 'absorber' of resources from the economy by raising taxes and cutting transfers to enterprises.

We have estimated price equations that include, among the regressors, public sector variables: these variables contribute to a remarkable improvement in the fit and predictive power of our estimates. Real current government spending seems able to account for the observed behaviour of inflation in the second half of the 1980s; the results for sectoral deflators confirm that this source of inflation was especially important for services.

REFERENCES

Attanasio, O. P., and Padoa Schioppa, F. (1990), 'Regional Inequalities, Migration and Mismatch in Italy, 1960–86', in F. Padoa Schioppa (ed.), *Mismatch and Labour Mobility*, Cambridge University Press.

Barca, F., and Visco, I. (1993), 'L'economia italiana nella prospettiva europea: terziario protetto e dinamica dei redditi nominali', in S. Micossi and I. Visco (eds.), *L'economia italiana nella prospettiva europea*, Il Mulino, Bologna.

Barrel, R., and Darby, J., and Donaldson C. (1990), 'Structural Stability in European Wage and Price Systems', *NIESR Discussion Paper*, 188.

Barro, R. J. (1990). 'Government Spending in a Simple Model of Endogenous Growth', in *Journal of Political Economy*, 5 (Oct.).

Bodo, G., and Sestito, P. (1991). *Le vie dello sviluppo*, Il Mulino, Bologna.

Cavazzuti, F. (1979). 'Inflazione e politica di bilancio', in F. Targetti (ed.), *Lezioni di economia dell'inflazione*, Feltrinelli, Milan.

Centro Studi Confindustria (1992*a*). 'Industria italiana e Mercato Unico Europeo', *XIV Rapporto*, SIPI, Roma.

—— (1992*b*), 'I servizi di pubblica utilita', in *Previsioni dell'economia italiana*, SIPI, Roma.

Cer (1991), *Le due inflazioni*, Rapporto, 5.

Cipolletta, I., and Heimler, A. (1989), 'Processi di ristrutturazione, progresso tecnologico e crescita economica', *Rivista di Politica Economica* (July–Aug.), 7/8.

De Grauwe, P. (1983), 'Symptoms of an Overvalued Currency: The Case of the Belgian Franc', in M. De Cecco (ed.), *International Economic Adjustment*, Blackwell, Oxford.

Dell'Aringa, C. (1993), 'Il mercato del lavoro italiano nel contesto internazionale', in S. Micossi and I. Visco (eds.), *L'economia italiana nella prospettiva europea*, Il Mulino, Bologna.

De Nardis, S., and Micossi, S. (1991), 'Disinflation and Re-Inflation in Italy and the Implications for Transition to Monetary Union', *BNL Quarterly Review*, 177 (June).

Egebo, T., and Englander, S. (1992), 'Institutional Commitments and Policy Credibility: A Critical Survey and Empirical Evidence from the ERM', *OECD Economic Studies*, 18 (Spring).

Ernst and Young (1992), *The Implications of Opening Up Public Procurement in the Excluded Sectors in Italy*, Report to the EC Commission Advisory Committee for Public Procurement (Jan.).

Ford, R., and Suyker, W. (1989). 'Industrial Subsidies in OECD Economies', *OECD Working Papers* (Jan.), 74.

Franco, D. (1992). 'L'espansione della spesa pubblica in Italia (1960–90)', in *Il disavanzo pubblico in Italia: natura strutturale e politiche di rientro*, i, Il Mulino, Bologna.

Froot, K. A., and Rogoff, K. (1991), 'The EMS, the EMU, and the Transition to a Common Currency', *NBER Working Paper*, 3684 (Apr.).

Giavazzi, F., and Spaventa, L. (1989), 'Italy: the Real Effects of Inflation and Disinflation', *Economic Policy* (Apr.), 8.

Gressani, D., Guiso, L., and Visco, I. (1987), 'Il rientro dell'inflazione: un'analisi con il modello econometrico della Banca d'Italia', in *Contributi all'analisi economica*, Banca d'Italia.

Guiso, L. (1985), 'Il dibattito sull'inflazione italiana negli ultimi quindici anni', in *Contributi all'analisi economica*, Banca d'Italia.

Katseli-Papaefstratiou, L. T. (1979), 'Nominal Tax Rates and the Effectiveness of Fiscal Policy', in *National Tax Journal*, 33/1.

Mediobanca (1992), *Dati cumulativi di 1790 societa italiane*, Milan.

Micossi, S., and Trau', F. (1989), 'Finanziamento delle imprese e trasformazioni produttive: il ruolo della politica monetaria nel processo di ristrutturazione', *Rivista di Politica Economica* (July–Aug.), 7/8.

Micossi, S., and Tullio, G. (1991), 'Fiscal Imbalances, Economic Distortions, and the Long Run Performance of the Italian Economy', *OCSM Working Paper*, 9, LUISS (Oct.), published in Italian in *Rivista di Politica Economica*, 82 (1992): 39–91.

OECD (1991), *Economic Surveys: Italy*.

Pellegrini, G. (1992), *La produttivita nei servizi destinabili alla vendita: nuove evidenze per un vecchio problema*, mimeo, Banca d'Italia (Apr.).

Prosperetti, L. (1992*a*), *La regolazione delle tariffe dei servizi pubblici italiani: alcune proposte*, mimeo, Politecnico di Torino.

—— (1992*b*), *Efficienza e qualita nei principali servizi di pubblica utilita: l'Italia nel contesto internazionale*, mimeo, Politecnico di Torino.

SVIMEZ (1992), *Rapporto 1991 sull'economia del Mezzogiorno*, Il Mulino, Bologna.

Tullio, G. (1986), *Taxation and Real Wages: an Empirical Analysis of Wage Behaviour in 8 Industrial Countries: 1960–83*, European Commission, Brussels, mimeo.

Visco, I. (1992), 'Caratteri strutturali dell'inflazione italiana (1986–91)', Relazione alla XXXIII Riunione Scientifica Annuale della Societa degli Economisti, mimeo (30–1 Oct.).

5

Inflation in Spain: A Two-sector Model Approach

IGNACIO MAULEÓN

JOSÉ LUIS RAYMOND BARA

I. INTRODUCTION

The purpose of this chapter is to account for the recent inflationary experience of the Spanish economy, which reveals some new features, and yet some old ones. We approach the problem by looking at the proper historical correlations, from a somewhat different perspective from those used up to now. In this way, we hope to explain current developments, and to offer some policy-orientated conclusions, having in mind the basic requirements of monetary union.

We start by describing what we think are the basic facts of the recent inflationary performance of the Spanish economy in the last twenty years (Section 2). We adopt an approach rather uncommon in Spanish applied research to this date, i.e. we look at data disaggregated in two sectors, industry and services (see Raymond (1992*a*) for such an approach). The different behaviour of prices in both sectors, more markedly since Spain joined the EEC, suggests that productivity shocks, as well as independent wage pushes, might be the essential clues. In Section 3 we consider the task of providing some theoretical background for the empirical models to be presented later. First, and starting from the work of Balassa (1964), Bruno (1976), and Frenkel and Razin (1987), we present a two-period model that explains the appearance of inflation and a trade balance deficit, as a joint result of a productivity shock in a framework of rational behaviour. This is in sharp contrast to the conventional demand-push explanation. Second, using a framework somewhat similar to that of Miller and Sutherland (1992), we show how a productivity shock can lead to lasting, and even accelerating inflation, under an exchange rate peg. The model used in the analysis is a two-sector model of wages and prices with overlapping contracts of the Taylor type, where the goods of one sector are perfectly traded, and the others imperfectly.

Next we tackle the problem of estimating a model inspired by the theoretical models just presented, and capable of giving a reasonable account of the disaggregated behaviour of wages and prices in industry and services in the last twenty years in Spain (Section 4). The empirical model takes account of the

The authors wish to acknowledge the comments of P. De Grauwe and G. Tullio. Any remaining errors are our own.

rational forward behaviour in wage equations of the Taylor (1980) type. Then, several kinds of simulations are presented to give a flavour for the kind of dynamic response that we might expect from the model, when subject to outside shocks (Section 5). This includes productivity shocks and foreign prices shocks. The likely effect of structural reforms of the labour market according to these results is also briefly discussed.

A last section gathers the main conclusions of the chapter. Some mathematical proofs, and the more detailed statistical results, are presented in three appendices.

2. THE BASIC FACTS

Some stylized facts about the inflationary performance of the Spanish economy are summarized in Tables 5.1 and 5.2 (the sample is split in 1986, the date of Spanish entry into the EEC). To start with, it is worth stressing the point (made clear by Table 5.2, col. 1), that the Spanish economy has become increasingly open. In the period spanning the last twenty years, approximately, the conventional measure of openness (the ratio of exports plus imports to GDP in real terms), has doubled, reaching a value close to 50 per cent (note that this result does not hold with current prices, because services inflation is faster than industrial inflation). As regards inflation, this increased openness must have had a 'discipline' effect on prices (in the sense that inflation in Spain has tended to be historically above that of its trade partners on average). If we look more closely at inflationary data, it is easy to check that this effect can be perceived more strongly in industrial than in service prices (col. 3, Table 5.2, and col. 1, Table 5.1). This suggests that the rough identification of industry with a traded sector, and services with a non-traded sector, might be a sensible approach. It is interesting to note also that industrial prices have grown less than prices in the service sector. That reinforces the appropriateness of looking at disaggregated data in both sectors, and suggests that we should be searching for some explanation in terms of the traded vs. non-traded models.

We next look at data on wages and productivity (cols. 3 and 4 in Table 5.1). The wage data show a considerable degree of convergence in both sectors, which is in sharp contrast to price behaviour. We also note that average productivity has been growing at a substantial rate, although decreasing in time. This growth has always been more pronounced in the industrial sector. One possible way to interpret this fact is as follows: prices in the traded sector are broadly determined by foreign competition (both grew at the same rate in the 1987–90 period), whereas in the non-traded-goods sector, wages were the main determinant of prices; productivity increases in the traded-goods sector led to higher wages in that sector (for given prices). Since wages tend to equalize in both sectors, this translates into higher wages in the non-traded sector. Finally, since productivity increases in the non-traded-goods sector are low, higher

TABLE 5.1. *Inflationary performance of the Spanish economy*

	Prices (1)	Unit labour costs (2)	Av. productivity per employee (3)	Nominal wage per employee (4)
Industry				
86/72	13.1	14.3	3.8	18.6
90/87	3.3	5.9	1.1	7.0
90/72	10.9	12.4	3.2	16.0
Services				
86/72	15.2	14.5	2.16	17.0
90/87	8.0	7.3	0.07	7.4
90/72	13.6	12.9	1.7	14.8

Note: Both sections of the table give the average annual growth rate for the period, of the corresponding variable.
Source: FIES.

TABLE 5.2. *Inflationary performance of the Spanish economy*

	(X + M)/Y (1)	Y_I/Y_T (2)	P_w (3)	P_I/P_S (4)
86/72	3.95	–0.37	16.1	–1.81
90/87	4.7	–1.18	3.3	–4.35
90/72	4.11	–1.55	12.4	–2.36

Notes: (X + M)/Y: ratio of exports plus imports over GDP.
Y_I/Y_T: ratio of industrial to total production.
Pw: world prices in domestic money units.
P_I/P_S: ratio of industrial to services prices.
The table gives the average annual growth rate for the period in cols. 1,3,4; in col. 2, the difference between the ending and starting values in the period is given.
Source: FIES.

wages lead to higher prices in that sector. This would explain the relative decrease of industrial prices compared to prices in the services sector.

The explanation in the previous paragraph goes some way towards understanding inflation in Spain in recent years. However, this cannot be the complete story, and that is why inflation is a more serious problem than this explanation would suggest.

There are at least two additional hypotheses that might have some explanatory relevance. The first is the credibility of the exchange rate commitment: if economic agents do not fully believe it, inflationary expectations will not be curtailed, as they would otherwise have been (see, for example, De Grauwe, 1993). The other is the impact of the government budget in a broad sense (see also Chapter 4 in this volume for the Italian case, and Froot and Rogoff, 1991).

As for the first hypothesis, it may be somewhat difficult to carry out an appropriate empirical test. Regarding the second one, however, there is some indirect evidence suggesting its potential relevance: for example, government expenditure in goods and services (excluding investment) as a proportion of GDP has increased by three points in the last decade; personal income tax and indirect taxes have also increased as a share of GDP, by three points each, during a similar period. This may have resulted in inflationary pressures running through several channels: government expenditure increases demand, mainly in the service sector; indirect taxation may increase the mark-up of prices over costs in both sectors (or may be translated downward into wages); and direct taxation may increase wage demands. All these possible impacts will be explored in the empirical section.

By way of summary, we might say that productivity differentials in the traded and non-traded-goods sectors, plus autonomous wage pushes and, perhaps, the government budget, are the key towards an understanding of the most salient features of Spanish inflation. The models proposed in the next two sections intend to give a more formal content to these hypotheses. Incidentally, it is worth noting that investment increased and the trade balance worsened during the period 1987–90.

3. INFLATION AND PRODUCTIVITY SHOCKS: SOME THEORETICAL RESULTS

This section is intended to present two theoretical models that provide the framework for the empirical research of the next section. The first model links productivity and inflation on the one hand, and productivity shocks and the trade balance deficit on the other. Both links have been investigated separately before in the literature (Balassa, 1964, and Bruno, 1976). Providing a simultaneous theoretical explanation for both of them may help understand the cause of recent macroeconomic disequilibria in the Spanish economy. Rebelo (1992) tackles the problem of explaining inflation in a related model: he picks the representative agent model in an infinite time-horizon with traded and non-traded goods (consumption and production are considered). Assuming that the stock of capital is below its optimum level, and that the non-traded-goods sector is relatively more labour-intensive than the traded-goods sector, he explains, among other things, the relative increase of non-traded vs. traded prices, and the persistence of inflation.

The model put forward in Section 3.1 is a two period-two sector model that explains relative price changes and the trade balance deficit. Also, investment is explained explicitly. The second model (Section 3.2) intends to explain the persistence of inflation in the context of a wage–price model of the labour market after an exchange rate peg. This is by no means trivial, as Miller and Sutherland show (1992). In their paper, it is shown that a Taylor type of wage bargaining only yields inflation for a number of periods equal to the length of the contract. They put forward an alternative model that explains inflation persistence as a result of the lack of credibility of the exchange rate peg commitment. This is a very powerful result, and the model presented in Section 3.2 intends to give yet another explanation for inflation persistence that might be relevant to the Spanish case.

The assumption of rational expectations underlies the results of the first model. As a result, the inflation and the trade balance deficit do not call for policy action. By contrast, the lasting inflation of the second model is caused by very definite features of the labour market that can be modified. Besides, inflation in this model is not innocuous, since it yields protracted unemployment. We believe that both models may have been at play in recent years in the Spanish economy. And although disentangling their relative weights may prove difficult, or impossible, they both point to some common conclusions: that the Spanish inflation and trade deficit are the results not only of macroeconomic disequilibria, but also of supply-side phenomena (notwithstanding other additional explanations, notably the possible impact of the government budget).

3.1. Inflation, the trade balance, and productivity shocks

The combination of a worsening trade balance and inflation in an open economy is customarily attributed to a demand shock. In a simple Keynesian model made up of the IS-LM block, plus a supply function with prices increasing with output, and a balance of trade equation with a fixed exchange rate, the demand shock explanation is, indeed, the most reasonable. Any supply shock would move prices and income in opposite directions, making the effect on the trade balance ambiguous, but always less pronounced in absolute value than under a demand shock. The purpose of this section is to show how a supply shock, and more precisely a productivity shock, can produce exactly those results, that is, inflation, a worsening of the trade balance, and an income expansion. We shall start by reviewing briefly the effect of productivity shocks in the two periods-one sector economy, proposed among others by Bruno (1976), Frenkel and Razin (1987), and Muellbauer and Murphy (1990). Then we shall combine this approach with the one period-two sector model of Balassa (see also Micossi and Milesi-Ferreti, Chapter 8 in this volume), in a two period-two sector model, where a productivity shock of the kind to be discussed later will yield exactly the results sought after.

Let us start, then, with a two-period economy, with one good that may be consumed or invested. The economy is open, and the good can be traded internationally, so that there can be a surplus or a deficit, that must be balanced in the two-period horizon. The optimality conditions in this case are,

$$\frac{u_1}{u_2} = F_k = 1 + r, \tag{3.1}$$

where the slope of the indifference curve between periods 1 and 2 must be equal to the slope of the production function, and to the real interest rate (plus one) given internationally. Let us assume simple production and utility functions of the type $y = a \cdot K^b$, and Cobb-Douglas respectively, and assume further, that the trade balance is in equilibrium. If there is a productivity shock, so that a increases, this leads to an increase in consumption and investment in period 1. Also, the trade balance turns into deficit (which equals the present value of the surplus in period 2).

This result is illustrated graphically in Fig. 5.1. Initially, the economy is endowed with fixed amounts of the one good in both periods. This can be understood as the result of constant labour employment in both periods. Therefore, the production function, valid for both periods, should be more properly written as $Y = a \cdot L^{1-b} \cdot K^b$. We take $L^{1-b} = 1$ with no loss of generality. In period 1, the good can be consumed, C_1, or invested, I_1, to yield an increased amount available for consumption in period 2. Equilibrium is reached at point E, where conditions (3.1) are fulfilled, and where the trade balance is assumed to equal zero for simplicity. Suppose now, that the economy becomes more

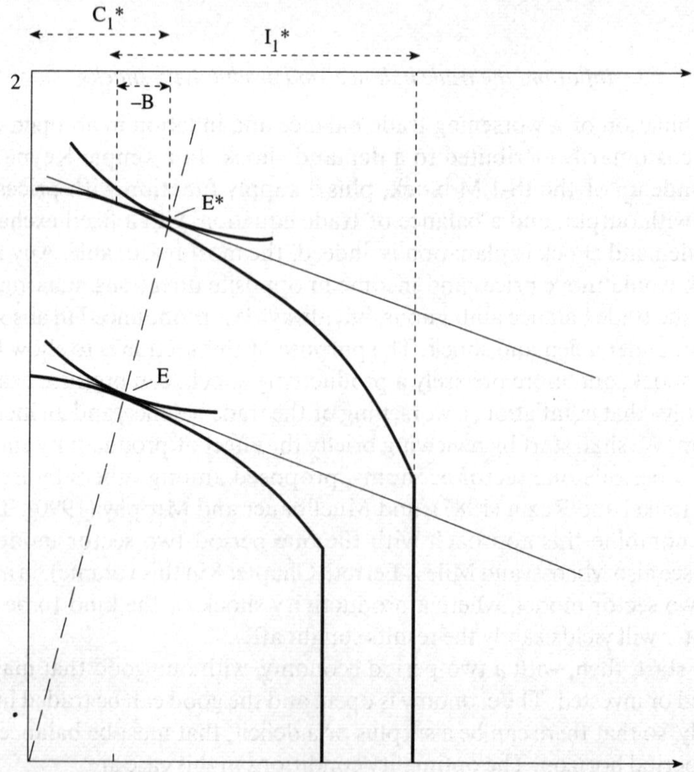

FIG. 5.1. Productivity shocks and trade balances

productive, in the sense that a increases. Then, the production frontier shifts rightwards (in a north-east direction). Clearly, the productivity of capital increases above the world rate of interest, making investment more attractive. In fact, the final equilibrium is obtained at a point as E*, where it is rational to borrow to invest more in period 1, and consume more in both periods. This is indicated in the upper front of the figure: investment in period 1 is determined by the tangency between the production frontier and the straight line, reflecting the rate at which it is possible to borrow or lend in international markets (I_1*); consumption is given by the tangency between this line and the new indifference curve (C_1*). Since total consumption plus investment is larger than domestic production, that implies a trade deficit equal to B (the horizontal distance between both tangency points).

The question is now, how to unify both results in the same model, that is, inflation and a trade balance deficit. The model should also explain the increase in consumption and investment. These four facts have happened recently in Spain, at least for some time, and therefore, the model put forward may help towards an understanding of some overlooked explanations for the recent inflationary experience. The proposed model for that purpose is a straightforward combination of the model presented in the above paragraphs and the Balassa model. We start with a two period–two sector model. We shall assume that the traded good can be invested in the own-traded sector, whereas the non-traded good can only be consumed (this fits the common identification of both sectors with the industrial and services sectors respectively). The current account must balance over the two-period horizon, and the exchange rate is fixed. The total labour supply is fixed in both periods, and employment in both sectors can be substituted perfectly. Finally, the economy derives utility from the consumption of both goods in both periods, under the usual marginal properties. The model can be formalized by the following set of equations,

$$
\begin{aligned}
&U(C_{T1}, Y_{N1}, C_{T2}, Y_{N2}) \\
&Y_{T1} = C_{T1} + I + B_1 \\
&Y_{T2} = C_{T2} + B_2 \\
&B_2 + B_1 (1 + r) = 0 \qquad (3.2) \\
&Y_{Nt} = f_N(L - L_{Tt}) \\
&Y_{Tt} = f_T(L_{Tt}, K_t) \\
&K_2 = K_1 + I \\
&f'_T / f'_N = P_N,
\end{aligned}
$$

where $Y_{Nt} = C_{Nt}$, f' (.) are first-order derivatives, subindices T and N refer to the traded and non-traded sectors respectively, L is labour supply, and K is the capital stock. Without loss of generality it is assumed for convenience that $P_T = 1$.

This set of equations allow us to write the utility function as depending on just four independent arguments: L_{T1}, L_{T2}, I, B, that is, employment in both periods in the traded sector, investment, and the trade balance in period one. To find a solution, we assume optimizing consumption and production behaviour, and we arrive at the following four first-order conditions,

$$\frac{\delta f_T}{\delta I} = \frac{\delta U/\delta C_{T1}}{\delta U/\delta C_{T2}} \tag{3.3}$$

$$(1 + r) = \frac{\delta U/\delta C_{T1}}{\delta U/\delta C_{T2}} \tag{3.4}$$

$$\frac{\delta f_T/\delta L_{T1}}{\delta f_N/\delta L} = \frac{\delta U/\delta C_{N1}}{\delta U/\delta C_{T1}} \tag{3.5}$$

$$\frac{\delta f_T/\delta L_{T2}}{\delta f_N/\delta L} = \frac{\delta U/\delta C_{N2}}{\delta U/\delta C_{T2}} \tag{3.6}$$

Conditions (3.3) and (3.4) are the equivalent in this model to conditions (3.1) in the two-period model; conditions (3.5) and (3.6) are the equivalent in both periods $t = 1$ and $t = 2$, to the first-order condition of the two-sector model.

The problem now is to work out the effect of a permanent productivity shock in the traded sector on the economy, and more specifically, on relative prices and the trade balance. This can be done tracking the impact of such a shock through equations (3.3) to (3.6) (that is, the optimality conditions). Doing that in a general way may prove rather difficult. For our present purpose it may be enough to specify simple, but reasonable functions, such as those given as follows:

$$U = U_1 + \beta \cdot U_2$$

$$U_t = C_N^{\alpha} \cdot C_T^{1-\alpha}; \qquad 0 < \alpha < 1$$

$$f_N = \gamma \cdot L_N = \gamma \cdot (L - L_T)$$

$$f_T = \rho \cdot K^{\theta} \cdot L_T^{1-\theta}; \qquad 0 < \ < 1 \tag{3.7}$$

that is, we assume a Cobb–Douglas utility function within a period, a constant time-discount factor β, a linear production function in the non-traded sector, and a Cobb–Douglas production function in the traded sector. The productivity shock can be formalized assuming a permanent increase in the value of the parameter ρ. Under these conditions, it can be shown that if initially $B = 0$, the shock yields the following results: (1) the relative price of non-traded goods increases in both periods; (2) the trade balance in period 1 turns into deficit; and (3) consumption of both goods and investment increase in period 1. (The proof of these results is left to Appendix 1.)

To summarize, the results of this section show that, both inflation and a trade balance deficit may be the result of rational behaviour under productivity shocks in the traded sector. They are equilibrium responses to a productivity shock and, therefore, do not call for policy action.

3.2. *A two-sector model of wage–price inflation*

The purpose of this section is to introduce a model where productivity shocks can generate long-lasting inflation under an exchange rate peg. Miller and Sutherland (1992) in an aggregate model of the Taylor (1980) overlapping contracts kind obtain the result that the exchange rate peg holds down inflation. In fact, positive inflation only lasts the number of periods of the overlapping wage contracts, and even becomes negative afterwards. The solution they propose to explain inflation sluggishness relies on a Bayesian learning model, whereby agents come to believe the exchange peg only slowly through time.

The model of this section starts by splitting the economy in two sectors: the first produces goods traded internationally under perfect competition, (T); the second produces goods traded internationally under imperfect competition (N). We describe the wage–price model of the T sector first. The price equation can be written as,

$$P_T = d(W_T - \rho) + (1 - d)(P_T^T + s), \tag{3.8}$$

where $1 > d > 0$, P_T and P_T^T are respectively the domestic and international price of traded goods, W_T is the wage in the traded goods sector, ρ average productivity per employee, and s the spot exchange rate (domestic units per foreign unit; all variables in natural logs). The perfect competition assumption implies that $P_T = P_T^T + s$. Also, we shall adopt the normalization $P_T^T = 0$ in what follows, with no loss of generality. Then we can write,

$$P_T = s = (W_T - \rho) \tag{3.9}$$

so that the nominal wage in this sector will be driven by the exchange rate and the productivity shock. There is no room, therefore, for an independent wage equation, although this can be easily arranged (see next section), and does not diminish the generality of the results.

The behaviour of the N sector is described by a two-period overlapping wage contracts model of the type proposed by Taylor, and given by equations,

$$P_N = \frac{1}{2}(W_N + W_{N,-1}) \tag{3.10}$$

$$W_N = \frac{1-\delta}{2}(P + P_{+1}^e + \beta(Y_N + Y_{N,+1}^e)) + \delta \cdot W_T \tag{3.11}$$

$$Y_N = \gamma^*(s - P_N) \tag{3.12}$$

$$P = \theta \cdot P_T + (1 - \theta) P_N, \tag{3.13}$$

where all variables are denoted in a self-evident way, and are defined in natural logs. We shall impose the obvious conditions $0 < (\theta, \delta) < 1$. Equation (3.11) is standard except for the term $(\delta \cdot W_T)$, which is introduced here to reflect the interdependence of wages in both sectors. The fact that Y_N instead of Y enters the equation reflects partly the lack of competition among the labour markets of the two sectors. The superscript e, means that the value of the variable in brackets is rationally forecasted with the information available up to time t.

Equation (3.12) reflects the imperfect competition assumption, and is introduced by Miller and Sutherland ($\gamma^* \rightarrow \infty$, would imply $s = P_N$, the perfect competition assumption). Finally, as all variables in both sectors are defined as deviations from long-run equilibrium we can omit constants.

In order to track the behaviour of inflation under different types of shocks, we are interested in deriving an aggregate model. First we define the average wage as follows,

$$w = \theta \cdot w_T + (1 - \theta) \cdot w_N. \tag{3.14}$$

The goods market equilibrium condition (3.12) can be written using (3.13) as,

$$\begin{aligned} Y_N &= \frac{\gamma^*}{1-\theta}(s - \rho) \\ &= \gamma(s - \rho), \end{aligned} \tag{3.15}$$

where we shall assume $(\gamma\beta) < 1$ to ensure dynamic stability. From now on we shall omit the subindex N in Y_N to simplify notation. We are now in a position to derive an aggregate wage–price inflation model. After some simple algebra, we obtain

$$w = a(s + \rho) + b(p + p^e_{+1} + \beta(Y + Y^e_{+1}) \tag{3.16}$$

$$p = (\frac{1 + L}{2})(w - \theta\rho) + \frac{\theta}{2}\Delta s \tag{3.17}$$

$$y = \gamma(s - \rho), \tag{3.18}$$

where

$$\begin{aligned} 0 < a &= \theta + (1 - \theta) \cdot \delta < 1 \\ 0 < b &= (1 - \theta)(1 - \delta) / 2 < 1/2 \\ a + 2b &= 1 \end{aligned} \tag{3.19}$$

and L is the lag operator ($Lx_t = x_{t-1}$).

In order to highlight the result of this section it is interesting to consider first the dynamics of inflation under an exchange rate peg, coming after a period of constant depreciation of the currency (as in Miller and Sutherland). The basic results are: (1) during the first period after the peg inflation falls at less than half its previous value, and (2) inflation becomes negative afterwards. These are the Miller and Sutherland's results (in fact, if $\delta = \theta = 0$, the model is the same; see Appendix 2). The short-run dynamic behaviour of inflation under a productivity shock in the traded goods sector is tackled next (this is the main purpose of this section). The shock considered is permanent and might be explained by increased investment placed in capital goods of newer and more productive vintages, generated in turn by an improvement of expectations associated with the exchange rate stability (that seems to be, at least, a plausible explanation for the Spanish case during the years 1986–90). Under these conditions, the shock can yield long and lasting overall inflation that may even accelerate in the first years.

The graphical comparison of the dynamic path of prices under an exchange rate peg, with and without a productivity shock, is shown in Fig. 5.2. The different inflation path in both cases is simply due to the fact that the equilibrium price level under the shock becomes positive, whereas it is zero without it. Finally, it may be worth remarking that the price of the *N* good increases relative to the *T* good, and that inflation in the *N* sector causes a protracted recession (and possibly a trade deficit too).

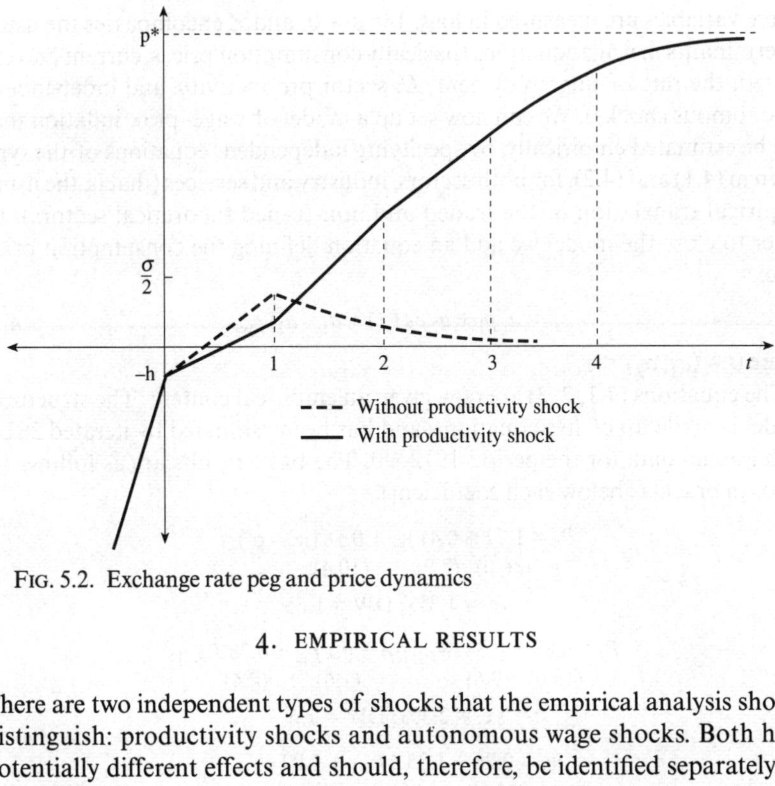

FIG. 5.2. Exchange rate peg and price dynamics

4. EMPIRICAL RESULTS

There are two independent types of shocks that the empirical analysis should distinguish: productivity shocks and autonomous wage shocks. Both have potentially different effects and should, therefore, be identified separately. In order to do this, we set up a model of wage–price inflation disaggregated in two sectors, industry and services. The price equation is standard and given by,

$$p = \phi \cdot (w - \rho) + (1 - \phi) \cdot P_{\mathrm{w}} \tag{4.1}$$

omitting the constant for simplicity, where variables are defined in logarithms, and where w are wages, ρ labour productivity ($w - \rho$, are unit labour costs), P_{w} world prices, and $0 < \phi < 1$. The equation is sufficiently general and may be understood as the result of a mark-up procedure, or a profit-maximizing behaviour, with constant foreign inputs in the short run. Since we are going to consider a two-sector model, the price of the remaining sector output could be introduced in (4.1). However, the output price of the other sector was never statistically significant, and therefore was not taken into account. We apply equation (4.1) to both the traded and non-traded goods sector. The degree of competition from the rest of the world is captured by the parameter ϕ. If $\phi = 0$, prices are completely determined by foreign competition (the labour unit cost disappears).

The wage equation assumes that wages are set through a bargaining process, where wages in the remaining sector are taken as reference. That is,

$$w_i = \mu z + (1 - \mu)\, w_j, \tag{4.2}$$

where variables are measured in logs, $1 > \mu > 0$, and Z encompasses the usual determinants in wage equations (basically consumption prices, current and expected, the rate of unemployment, U, sector productivity, and independent autonomous shocks). We can now set up a model of wage–price inflation that can be estimated empirically, by specifying independent equations of the type given in (4.1) and (4.2), for both sectors, industry and services (that is, the usual empirical translation of the traded and non-traded theoretical sectors). In order to close the model we add an equation defining the consumption price index:

$$p = a_1 p_{\mathrm{I}} + a_2 p_{\mathrm{S}} + (1 - a_1 - a_2)\, p_{\mathrm{w}}, \tag{4.3}$$

where $0 < (a_1, a_2) < 1$.

The equations (4.1, 2, 3) are now given an empirical content. The structural model is made up of five equations, and has been estimated by iterated 3SLS with annual data for the period 1972–90. The basic results are as follows (t-ratios in brackets below each coefficient):

$$\underset{}{P_S} = \underset{(36.0)}{1.77} + \underset{(7.9)}{0.41}\, w_s + \underset{(10.4)}{0.58}\, (w_s - \rho_s)_{-1}$$

s.e. = 1.3%; DW = 1.65

$$P_I = \underset{(13.0)}{0.88} + \underset{(9.6)}{0.38}\, (w_I - \rho_I) + \underset{(1.6)}{0.1}\, p_w + \underset{(8.4)}{0.38}\, P_{w-1}$$

s.e. = 2.3%; DW = 1.6

$$w_{\mathrm{I}} = \underset{(4.4)}{0.26} + \underset{(8.0)}{1.85}\, \Delta P_{+1} + \underset{(82.0)}{1.09}\, w_{s-1}$$

s.e. = 3.4%; DW = 2.2

$$w_{\mathrm{S}} = \underset{(6.6)}{-1.58} + \underset{(4.5)}{0.46}\, P - \underset{(6.9)}{0.14}\, U + \underset{(5.6)}{0.49}\, w_{\mathrm{I}-1} + \underset{(6.8)}{1.41}\, \rho_s$$

s.e. = 1.7%; DW = 2.0

$$P = \underset{(1.6)}{-0.07} + \underset{(3.8)}{0.335}\, P_I + \underset{(10.0)}{0.539}\, P_S + \underset{(2.5)}{0.12}\, p_w \tag{4.4}$$

s.e. = 1.2%; DW = 1.38

All variables are in logs and defined in a self-evident way (see also the notation above). The term ΔP_{+1} has been dealt with by means of instrumental variables (Sargan, 1982 discusses alternative estimation procedures). All equations are estimated in levels, since co-integration tests do not give a clear indication to the contrary. That also implies that R^2's are generally close to one, but otherwise meaningless, and therefore are not reported. It may be worth pointing out that all equations can be rewritten in the error-correction mechanism way (see Appendix 3). However, that empirical specification strategy led, in this case, to a substantial loss of degrees of freedom, in the sense that too many variables (lags) had to be added, relatively to the few observations (twenty annual observations). Besides, recent Monte Carlo experiments (Brett, 1993), seem to indicate that the best procedure to estimate long-run coefficients and *t*-ratios, when only a moderate sample size is available, is the traditional approach, that is, apply OLS to the equation with all variables specified in levels (or in logs). All equations have been tested against a standard battery of possible misspecifications, which did not detect any serious trouble. The details of the econometric procedures, and other empirical results are discussed in Appendix 2.

As for stability, it may be worth stressing, however, that it may go uncovered by formal, and otherwise correct, statistical procedures, due to a lack of sample power. Another interesting aspect of the problem refers to the possible time-varying feature of the industrial price equations, as a result of an increasing degree of openness. This feature can be captured by means of the following estimated model,

$$P_I = \underset{(10.0)}{0.98} + \underset{(8.2)}{0.59}\,(w_I - \rho_I) + \underset{(3.0)}{0.22}\,p_w - \underset{(6.6)}{0.074}\,\mathrm{Log}(t)\,(w_I - \rho_I - P_{w-1})$$

$$\text{s.e.} = 1.7\%\,;\ \text{DW} = 1.9\,;\ \text{T} = 1972\text{–}90 \qquad (4.5)$$

This specification ensures long-run constancy of the sum of all coefficients. Yet it allows for a redistribution of the total sum between both variables, unit labour costs, and world prices, along time. According to the results of (4.5), the coefficient of the labour cost appears to have decreased by 0.06 points between 1972 and 1990, and the coefficient for world prices would have increased by the same amount (from 0.45 to 0.51). Since this effect, although significant, is not too strong, the simpler specification of (4.4) will be adopted.

The several potential effects of the government budget have also been explored: the government expenditure variable was tried in the service price equation, the personal income effective tax rate in both wage equations, and the indirect effective tax rate in all wage and price equations. The only slightly significant coefficients were those of the indirect tax rate in the industrial price equation and in the wage equation (in the latter it was negative, indicating backward shifting). Taking together all these effects, and after working out the final impact of the tax rate in the consumer price equation, the equilibrium indirect tax elasticity reaches a value of 0.055. Since the effective indirect tax rate has increased approximately from 1.3 to 4.5 per cent over the last ten years, this means an average contribution to inflation of indirect taxation of 0.4 per cent per year (assuming an average weight of industry in total production of 35 per cent). This does not seem completely unreasonable. But the budget variables employed in the estimation are of a very aggregative kind, and therefore, it is not totally clear what they mean in disaggregated equations. Also, the coefficients were only slightly significant. For these reasons, the specification of (4.4) is retained in what follows.

We continue the discussion by considering the long-run solution of the wage equations given next,

$$w_I = 1.07\,p + 3.03\,\rho_s - 0.301\,U$$
$$w_S = 0.99\,p + 3.03\,\rho_s - 0.301\,U \qquad (4.6)$$

(constants omitted for simplicity). As expected, the consumer price elasticity is close to one in both equations. The remaining determinants are exactly the same in both cases: this lends support to the hypothesis that there is substantial rigidity in the labour market, since any improvement in any sector spreads immediately to the other sector. It is also interesting to remark that it is the level of wages which is made to depend on the rate of unemployment, rather than the rate of wage inflation itself, as in the traditional Phillips curve. This may look unusual, but the idea goes back at least to 1964 (see, for example, Sargan, 1964). The other somewhat striking feature of these equations is the strong responsiveness of wages to increases in productivity. This is due to the 1.47 productivity elasticity in the services wage equation. This last elasticity is too high, since employers would not implement the change leading to a productivity increase, knowing that the unit labour cost would increase. Therefore, it should have a value less than one. The fact that it turns out to be higher may be due to a reverse causation effect: a wage increase reduces the demand for labour, and increases labour productivity. Since the demand for labour can be written empirically as depending on output with elasticity one, and real wages with elasticity –0.5 (Raymond Bara, 1992*b*), this would match the explanation just proposed. Therefore, the value of this coefficient reflects, to a large extent, the difficulty in modelling wage equations, which come out as a result of a bargaining process and are, therefore, intrinsically unstable. The other potential explanation is that it is simply picking an upward-trend effect, which is certainly an empirical feature of Spanish wage behaviour (although trying to capture this effect by means of several trend specifications proved to be empirically difficult).

The price equations are fairly reasonable, and accord roughly with what should be expected. The industrial sector is considerably open to foreign competition (0.48 world prices elasticity in the long run), and the service sector is completely shielded, according to these estimates (zero long-run elasticity to foreign prices). Finally, the sum of the coefficients in the consumer price equation (*P*), is almost one (0.994), as it should be, and the sum of all coefficients in the other two equations is near one, too.

One last point that should be briefly discussed is the stability of the model. Formal tests accept the stability of the model as a whole. However, although the sample is short, estimating the model with the last ten or twelve years shows some changes in the wage equations. In particular, industrial productivity becomes significant in the industrial wage equation with a coefficient of 0.85, and service productivity disappears. This last value has been used in some simulations. The price equations, on the other hand, are stable.

5. DYNAMIC ANALYSIS

The next step in our analysis has to do with the dynamics of the system. We first study the stability of the system, and second, we work out the short-run dynamics of inflation under several shocks. The system can be written compactly as

$$(\mathbf{B_0} + \mathbf{B_1} \cdot \mathbf{B_2} \cdot F)\, y_t + (\mathbf{c_0} + \mathbf{c_1} L)\, z_t = u_t, \tag{5.1}$$

where $\mathbf{B_0}$, $\mathbf{B_1}$, $\mathbf{B_2}$ are square matrices of order 5, $\mathbf{c_0}$ and $\mathbf{c_1}$ (5×7) matrices, and where y_t and z_t are the vectors of endogenous and exogenous variables respectively; L is the lag operator, F the forward operator, and they fulfil the property $L \cdot F = 1$. The dynamic stability condition of a system such as (5.1) starts by finding the roots of the equation obtained equating to zero the determinant of $(\mathbf{B_0} + \mathbf{B_1} \cdot \mathrm{L} + \mathbf{B_2} \cdot \mathrm{L}^{-1})$. In this case, the system has three roots, and since there are two initial conditions (two lagged endogenous variables), there are three roots for L. If the system is to be stable, there must be one inside the unit circle, and two outside (the last two are solved backwards and the other forward; see, for example, Wallis (1987), and Blanchard *et al.* (1980)). The roots of the system (4.4) are in fact $L = (0.283, -2.717, 1.244)$, so that we conclude that the system is indeed stable.

Once dynamic stability is ensured, it makes sense to discuss the long-run solution. This is easily obtained by making $L = F = 1$ in (5.1), and solving the resulting system of linear equations. That is,

$$\begin{aligned} y^* &= -(\mathbf{B_0} + \mathbf{B_1} + \mathbf{B_2})^{-1} (\mathbf{c_0} + \mathbf{c_1})\, z^*. \\ &= \pi \cdot z^* \end{aligned} \tag{5.2}$$

The values of π are long-run elasticities, since all variables are measured in natural logarithms (see Table 5.3). It may be also of some interest to work out explicitly the value of independent shocks in the wage equations. If we establish the ordering $y'_t = (p_{st}, p_{It}, w_{It}, w_{st}, p_t)$, the coefficients that we are looking for are given by the third and fourth columns of the matrix $-(\mathbf{B_0} + \mathbf{B_1} + \mathbf{B_2})^{-1}$, respectively. Finally, the effect of productivity shocks in the industrial wage equation seems to have been rather crucial in later years (see also, estimates below). Therefore, this effect has also been worked out assuming a coefficient of 0.85. The values of all these coefficients are presented in Table 5.4.

TABLE 5.3. *Values of long-run elasticities*

	p_w	ρ_I	U
p_s	0.83	–0.379	–0.89
p_I	0.83	–0.539	–0.37
w_I	0.91	–0.417	–0.98
w_s	0.84	–0.383	–0.90
p	0.85	–0.388	–0.61

TABLE 5.4. *Values of coefficients* (assuming coefficient of 0.85)

	ε_i	ε_s	ρ_I	ρ_{i*}
p_s	3.5	6.38	2.98	2.6
p_I	1.85	2.67	1.57	1.03
w_I	4.86	7.02	4.13	3.71
w_s	3.54	6.44	3.01	2.63
p	2.52	4.35	2.14	1.75

Notes:
ε_I: industrial wage shock.
ε_s: service wage shock.
*: adding both columns ρ_I in Tables 5.3 and 5.4.

The world price elasticity of the general price index is close to one as expected. The elasticities of the remaining variables possess the correct sign, and are generally very high: high interdependence of wages in both sectors accounts for this fact (see 4.6), and the elasticities are probably overstated. In any case, and according to these estimates, autonomous wage shocks have a multiplied impact on the general price level, and should therefore be the first target in any anti-inflationary programme. It is also worth remarking that shocks in industrial wages have a substantially smaller effect across the economy than shocks in services wages (compare cols. ε_I and ε_S in Table 5.4). This is due to the fact that the services sector is almost perfectly closed to foreign competition in this model, so that wage shocks are fully passed on to prices, whereas in the industrial sector, shocks are partially absorbed by reduced profits, because foreign competition is strong. The impact of productivity in the services sector is omitted because its coefficient in the corresponding wage equation has probably been overstated as discussed before. As for industrial productivity, its impact is positive on inflation: this may seem surprising, but it is just the result predicted by the models of Section 3.2, and the non-competitive behaviour of the labour market. As soon as this last feature is removed, this positive impact simply disappears.

To complete the study of shocks to the model, we must analyse its dynamics. The analytic solution of a model such as (4.4) is complicated because of the future expectation of *P* in the industrial wage equation: this implies that one of the dynamic roots has to be solved forward. We shall focus in what follows on the general price level *P*. Its associated dynamic polynomial is common to all endogenous variables in the model, and equal to the determinant of ($\mathbf{B_0} + \mathbf{B_1}$L + $\mathbf{B_2}$F). Once the roots of this polynomial are worked out, it is possible to split appropriately the roots into those to be solved backwards, and the forward root. The simplest way to derive the dynamic equation is by direct substitution. After all these derivations, one gets the general solution given by:

$$
\begin{aligned}
&(1 - 0.436L - 0.296\,L^2)\,P = 1.2 \sum_{s=0}^{\infty} 0.283^S F^s \\
&[(0.1535 + 0.127L - 0.082\,L^2 - 0.067\,L^3)\,P_w \\
&\quad + (0.312 + 0.324\,L + 0.166\,L^3)\,\rho_s \\
&\quad + (-0.019 + 0.093\,L + 0.198\,L^2)\,\rho_I \\
&\quad + (0.127 + 0.108\,L + 0.153\,L^2)\,\varepsilon_I \\
&\quad + (0.221 + 0.451\,L)\,\varepsilon_S]
\end{aligned} \tag{5.3}
$$

The shocks in Table 5.4 have also been taken into account. More specifically, it has been assumed that both industrial and services wage equations embody autonomous shocks, and that the industrial productivity elasticity of the industrial wage is 0.85 (estimating the model in the last part of the sample yields that value; the estimates are not very significant, however, since they are based on a few observations). From this last equation, we can simulate the dynamic response of the price level, when the model is perturbed by different types of shocks. Since variables are measured in natural logarithms, we can get the dynamics of inflation simply by first-order differencing the simulated values for the price level. The kind of shock considered is of the permanent and fully anticipated type (because the model assumes rational expectations). The simulation of the model under these conditions is not standard, and is briefly discussed in Appendix 2 (see also Wallis *et al.*, 1987). Fig. 5.3 summarizes the main results. Interestingly enough, inflation persists after several years, in spite of the possible peg of the exchange rate. The other striking result is that inflation can even accelerate in the first years after the shock, at least after some of them. This is specially the case after an industrial productivity shock. These two properties of the model seem to be roughly in agreement with the recent inflationary experience in Spain.

The high sensitivity of inflation to wage shocks in the empirical results presented is mainly due to (1) the strong interdependence of wages in both sectors, and (2) the fact that the service sector is shielded from foreign competition to a large extent. This sensitivity can be substantially reduced by policy actions addressed to modifying these two features. The long-run elasticity of the empirical model presented in (4.4) can be obtained as in (5.2) under a variety of assumptions, and the simulations yield the expected results: opening the service sector to foreign competition, and decreasing the interdependence of wages, reduces the sensitivity of inflation to all kind of shocks. In particular,

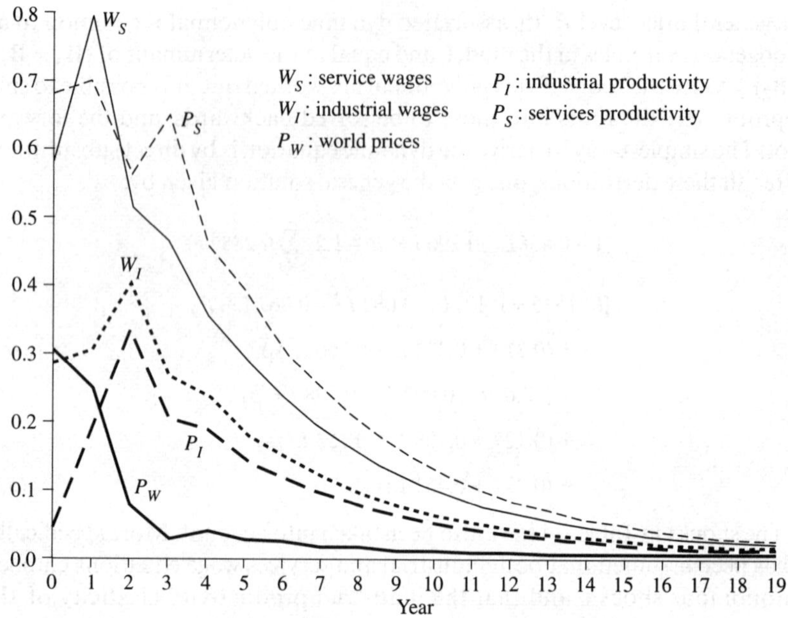

FIG. 5.3. Consumer price inflation (1% shocks)

the impact of productivity shocks in the industrial sector vanishes if wages are set independently.

6. CONCLUSIONS

One way to start this last section may be to recall that inflation is costly in the context of a monetary union because it entails a loss of competitiveness (apart from being possibly self-accelerating and distorting relative prices). The question is then, how to stop it from running above world or average European inflation. The results of this chapter point to two clear ways to address this target, and throw light on a third alternative frequently proposed outside government institutions. The first policy recommendation is simply to open up the services sector to foreign competition. This can only be done by achieving a real common market, inside which goods, services, and factors of production can move freely. The mobility of services and its productive factors will always remain low, so that it will be difficult to increase international competition in the services sector. It is also worth pointing out that, even under a situation where wages are set in each sector quite independently from the remaining sector, autonomous wage shocks in the services sector feed into industrial prices through consumption prices and industrial wages. Services are also an input to industry, and this is another channel for inflation in services to affect industrial prices. If the services sector is more open to foreign competition, this translation would be dampened: therefore, we get the result that one way to improve the competitiveness of the industrial sector is to open the services sector to foreign competition.

The second policy recommendation is simply to reduce the degree of interaction among the wage-setting processes of both sectors. This would lead to a general decrease of inflation sensitivity to all kinds of shocks. More specifically, tying real wage increases to productivity increases in each sector would dampen considerably any autonomous wage shock, should it occur. Besides, the positive impact of productivity on inflation would vanish.

The third policy measure is more properly related to fighting the consequences of inflation itself, and it is simply to depreciate the currency in order to reverse the trade balance deficit provoked by inflation. In the long run it is clear that this measure is ineffective, since the world price elasticity of all domestic prices is around 85 per cent (industry, services, and consumption prices). On the other hand, it is also clear that simply pegging the exchange rate does not ensure a domestic inflation equal to foreign inflation. The reason is that other forces are at work in the domestic price-fixing process (notably, productivity and wage shocks). Therefore, long-run competitiveness in a fixed exchange rate environment can only be achieved by structural reforms (of the labour market and the production process itself). The long-run ineffectiveness of a depreciation does not imply that realignments may not be called upon occasionally. The fact that prices are sticky in the short run makes it possible to depreciate as a measure to cope with a trade balance deficit crisis, provided the trade balance reacts sufficiently fast, as seems to be the case in Spain (Mauleón, 1988, 1993). Nevertheless, depreciation does not have much to recommend it as a permanent solution to gain competitiviness (in fact, it can be shown that in the long run it leads to accelerating inflation).

APPENDIX 1

This appendix proves the proposition discussed in Section 3. Under the specification of the utility and production functions for both sectors proposed in (3.7), the first-order conditions for an optimum become,

$$1 + r = \rho \, . \, \theta \, . \, (k + I)^{\theta - 1} \, . \, L_2^{1 - \theta} = \theta \, . \, \frac{Y_2}{I + k} \qquad \text{(A.1.1)}$$

$$\beta (1 + r)^{\frac{1}{\alpha}} \, . \, \frac{Y_1 - I - B}{Y_2 + B\,(1 + r)} = \frac{L - L_1}{L - L_2} \qquad \text{(A.1.2)}$$

$$\frac{1 - \theta}{\gamma} \, . \, \rho \left(\frac{k}{L_1}\right)^{\theta} = \frac{\alpha}{1 - \alpha} \, . \, \frac{Y_1 - I - B}{\gamma (L - L_1)} \qquad \text{(A.1.3)}$$

$$\frac{1 - \theta}{\gamma} \, . \, \rho \left(\frac{k + I}{L_2}\right)^{\theta} = \frac{\alpha}{1 - \alpha} \, . \, \frac{Y_2 + B\,(1 + r)}{\gamma (L - L_2)} \qquad \text{(A.1.4)}$$

after relevant substitutions, so that we end up with a four-equation system in four unknowns (L_1, L_2, I, B). For simplicity and from now on, we shall write $B = B_1$, $L_{Tt} = L_t$, $Y_{Tt} = Y_t$.

We start by noting that from (A.1.1) we get,

$$(1 + r) = \rho \, . \, \theta \, . \left(\frac{L_2}{I + K}\right)^{1 - \theta} \qquad \text{(A.1.5)}$$

so that if ρ increases, so does ($(I + D) / (L_2)$).

Secondly, dividing (A.1.3) by (A.1.4) and using (A.1.1) we immediately obtain,

$$\left(\frac{K}{K + I}\right)^{\theta} \left(\frac{L_2}{L_1}\right)^{\theta} = (\beta (1 + \mathrm{r})^{\frac{1}{\alpha}})^{-1} \qquad \text{(A.16)}$$

Now, since ($L_2 / (I + K)$) goes up from (A.1.5), then ($1/L_1$) goes up too, so that finally we get the result that L_1 decreases. Thirdly, from (A.1.4) and the specified production function for Y_T in (3.7), we get

$$\frac{(1 - \theta)(1 - \alpha)}{\alpha} \, . \, \rho \left(\frac{K + I}{L_2}\right)^{\theta} = \rho \left(\frac{K + I}{L_2}\right)^{\theta} \cdot \frac{L_2}{L - L_2} + \frac{\beta}{L - L_2} (1 - \mathrm{r})$$

$$\frac{(1 - \theta)\,(1 - \alpha)}{\alpha} = \frac{L_2}{L - L_2} + \frac{\beta}{L - L_2} \cdot \frac{1 + r}{\rho} \cdot \left(\frac{L_2}{k + I}\right)^{\theta} \qquad \text{(A.17)}$$

$$= \frac{L_2}{L - L_2} + \frac{\beta}{L - L_2} \cdot \left(\frac{L_2}{K + I}\right)^{\theta}$$

where use has been made of (A.1.1) in the last step. It is immediate from here that

$$\beta_2 \, . \, \frac{L_2}{I + K} = \frac{(1 - \theta)\,(1 - \alpha)}{\theta \, \alpha} \, . \, (L - L_2) - \frac{L_2}{\theta}$$

$$d\left(\beta \, . \frac{L_2}{I + K}\right) = -\left(\frac{(1 - \alpha)\,(1 - \theta)}{\alpha \, \theta} + \frac{1}{\theta}\right) dL_2 \qquad \text{(A.18)}$$

$$= -\gamma \, . \, dL_2,$$

where $\gamma > 1$. From this result we now obtain

$$dB = d\left(\frac{I+K}{L_2}\right).\left(B\frac{L_2}{I+K}\right) + \frac{I+K}{L_2}(-\gamma).dL_2$$

$$= -\gamma.\frac{I+K}{L_2}.dL_2 \tag{A.19}$$

assuming $B = 0$ before the productivity shock. From (A.1.9) it follows that showing that $dL_2 > 0$, implies $dB < 0$. In order to prove this, we first differentiate (A.1.2) and make some simple substitutions. Thus,

$$B(1+r)^{1/\alpha}.\frac{L-L_2}{L-L_1} = \frac{Y_2 + B.(1+r)}{Y_1 - I - B}$$

$$= \frac{\rho(K+I)^{\theta}L_2^{1-\theta}\left(1+\frac{B\theta}{I+K}\right)}{\rho k^{\theta}L_1^{1-\theta} - I - B}, \tag{A.1.10}$$

where use has been made of the production function assumed for tradeables in (3.7). Defining now $\delta = \beta(1+r)^{1/\alpha}$, and using (A.1.1) and (A.1.6), taking logs and differentiating

$$0 = \frac{dL_2 + \theta.d\left(\frac{L_2B}{I+K}\right)}{N}$$

$$-\frac{\delta.dL_1 - \frac{\theta}{1+r}\left(d\left(\frac{IL_2}{I+K}\right) + d\left(\frac{BL_2}{I+K}\right)\right)}{D} \tag{A.1.11}$$

$$-\frac{dL_1}{L-L_1} + \frac{dL_2}{L-L_2}$$

where $N = L_2 + B \cdot \Theta \cdot L_2/(I+K)$, and $D = \delta \cdot L_1 - (I+B) \cdot \Theta \cdot L_2/((1+r)(I+K))$. To solve this last expression we need to work out $d(I \cdot L_2/(I+K))$. We note first,

$$d\frac{I.L_2}{I+K} = (dI).\frac{L_2}{I+K} + I.d\left(\frac{L_2}{I+K}\right) \tag{A.1.12}$$

Taking logs of (A.1.1) and differentiating, we get

$$dI = \frac{K+I}{L_2}.dL_2 + \frac{K+I}{\rho(1-\theta)}.dp$$

$$d\left(\frac{I.L_2}{I+K}\right) = -\frac{d\rho}{\rho}.\frac{L_2}{(I+K)(1-\theta)}, \tag{A.1.13}$$

and substituting these results in (A.1.12), leads to

$$d\left(\frac{I.L_2}{I+K}\right) = dL_2 + \left(\frac{L_2}{I+K}\right).\frac{k}{\rho(1-\theta)}, \tag{A.1.14}$$

$$= dL_2 + \sigma$$

where $\sigma > 0$. Substituting now (A.1.8) and (A.1.14) in (A.1.11) we get:

$$0 = \frac{dL_2 - \theta\gamma dL_2}{N} - \frac{\delta \, . \, dL_1 - \dfrac{\theta}{1+r}(dL_2 + \sigma - \gamma dL_2)}{D} - \frac{dL_1}{L-L_1} + \frac{dL_2}{L-L_2}$$

$$= \left(\frac{\theta\gamma - 1}{N} + \frac{\theta(\gamma - 1)}{(1+r)\,D} - \frac{1}{L-L_2}\right) . \, dL_2 + \left(\frac{\delta}{D} + \frac{1}{L-L_1}\right) dL_1 - \frac{\theta\sigma}{(1+r)} \, . \, D$$

$$= a \, . \, dL_2 + b \, . \, dL_1 - c.$$

Now, a must be different from zero, because otherwise that would imply that $dL_1 = 0$, which cannot be true from (A.1.6). Therefore we can write:

$$dL_2 = -\frac{b}{a} \, . \, dL_1 + \frac{c}{a} \, . \tag{A.1.16}$$

We know that $(b, c) > 0$, $dL_1 < 0$. We now show that $a > 0$. Substituting the values of γ given in (A.1.8), N and D given in (A.1.11), and under the assumption that $\beta = 0$, and using (A.1.11), the hypothesis that $a > 0$ amounts to proving the following inequality,

$$\frac{(1-\alpha)(1-\theta)}{\alpha} + \delta\left(\frac{L-L_2}{L-L_1}\right)\left(\frac{1}{1+r}\right)\left(\frac{(1-\alpha)(1-\theta)}{\alpha} + 1 - \theta\right) > \frac{L}{L-L_2} = \frac{(1-\theta)(1-\alpha)}{\alpha}, \tag{A.1.17}$$

where the last equality has been obtained from (A.1.7). It is immediate that the inequality holds, so that $a > 0$. Given that $a > 0$, it is immediate from (A.1.16) that $dL_2 > 0$, and therefore $dB < 0$ from (A.1.9), which is the result that was to be proved.

As a corollary, we note from (A.1.3) that the consumption of tradeables in the first period goes up, that is C_{T1} increases. Also, since L_{T1} decreases, L_{N2} must increase by the same amount, and therefore so must do D_{N1} too. Finally, dividing (A.1.3) by (A.1.4) and from the general expression for the first-order conditions, we get that P_N goes up in both periods, and by the same amount. Summarizing, we have proved the following results under a productivity shock, starting from a trade balance in equilibrium: (1) consumption increases, (2) investment increases, (3) the trade balance turns into deficit, and (4) the price of non traded goods increases. So, inflation and a trade deficit can be induced by a supply shock, which was the result we wanted to prove.

APPENDIX 2

We consider first, the steady-state inflationary solution assuming a constant rate of depreciation of the currency, $\Delta s_t = \sigma > 0$ (as in Miller and Sutherland). This can be done by taking first-order differences of all variables in model (3.16)–(3.18), and imposing dynamic equilibrium (that is, $\Delta x_t = \Delta x_{t-n}$, for all n). The solution for the rate of change of all variables involved is:

$$\Delta p = \Delta w = \Delta s = \sigma > 0 \qquad \text{(A.2.1)}$$
$$\Delta y = 0.$$

Now we can solve for the levels, and after substituting the aggregate model this leads to,

$$P_t = s_t + \eta \qquad \text{(A.2.2)}$$
$$w_t = s_t + \phi,$$

where η, ϕ, are proportional to σ, and fulfil,

$$n < 0$$
$$0 < \phi < \sigma/2 \qquad \text{(A.2.3)}$$
$$\phi - \eta = \left(\frac{1-\theta}{2}\right)\sigma. \qquad \text{(A.2.3)}$$

From there we get $(w -) > 0$, and $y = -\gamma\eta > 0$, that is, output in the N sector is above the non-inflationary steady-state value.

We seek now the solution of the model, and more specifically, the short-run dynamics of inflation when there are input shocks. We then have to deal with the rational expectation variables. After some substitutions we get,

$$w_t = (1-\alpha_4)^{-1} \cdot ((\alpha_4/2) \cdot w_{t-1} + (\alpha_4/2)\, w^e_{t+1}$$
$$+ (\alpha_3 - \alpha_4 \cdot \theta) . \rho_t - \alpha_4 \theta \rho^e_{t+1} \qquad \text{(A.2.4)}$$
$$+ \alpha_1 . S_t - \alpha_4 . S_{t-1} + (\alpha_4 + \alpha_2) . S^e_{t+1}$$

$$0 < \alpha_1 = a + b \cdot \beta \cdot \gamma < 1.5$$
$$0 < \alpha_2 = b \cdot \beta \cdot \gamma < 1/2$$
$$0 < \alpha_3 = a < 1 \qquad \text{(A.2.5)}$$
$$0 < \alpha_4 = b(1 - \beta\gamma) < 1/2,$$

where the α's are parameters given by (A.2.5).

To solve equation (A.2.4) we note first that the solution to an equation of the following form:

$$\Phi w_t - w_{t-1} - w^e_{t+1} = z; \quad z < \Phi = 2\left(\frac{1-\alpha_4}{\alpha_4}\right) \qquad \text{(A.2.6)}$$

is given by,

$$(1 - \lambda L) . w_t = \frac{\lambda}{1 - \lambda F} \cdot z_t \qquad \text{(A.2.7)}$$

$$0 < \lambda = \Phi - (\Phi^2 - 4)^{1/2} < 1,$$

where F is the forward operator, that is, $FX_t = X_{t+1}$. We can consider now the dynamics of inflation after the exchange rate peg. Let us assume then that $S_0 = 0$, but the peg is not announced beforehand, so that agents only become fully aware of it at $t = 1$. Then we shall have from (A.2.3). $w_0 = \phi > 0$, and $P_0 = \eta < 0$. If there are no productivity shocks from (A.2.4) and (A.2.7) it is immediate that

$$w_n - \lambda w_{n-1} = 0 \qquad \text{(A.2.8)}$$
$$w_n = \lambda^n \cdot w_0 > 0, \quad n > 0.$$

Thus,

$$P_1 - P_0 = \frac{1}{2}(1 + \lambda)\, w_0 - \eta$$
$$= 1/2\,(1 + \lambda)\,\phi - \eta < \phi - \eta = \frac{1 - \theta}{2} \cdot \sigma < \frac{\sigma}{2}, \qquad \text{(A.2.9)}$$

so that inflation at $t = 1$ is positive, but falls at less than half its previous value. Also,

$$P_n - P_{n\text{-}1} = \frac{1}{2}(1 + \lambda)\, \lambda^{n-2} (\lambda - 1)\, w_0 < 0, \quad n > 2 \qquad \text{(A.2.10)}$$

so that inflation becomes negative after $t = 1$. These results are the same as those of Miller and Sutherland (in fact, if $\delta = \theta = 0$, the model is the same).

We finally tackle the main problem, that is, the short-run dynamic behaviour of inflation under a productivity shock in the traded sector. As for the source of the shock, we might explain it by increased investment placed in capital goods of newer and more productive vintages, generated in turn by an improvement of expectations associated to exchange rate stability (that seems to be at least a plausible explanation for the Spanish case during the years 1986–90). As before, we have that $s_0 = 0$, $w_0 = \phi > 0$, $p_0 = \eta < 0$. But now the wage behaviour differs, and from (A.2.4), (A.2.7) is given by,

$$w_n - \lambda \cdot w_{n-1} = \frac{\lambda}{1 - \lambda}(\alpha_3 - 2\alpha_4\theta)\, \rho\, \cdot, \quad n > 0, \qquad \text{(A.2.11)}$$

and for $\rho > 0$, we have $w_n > 0$, as can easily be checked. It will be convenient later to use the long-run values of wages and prices (written as starred variables in what follows). First and from (3.10) and (3.13) we immediately get,

$$p^* = (1 - \theta) \cdot P^*_{\mathrm{N}} \qquad \text{(A.2.12)}$$
$$P^*_{\mathrm{N}} = w^*_{\mathrm{N}}.$$

We can obtain the value for w^*_{N} directly from the equations that define the model for the N sector given in (3.10) to (3.13), in the usual way. Thus

$$w^*_{\mathrm{N}} = \frac{\delta \,.\, \rho}{1 - (1 - \delta)(1 - \theta)(1 - \beta\gamma)} > 0, \qquad \text{(A.2.13)}$$

and therefore $P^* > 0$. Also $w^* = \theta\rho + (1 - \theta)w^*_{\mathrm{N}}$ will be greater than zero, too. Besides, we shall consider productivity shocks large enough to ensure $w^* > w_0$. The dynamics of the aggregate wage can be written now as,

$$w_n = \lambda \cdot w_{n-1} + (1 - \lambda) \cdot w^*$$
$$(w^* - w_n) = \lambda\,(w^* - w_{n-1}) \qquad \text{(A.2.14)}$$
$$= \lambda^n (w^* - w_0) > 0, \qquad n > 0,$$

and the price dynamics as

$$P_1 = \frac{1}{2}(w_1 + w_0 - \theta\rho) \tag{A.2.15}$$

$$P_n = \frac{1}{2}(1 + \lambda)\, w_{n-1} + \frac{1-\lambda}{2} \cdot w^* - \theta\rho, \quad n > 1$$

(note that $\rho_0 = 0, \rho_n = \rho, n > 0$). From here it is straightforward to derive the dynamics of inflation as

$$P_2 - P_1 = \frac{1}{2}(1 - \lambda^2)(w^* - w_0) - \theta \cdot \rho/2$$
$$P_n - P_{n-1} = \frac{1}{2}(1 - \lambda^2)\,\lambda^{n-2}(w^* - 2)(w^* - w_0) \quad > 0 \quad n > 2, \tag{A.2.16}$$

so that inflation will be positive at least after $t = 2$, whereas it was negative without the productivity shock.

It can also accelerate between $t = 1$, and $t = 2$, if the productivity shock is large enough. For $t = 1$, we have

$$2(P_1 - P_0) = (1 + \lambda) \cdot w_0 - 2\eta + (1 - \lambda)\, u^* - \theta u. \tag{A.2.17}$$

In order to analyse this expression, we shall consider different values of θ (the weight of the traded sector in the economy). When $\theta \to 1$, it is easily checked that $\alpha_4 \to 0$ (see (3.18) and (A.2.5)), and $\lambda \to 0$ (see (A.2.6), and (A.2.7)). Then (A.2.17) becomes,

$$2(P_1 - P_0) = 2(w_0 - \eta) + (w^* - w_0) - \eta = 0 \tag{A.2.18}$$

from (A.2.2), (A.2.3), the definition of w^*, and the fact that $\phi = 0$, if $\theta = 1$. Conversely, if $\theta \to 0$ it is self evident that inflation on $t = 1$ will be positive. So, in general, a positive inflation at time $t = 1$, will be ensured. Finally,

$$(P_2 - P_1) - (P_1 - P_0) = \frac{1}{2}(\lambda(1 - \lambda)w^* - (1 + \lambda)(2 - \lambda) \cdot w_0) + \eta \tag{A.2.19}$$

and a large enough productivity shock will ensure a sufficient difference between w^* and w_0, so that the inflation differential between $t = 1$ and $t = 2$ is positive.

APPENDIX 3

This appendix presents and discusses the relevant statistical information to the models presented in Section 4. It also discusses some other technical aspects concerning simulations of dynamic models with rational forward-looking expectations (see also Wallis, 1980).

We shall start by considering the last point first. Let us start then by a forward-looking model under rational expectations given by:

$$Y_t = \alpha Y^e_{t+1} + \beta x_{t-n}, \tag{A.3.1}$$

where $(\cdot)^e$ means expectations of the variable in question, under information up to time t, and $0 > \alpha > 1$. Solving forward we get,

$$Y_t = B \cdot \sum_{s=0}^{\infty} \alpha^s \cdot x^e_{t-n+s} \tag{A.3.2}$$

where $x^e_{t-n+s} = x_{t-n+s}$ for $s < (n + 1)$. Suppose now that we start from a long-run static equilibrium where $x = y = 0$, and that at $t = 0$, x is made equal to k for ever. Then

$$y_0 = \frac{\beta}{1-\alpha} \cdot \alpha^n \cdot k \tag{A.3.3}$$

and in general

$$y_r = \frac{B}{1-\alpha} \cdot K \cdot \begin{cases} \alpha^{n-r}; & \text{n} > r-1 \\ 1; & n < r. \end{cases} \tag{A.3.4}$$

With this result conveniently adapted, the dynamic simulation of the model (5.1) can be handled with no further problems.

The precise definition of the variables implied in the empirical results is the following (all variables are in natural logarithms):

- P_S: prices of services.
- W_S: wages in the service sector.
- ρ_S: average productivity for employee in the services sector.
- P_I: industrial prices.
- W_I: industrial wages.
- ρ_I: average productivity for employee in the industrial sector.
- P_W: index of world prices.
- P: consumer price index.
- U: unemployment rate.

The statistical sources are the Statistics National Institute (INE) and the FIES foundation. We proceed now to the discussion of other empirical results pertaining to the estimated models presented in Section 4.

The estimation of models with forward-looking rational expectations poses also very difficult problems (Sargan (1982) discusses alternative estimation procedures). One possibility consists of solving explicitly the model. This leads to a model which is highly non-linear in parameters, with cross-equation restrictions. But this requires the specification of autoregressive models for the exogenous variables. This may be a rather restrictive statistical description of these variables and, indeed, it may be that they do not follow any statistical model at all. Alternatively, we can apply instrumental variables procedures (viewed as special cases of the generalized method of moments methodology). To put it simply, let us consider the simplified equation:

$$\begin{aligned} w &= \alpha \cdot P^e_{+1} + \varepsilon \\ &= \alpha \cdot p_{+1} + (\varepsilon - \alpha u_{+1}) \\ &= \alpha \cdot P_{+1} + v, \end{aligned} \tag{A.3.5}$$

where $P = P^e + u$. But now,

$$E(v\,v_{-1}) = -\alpha\, E(\varepsilon u), \tag{A.3.6}$$

and this will not be zero in general if there is contemporaneous correlation in the error term, as seems to be the case with model (4.4). Also, P will be correlated with the error of the equation. Therefore, we face two joint problems: simultaneity and autocorrelation. The last problem was tackled estimating the W_I equation with a first-order moving-average error, under instrumental variables (instruments: w_{s-1}, P_{W+1}, P_W, P_{W-1}). The t-ratio of the moving average was 0.15. Therefore, and although the error must follow a first-order m.a. process according to (A.3.6), it is clearly not a serious problem, and so it was neglected. Finally, the simultaneity problem can be handled easily by means of the instrumental variable technique. The system (4.4) was therefore estimated by iterated three stages least-squares, using as instruments, w_{s-1}, ρ_{s-1}, ρ_I, P_W, P_{W-1}, P_{W+1}, U, W_{I-1}, ρ_s, ρ_{s+1}. The estimation is not equivalent to the maximum likelihood method: this would require solving forward the model, and using as instruments all future values of the exogenous variables. Clearly this is not possible since the matrix of instruments would be singular. So, unless we are willing to specify a statistical model for the exogenous variables, optimum methods are not applicable, and one has to resort to simple estimation methods. The last qualification that must be made is that the general price equation was not estimated by instrumental variables. In fact, the results presented come from a joint estimation of the five equations by the seemingly unrelated equations technique. The explanation is that this procedure gave the most reasonable results for the equation. On the other hand, this is not a structural equation, and is estimated only to close the model.

The residual correlation matrix of the iterative 3SLS procedure implemented with the equations for the variables P_S, P_I, W_I, W_S (in that order) is:

$$\Sigma = \begin{bmatrix} 1 & -0.037 & 0.45 & -0.41 \\ & 1 & 0.47 & -0.32 \\ & & 1 & -0.6 \\ & & & 1 \end{bmatrix} \tag{A.3.7}$$

The relatively sizeable values of the off-diagonal elements confirms the advisability of a joint estimation procedure (which comes as no surprise with annual data).

The stability of the model can be judged by the predictive ability of its equations independently. The test based upon the last three observations (1987–90) is asymptotically distributed as a X^2 with three degrees of freedom. The values of the test are the following:

$$\begin{aligned} &\textit{equ. } P_S,\ X^2(3) = 1.37 \\ &\textit{equ. } P_I,\ X^2(3) = 0.97 \\ &\textit{equ. } W_I,\ X^2(3) = 0.53 \\ &\textit{equ. } W_S,\ X^2(3) = 1.04 \\ &\textit{equ. } P,\ X^2(3) = 0.98. \end{aligned} \tag{A.3.8}$$

Therefore, we can conclude that the equations are formally stable.

The serial autocorrelation can be tested easily by the Lagrange multiplier technique. Since in all cases the lagged dependent variable does not belong to the set of regressors, and the lagged values of dependent and independent variables are not contained in the instrument set, the test is equivalent to the t-ratio of the lagged error, after regressing the error of the equation on its own lagged value. Finally, the equation must be estimated by instrumental variables, using the same set of instruments as in the estimation of the structural equation. The values of the test are the following:

$$\begin{aligned} &equ.\ P_S,\ t = 0.92 \\ &equ.\ P_I,\ t = 1.2 \\ &equ.\ W_I,\ t = -0.17 \\ &equ.\ W_S,\ t = 0.07 \\ &equ.\ P,\ t = 1.26 \end{aligned} \qquad \text{(A.39)}$$

(simple ordinary least-squares applied to the errors of the equation for P). Since the sample is somewhat short, the small sample results might be away from their asymptotic counterparts. The instrumental variable technique is more sensitive to this kind of problem than ordinary least-squares. Therefore, the test was also run omitting the instruments, and the results, although different, did not give any sign of serial autocorrelation.

As regards the specification of the lag structure and selected variables, a combination of approaches was followed (general to particular and the opposite). The final equations were tested against omitted variables with no sign of misspecification error. The equation can also be respecified in the error-correction-mechanism form, once the proper co-integration test confirms the adequacy of the level specification (see below). For example, the services price equation in model (4.4) can be written as:

$$\Delta P_S = 1.77 + 0.41\,\Delta W_S - (P_S - 0.99\,W_S + 0.58\,\rho_s)_{-1}. \qquad \text{(A.3.10)}$$

As the normality of the errors is concerned, there are no outliers, the model is not going to be used for predictive purposes, and the stability test of (A.3.8) is not seriously biased, because the usual empirical result otherwise would have been an overstatement of instability (because of thicker error-distribution tails, which is the usual result). Therefore, it was not thought necessary to run this type of test. Heteroskedasticity tests were not run either because that type of problem is more likely to happen in financial series. Besides, the error did not give any warning in this direction.

The final question to be discussed in this appendix is the order of integrability and co-integrability of the variables involved. We now turn to this question. To investigate the order of integrability, regressions of the type proposed in the augmented Dickey–Fuller statistic were run (with a constant, one lag of the differenced variables, and no trend). The values of the coefficient and the associated t-statistic for the level of the lagged dependent variable are given in Table 5.A1 (variables in logs, sample, 1972–90).

Given that available significant statistical values are always obtained by simulations, we can conclude that a value of the t-statistics below 3 is a clear sign of a unit root, a value above 4 a sign of no unit root, and values between 3 and 4 may not have a clear-cut answer. Then, and in view of the results, we might say that wages seem to be stationary, and also perhaps productivities. Thus, one should test for co-integration of the non-stationary variables entering the wage equations. Note, however, that the dynamic root in both wage regressions of Table 5.A1 is above 0.95, so that a more sensible conclusion may be just that the unit root tests have a low power.

TABLE 5.A1. *Unit root tests*

Variable	Coefficient	*t*-ratio
w_S	–0.039	–3.7
w_I	–0.048	–6.1
p_C	–0.02	–2.8
p_I	–0.027	–2.7
P_S	–0.021	–2.4
P_W	–0.031	–1.4
ρ_S	–0.13	–4.3
ρ_I	–0.09	–3.1
U	–0.03	–1.4

The co-integration of the variables in each of the five equations of the model is tested next. In all cases the values presented in Table 5.A2 are the *t*-statistics of a regression on the errors of the co-integration vector of the type $\Delta err = a + b \cdot err_{-1}$. The significant values are MacKinnon's, and the value of the coefficient *b* is also given.

TABLE 5.A2. *Co-integration tests*

Variable	Coefficient	*t*-statistic	critical value (5%)
p_c	–0.66	–2.95	–4.7
w_S	–0.98	–4.1	–5.2
w_I	–0.73	–3.1	–3.7
P_I	–0.996	–4.15	–4.3
P_S	–0.94	–3.22	–4.3

According to these results, therefore, and since the null of a unit root is never rejected, equations should be specified in first differences. However, when tests of first-order autocorrelation were run, the null of a zero autoregressive coefficient was never rejected (results presented above). This matches the results of Table 5.A2, where the very high absolute values of *b* close to –1 indicate almost without doubt that the dependent variable has been overdifferenced. Interestingly enough, these comments are also applicable to wage equations.

The conclusion to be drawn from all these results is that the power of unit root tests in this context is too low to be of any practical use. Perhaps for this reason, it may be advisable to re-estimate the basic model differencing all variables, but keeping the same specification and estimation method (that is, iterative 3SLS, with the same instruments differenced too; note that estimating by a proper instrumental variables procedure is important now, since variables are not trending). The results are the following:

$$\Delta P_S = \underset{(0.6)}{-0.006} + \underset{(4.6)}{0.3}\,\Delta w_S + \underset{(8.3)}{0.73}\,\Delta(w_s - \rho_s)_{-1}$$

s.e.: 1.5% ; DW: 1.81

$$\Delta pI = \underset{(1.5)}{0.018} + \underset{(4.5)}{0.38}\,\Delta(w_I - \rho_I) + \underset{(2.4)}{0.16}\,\Delta P_W + \underset{(2.9)}{0.18}\,\Delta P_{W-1}$$

s.e.: 2.3% ; DW: 2.19

$$\Delta w_I = \underset{(0.3)}{0.008} + \underset{(4.4)}{1.97\,\Delta^2 P_{+1}} + \underset{(5.1)}{1.01 \Delta w_{s-1}}$$

s.e.: 5.4% ; DW: 2.73

$$\Delta w_s = \underset{(0.8)}{0.015} + \underset{(2.0)}{0.54\,\Delta P} - \underset{(0.4)}{0.03\,\Delta U} + \underset{(1.84)}{0.26\,\Delta w_{I-1}} + \underset{(3.6)}{1.4\,\Delta \rho_s}$$

s.e.: 3.2% ; DW: 1.4

$$\Delta P = \underset{(3.7)}{0.37\,\Delta p_I} + \underset{(5.9)}{0.58\,\Delta P_S} + \underset{(0.1)}{0.01\,\Delta P_W}$$

s.e.: 1.2% ; DW: 2.1 (A.3.11)

The model performs acceptably well, noting that no specification search has been conducted. In fact, there are only two coefficients that lose their significance: U in the Δw_I equation, and ΔP_W in the equation for P (and both were small before, after all). The standard errors, however, increase in all cases, so the fit is worse (and the R^2's decrease, although they remain high and in the neighbourhood of 0.8 to 0.9). The DW statistics get larger in all equations except the fourth: in the equations for P_S, P_I, and P, the final value gets closer to the theoretically desired value of 2 than before. In the equation for W_I, however, the new value gets close to 3, which is exactly what we would get under overdifferencing. So it seems that we might accept the differenced model too. However, there are some advantages in the level specification that finally made us choose it: (1) the indication of overdifferencing in the equation for W_I, (2) the loss of statistical significancy of two variables and the larger s.e'.s in the differenced model, and (3) the level specification allows us to obtain the long-run solution (note, by contrast, the loss of significance of all constants in the differenced version). Finally, another possible alternative would haven been to specify some equations in levels and some in differences. But that would have made it very difficult, and sometimes impossible, to set up and work with a joint model.

REFERENCES

Balassa, B. (1964), 'The Purchasing Power Parity Doctrine: A Reappraisal', *Journal of Political Economy*, 62.

Blanchard, O., and Kahn, C. (1980), 'The Solution of Linear Difference Models under Rational Expectations', *Económétrica*, 48: 1305–11.

Bruno, M. (1976), 'The Two-Sector Open Economy and the Real Exchange Rate', *American Economic Review*, 57.

Campbell, J., and Perron, P. (1991), 'Pitfalls and Opportunities: What Macroeconomists Should Know about Unit Roots', NBER, *Macroeconomics Annual, 1991*, MIT Press.

Cochrane, J. (1991), 'Comments', NBER, *Macroeconomics Annual, 1991*, MIT Press.

De Grauwe, P. (1993), 'Inflation Convergence during the Transition to EMU', Ch. 7 in this volume.

Frenkel, J., and Razin, A. (1987), 'Fiscal Policies and the World Economy', MIT Press.

Froot, K., and Rogoff, K. (1991), 'The EMS, the EMU and the Transition to a Common Currency', *NBER Macroeconomics Annual, 1991*, MIT Press.

MacKinnon, J. (1991), 'Critical Values for Co-integration Test', in R. F. Engle and D. Granger (eds.), *Long-Run Economic Relationships*, OUP.

Mauleón, I. (1988), 'A Quarterly Econometric Model for the Spanish Economy', in H. Motamen (ed.), *Economic Modelling in OECD Countries*, Chapman & Hall, London.

—— (1993), 'Una perspectiva diferente sobre el deficit exterior', *Revista de Economia Aplicada*, 2.

Micossi, S., and Milesi-Ferreti, G. M. (1993), 'Real Exchange Rates and the Prices of Non-Tradeables', Ch. 8 in this volume.

—— and Papi, L. (1993), 'Inflation in Italy: Some Evidence on the Role of the Public Sector', Ch. 4 in this volume.

Miller, M., and Sutherland, A. (1992), 'Contracts, Credibility and Common Knowledge: Their Influence on Inflation Convergence', in Torres and Giavazzi (eds.), *The Transition to EMU in Europe*, Center for Economic Policy Research.

Muellbauer, J., and Murphy, A. (1990), 'Is the UK Balance of Payments Sustainable?', *Economic Policy*, 5: 347–96.

Raymond Bara, J. L. (1992*a*), 'La inflación dual en España', *Papeles de Economia Española*, 52/53.

—— (1992*b*), 'Salarios reales y empleo', *Papeles de Economia Española*, 52/53.

Rebelo, S. (1992), 'Inflation in a fixed exchange rate regime: The recent Portuguese experience', in Torres and Giavazzi (eds.), *The Transition to EMU in Europe*, CEPR.

Sargan, J. D. (1964), 'Wages and Prices in the United Kingdom: A Study in Econometric Methodology', in Hartland Mills (eds.), *Econometric Analysis for National Economic Planning*, Butterworth & Co., London.

—— (1982), 'A comparison of different methods of estimating and testing the specification of rational expectation models with one endogenous and one exogenous variable', mimeo, London School of Economics (also as a Working Paper, Univ. Carlos III, Madrid).

Taylor, J. (1980), 'Aggregate Dynamics and Staggered Contracts', *Journal of Political Economy*, 88/1: 1–24.

Wallis, K. (1980), 'Econometric Implications of the Rational Expectations Hypothesis', *Econométrica*, 48: 49–73.

—— and Whitley, J. (1987), 'Long-Run Properties of Large-Scale Macroeconometric Models', *Annales d'Economie et de Statistique*, 6/7: 207–24.

6

Inflation Control in Small EMS Countries: The Case of Belgium and The Netherlands

HENK JAGER

I. INTRODUCTION

The effect of EMS membership on controlling inflation is approached in three chapters in Part II of this volume by analysing the effect of Germany on one specific economic variable—price expectations (De Jong), prices and wages (Artis and Ormerod), and the interest rate (Wolters)—for a large set of EMS countries. In this chapter, however, we focus on only two member countries, viz. Belgium and the Netherlands, by looking at EMS effects on Belgian and Dutch inflation, via several economic variables—prices, wages, unemployment, and long-term interest rates.

Belgium and the Netherlands are quite similar in terms of many economic aspects. The two most important of their common features are their smallness and economic openness. Consequently, these two countries have a negligible influence on the partner countries in the EMS, whereas the latter countries substantially affect the former. Moreover, the two countries display a strong economic dependence on a specific large neighbour country: Germany. Additionally, it is the central country of the EMS and, above all, it leads the fight against inflation in the EMS area.

It is remarkable that, despite their similarities, in particular in their economic dependence, the two countries concerned have had the opportunity as well as the preference to go their own way in controlling inflation. This is chiefly demonstrated by the diverging paths of currency devaluations carried out against the key currency, the Deutschmark. Nevertheless, eventually both ways of controlling inflation have proved to be successful. In this context three essential questions arise.

First, did the EMS membership contribute essentially to the achievement of a moderation in inflation in the two countries and are there any inter-country differences? The 1980s showed a worldwide reduction in inflation. Is there an

This chapter is part of a research project on the Control of Inflation in the EMS during the Transition to Monetary Unification. Research support by the Commission of the European Communities (grant: SPES CT91-0053) is gratefully acknowledged. I am also indebted to Jolanda Heemskerk and Wendy Smits for their research assistance and to Paul De Grauwe, Eelke de Jong, Bertholt Leeftink, Jan Kees Martijn, and Giuseppe Tullio for their helpful comments.

additional and differentiated EMS effect? Economic theory is ambiguous with respect to the impact of fixed exchanges rates on inflation in the area concerned. Of course, as a fixed exchange rate area the EMS has the additional advantage that the central country is inflation-shy. But even that advantage does not preclude that the adjustment process to restore balance-of-payments equilibrium under fixed exchange rates may have an built-in inflation bias. It arises when the adjustment process of a balance-of-payments disequilibrium under fixed exchange rates is asymmetrical. This asymmetry results from the fact that in the deficit countries money wages show a downward rigidity, so that their domestic prices cannot fall. Then the main contribution to the adjustment must come from price rises in the surplus countries—inflation-shy or not. This asymmetry will be enhanced if the international liquidity position of deficit countries is ample.[1]

Second, if the EMS does appear to have contributed significantly to lower inflation, were the adjustment costs perhaps not too high? In this respect it is relevant to get an impression of the sacrifice ratios of lower inflation. It is important to detect the nature of the costs. Long-term costs are incompatible with a vertical Phillips curve. An alternative cost source of lower inflation is the real interest rate. This variable appears to be strikingly high in the 1980s, not only for Belgium and the Netherlands but indeed for Germany too: this high level exhibits prolonged features. If this is true, it could undermine the idea of a vertical Phillips curve.

Third, in line with the previous remark: what is the effect of the EMS membership on the level of the nominal interest rate? One aspect of this effect is whether the Walters dilemma occurs. The latter suggests that if a relatively high-inflation country joins the EMS, it will initially be faced with an upward impulse to inflation. For, the very entry is deemed to be associated with an additional amount of credibility. As devaluation expectations are reduced, the outcome is a huge capital inflow. As long as the country maintains its anti-inflationary, high-interest rate this situation will continue. Through the necessary official foreign exchange market interventions, however, the capital inflow will tend to add to the domestic money supply. The final result may well be additional economic growth but, important in this context, at the cost of higher inflation. In essence, it is a consequence of joining the EMS. On the other hand, there are several factors which may undermine the Walters effect. They include imperfect capital mobility, the absence of credibility related to the sustainability of the country's membership of the EMS, as well as offsetting negative expenditure impulses due to an appreciation of the real exchange rate and to a higher real interest rate related to a rapid reduction in inflation expectations.

[1] Corden (1985: 76) calls it the Haberler argument. Goldstein (1984: 15–19) gives a modest support from an opposite starting-point. He summarizes the arguments which underlie the view that floating, rather than fixed, exchange rates have an inflation bias. Eventually, he had to refute these arguments.

In the Walters dilemma the credibility of the chosen fixed exchange rate plays a crucial role. Built on the same footing is the idea that an irrevocable link of a currency to a strong currency, like the Deutschmark, is a feasible strategy to realize a low-interest rate in the longer run. Particularly, it was defended and put into practice by the Dutch central bank, De Nederlandsche Bank, at the beginning of the 1980s.

In order to answer these questions for Belgium and the Netherlands, several economic relations will be quantified. They are described and presented in the Appendices. The direct influence of the EMS on inflation will be investigated in Section 6 through an analysis of the estimated price and wage relations. An attempt to materialize the costs of inflation moderation will be made in Section 7 by means of the estimated unemployment relations. The consequences for the interest rate of stabilizing initially weak currencies will be analysed in Section 8 with the help of relations for the long-term interest rate. But first we will look at the economic developments of Belgium and the Netherlands more closely in Section 2, followed in Section 3 by a justification of the method used, which is built on a combination of recursive parameter estimation and Chow tests. Sections 4 and 5 contain a survey of the relevant policy measures in the two countries in the period to be investigated: from the second half of the 1970s up to the beginning of the 1990s. This survey is important to prevent erroneous conclusions being made in the later sections that possible structural changes in the inflation process must necessarily be ascribed to the EMS, whereas in fact other domestic policy changes which occurred during the same time-span may prove to be plausible explanations too.

2. COUNTRY SIMILARITIES AND DIFFERENCES

Long before the start of the EMS in March 1979 the Belgian franc and Dutch guilder had close relations with the Deutschmark. Without any interruption these two currencies participated in the European Snake arrangement which had already been introduced in May 1972. In that adjustable peg system the mutual fluctuation margins for the participating currencies amounted to 2¼ per cent on both sides of the central rate. The two currencies have continued to show these features in the exchange rate mechanism of the EMS. For that reason the EMS cannot really be considered to be a break with the past for the Belgian franc and guilder.

Since both the Snake arrangement and the exchange rate mechanism of the EMS are of the adjustable peg type, currency re- and de-valuations were allowed. Tables 6.1 and 6.2 demonstrate that the membership to these two exchange rate systems over the same time-period did not prevent important differences for the two currencies in terms of both frequency and also accumulation of devaluations against the key currency, the Deutschmark. According to Table 6.1, the paths of the Belgian franc and the guilder started to diverge in

TABLE 6.1. *Realignments of the Belgian franc and guilder against the mark* (1976–1990) (%)

Currency	Date								
	18.10. 1976	16.10. 1978	24.09. 1979	05.10. 1981	22.02. 1982	14.06. 1982	21.03. 1983	07.04. 1986	12.01. 1987
Franc	–2.0	–2.0	–2.0	–5.5	–8.5	–4.25	–4.0	–2.0	–1.0
Guilder	–2.0	–2.0	–2.0	0.0	0.0	0.0	–2.0	0.0	0.0

TABLE 6.2. *Cumulative realignments against the Deutschmark*

Currency	Period		
	1979–81	1982–3	1984–9
Belgian franc	–7.5	16.75	–3
Dutch guilder	–2.0	–2.0	0

October 1981. In all three EMS subperiods distinguished in Table 6.2 the franc devalued substantially more than the guilder. The largest difference was recorded in the years 1982–3 when the franc was devalued by almost 17 per cent. This contrasts with the 2 per cent devaluation of the guilder. After that period the guilder did not weaken at all against the mark.

Belgium and the Netherlands have been successful in combating inflation since the onset of the EMS. Table 6.3 shows the decline in their inflation rates. The final outcome is cheering although the time-span which was needed is rather long. As a matter of fact from 1983 onwards the Netherlands has proved to be much more effective than Belgium. In 1987–9 Dutch inflation even came near to a standstill. In response to that, the guilder depreciated substantially in real terms in the 1980s, although it endured a nominal effective appreciation in that period.[2]

Despite these country differences in devaluation and inflation rates, the economic growth and unemployment rates of these two countries hardly differed. Table 6.4 shows the similarity of real economic growth and unemployment in

TABLE 6.3. *Average annual inflation (consumer price)* (%)

Country	Period			
	1975–8	1979–82	1983–6	1987–9
Belgium	8.4	6.9	5.0	2.0
The Netherlands	7.5	5.8	2.1	0.3

2 See e.g. De Grauwe and Vanhaverbeke (1990: 138).

TABLE 6.4. *Average annual growth (Y) and unemployment (U) (%)*

Country	Period					
	1971–80		1981–6		1987–9	
	Y	*U*	*Y*	*U*	*Y*	*U*
Belgium	3.2	4.9	0.9	11.8	3.4	10.4
The Netherlands	2.9	4.2	1.2	11.0	2.6	10.1

the countries concerned for various subperiods. The high levels of unemployment look alarming and raise the question whether, apart from the Eurosceloris, it is possible to discern an EMS effect on this unsatisfactory situation.

3. METHOD

Because in terms of exchange rate policies the transition to the EMS was a smooth process for Belgium and the Netherlands, it is not at all self-evident that the inception date of that system represents a clear break into periods with substantial differences in both countries' exchange rate stability. It is to be expected that if there is any change in this respect it will only be a gradual one. Then the same argument must also hold for the associated rise in credibility of the new exchange rate policy. This idea is reinforced by the fact that the more stable exchange rates in the two countries were accompanied by supporting policy measures, which usually only gradually appear to be convincing for the private sector. As a consequence, if the membership of the exchange rate mechanism of the EMS does have an anti-inflationary drift for the participating countries, it is probable that for Belgium and the Netherlands the awareness in the private sector has arisen neither immediately nor shockwise.

It is not only the gradual nature of achieving exchange rate stability for Belgium and the Netherlands that suggests that there are occasions other than the actual start of the EMS to account for a growing awareness of lower future inflation. There is also another way in which March 1979 competes with other dates with respect to a change in private sector behaviour against inflation. Both prior to and after the beginning of the EMS, these countries may have reassessed and adapted their anti-inflation policy. Such policy decisions may have been taken for reasons which have nothing to do with the process of European monetary integration. Therefore, the next two sections provide a chronological description of such potential events for Belgium and the Netherlands. We will concentrate on all measures which may affect the inflation outlook and the position of the national currency on the foreign exchange markets and, in doing so, may modify private sector behaviour with respect to inflation.[3]

The private sector's belief in the probability of a policy change, in this case a change in anti-inflation policy, emerges not so much in the quantitative economic determinants of inflation, but particularly in the values of their coefficients in behavioural relations. A credible anti-inflation policy change, for example, is expected to shift the emphasis in inflation determination away from backward-looking explanatory variables in favour of forward-looking ones. The well-known Lucas critique (Lucas, 1976) has drawn the attention to the possibility that policy regime changes especially affect the model parameters. The policy changes aimed at above, including the start of the EMS, can be regarded as such changes of the policy regime. They can have an announcement impact and an implementation effect on the inflation level.[4] It is likely that in particular the implementation of an anti-inflation policy action affects the rate of inflation itself with a delay, because the gain in anti-inflation credibility is usually obtained only gradually.

There are several methods of measurement available to assess the immediate occurrence or gradual increase of credibility.[5] As the idea of a gradual process is judged to be quite topical here, we will apply a method which is closely allied to the approach of time-varying parameters. It consists of the following three steps. First, a linear equation is estimated for the period which starts at the beginning of the 1970s and ends in 1990. Its coefficients are deemed to represent the average effect of the variable involved during the entire estimation period. Second, the equation with the best fit for the entire period is subjected to a recursive estimation experiment. This means that the specification with the best fit for the entire period is re-estimated, at first for a relatively short period. This period has the same starting-date and ends as early as is allowed in view of the degrees of freedom in the regression analysis. In any case the last observation is prior to the start of the EMS. This estimation is followed by re-estimating rounds in which the estimation period is continually extended with one new observation until the estimation period from the first step is attained. Third, the development over the course of time of the parameters obtained in the second step is examined with emphasis on the parameters attached to those variables which are considered to express the EMS effect. This method will be supplemented with the application of the Chow test on structural breaks for each equation. This information will be considered here as only additional, since the Chow test analyses the complete equation and not specific coefficients and, thus, not the impact of specific events.

Parameter instability may occur. It signifies two consequences. The equation's value for prediction purposes will be small. Moreover, and essential for

[3] The description is mainly based on the country surveys of the OECD for the two countries.

[4] For this distinction, see e.g. Agénor and Taylor (1992: 549–50).

[5] A clear recent survey with an emphasis on the pros and cons of each method is Agénor and Taylor (1992).

our analysis, at the moment when the parameter value starts to change substantially, a relevant and credible change in the policy stance or regime may have taken place. The reason is that only if the private sector is becoming convinced of the policy change will it be incorporated in the private sector's behaviour, and thus it will become perceptible when this behaviour is quantified. In combination with the outline of policy measures in Belgium and the Netherlands in the next two sections, the signals furnished by a parameter change may be given convincing support.

The evidence in the Sections 6, 7, and 8 will show that with this method there will never be a parameter value which changes to such an extent that its value crosses the limits of the two-sigma band at a certain moment in the estimation period.[6] We should, therefore, be guided by more moderate but salient changes rather than use statistically significant changes in the parameter values as a yardstick. This wrongly seems to be a weak 'criterion': after having included many observations in the preceding estimation in the recursive estimation method, an additional observation has to incorporate a rather strong change in behaviour in order to achieve a clearly observable change in the coefficient attached to an explanatory variable.

4. POLICY MEASURES IN BELGIUM

In the 1970s Belgium, like many other industrial countries, experienced steeply rising labour costs. This was evident, particularly, in the years 1972–6. Then the cumulative rise of unit labour costs in Belgium relative to Germany amounted to some 40 per cent. It undermined the stability of the Belgium economy: the rate of unemployment reached a level of over 7 per cent at the end of that decade and subsequently it rose steeply to over 13 per cent in 1983–4.

Economic policy in the 1970s was mainly directed at reducing unemployment through supplementary public investment programmes and at suppressing inflation by means of temporary price freezes, prior notices of price increases, and maximum price directives. Fiscal policy was strengthened in the middle of 1978 by two so-called 'anti-crisis laws' to check the growth of current government expenditure and to stimulate private investment. Despite that, the government's budget deficit continued to increase and in 1981 it was over 12 per cent of the Belgian GDP. This huge budget deficit can be explained by a combination of a worldwide economic recession and strong automatic stabilizers in the government budget. On the external front, the stability of the Belgian franc was a priority objective, especially after 1978. The franc was defended by several exchange market interventions and a higher interest rate. None the less, in

[6] The phenomenon that the limits of the band tend to converge contains no relevant information about the EMS effect. It need not be the expression of more certainty about the effect; the convergence can be fully explained by the lower value of the standard deviation of a parameter estimation as the estimation period increases.

the years 1976–9 three devaluations appeared to be necessary, each of 2 per cent against the Deutschmark. In each of these devaluations the franc was accompanied by the Dutch guilder (see Table 6.1).

In February 1981 the government launched a 'recovery plan' containing various reliefs in combination with restrictions on the growth of the purchasing power of wages for two years. In April 1981 retail prices were frozen for half a year. In order to combat pressures on the foreign exchange market, in the same month the National Bank issued a recommendation to the financial intermediaries to hold a specified minimum portfolio of Belgian government securities equal to at least the amount of holdings of securities of other governments. It did not prevent a new devaluation: in October the franc devalued against the mark and the guilder by 5.5 per cent. These measures were prompted by the bad state of the balance of payments. However, after this the current account, which had still been roughly in equilibrium in 1978, worsened and showed in 1981 a deficit of 4 per cent of the country's GDP.

In February 1982 even a kind of shock therapy was applied in an attempt to redress the growing disequilibria in the Belgian economy. The central rate of the franc was devalued by 8.5 per cent against all EMS currencies except the Luxembourg franc and the Danish krone. In doing so, the hard-currency objective was abandoned and Belgium, in fact, switched to the soft-currency option. This step was accompanied by selective price and wage indexation freezes. Subsequently, the price freeze was extended until the end of 1983 and the wage restraint until end 1984. In June 1982 and March 1983 new devaluations of the franc against the Deutschmark followed of 4¼ and 4 per cent, respectively. In April 1983 'competitiveness norms' were laid down by act for the years 1983 and 1984. Under these norms labour costs in Belgium were not allowed to exceed the weighted average rise of the labour costs in the country's seven main trading-partners.

In January 1984 the rate of source tax on share income was raised from 20 to 25 per cent. In March 1984 a multi-year plan was adopted with further measures to reduce the public finance deficit. The plan decreed partial deindexation for wages and social security benefits. The revenue from the former augmented by the concomitant drop of employers' social security contributions had to be donated to the institution responsible for collecting the social security contributions.

In June 1986 the price controls were eased. Small and medium-sized enterprises with turnovers not exceeding a certain amount were henceforth exempted from the obligation to announce price increases. This was followed by an agreement in September to return to free bargaining of real wages in 1987. However, the government retained the right to intervene in wage formation should unit labour costs in Belgium rise more rapidly than in the main competitor countries. In July 1989 and March 1990 the Council of Ministers adopted two series of budget adjustment measures in order to achieve targets for a budget deficit of 6.5 and 6.3 per cent of GDP for those years. In January

1990 it was announced that the withholding tax on interest income would be reduced from 25 to 10 per cent, with effect from 1 March 1990.

In March 1990 the two-tier exchange market was abolished. For many years this way of channelling the international payments for trade and capital flows into distinct foreign currency markets had suppressed the impact of currency speculation on international trade flows. Particularly in March and May 1971, when the Bretton Woods system of the adjustable peg was in trouble, Belgium had considerably strengthened this dual exchange market system. In June 1990 it was decided that the Belgian franc would be pegged more closely to the Deutschmark. The fluctuation band would be reduced informally to 1 per cent on both sides of the parity in an attempt to increase foreign investors' confidence in the franc. The result was supposed to be lower interest rates and according to some it actually happened (e.g. In't Veld, 1992: 158).

5. POLICY MEASURES IN THE NETHERLANDS

Earlier than Belgium, the Netherlands government conducted a stringent price and wage policy. For example, when in December 1977 price policy for 1978 was announced, the scope of price control measures was widened. Prices in industry were allowed to include external cost increases in full but to rise by not more than 2 per cent in response to higher wage costs. In January 1978 fees charged by the liberal professions were allowed to rise by 4½ per cent. In February a new law established government regulation of wage increases not covered by collective agreements. In December 1978 the Minister of Social Affairs suggested a flat rate ceiling on the price compensation for wage-earners and further moderation in contractual wage rises in order to finance early retirement schemes. Also price guidelines were given for 1980. These price measures seem to have been successful. While at the end of 1975 the increase of Dutch producer prices was some 4 per cent larger than the German price rise, by mid-1978 the Dutch price rise was already lower than the German rise. The same holds for Dutch wages relative to German wages. This situation remained for prices until the beginning of 1980 and for wages even until the end of 1981.

At the beginning of 1979 wage cost subsidies were granted for the employment of persons who were unemployed for a long period. In December 1979 trade unions claimed wage increases for 1980 ranging from 1 to 2 per cent on top of indexation as well as the transformation of the semi-annual price compensation into flat-rate payments. However, after gloomy forecasts of export volumes and the general government deficit, a two-months' wage freeze was decreed in January 1980. In March a bill was passed by parliament which provided for temporary powers granted to the Minister of Social Affairs to regulate changes in wages and other conditions of employment affecting all employees. The cost-of-living adjustments were restricted in mid-1980.

In July 1981 De Nederlandsche Bank announced a relaxation of exchange controls on capital imports. In principle, the Bank would grant permission for foreign loans with an average period to maturity of at least two years instead of 5½ years, the lower bound until then.

On the occasion of the installation of a new government, an economic programme was proposed in November 1981. One of its elements was that, in essence, the price compensation system during the period 1981–5 would be maintained. But 1 per cent of the annual price increase would no longer be compensated in wages. Besides the price compensation, there would be room for an annual wage drift of 2 per cent. In practice, the government appears to have abstained from further interventions in the wage negotiations in that period. Only government decisions about social benefits and the minimum wage were still made. At the end of 1982 price controls for manufacturers and traders were abolished.

On 21 March 1983 a realignment of EMS currencies occurred which raised a dust. The guilder was devalued by 2 per cent relative to the Deutschmark. That decision was attended by an agitated polemic between the Dutch Ministry of Finance and De Nederlandsche Bank. The former pushed the devaluation through against the will of the Bank. The latter painted the disadvantages of the decision in vivid colours; the most important drawback was the need for higher interest rates in the longer run, as the devaluation would diminish the private sector's confidence in the guilder.[7] The Ministry, in turn, emphasized the chief benefit of the devaluation: the improved competitiveness, which would give indispensable support to Dutch employment. After the overt critique of the Bank following the devaluation, the Dutch Minister of Finance declared that in the case of future realignments in the EMS, devaluations of the guilder against the mark would no longer be considered.

In November 1984 the Dutch government reduced the rate of corporation tax from 48 to 43 per cent. With respect to wage determination, there were two signs of a non-interventionist government in 1985. In June an amendment to the Wage Determination Act was presented to parliament. It redefined the criterion for government interventions as a sudden emergency situation of the national economy caused by one or more sharply changed factors. In September the paper on Income Policy 1986 did not go any further than the statement that moderate private sector wage growth was important. In November 1985 a further deregulation of the Netherlands capital market was announced with effect from 1 January 1986. It entailed more opportunities for foreign banks to operate in the Netherlands' capital market. Moreover, a more flexible choice of the date of issue of loans was allowed. Issues of bullet loans, loans with an adjustable interest rate, and commercial paper as well as bank issues of certificates of deposit were tolerated.

7 According to De Nederlandsche Bank (1986) and, for example, In't Veld (1992), the devaluation led to a small increase in the interest-rate differential against Germany. Koen (1991) found that the hard-currency policy in the Netherlands only became credible by early 1986, about three years after the promise of an irrevocable link between the guilder and the Deutschmark.

In May 1986 the General Public Service Pension Fund, one of the largest institutional investors in the world, was allowed to start investing abroad, though with an upper limit of only 5 per cent of its assets. In June a bill was published in which the VAT tariffs were proposed to increase by 1 percentage point. This proposal took effect from 1 October 1986. Moreover, in September De Nederlandsche Bank announced, with effect from 1 October, the lifting of regulations on borrowing by non-residents in the Netherlands' capital market. In January 1988 the Netherlands' capital market was further liberalized when zero-interest bonds and discount bonds were allowed, while in May the transaction costs in the primary market for commercial paper in guilders were reduced. On 1 January 1989 VAT rates were lowered by 1 percentage point. In November 1990 the private sector was granted permission to issue loans with the nominal rate of interest indexed against inflation. This financial instrument had been forbidden until then because it was considered to undermine the fight against inflation.

6. THE INFLATION EFFECTS OF THE EMS

6.1 Belgium

In this section we will examine the relationships between wages and prices on the one hand and the variables driving the inflationary process on the other hand. The basic idea is that a government possesses an anti-inflationary reputation to a certain degree established by a track record of continuous low-inflation policy. This reputation determines some parameter values in these relations.

For a discussion of the inflation process, we will concentrate on an explanation of the producer price and the wage rate. The producer price has the advantage over the consumer price in that it undergoes a more moderate influence of changes in tax rates. The latter form an exogenous disturbance, which is not due to private sector behaviour.

The specifications and statistical characteristics of the price and wage equations for the Belgian economy are presented in Appendices 1 and 2. The Belgian inflation is adequately explained by only two explanatory variables: the Belgian import price and the German producer price. The former is part of the input costs for producers and the latter is an indicator of the foreign competitive position of the Belgian producers. Of course, in practice these effects are not so strictly separated. The extent of cohesion between Belgian and German inflation is conceived as the gauge for the EMS effect on Belgian inflation. A credible EMS necessitates Belgian producers to keep their price more in line with the German price than before.

Fig. 6.1(*a*) displays the value over the course of time of the coefficient attached to German inflation in the equation of Belgian inflation. From a

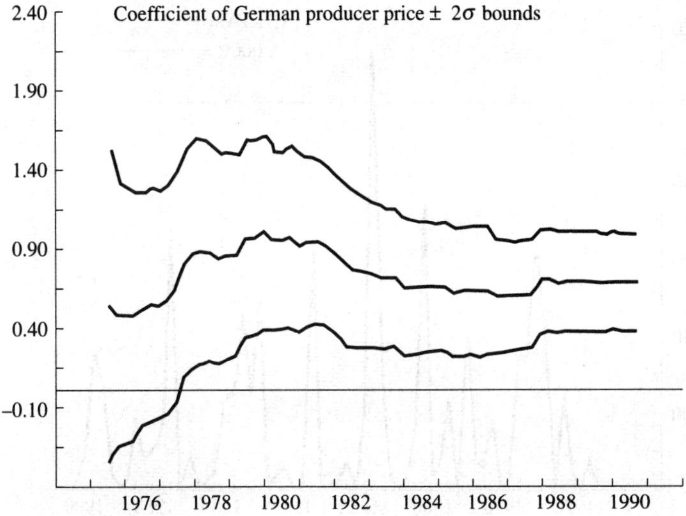

(*a*) Producer price

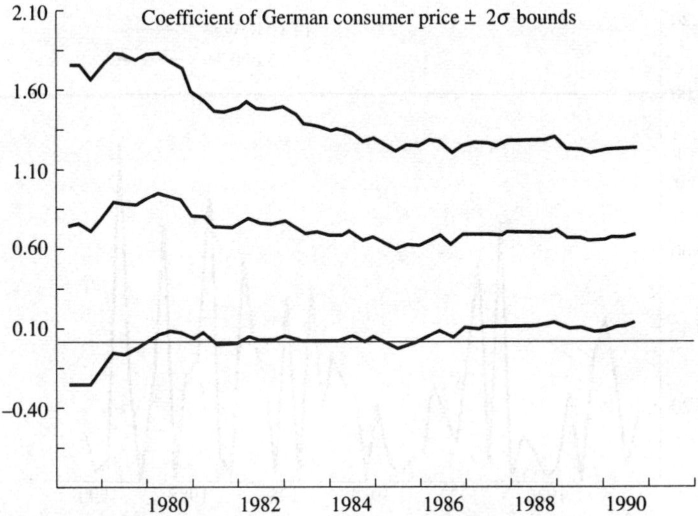

(*b*) Wage level

FIG. 6.1. Belgian inflation process and the EMS effect

statistical viewpoint a significant change is not observable: the estimated coefficient remains within the zone determined by the minimal distance between the bounds of twice the standard deviation. But, as argued before, significance of the change of the coefficient seems to be too strong as a test. A clearly discernible change of the coefficient due to one added observation implies a substantial change in the effect of the explanatory variable involved in the last observation period. The coefficient of the German producer price does

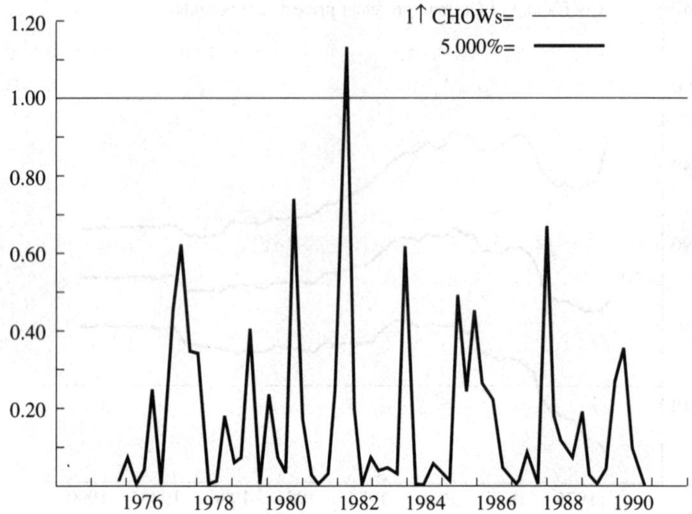

(*c*) Belgian producer price equation

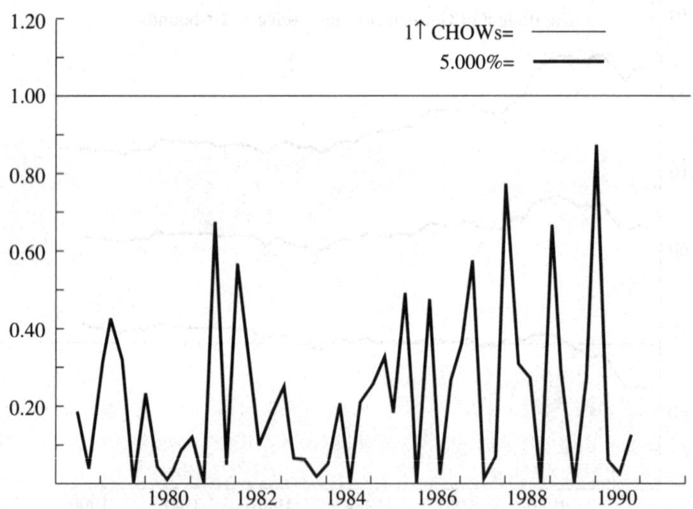

(*d*) Belgian wage equation

FIG. 6.1. (*cont.*)

show some noticeable changes: until 1980 a rise and after 1981 a fall. The Chow test, depicted in Fig. 6.1(*c*), points at the presence of one structural break for the Belgian price equation, namely in 1982(2).

The rise in the coefficient of German inflation until 1978 cannot be imputed to the EMS, but seems to be a response to the growing credibility of the Snake arrangement for Belgium. In 1979 the coefficient shows a new, small upward jump. The only possible explanation is an EMS effect, though only of short duration. It was the 'shock' therapy which was initiated at the beginning of 1982 that resulted in a real breakthrough in the direction of a recovery of the internal and external balance: the decline in Belgian inflation (measured by producer prices) was in the period 1982–6 much larger than the decline of inflation in Germany. The shock therapy and particularly the devaluation of the Belgian franc by 8.5 per cent in February seems to have convinced the private sector that the Belgian government had made a break with the past characterized by similar inflation developments in Belgium and Germany. This led to a fall in the coefficient of German inflation and the only structural break according to the Chow test. Starting in 1988 one observes in Fig. 6.1(*a*) a slight increase in the role of German inflation rate. This may be explained by the end of price controls, the increased stability of the Belgian franc and the greater credibility of the exchange rate band.

The Belgian wage is adequately explained by the following variables: the wage itself but with a four-quarter lag, the consumer price, labour productivity, the German consumer price with a one-quarter lag, and the rate of unemployment lagged two periods. The autoregression term with a four-quarter lag is plausible since the wage negotiations usually take place annually. The coefficient of the German consumer price is considered to be an indicator of an EMS effect: as the EMS is felt to be more binding, the Belgian wage needs to be more competitive and requires a closer relation with price developments in Germany. Fig. 6.1(*b*) shows that there is no significant change in the coefficient of the German price. It remains within the smallest distance between the two bounds. Neither does the Chow test in Fig. 6.1(*d*) indicate a structural break.

In the size of the German effect on the Belgian wage growth an EMS effect is initially observable, as illustrated in Fig. 6.1(*b*). In the first half of 1979 the influence of German prices grew, at the cost of the impact of Belgian prices. Apparently, in the wage negotiations the inflation compensation was determined with more emphasis on German inflation than before the inception of the EMS. In the second half of 1980 this emphasis fades away again. The growing Belgian deficits probably undermined the confidence in the EMS venture. An additional explanation is perhaps the recovery plan of the beginning of 1981, which reduced the possibility of compensating wages for higher prices. After a lowest point in 1985, Fig. 6.1(*b*) points at a certain recovery of the influence of the German price since then. The same appears to hold for the Belgian price in the wage equation. These stronger price influences since 1985 seem to be a response to the gradual liberalization of wage negotiations after 1984. But the increases of the two price effects are so small that at the end of 1990 the two influences did not succeed in matching their levels prior to the beginning of the EMS.

It is worth stressing that the coefficients of German inflation in the two Belgian equations are on average very high and higher than in the corresponding Dutch equations.

6.2 The Netherlands

The outcome of the regression analysis for the Dutch producer price is depicted in Appendix 1. The Dutch price appears to be influenced significantly by the unit labour costs, the import price, the German producer price, and a constant term. An increase in the coefficient of the German price at the expense of the remaining explanatory variables will be interpreted as a possible EMS

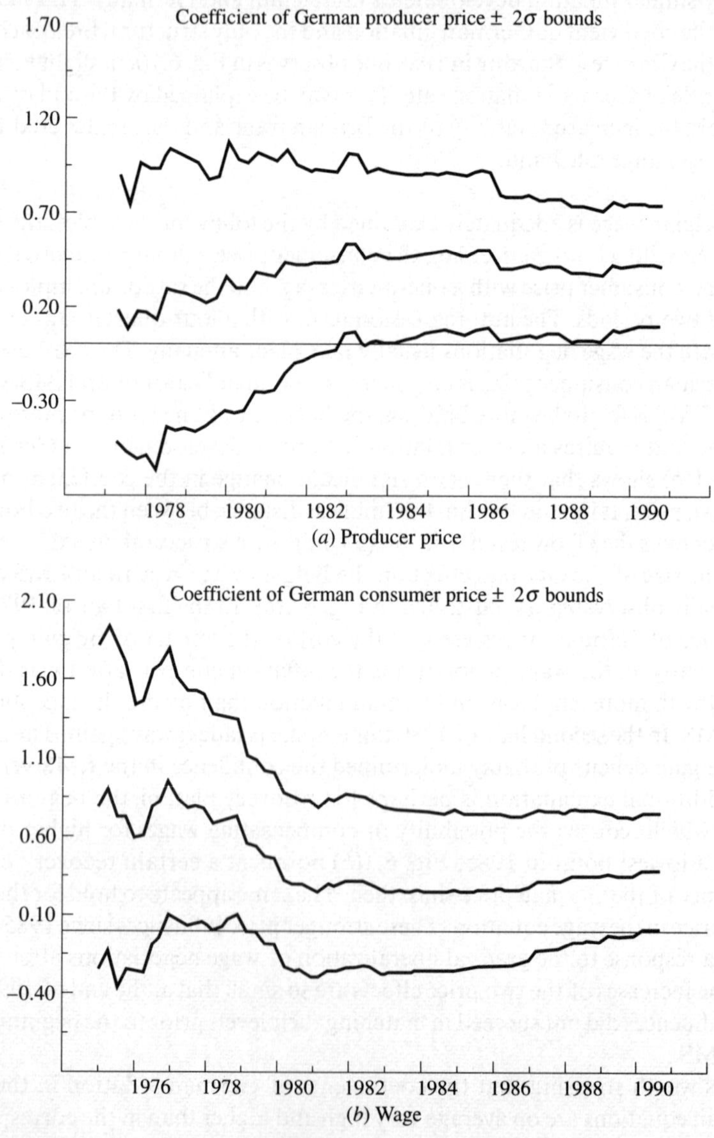

FIG. 6.2. Dutch inflation process and the EMS effect

effect on the Dutch price. As in the case of the analysis of the Belgian price, alternative explanations for a rise of the coefficient of the German producer price will be considered. Fig. 6.2(*a*) shows the quantitative development over the course of time of the German price parameter in the Dutch price equation. During the entire period the coefficient stays within the minimum width of the two standard deviation band. The Chow test, shown in Fig. 6.2(*c*),

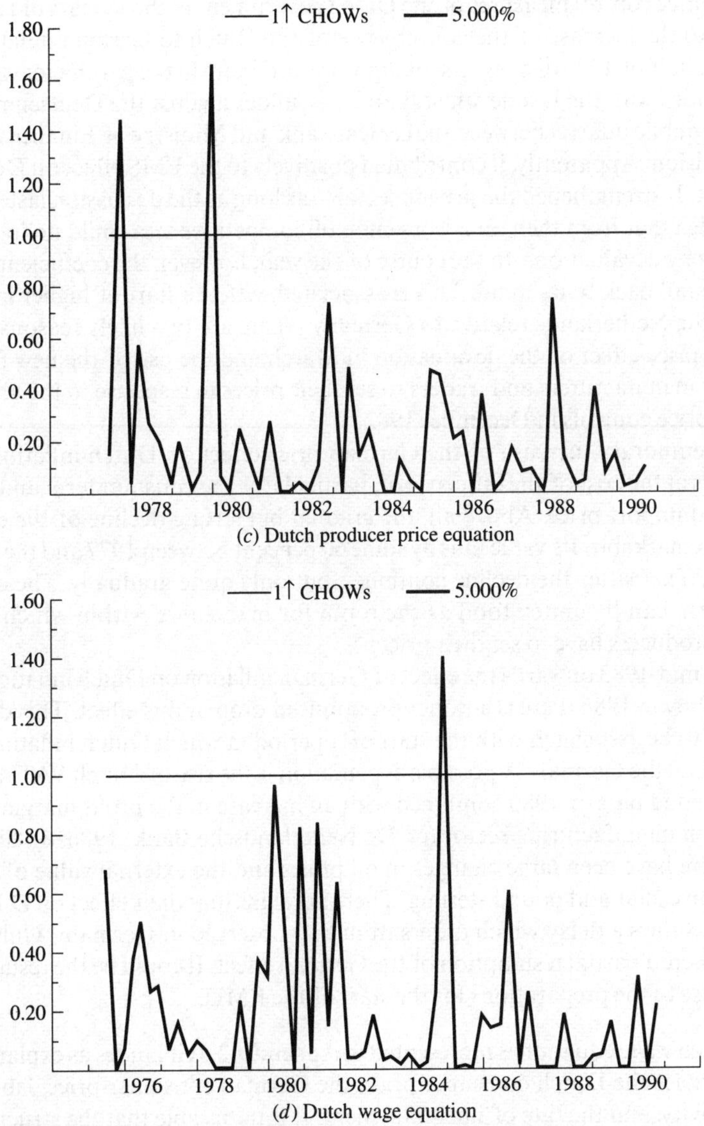

(*c*) Dutch producer price equation

(*d*) Dutch wage equation

FIG. 6.2. (*cont.*)

appears to indicate two possible structural breaks, one in 1977(4) and another in 1980(1).

It appears that between mid-1978 and 1983 the impact of the German price gradually increased. The parameter value rose from some 0.15 to about 0.45. From then on the impact remained roughly unchanged. In the middle of 1978 a dialogue on the EMS was already underway. Therefore, this gradual rise of the German influence might have been an EMS effect. Undoubtedly, the successful price control measures of the Dutch government in those years did contribute to the increase of the convergence of the Dutch to German inflation. The first half of 1983 displays a strikingly upward jump in the parameter value. It coincides with the last devaluation of the guilder against the Deutschmark and the public quarrel between the central bank and Ministry of Finance over that decision. Apparently, it contributed positively to the EMS effect on Dutch inflation. It strengthened the private sector—as long as the discussion lasted—in the idea that from then on a worsening of competitiveness could no longer be offset by devaluations. In the course of the year, however, the coefficient appears to fall back to its trend. This is associated with the start of higher inflation in the Netherlands relative to Germany. There are two likely reasons: an upward price effect of the devaluation in March and the use of the new freedom for manufacturers and traders to set their prices in response to the abolition of price controls in December 1982.

The temporary increase of the German price effect on Dutch inflation in 1983 was at the cost of the influence of, particularly, the constant term and the unlagged import price. Above all, the gradual but strong decline of the constant is remarkable. Its value falls by some 60 per cent between 1977 and the end of 1981. Thereafter the decline continues, but only quite gradually. The constant term can be understood as the room for manœuvre within which the Dutch producers have to set their prices.[8]

From mid-1983 onwards the effect of German inflation on Dutch inflation is stable. Only in 1986 there is a rather pronounced drop in this effect. This drop appears to be associated with the start of a period in which Dutch inflation is higher than the German. A possible explanation is the rise of Dutch VAT rates in the second part of 1986 combined with an increase in the profit margins of the Dutch manufacturing sector (cf. De Nederlandsche Bank, 1986: 8). Since 1985 there have been large changes in oil prices and the external value of the American dollar and pound sterling. There are signs that their effect on Dutch inflation shows a delay which differs from that observed in Germany. Only in 1989 is there a partial resumption of the German effect. It could be the result of a response to the preparations for the start of the EMU.

The Dutch wage equation is represented in Appendix 2. It includes as explanatory variables the Dutch consumer price, the German consumer price, labour productivity, and the rate of unemployment. It is noticeable that the structure

[8] See De Jong's contribution in this volume.

of the equation is quite similar to that of the Belgian wage equation. There are only small differences in the lag structure. Only in the first years, until 1977, did the coefficient of the German consumer price fall outside the minimum width of the two standard-deviations band, as Fig. 6.2(*b*) shows. As usual the minimum width occurs at the end of the estimation period. This coefficient of the German consumer price has been chosen as the EMS-effect indicator. The Chow test in Fig. 6.2(*d*) points at one structural break, namely in 1985(1).

The Dutch equation gives the impression that, if there is an EMS effect, it only starts at the end of 1986. Then the coefficient of the German price begins to rise, although gradually. In the same time-span the Dutch price loses some of its impact. Its coefficient falls from .60 to .40. The reduced domestic influence is enhanced by a small reduction in the contribution of the unemployment rate to Dutch wage changes in the same period. For the turn of the tide in 1986 there is, in fact, no domestic explanation. This gives some indirect support to the assumption that albeit with a substantial lag, the credibility of an irrevocable link of the guilder to the mark grew among Dutch trade unions. However, the length of the lag weakens somewhat this proposition.

An important by-product of the quantitative results for Dutch wages is that also in a situation of liberal wage negotiations it is quite possible to have only a moderate wage growth, even to the extent that in the second half of the 1980s Dutch wage growth stayed behind that of Germany by some 2 per cent per annum. Such a flexibility of nominal wages makes, in effect, exchange rate adjustments superfluous.

7. THE SACRIFCE RATIO

7.1 Belgium

Because of the non-stationarity of the time-series of the rate of unemployment and its potential determinants both for Belgium and the Netherlands, we had to have recourse to the first difference of these series as the dependent variable. The value of the coefficient of determination suffered from this transformation. The best fit for the explanation of Belgian unemployment contains the following determinants, with statistically significant contributions: the unemployment itself with a one-quarter lag, the real interest rate, unit labour costs, an inflation indicator (introduced to allow the Phillips curve effect in the equation), the second-quarter dummy, and a constant term. Appendix 3 contains the statistical specification of this equation. The Phillips curve effect has been measured by the growth rates of producer prices or wages. Only the wage growth turned out to be significant. The coefficient of the inflation-indicator term is represented in Fig. 6.3(*a*). It can be considered to be an indicator of the costs in terms of unemployment of inflation reduction; in other words, a measure of the sacrifice ratio. With reference to the two standard-deviations bounds, the figure reveals no significant changes in the coefficient. In contrast, in Fig. 6.3(*c*) the Chow test suggests two large structural breaks in the unemployment equation: in 1984(4) and 1985(2).

The coefficient's most remarkable feature is that its stability is interrupted in the period between the second half of 1980 and 1985. Then its absolute value is about 50 per cent higher than both before and after the period concerned. The abrupt change of this coefficient more than one year after the inception of the

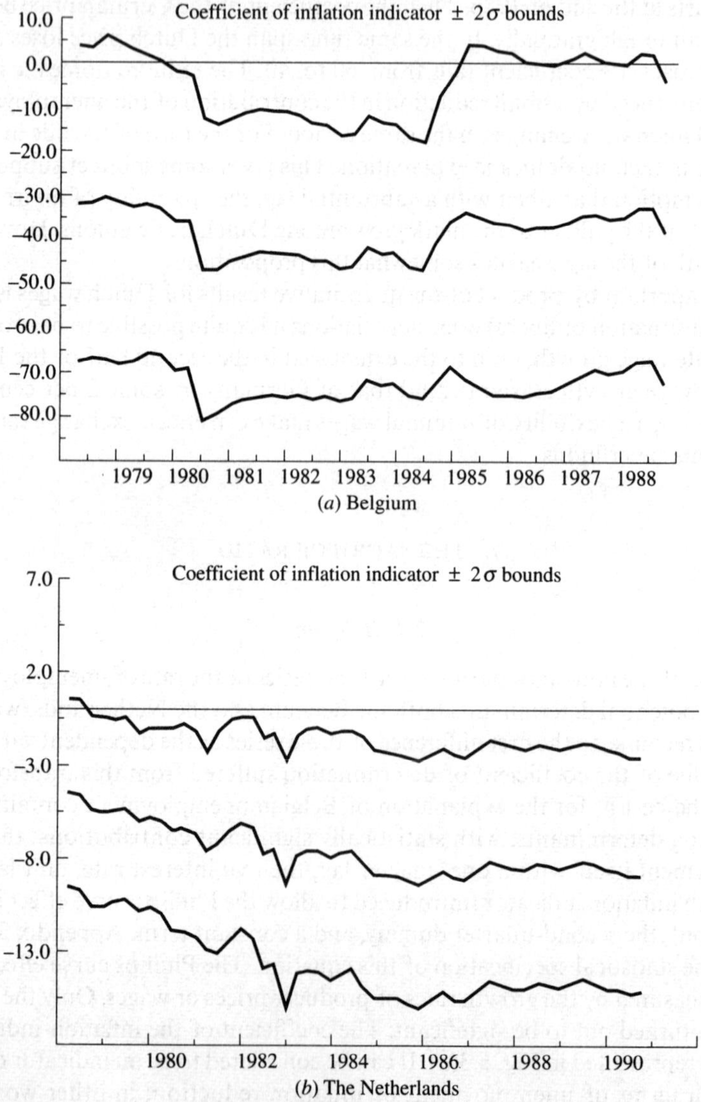

FIG. 6.3. Unemployment and the EMS effect

EMS weakens the idea that the higher coefficient has anything to do with the transition to the EMS. Moreover, it is to be expected than through an increased credibility of the anti-inflation policy as a corollary of EMS membership the costs of that policy in terms of unemployment would decline rather than increase. Closer investigation, indeed, points to a different origin. It is roughly the period in which the Belgian government through a recovery plan (February 1981) and a kind of shock therapy (as described in Section 4, beginning in 1982

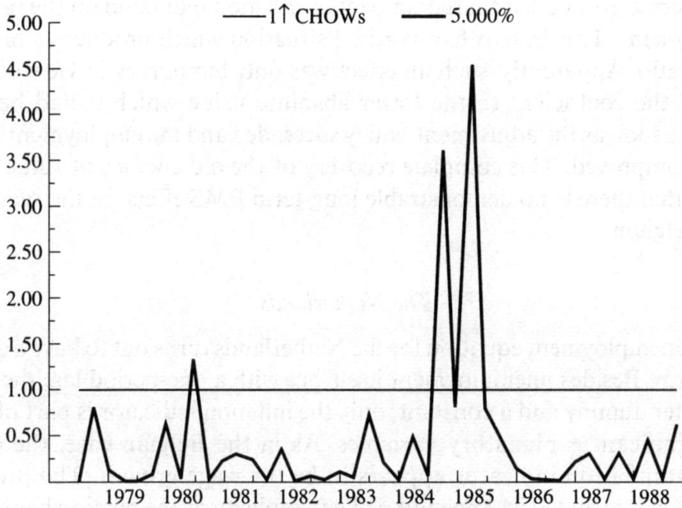

(*c*) Belgian unemployment equation

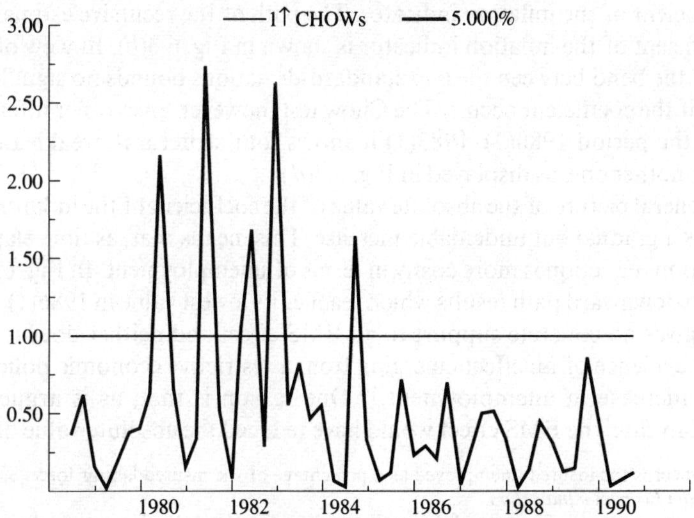

(*d*) Dutch unemployment equation

FIG. 6.3. (*cont.*)

and lasting until the end of 1984) successfully attempted to reduce the fiscal and balance-of-payments deficits. Probably, these policies are the main reason why in Belgium between 1980(1) and 1984(1) the rate of unemployment rose dramatically from some 11.3 to 19.3 per cent.[9] At the beginning of 1985 a steep fall in the rate occurred. This period conforms with the quarters for which the Chow test suggested structural breaks.

Evidently, a period characterized by a restrictive budgetary policy, supplemented with wage and price freezes, and a strong increase in the unemployment rate, is a fertile ground for a larger impact of inflation reduction on the rate of unemployment. This is, in other words, a situation which produces a higher sacrifice ratio. Apparently, such an effect was only temporary in view of the return of the coefficient to the lower absolute value which it had before 1979–80 as soon as the adjustment policy succeeded and the employment situation had improved. This complete recovery of the old coefficient value also indicates that there is no demonstrable long-term EMS effect on the sacrifice ratio in Belgium.

7.2 The Netherlands

The best unemployment equation for the Netherlands turns out to have a quite simple form. Besides unemployment itself but with a one-period lag, the second-quarter dummy and a constant, only the inflation indicator is part of the set of significant explanatory variables. As in the Belgian case, the only significant inflation indicator appears to be the wage growth. The precise specification is included in Appendix 3. The simplicity of the relation has some drawbacks when we try to unravel the factors behind the shifts in the value of the coefficient of the inflation indicator. The path of the recursive estimate of the coefficient of the inflation indicator is shown in Fig. 6.3(*b*). In view of the width of the band between the two standard-deviations bounds no significant change of the coefficient occurs. The Chow test, however, gives other information. In the period 1980(3)–1983(1) it shows four structural breaks and in 1984(4) another one, as displayed in Fig. 6.3(*d*).

The general picture of the absolute value of the coefficient of the inflation indicator is a gradual but undeniable increase. This means that, as time elapses, the inflation reduction is more costly in terms of unemployment. In Fig. 6.3(*b*) a smooth downward path results which reaches its lowest value in 1986(1). The pattern gives no concrete support to an EMS effect and neither does it provide any evidence of an effect emerging from a restrictive economic policy or a sharp increase in unemployment.[10] One reason is that, as is argued in the Belgian case, the EMS effect would have reduced the absolute value of the

9 It concerns the insured unemployed as a percentage of the insured labour force. Source: OECD, *Main Economic Indicators*.

10 A sharp increase in the rate of unemployment in the Netherlands arose in the period 1980(1)–1984(1). In those years the registered unemployed as a percentage of civilian labour force grew from 5.2 to 18.2 per cent. Source: OECD, *Main Economic Indicators*.

coefficient. Another reason is that the course of the coefficient involved lacks clear turning-points necessary to be able to relate coefficient changes to policy-regime changes. The coefficient value almost doubled between 1978 and 1990, but the level remains very low compared to the value of the corresponding Belgian coefficient. A potential cause for this gradual increase in the coefficient value may be the presence of slow structural changes, like higher unemployment benefits and increased rigidity in the labour market.

8. EMS EFFECTS AND INTEREST RATES

8.1 Belgium

In the analysis of the EMS effect on interest rates, the preference is given to the long-term interest rate over the short-term rate. This is because the former has much more relevance for the real side of the economy. As a consequence of the non-stationarity of the time-series of the interest rate itself, we had to have recourse to the first difference of that variable as the dependent variable, both for Belgium and the Netherlands.

The Belgian long-term interest rate is best explained by three variables, besides the constant term. These are the interest rate itself lagged one quarter, the German long-term interest rate, and a weighted average of the Belgian consumer price in the recent past with lags between zero and two quarters. The detailed specification of the equation is included in Appendix 4. In this relation the regression coefficient of the German interest rate unfolds the EMS effect. Fig. 6.4(*a*) displays the course of its value over time, obtained by the recursive estimation method. It appears that at the start of the curve in the first half of 1978 the German impact is negligible. From then on the coefficient rises, especially in 1980 and 1981. One of the consequences is that the statistical stability of the coefficient is absent: the coefficient is not always in the band between the highest value of the lower boundary and the lowest value of the upper boundary of the two-standard-deviation limits. Also according to the Chow test there are structural breaks: according to Fig. 6.4(*c*) they occur in 1979(4), 1980(3), 1985(4), 1986(2), 1989(4), and 1990(2).

The initial rise of the coefficient of the German interest rate changes into a temporary stagnation in the first half of 1979, but then the coefficient endures an accelerated growth in the second half of 1980. The significant upward move of the German interest rate coefficient in 1980 and 1981 has no other plausible explanation than the inception of the EMS.

The coefficient of the German interest rate continued to rise in 1982, but only slightly, until the severe devaluation of the Belgian franc in March 1983. The end of the successful recovery period of the Belgian economy, and the concomitant support for a stable Belgian franc, might be the explanation for a renewed rise of the coefficient of the German interest rate from 1986 onwards. At last, from 1989(3) there is a non-negligible upward jump in the coefficient of

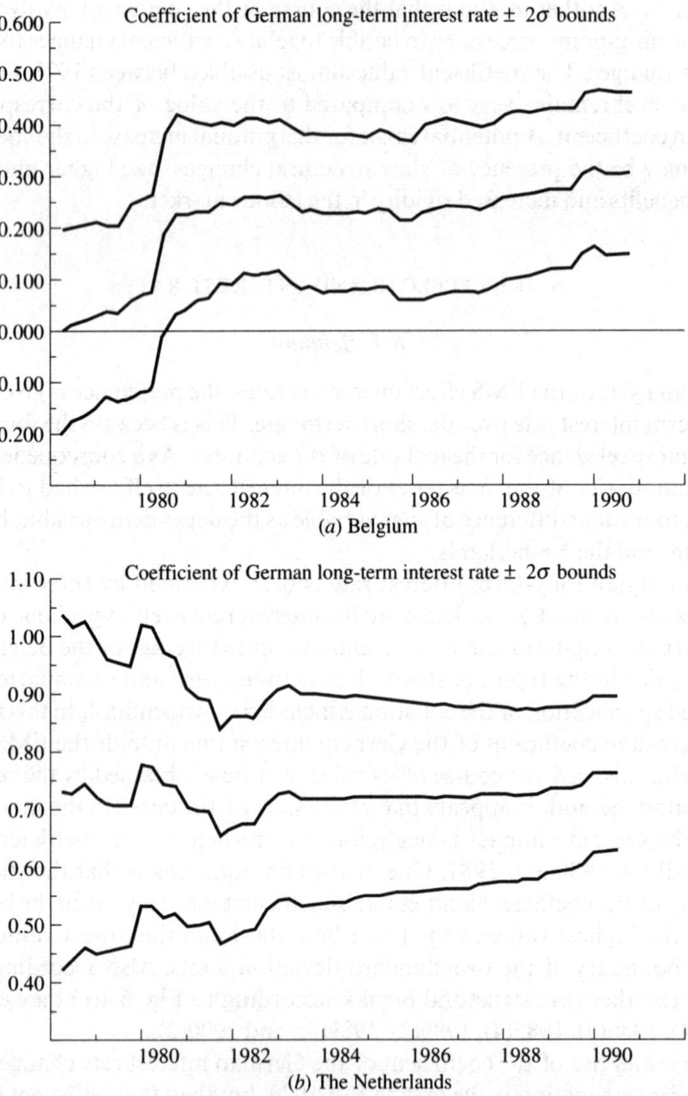

FIG. 6.4. Long-term interest rate and the EMS effect

the German interest rate from 1986 onwards. It is associated with the last two breaks in the Belgian interest rate equation, according to Fig. 6.4(*c*). It seems that the jump can be ascribed to the additional credibility generated by the EMU preparations.

In sum, the EMS effect seems to have been a tremendously large on the Belgian long-term interest rate. The coefficient that expresses that effect rose from zero in 1978 to around 0.30 in 1990. This development is attended by a

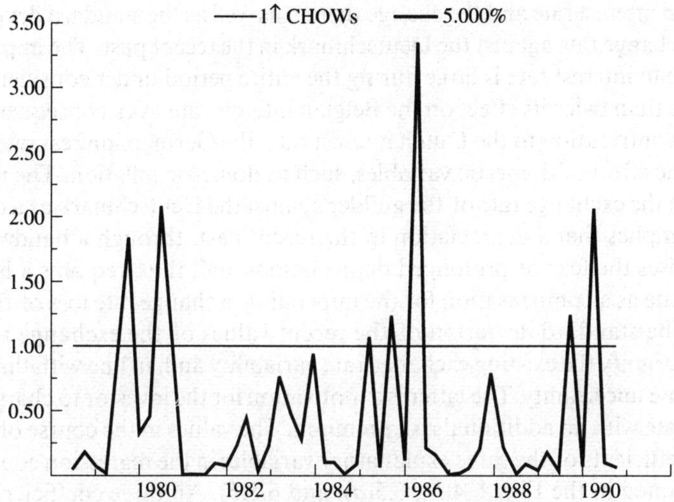

(*c*) Belgian interest rate equation

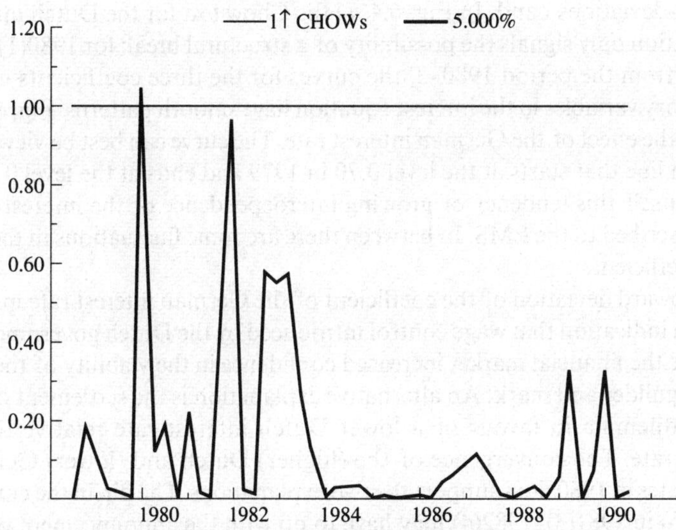

(*d*) Dutch interest rate equation

FIG. 6.4. (*cont.*)

slow convergence of the Belgian and German long-term interest rates in the same period, although the Belgian rate remained higher than the German one.

8.2 The Netherlands

The Dutch equation for the long-term interest rate is also shown in Appendix 4. It has an interesting structure. The explanatory variables are the German long-term interest rate and the change therein as well as the standard deviation of the exchange rate against the Deutschmark in the recent past. The impact of the German interest rate is large during the entire period under consideration and more than twice its effect on the Belgian interest rate. As a consequence of the high contribution to the Dutch interest rate, the German interest rate suppresses the effect of domestic variables, such as domestic inflation. The recent change in the exchange rate of the guilder against the Deutschmark as a determinant implies that a depreciation in the recent past, through a bandwagon effect, raises the fear of prolonged depreciations and, thus, requires a higher interest rate as a compensation for the impending exchange rate loss of the investor. The standard deviation of the recent values of the exchange rate is meant to signify the existing exchange rate variability and, in line with that, exchange rate uncertainty. The latter is a motivation for the investor to charge the interest rate with an additional risk premium. The values in the course of time of the coefficients of the three explanatory variables in the regression equation are illustrated in the Figs. 6.4(*b*), 6.5(*a*), and 6.5(*b*). All three coefficients remain in the entire estimation period within the minimum width of the two standard-deviations band. In Fig. 6.4(*d*) the Chow test for the Dutch interest rate equation only signals the possibility of a structural break for 1980(1).

Apart from the period 1980–3, the curves for the three coefficients of the explanatory variables in the interest equation have smooth patterns. Fig. 6.4(*b*) contains the effect of the German interest rate. The curve can best be viewed as a smooth line that starts at the level 0.70 in 1979 and ends at the level 0.78 in 1990. In itself this tendency of growing interdependence of the interest rates may be ascribed to the EMS. In between there are some fluctuations in the size of the coefficient.

The upward deviation of the coefficient of the German interest rate in 1980 can be an indication that wage control introduced by the Dutch government in 1980 gave the financial market increased confidence in the viability of the link between guilder and mark. An alternative explanation is the settlement of the Walters dilemma in favour of a lower Dutch interest rate relative to the German rate. The convergence of the (higher) Dutch and (lower) German interest rates in 1980 does support the two explanations. The dip in the curve in Fig. 6.4(*b*) in 1981(3)–1982(4) may have to do with the announcement of the central bank relaxing capital import controls. This announcement of capital liberalization may have strengthened the fear of exchange rate instability and may, thus, have reduced the close linkage of the interest rates. This hypothesis is refuted, however, by the fact that in this period the positive difference between the Dutch and the German interest rates diminished. The small increase of the coefficient, relative to the trend, in the period between 1982(4) and 1983(3) may be due to the official promise that the devaluation of the guilder of March 1983 would be the last one. This might have increased the conviction of a permanent link between the currency values and thus also between the interest rates. In any case, it is clear that this devaluation did not undermine the correlation between the two interest rates as De Nederlandsche Bank feared it would. These inferences about the consequences of Dutch policy in the period 1981–3 must be viewed in the light of absence of structural breaks, as Fig. 6.4(*d*) exhibits. Finally, the upward movement of the coefficient in 1990 can be considered to be the EMU effect, as in the case of Belgium.

Since the close linkage in the 1980s between the guilder and the Deutschmark, including the synchronization of Dutch monetary policy with that of Germany, has a growing similarity with a monetary union, it is instructive to look in somewhat more detail at the explanatory variables of the Dutch interest rate. It may be a manifestation of the future situation for other countries in the EMU. For that purpose Fig. 6.5 depicts the time-paths of the coefficients of the two other determinants of the Dutch interest rate. Fig. 6.5(*a*) reveals that the impact of the recent change in the exchange rate on the Dutch long-term interest rate gradually increases. When we move in the direction of a monetary union, apparently a weakening of the currency, even if it is a very small intra-band change, has an upward effect on the interest rate to a larger extent. In effect, the adjustment costs of the EMS membership increase as the integration advances. Starting from 1983, the outcome for the exchange rate uncertainty is just the other way around: a considerable but gradual decline of the coefficient in the interest rate equation. This means that a certain amount of exchange rate variability is less dangerous for the system the farther we are on the way towards a monetary union. Obviously, the credibility which has gradually been gained suppresses the impact of exchange rate uncertainty.

What about the upward effect of devaluation on the interest rate, as has been argued by the Dutch central bank? In the period under investigation three guilder devaluations occurred, as we can see in Table 6.1, viz. on 16 October 1978, 24 September 1979, and 21 March 1983. Prior to this period guilder devaluations also occurred. Until the last devaluation, in March 1983, the coefficient in Fig. 6.5(*a*) remained more or less the same. It was only in the year after that devaluation that the coefficient value shifted to a somewhat higher level. From then on the value remained stable. Thus, there is no evidence of an impact of a devaluation on the coefficient in Fig. 6.5. On the contrary, only as devaluations are things of the past, a certain weakening of the currency against the Deutschmark proves to have a more forceful upward effect on the long-term interest rate.

The coefficient of exchange rate variability against the Deutschmark in the long-term interest rate equation displays a peak in the period around the devaluation of March 1983. The preceding two devaluations appear to have no effect on this coefficient. Subsequently, after 1983 the coefficient value decreases slowly again. In the period analysed this lowering does not end. Here we seem to have the effect of a devaluation on the interest rate which De Nederlandsche bank presaged. However, it is then not so much the devaluation, but the increased variability of the exchange rate that caused the higher interest rate. Moreover, there is no strict coherence between a devaluation and

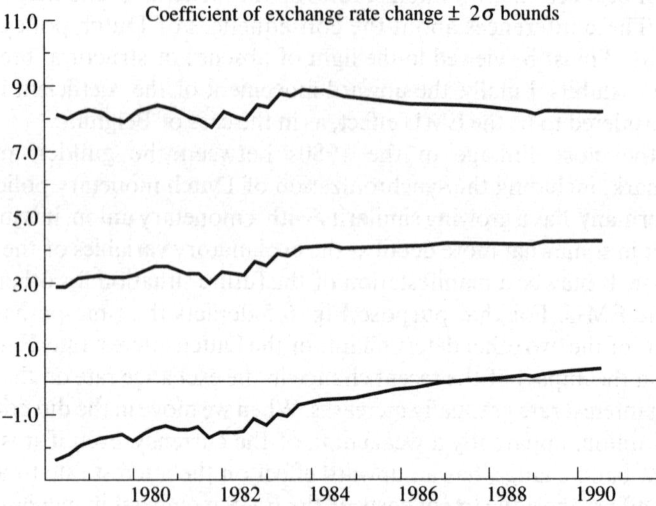

(*a*) Band wagon effect

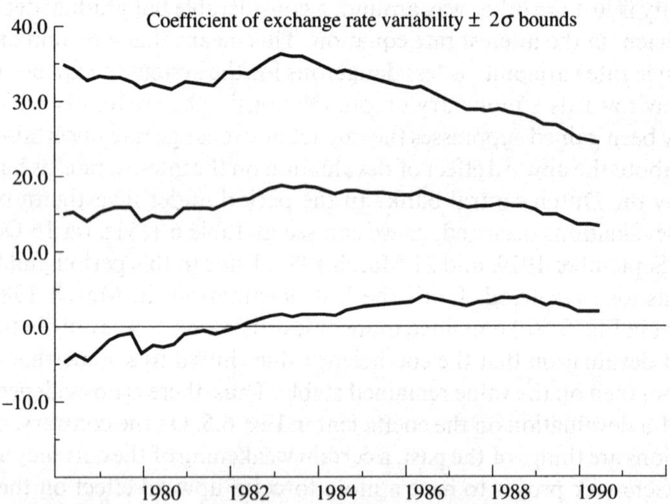

(*b*) Exchange rate uncertainty effect

FIG. 6.5. Exchange rate effects on Dutch interest rate

this variability. The first two devaluations in the period under study failed to have a visible effect. Therefore, the idea is supported that it is the overt attack of the Dutch central bank on the Ministry of Finance that caused the increase in the coefficient value in 1983. As the Bank predicted, it appeared to last some years before the upward impulse on the effect disappeared. It costs time to regain credibility.

The preceding conclusions are irrespective of the fact that through increases in the two explanatory variables themselves in the Dutch interest rate equation the change in the exchange rate in the preceding period is higher for the quarters just after the devaluation occurs. But this bandwagon effect holds only for one quarter. The exchange rate variability works for a period of four quarters following the devaluation. These upward impulses on the interest rate are only temporary and not of a more permanent character, contrary to what De Nederlandsche Bank expects.

9. CONCLUDING REMARKS

The preceding sections have sketched the economic policy measures in Belgium and the Netherlands, while the behaviour of the private sector in these two countries has been analysed by means of regression equations for prices, wages, unemployment rates, and long-term interest rates. By using the changes in the coefficients obtained by means of the estimation method of recursive regression, supported by the Chow test for structural breaks in the equations, it appeared to be possible to determine changes in private sector behaviour. Subsequently, an attempt was made to connect these changes with changes in the policy stance, in policy measures, or in the policy regime. For the purpose of the present analysis, which concerns the anti-inflationary character of the EMS, the consequences of the inception of the EMS—as a policy regime switch—were treated as the focal point. In each equation the value of the coefficient of a well-chosen German explanatory variable has been used as the yardstick for the EMS effect.

In the case of Belgium, the wage and price equations show a small and temporary EMS effect in 1979 and 1980; the coefficient of the German explanatory variable increased. Soon, however, the initial quantitative relation of the Belgian price and wage levels with their German explanatory variables had been restored. This happened at first for the wage rate in 1981, probably due to a reduced confidence in the continuation of the EMS membership in view of the growing deficits in the Belgian economy. Later on, the Belgian shock therapy, which started at the beginning of 1982, lessened the EMS effect on Belgian prices. After this policy was ended, we see in 1987 a certain rebound of the EMS effect in Belgian wages and prices, but at a lower level than initially in 1979–80. The overwhelming contribution to lowering Belgian inflation came from the shock therapy in the period 1982–6, which included wage and price freezes and some large devaluations against the Deutschmark. So it was mainly conscious, internal anti-inflationary policy, and not the phenomenon of borrowed EMS credibility, which reduced the rate of inflation in Belgium. Indirectly, it may have been an EMS effect, in so far as the shock therapy has been motivated by the wish to minimize the number of EMS devaluations of the Belgian franc and to maintain the franc in the exchange rate mechanism of the EMS.

The empirical results for the Belgian unemployment equation do not give support to the idea that monetary integration entails lower anti-inflation costs in terms of unemployment. In the period 1980(3) to 1984(4) this so-called sacrifice ratio is even temporarily substantially higher. But this period coincides much more with the period of the Belgian recovery policy than with the first years of the EMS, so that, again, an EMS effect is not observable.

In contrast, the EMS effect on the Belgian long-term interest rate has been quite large, judging from the substantial increase in the coefficient of the German interest rate in 1979 and 1980. From this it follows that the two interest rates have moved much more in parallel with each other since the inception of the EMS. The large devaluations of the Belgium franc in 1982 and 1983 temporarily reduced the dependence of the Belgian interest rate on the German rate. On the other hand, in 1989 the announcement effect of the EMU seems to have reinforced the dependence of the Belgian interest rate relative to the German one.

The wage and price behaviour in *the Netherlands* shows contrasting EMS effects. In the price behaviour there is a slowly increasing EMS effect over the years after March 1979, which, in fact, is a continuation of the positive effect under the Snake arrangement. In the first half of 1983 there is an upward jump in the EMS effect. This can be attributed to the official promise that the devaluation of March 1983 of the guilder against the Deutschmark would be the last one. In contrast to the expectations, this effect in 1983 appeared to be only temporary. In the second half of 1986 there is a pronounced drop in the coefficient which measures the EMS effect. The increase of VAT rates and different lags in the effect of the fall of the dollar and oil prices on producer prices in the Netherlands and Germany seem to be responsible for this drop. This lower influence of German prices on Dutch prices is partly compensated by a small positive and permanent EMU effect at the beginning of 1989. Dutch wages, on the other hand, have not demonstrated a convincing EMS effect since 1979. For the Netherlands the anti-inflation costs slowly increase during the whole period 1978–90. Both the direction and speed of this development suggest that the steady increase in the sacrifice ratio cannot be attributed to the EMS. In so far as in the Netherlands the Walters dilemma emerged at the start of the EMS, the Dutch solution was a temporary downward impact on the Dutch interest rate.

The Netherlands is an instructive example of what the path towards a monetary union may look like. In the Dutch interest rate one can distinguish slight EMS and EMU effects in the form of somewhat increased dependence of the Dutch long-term interest rate on the German rate. Additionally, it appears that, according to the Dutch experience, on the path towards monetary union the occurrence of a bandwagon effect in the exchange rate exerts a larger effect on the Dutch interest rate, whereas exchange rate variability exhibits a reduced impact. Moreover, it appears that isolated devaluations of the guilder do not affect the structure of the behaviour of the Dutch interest rate. This outcome contrasts with the view of the Dutch central bank.

APPENDIX 1

Price Equations

As an indicator of inflation the growth rate of producer prices has been chosen. For this purpose consumer prices have the drawback that they are more strongly influenced by tax changes, which are difficult to quantify in the form of a time-series.

Prices are assumed to depend on three categories of variables: input costs, international competitiveness, and a slack variable. In order to approach input costs, use has been made of unit labour costs and import prices. The German producer price has been introduced as an indicator of the foreign competition position of the two small, German 'satellite' countries under investigation. Two variables have been tried to portray the slack in the production process: the degree of capacity utilization and the rate of unemployment. Lags were restricted up to four quarters.

These considerations imply the following starting equation:

$$\Delta p = \alpha\Delta p_{-1} + \sum_{i=0}^{4}\beta_i\Delta ulc_{-i} + \sum_{i=0}^{4}\gamma_i\Delta pm_{-i} + \sum_{i=0}^{4}\delta_i\Delta pg_{-i} + \sum_{i=0}^{4}\eta_i . cu_{-i} + \sum_{i=0}^{4}\omega_i . u_{-i} + C.$$

Lower-case variables are in the form of natural logarithms. Δ indicates the first difference of the variable involved. The meaning of the other symbols is:

p = producer price
ulc = unit labour costs
pm = import price
pg = German producer price
cu = capacity utilization
u = unemployment
C = constant

Table 6.5 contains the best fits for Belgium and The Netherlands

TABLE 6.5. *Price equations*

Belgium: 1972 (2)–1990 (4)

Variable	Coefficient	*t*-value
Δpm	0.347	6.96
Δpg	0.685	4.51
C	–0.0002	–0.14
R^2	0.78	
DW	1.13	
Serial correlation:		
CHI²(5)	19.58*	
F(5,67)	4.73*	
ARCH		
CHI²(4)	4.90	
F(4,64)	1.19	
Normality:		
CHI²(2)	0.08	
Heteroscedastic errors:		
F(4,67)	1.31	

The Netherlands: 1973(2)–1990 (4)

Variable	Coefficient	*t*-value
Δulc_{-3}	0.003	2.34
Δulc_{-4}	0.004	2.58
Δpm	0.094	2.09
Δpm_{-2}	0.060	2.05
Δpg	0.414	2.60
C	0.004	3.02
R^2	0.65	
DW	1.93	
Serial correlation:		
CHI²(5)	5.20	
F(5,60)	0.95	
ARCH		
CHI²(4)	0.47	
F(4,57)	0.10	
Normality:		
CHI²(2)	4.71	
Heteroscedastic errors:		
F(10,54)	0.35	

*** The corresponding test value rejects the null hypothesis of absence of correlation or heteroscedasticity at the 0.01 level.**

APPENDIX 2

Wage Equations

Wages are assumed to depend on three kinds of variables: first, the variables which usually play a central role in wage negotiations: inflation and the development of labour productivity; second, international competitiveness, including the EMS effect—this is indicated by the German inflation; third, the tensions on the labour market. The indicators tried are the rate of unemployment and the rate of capacity utilization. Since in the estimation period wage adaptions were made semi-annually or annually, additionally the estimation procedure allowed that the wages two and four quarters ago affect the current wage.

Consequently, the starting equation for the explanation of wages on a quarterly basis was:

$$\Delta w = \alpha_1 \Delta w_{-2} + \alpha_2 \Delta w_{-4} + \sum_{i=0}^{4} \beta_i \Delta pc_{-i} + \sum_{i=0}^{4} \gamma_i \Delta lp_{-i} + \sum_{i=0}^{4} \delta_i \Delta pcg_{-i} + \sum_{i=0}^{4} \varepsilon_i U_{-i} + \sum_{i=0}^{4} \tau_i \Delta u_{-i} + \sum_{i=0}^{4} \omega_i \Delta cu_{-i} + C.$$

All lower-case variables in this equations are expressed in natural logarithms, while Δ indicates a first difference. The meaning of the other symbols is:

w = wage level
pc = consumer price
lp = labour productivity
pcg = consumer price in Germany
u = unemployment
cu = capacity utilization
C = constant

Table 6.6 shows the best fits for the wage equations for Belgium and the Netherlands.

TABLE 6.6. *Wage equations*

Belgium: 1970 (4)–1990 (4)

Variable	Coefficient	*t*-value
Δw_{-4}	0.430	5.62
Δpc	0.583	2.83
Δlp	0.243	5.95
Δpcg_{-1}	0.662	2.37
ΔU_{-2}	–0.011	–3.62
C	–0.005	–1.59
R^2		0.74
Serial correlation:		
$CHI^2(5)$		10.95
F(5.68)		2.19
ARCH		
$CHI^2(4)$		10.06*
F(4,67)		2.52*
Normality:		
$CHI^2(2)$		0.37
Heteroscedastic errors:		
F(10,58)		1.28

The Netherlands: 1971 (2)–1990 (4)

Variable	Coefficient	*t*-value
Δw_{-4}	0.464	5.21
Δpc_{-1}	0.408	2.32
Δlp_{-4}	0.099	1.98
Δpcg_{-1}	0.484	2.40
Δu_{-3}	–0.024	–2.61
C	–0.002	–1.20
R^2	0.71	
Serial correlation:		
$CHI^2(5)$	8.88	
F(5,68)	1.72	
ARCH		
$CHI^2(4)$	4.66	
F(4,65)	1.08	
Normality:		
$CHI^2(2)$	1.27	
Heteroscedastic errors:		
F(10,62)	1.43	

* The corresponding test value rejects the null hypothesis of no correlation, etc. at the 0.05 level.

APPENDIX 3

Unemployment Equations

Unemployment is considered to be determined by: the demand for and supply of domestically produced goods, seasonal fluctuations in the demand for labour, a Phillips curve effect, and a trend variable. The demand for domestic goods is deemed to depend on competitiveness, materialized here by the ratio between domestic producer prices and import prices. The supply side has been introduced by using the capital costs in the form of the long-term real interest rate and labour costs by means of unit labour costs. The Phillips curve effect on unemployment has been included through inflation or wage growth. Since the rate of unemployment appeared to be non-stationary the change in that rate has been explained.

Therefore, the general form of the equation was:

$$\Delta u = \alpha \Delta u_{-1} + \sum_{i=0}^{4} \beta_i \Delta comp_{-i} + \sum_{i=0}^{4} \gamma_i \Delta RIR_{-i} + \sum_{i=0}^{4} \delta_i \Delta ulc_{-1} + \sum_{i=0}^{4} \eta_i \Delta\Delta w_{-i} + \sum_{i=0}^{4} \omega_i Q_i + C.$$

Lower-case variables are in the form of natural logarithms. A Δ indicates the first difference of the variable involved. The meaning of the other symbols is:

u = unemployment rate
$comp$ = international competitiveness
RIR = real interest rate
ulc = unit labour costs
p = producer price
w = wage
Q_i = quarter i
C = constant

Table 6.7 contains the best fits found for Belgium and the Netherlands.

TABLE 6.7. *Unemployment equations*

Belgium: 1971 (2)–1988 (4)

Variable	Coefficient	*t*-value
Δu_{-1}	0.210	2.40
ΔRIR_{-1}	0.095	2.88
Δulc	8.651	3.13
$\Delta\Delta w_{0,-1,-2}$†	–38.319	–2.25
Q_2	–0.924	–7.47
C	0.260	4.02
R^2		0.57
Serial correlation:		
CHI²(5)		21.35**
F(5,60)		5.16**
ARCH		
CHI²(4)		11.63*
F(4,57)		2.99*
Normality:		
CHI²(2)		11.95
Heteroscedastic errors:		
F(9,55)		0.64

The Netherlands: 1971 (1)–1990 (4)

Variable	Coefficient	*t*-value
Δu_{-1}	0.309	3.72
$\Delta\Delta w_{-1}$	–8.820	–2.80
Q_2	–0.846	–5.54
C	0.295	4.46
R^2		0.54
Serial correlation:		
CHI²(5)		30.62**
F(5,61)		8.80**
ARCH		
CHI²(4)		10.54*
F(4,68)		2.74*
Normality:		
CHI²(2)		4.43
Heteroscedastic errors:		
F(5.70)		1.62

*, ** The corresponding test value rejects the null hypothesis of absence of correlation or heteroscedasticy at the 0.05 or 0.01 level, respectively.

† The variable $w_{0,-1,-2}$ is a composite consisting of: $0.5\,w + 0.25\,w_{-1} + 0{,}25\,w_{-2}$.

APPENDIX 4:

Interest Rate Equations

For the interest rate preference has been given to the long-term interest rate in the form of the government bond yield. The potential determinants can be split up into several categories. First, the inflation expectations. These are materialized through the recent developments in the national inflation rates. Second, exchange rate expectations. They are approached by employing recent trends in the rate of the national currency against the Deutschmark. Third, tensions in the capital market. As an indicator the fiscal deficit of the government has been used. Fourth, the interrelations, and thus the interdependence, of interest rates for assets with different maturities have been introduced by means of the short-term interest rate, viz. the call money rate as a potential determinant. Fifth, the idea of a strong dependence of the interest rate with respect to the German one has been concretized through the inclusion of the German government bond yield. Sixth, the notion of risk premia in the interest rate is the background to using indicators of variability, and thus uncertainty, around both the rate of inflation and the exchange rate. Use has been made of the standard deviation of the two variables in the last four quarters. The recent trend in the exchange rate is deemed to be another indicator of the risk premium. A depreciation tendency is expected to raise the long-term interest rate.

The series for the two interest rates to be explained proved to be non-stationary. Hence, their first differences have been chosen as the dependent variables. They appeared to be stable. Only a small set of explanatory variables was left with a significant influence, as is visible in Table 6.8. The estimation period was started in 1971(3) just after the inception of the Snake arrangement to avoid an immediate break.

TABLE 6.8. *Long-term interest rate equations*

Belgium: 1971 (3)–1990 (4)

Variable	Coefficient	*t*-value
Δlr_{-1}	0.3915	4.43
Δlrg	0.3064	3.88
$\Delta\Delta cp_{0,-1,-2}$	27.8349	2.13
C	0.0180	0.48
R^2	0.45	
DW	—	
Serial correlation:		
$CHI^2(5)$	7.24	
F(5,69)	1.41	
ARCH		
$CHI^2(4)$	6.74	
F(4,66)	1.65	
Normality:		
$CHI^2(2)$	7.75*	
Heteroscedastic errors:		
F(6,67)	0.57	

The Netherlands: 1971 (3)–1990 (3)

Variable	Coefficient	*t*-value
Δlrg	0.7626	11.47
$\Delta\Delta s_{-1}$	4.2455	2.17
sds	13.0320	2.31
C	–0.0695	–1.41
R^2	0.67	
DW	2.30	
Serial correlation:		
$CHI^2(5)$	7.20	
F(5,68)	1.40	
ARCH		
$CHI^2(4)$	9.44	
F(4,65)	2.41	
Normality:		
$CHI^2(2)$	1.66	
Heteroscedastic errors:		
F(6,66)	7.05**	

*, ** The corresponding test value rejects the null hypothesis of absence of heteroscedasticity etc. at 0.05 and the 0.01 level, respectively.

The meaning of the symbols is:

Δ	=	first difference
lr	=	long-term interest rate
lrg	=	German long-term interest rate
cp	=	consumer price
C	=	a constant
s	=	exchange rate
sds	=	standard deviation of the exchange rate in the preceding four quarters.

$cp_{0,-1,-2}$ is defined as $0.5\,cp + 0.3\,cp_{-1} + 0.2\,cp_{-2}$

APPENDIX 5:

Sources of the Data

The main sources are: International Monetary Fund, *International Financial Statistics* (*IFS*) (various issues) and Organization for Economic Co-operation and Development, *Main Economic Indicators* (*MEI*) (various issues):

Capacity utilization: for Belgium and the Netherlands: MEI (Capacity utilization of manufacturing industry)

Consumer price: for Germany, Belgium, and the Netherlands: *IFS*, line 64

Producer price: for Germany, Belgium, and the Netherlands: *IFS*, line 63

Wage level: for Germany, Belgium, and the Netherlands: *IFS*, line 65

Exchange rate: the dollar rate for Germany, Belgium, and the Netherlands: *IFS*, line 'af'

Import price: for Belgium: *IFS*, line 76-x; for the Netherlands: *IFS*, line 75

International competitiveness: for Belgium and the Netherlands: producer price/import price

Labour productivity: for Belgium: hourly earnings/unit labour costs, with hourly earnings in *MEI*; for the Netherlands: De Nederlandsche Bank, Kwartaalberichten

Long-term interest rate: for Germany, Belgium and the Netherlands: *IFS*, line 61 (government bond yields)

Real interest rate: for Belgium and the Netherlands: long-term interest rate—growth of produce price.

Unemployment: for Belgium and the Netherlands: *MEI*; because of a break in the series it is adapted for the Netherlands for the years 1989 and 1990 by means of data from the Dutch Central Bureau voor de Statistiek

Unit labour costs: for Belgium and the Netherlands: *IFS*, line 65 um

REFERENCES

Agénor, P.-R. and M. P. Taylor (1992). 'Testing for Credibility Effects', *IMF Staff Papers*, 39/3: 545–71.

Chadha, B., P. R. Masson and G. Meredith (1992). 'Models of Inflation and the Costs of Disinflation', *IMF Staff Papers*, 39/2: 395–431.

Corden, W. M. (1985). *Inflation, Exchange Rates and the World Economy*, 3rd edn., Oxford, 1985.

De Grauwe, P. and W. Vanhaverbeke (1990). 'Exchange Rate Experiences of Small EMS Countries: Belgium, Denmark, and the Netherlands', in V. Argy and P. De Grauwe (eds.), *Choosing an Exchange Rate Regime: the Challenge for Smaller Industrial Countries*, IMF, Washington, DC: 135–55.

De Nederlandsche Bank (1986). *Kwartaalbericht* 1986/2, Amsterdam.

Goldstein, M. (1984). 'The Exchange Rate System: Lessons of the Past and Options for the Future', *IMF Occasional Paper*, 30, Washington, DC.

Koen, V. R. (1989). 'Testing the Credibility of the Belgian Hard Currency Policy', *IMF Working Paper*, 89/36, Washington, DC.

In't Veld, J. W. (1992). 'The Diverse Experience of the Netherlands, Belgium and Denmark in the ERM', in R. Barrell (ed.), *Economic Convergence and Monetary Union in Europe*, London: 154–73.

Kremers, J. M. (1990). Gaining Policy Credibility for a Disinflation: Ireland's Experience in the EMS', *IMF Staff Papers*, 37/1: 116–45.

Lucas, R. E. (1976). 'Econometric Policy Evaluation: A Critique', in K. Brunner and A. H. Meltzer (eds.), *The Phillips Curve and Labor Markets, Carnegie-Rochester Series on Public Policy*, i, Amsterdam.

OECD, Economic Surveys, BLEU and the Netherlands, various issues.

PART II

Systematic Studies on Convergence, Financial Integration, and the Role of the EMS

7

Inflation Convergence during the Transition to EMU

PAUL DE GRAUWE

1. INTRODUCTION

The historic Maastricht Treaty has set out a strategy and timetable for monetary union in the Community. Its basic philosophy was influenced by the Delors Report and is one of gradualism. The steps towards EMU, and in particular, the last step into full union are made conditional on achieving sufficient convergence in inflation, interest rates, and budgetary indicators (deficits and debt levels).

This chapter concentrates on the required convergence of inflation rates. According to the Maastricht Treaty, EMS countries will be able to join EMU if their inflation rates are not more than 1.5 per cent higher than the average of the three lowest inflation rates in the EMS. We analyse first, whether it is likely that inflation rates will converge to the levels set out in the Maastricht Treaty. Second, we ask the question whether the Maastricht convergence requirement for inflation rates is not needlessly tight.

In order to shed some light on these issues we will compare the inflation convergence within the EMS with inflation convergence during the 1960s. In addition, we compare it with inflation convergence between regions of the same country.

2. INFLATION CONVERGENCE IN THE 1980S

One of the remarkable achievements of the EMS has been the degree to which inflation rates have converged within the system. We show the evidence in Fig. 7.1. It can be seen that the yearly standard deviations and the range of national inflation rates declined substantially during the period 1981–91. From this evidence one could be tempted to conclude that all looks fine, and that in a few years the Maastricht criterion will be met by all EMS countries. Is such optimism warranted? Not necessarily. Convergence in yearly inflation rates can hide increasing divergences of trends in price *levels*, when the same countries have small but consistently higher inflation rates than other countries. This is exactly

I am grateful to Danny Decupere for research assistance, and to Casper de Vries for his comments.

what happened within the EMS during the 1987–91 period (a period during which no realignments occurred). We show evidence in Fig. 7.2 for a selected group of EMS countries. One observes that during 1987–91 some countries, in particular Italy and Spain, experienced a cumulative increase in their price level against Germany of close to 15 per cent. Note that Spain has been a member of the EMS since 1989 only. However, during 1987–91 the peseta has actually experienced a (nominal) appreciation of approximately 10 per cent against the other EMS currencies. Thus, the *real* appreciation of the peseta from 1987 to 1991 is larger than appears from Fig. 7.2 (i.e. it is close to 25 per cent of September 1992).

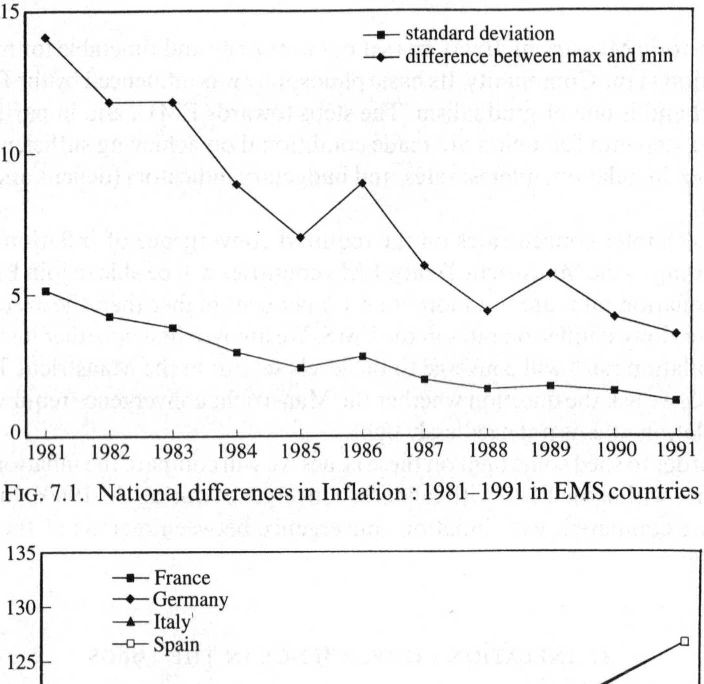

FIG. 7.1. National differences in Inflation : 1981–1991 in EMS countries

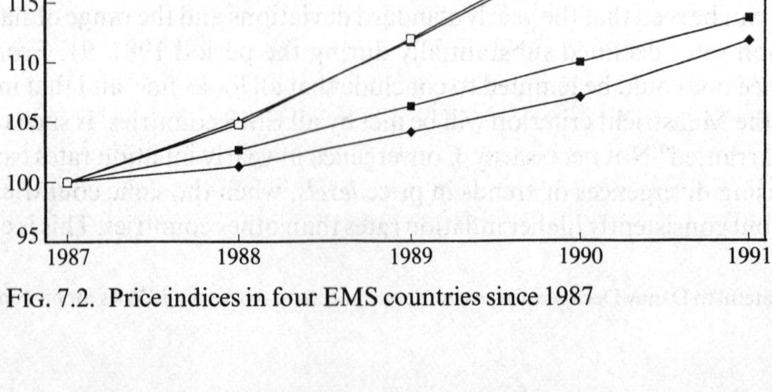

FIG. 7.2. Price indices in four EMS countries since 1987

Prior to the foreign exchange crisis which led to the depreciation of the lira and the peseta, the sustainability of these price trends was hotly debated. The drafters of the Maastricht Treaty, who could observe these trends when they signed the Treaty in December 1991, must have been convinced that such diverging price trends were sustainable.

The argument that such diverging price trends were sustainable is based on a model where differences in productivity growth occur between countries. We set out this model in the next section. We then evaluate whether this model can explain the observed price trends. We formulate an alternative explanation based on differences in credibility of national monetary authorities.

2.1 Structural differences

The best-known structural factor that can produce systematic differences in inflation rates (and thus diverging trends in national price indices) has to do with differences in productivity growth.[1] A country that experiences a high-growth rate of productivity in the tradable-goods sector can allow the growth rate of nominal wages to reflect this, without losing competitiveness. These high nominal wage increases in the tradable-goods sector will be transmitted to the non-tradable-goods sector, so that also prices in that sector increase fast. As a result, the increases in the CPI-index in that country will tend to be high. We will, therefore, also measure a high rate of (CPI)-inflation. This high inflation rate, however, does not represent a problem. It should be considered as an equilibrating mechanism. Without it, the high-productivity-growth country would progressively gain competitiveness and would accumulate current account surpluses. Thus, if productivity growth is the source of systematically higher inflation in some EMS countries, it can be sustained without the need for realignments.

In an Appendix we present a well-known two-country model of inflation with traded and non-traded goods. It is shown there that the inflation differential between two countries (called Spain and Germany) that can be explained by the productivity differentials can be written as follows:

$$\pi_S - \pi_G = a(q_S - q_G), \qquad (1)$$

where π_S and π_G are the inflation rates in Spain and Germany, respectively; and q_S and q_G are the rates of productivity growth in the tradable-goods sectors of Spain and Germany respectively; a is the share of non-traded goods in the two countries (assumed to be equal in the two countries).

How far can we go with this model in explaining inflation differentials within the EMS? In Table 1 we show some evidence about the growth rates of productivity in a number of EMS countries. It can be seen that in Southern

[1] This is sometimes called the Balassa effect. See Balassa (1964).

countries like Italy and Spain the productivity growth rates in the tradable-goods sector tended to be higher than in the Northern EMS countries. Thus, the systematically higher rates of inflation of Italy and Spain could be said to be related to this productivity effect. However, it is unlikely to explain the full difference of inflation. During 1987–91 the Italian and Spanish inflation rates exceeded the German inflation rate by approximately 3 per cent per year. The productivity-growth differential between Italy and Spain on the one hand and Germany on the other hand is likely to be too low a differential to fully explain why these Southern countries' inflation rates exceeded Germany's by 3 per cent per year. This is also made clear from equation (1): a productivity-growth differential of 0.5 to 1.2 per cent between these Southern countries and Germany can explain something like 0.3 to 0.7 per cent inflation differential (assuming that $a = 0.6$).

There is of course a great deal of uncertainty about these productivity measurements. In general the statistical quality of productivity indices is low and certainly much lower than that of the price indices. In particular, the productivity growth of the Spanish manufacturing sector may be biased downwards in Table 7.1.[2] Nevertheless, it is unlikely that productivity-growth differentials suffice to explain the full inflation differential. This can also be seen as follows. Equation (1) can be rewritten as follows:

$$q_S - q_G = (1/a)(p_S - p_G) \tag{2}$$

TABLE 7.1. *Average yearly growth in labour productivity during the 1980s manufacturing (%)*

France*	2.5
Germany	3.0
Italy	4.2
Spain*	3.5

* Productivity growth in industry.

Source: OECD, *Economic Outlook*.

Equation (2) now tells us how large the productivity-growth differential can be in order to sustain a given inflation differential. Given that the yearly inflation differential of Spain and Italy in relation to Germany amounted to 3 per cent on average, one finds that the required differential in productivity growth was 5 per cent per year (assuming $a = 0.6$). It is very unlikely that the productivity-growth differential between these Southern countries and Germany was of that order of magnitude during 1987–92. We conclude that the higher inflation rates in Italy and Spain since 1987 can only partially be

[2] Evidence given in Danthine *et al.* (1991) over the period 1980–8 indicates a somewhat higher rate of labour productivity in Spain than the one obtained in Table 1. For more evidence see Danthine *et al.* (1991).

explained by productivity differentials. This also means that the view implicit in the Maastricht Treaty that the differences in inflation rates were sustainable should be questioned. The speculative crisis of September 1992 indicates that the markets also considered these price trends to be unsustainable.

2.2 *Credibility and inflation*

The second major explanation of persistent inflation differentials between countries in a fixed exchange rate system is based on differences in credibility of the monetary authorities.[3] In fixed exchange rate systems in which countries maintain their own central banks, the authorities will have very different credibilities. As a result, expectations of inflation will not be equalized easily. Only, if these monetary authorities were to merge (which is a monetary union) would inflationary expectations be the same in all the countries. Thus, as long as national monetary authorities, with different credibilities concerning inflation, remain in place, residual differences in inflation expectations, and therefore, in observed inflation will remain. These, however, lead to cumulative divergencies in price indices, and to unsustainable trends in competitiveness. In the next section a simple Barro–Gordon model of two open economies is presented which formalizes these ideas (Barro and Gordon, 1983). The model is kept extremely simple. For example, it does not explicitly incorporate the role played by the permissible band of fluctuations in the EMS.[4] Its purpose is to indicate how differences in credibility of autonomous central banks can lead to persistent inflation differentials.

3. A TWO-COUNTRY MODEL OF INFLATION

Consider two countries A and B whose authorities minimize the following loss functions:

$$V_A = (U_A - U_A^*)^2 + b_A(\pi_A - \pi_A^*)^2$$

$$V_B = (U_B - U_B^*)^2 + b_B(\pi_B - \pi_B^*)^2,$$

where U_A and U_B are the unemployment rates in countries A and B, U_A^* and U_B^* are the target unemployment rates in countries A and B, π_A and π_B are the inflation rates, and π_A^* and π_B^* are the target inflation rates.

The authorities aim at minimizing deviations of the observed unemployment rate U from the desired level of unemployment U^*, and they minimize the deviation of the observed inflation rate π from the desired rate π^*. It will be assumed that in the two countries the desired rate of inflation is equal to zero.

[3] This problem has already been identified before by, among others, Walters (1985), Giavazzi and Giovannini (1989), Giavazzi and Spaventa (1990), Artis (1992).

[4] For such an analysis, see Lambertini *et al.* (1991).

The coefficient b expresses the weight the authorities attach to the inflation objective. It will be assumed that this weight is different in the two countries. It is this difference in preferences of the two authorities that will be responsible for persistent inflation differentials.

The level of unemployment desired by the authorities is assumed to be different from the natural unemployment rate in the following way:

$$U_A^* = (1 - c_A)U_{N,A}$$

$$U_B^* = (1 - c_B)U_{N,B},$$

where $U_{N,A}$ and $U_{N,B}$ are the natural unemployment rates in countries A and B and where $0<c<1$.

This specification is generally rationalized by the fact that there are distortions in the labour market so that the natural rate of unemployment tends to be too high, at least in the eyes of the authorities. The latter therefore tend to target an unemployment rate that is lower than the natural unemployment rate. The Philips curve in the two countries has the usual specification:

$$U_A = U_{N,A} - k_A(\pi_A - \pi_A^e)$$

$$U_B = U_{N,B} - k_B(\pi_B - \pi_B^e),$$

where π_A^e and π_B^e are the expected inflation rates in countries A and B.

This specification of the Philips curve assumes that only unanticipated inflation $(\pi - \pi^e)$ affects the unemployment rate. If expectations are rational, economic agents will not make systematic errors in predicting inflation, so that the authorities cannot systematically exploit the Phillips curve.

The rational expectations, time-consistent, solution of this model can be computed as follows. The authorities minimize their loss function, subject to the constraint that private agents set $\pi = \pi^e$. This means that private agents anticipate the authorities' actions. The rational expectations solution can then be written as follows:[5]

$$\pi_A = (k_A c_A / b_A) U_{N,A}$$

and

$$\pi_B = (k_B c_B / b_B) U_{N,B}.$$

It follows that the equilibrium inflation rates of the two countries will be different if the underlying parameters of the model differ. We concentrate on the parameter b here[6]. If $b_B < b_A$, i.e. if country B's authorities attach a smaller weight to inflation in their objective function than country A, the equilibrium

[5] See Barro and Gordon (1983).

[6] Obviously, the other parameters are equally important. In particular, differences in the natural unemployment rates can lead to 'structural' differences in inflation rates. Similarly, differences in labour market distortions affect the parameters c_A and c_B, and can lead to different inflation rates between countries. Note, however, that in this model these differences in inflation rates ultimately arise from the fact that the authorities are different.

inflation rate in country B will be higher, *ceteris paribus*. This must be so because rational agents take into account the higher incentive the authorities of country B have in producing surprise inflation. One can say that country A and B will have a different reputation[7] in the eyes of economic agents leading to systematic differences in inflation.

Such differences in inflation rates due to differences in reputation will inevitably lead to issues of sustainability of the fixed exchange rate commitment. We conclude that as long as monetary authorities with different preferences, and therefore different reputations, maintain their autonomy, a fixed exchange rate system will find it difficult to eliminate systematic differences in inflation rates. This is likely to be the fundamental source of persistent inflation differentials within the EMS. It also explains why in September 1992 speculators took positions against currencies like the lira and the peseta.

4. INFLATION CONVERGENCE IN THE 1960S

The difficulty in achieving complete convergence of inflation rates in fixed exchange rate systems is also illustrated by the experience of the 1960s. In this section evidence of inflation convergence among European countries that kept a fixed exchange rate during the 1960s is presented.[8] Since the margins of fluctuations in the Bretton-Woods system were smaller than in the EMS, the fixity of the exchange rates during the 1960s was quite constraining on the countries participating in the system. The data on the convergence of inflation during the 1960s are shown in Fig. 7.3

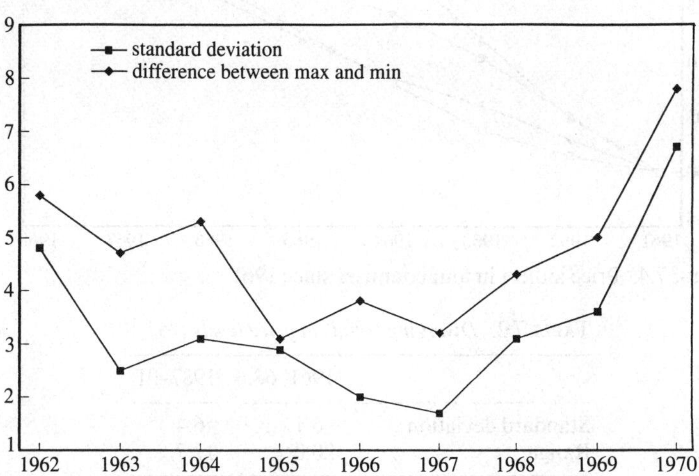

FIG. 7.3. National differences in Inflation : 1962–1970 in EMS countries

[7] We use the word 'reputation' in a loose sense. In the literature following the Barro–Gordon publication this term has been used in the context of dynamic games.

[8] Austria, Belgium, Greece, Italy, France, The Netherlands, Norway, Sweden, Switzerland.

It is interesting to observe that until 1967, a similar inflation convergence was observed as in the EMS during the 1980s. After 1967, however, inflation rates started to diverge, to become very large in 1970. This is also the time when devaluations and revaluations occurred, i.e. in 1969 and 1970. Thus, the fixity of the exchange rates remained in place only until 1968.

How can it be explained that although in 1967 and 1968 the differences in national inflation rates had declined to relatively low levels (which were comparable to the situation reached today in the EMS), one year later major realignments were necessary? The answer here also has to do with persistence of inflation differentials which led to diverging movements in price levels.

We show the evidence first in Fig. 7.4 which presents the price indices of a selected group of countries. It can be seen that a similar divergence in price trends occurred as in the EMS during 1987–91. Table 7.2 presents more systematic evidence of price level divergencies during the two periods. It can be seen that from 1961 to 1968 (the last year of the truly fixed exchange rate period), national price indices diverged on average by 6.1 per cent (as measured by the standard deviation of the national indices in 1968). More significantly, in 1968

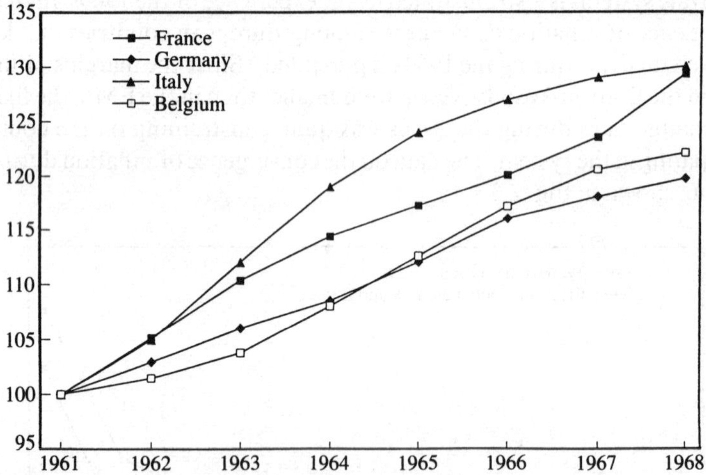

FIG. 7.4. Price indices in four countries since 1961

TABLE 7.2. *Diverging trends in price levels (%)*

	1961–68	1987–91
Standard deviation	6.1	6.4
Range	20.0	17.7

Note: Standard deviation of the price indices in 1968 and 1991 respectively. Range is the difference between the price index of the country with the highest rate of inflation and the price index of the country with the lowest rate of inflation in 1968 and 1991 respectively.

the difference in the price indices of the highest- and the lowest-inflation countries amounted to about 20 per cent (France and Italy on the one hand and Germany on the other). This phenomenon contributed to putting pressure on the existing structure of exchange rates. This pressure finally led to exchange rate adjustments at the end of the decade.

Table 7.2 also makes clear that these divergencies in price indices observed during the 1960s are of the same order of magnitude as those observed during the 1980s. Thus, the situation in the EMS in 1992 was not unlike the one observed during the second half of the 1960s.

From the preceding discussion one can conclude that the underlying price trends during the fixed exchange rate episode of the EMS were comparable to those observed during the fixed exchange rate episode of the 1960s. It is clear that such a situation was unsustainable. The loss of competitiveness of certain countries in the EMS made devaluations necessary.

These devaluations introduce new problems with the Maastricht inflation convergence requirement. It is almost inevitable that these devaluations will introduce a renewed divergence of inflation rates in the future. This was also observed at the end of the 1960s when the exchange rate adjustments which were necessary to correct for diverging developments in competitiveness, led to a renewed divergence of the national inflation rates.

The previous analysis leads to the view that the degree of inflation convergence achieved in the period 1991–2 in the EMS was probably at a historically high level, and that hopes of a further narrowing of the differences in national inflation rates are unrealistic. A renewed divergence in inflation rates during the 1990s is more likely to happen than the contrary. This leads to the question of whether the Maastricht inflation convergence requirement is not too tight. We analyse this question further in the next section by looking at the inflation convergence in existing monetary unions.

5. CONVERGENCE OF INFLATION RATES WITHIN MONETARY UNIONS

In order to evaluate the tightness of the inflation convergence criterion in the Maastricht Treaty it is useful to analyse the degree of inflation convergence observed between member states of existing monetary unions. We present evidence relating to the Länder in Germany. In Fig. 7.5 we show measures of convergence of inflation rates between these Länder. We observe that quite often the yearly differences in regional inflation rates in Germany are around 1 per cent, and sometimes come close to 1.5 per cent. This tight convergence, however, is the result of a full monetary union, i.e. the use of one currency and one central bank.[9]

[9] In the case of Canada larger differences in regional inflation rates are observed. Poloz (1990) finds that the average yearly differences of inflation rates (CPI) between major Canadian cities is between 1 and 2%. See Poloz (1990), 11.

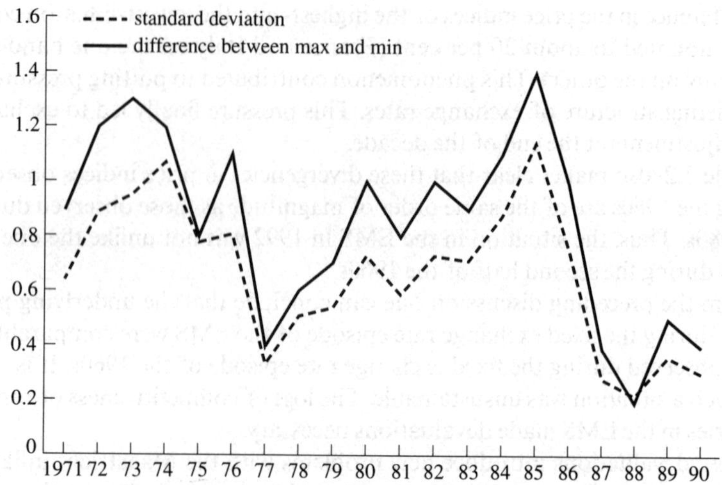

FIG. 7.5. Regional differences in inflation in Germany (%) (Northrhine-Westphalia, Baden-Würftemberg, Bayern, Hesse, West Berlin) (%)

In Table 7.3 we present measures of long-term price trends in the German Länder, and compare those with the price trends observed in the EMS (Table 7.2). The differences are striking. During the period 1986–90 the price indices diverged (cumulatively) by only 0.5 per cent between the German Länder. This compares with 6.4 per cent between the EMS-countries (during 1987–91). Similarly, the range between the price indices of the highest- and the lowest-inflation Land in Germany was only 1 per cent versus 17.7 per cent in the EMS. Thus, the tight convergence of yearly inflation rates between German Länder goes together with a tight convergence of price trends over longer periods. This is made possible by the fact that not always the same Länder happen to have a higher rate of inflation than the others. This is not the case in the EMS where such systematic biases in inflation rates are observed.

The German example suggests that the Maastricht inflation convergence criterion is probably too tight. It imposes as a condition for entry in EMU a degree of convergence that is only observed in a full monetary union, where

TABLE 7.3. *Diverging trends in price levels between German Länder (%)*

	1986–90
Standard deviation	0.5
Range	1.0

Note: Range is the difference between the price index of the Land with the highest rate of inflation and the price index of the Land with the lowest rate of inflation in 1990 (base year 1986).

a common currency and a common central bank impose the necessary discipline to achieve the Maastricht convergence criterion. It seems quite unreasonable to expect that such a tight inflation convergence can be achieved among countries that maintain their own currency and central bank.

The previous analysis leads to the view that there is no benefit to be obtained from stretching the final stage of EMU to 1996, let alone 1999. On the contrary, such a long transition period makes further accidents on the road to EMU almost inevitable. Each time such an accident (realignment) occurs, countries move away from the convergence criterion spelled out in the Maastricht Treaty.

6. IS INFLATION CONVERGENCE PRIOR TO EMU NECESSARY?

In the previous sections it was argued that the Maastricht inflation criterion is too tight, and that some EMS countries will have great difficulties in achieving this convergence requirement. The issue that arises now is whether such a stringent convergence criterion is really necessary as a condition for a successful entry into a monetary union. Two views about this question can be formulated.

6.1. Monetary union is a monetary reform

The first view equates monetary union with monetary reform, and argues that a stringent convergence criterion for inflation is not a necessary condition for entry in a monetary union. When countries join a monetary union, they abolish their national currencies so as to acquire a new and common currency. Since the old currencies disappear, so does the whole history of inflationary expectations associated with these currencies. The past history of these currencies becomes irrelevant. As a result, it is quite conceivable that a country with an inflation rate of say 6 per cent EMU with countries having an inflation rate of say only 2 per cent without major problems. When the high-inflation country joins EMU, its currency disappears. The fact that this currency used to experience a loss of purchasing power of 6 per cent per year becomes irrelevant.

In this view, the only serious problem that will exist is the choice of the rate at which the old currencies will be converted into the common currency. But this problem will also have to be addressed in the Maastricht framework of a long transition to EMU. In 1996 (or 1999) the national price levels will have diverged sufficiently to necessitate the choice of conversion rates implying a devaluation for some and a revaluation for other currencies, in order to avoid locking in some countries in unfavorable competitive positions. The long transition period to EMU that the European leaders have chosen does not solve that problem—on the contrary.

There are certainly a number of problems with this view of a monetary union. First, the problem of the conversion of old debt contracts into new ones is made more difficult when countries with different inflation rates form a monetary union. When the monetary reform is instituted the old debt contracts must be expressed in the new numeraire. This poses problems of transition which are made more difficult when the countries joining the union have different inflation rates, and therefore, also different interest rates on debt contracts. It is clear, however, that this can be solved relatively easily, certainly when inflation differentials are of the order of magnitude as observed today.

A second more serious problem has to do with the fact that, even after monetary union, some inertia in prices may continue to exist. For example, wage indexing and overlapping wage contracts introduce inertia in wages. When inflation rate differentials between countries are sizeable at the moment of the monetary reform, prices in these countries may continue to diverge after the introduction of the monetary union. Again these problems can be solved by introducing transitional clauses of contract adjustment (e.g. the tablita in some Latin American countries). High-inflation differentials, however, make these transitional problems more serious.

The tight Maastricht inflation-convergence criterion not only reflects a concern for these problems of transition. It also reflects a basic ambiguity about the nature of the future monetary union in Europe. From the text of the Treaty it cannot be determined whether in 1996 (or in 1999), when the final stage sets in, the ECU will replace the national currencies and be the sole currency used by the countries participating in EMU, or whether the national currencies will circulate alongside the ECU, albeit at 'irrevocably' fixed exchange rates. If the first solution is envisaged, we will have a true monetary union, which will have to be instituted by a monetary reform. In that case, as argued before, the inflation-convergence requirement as a condition for entry is superfluous.

If, however, it is the second solution which is envisaged by the drafters of the Treaty, we will have a very different monetary union. Problems of confidence about the irrevocability of the fixity of the exchange rates will continue to exist. In that case the inflation-convergence requirement is important, because the national currencies will remain in existence. As a result, the past inflationary experiences of these currencies will continue to influence inflationary expectations. Therefore, in order to fix the exchange rates of these currencies once and for all, the inflation rates to start with should be the same, lest the confidence in the irrevocable fixity will be questioned right from the start.

There is now a consensus among economists that this second form of monetary union has nothing to recommend it. It puts the same kind of constraint on national policies, and has the disadvantage of not being fully credible. In addition, if one can achieve this stage, one can as well go all the way to a full monetary union with one currency and one central bank.

6.2. The 'German' View

There is a second possible view about the desirability of stringent inflation-convergence criteria as a condition for entry in EMU. This can be called the German view, and can be formulated as follows.

The problem of the low-inflation country, Germany, is that it stands to lose its brand name, the strong Deutschmark, by joining EMU. It is very likely that the European central bank will not have the same low-inflation reputation as the Bundesbank has today. As a result, the incentives of Germany for joining the union are weak. The German authorities are suspicious about the inflationary intentions of the future members of the union. One way to allay these fears is for the other potential members to prove by facts that they are serious about their commitment to a low inflation. Thus, the stringent inflation-convergence requirement can be considered as a 'rite of passage' for the potential members of the union, by which they demonstrate to the sceptical leader that they are converted to a low-inflation policy.

There is another political benefit for Germany from imposing unrealistically tight entry conditions. These conditions will necessarily restrict the union to a limited number of countries. In such a small European monetary union, the position of Germany will continue to be strong. In a monetary union with fifteen members, however, the position of Germany in determining the monetary policies will be considerably weakened. Thus, a monetary union with the fifteen EU members looks quite unattractive to the leading country. Germany has everything to gain from restricting the membership in the union.

This political interpretation goes a long way in explaining why the Maastricht convergence criterion was instituted. The reason why tight inflation-convergence was imposed has very little to do with a technical necessity for a monetary union. It has everything to do with allaying the fears and the suspicions of the low-inflation country which stands to lose a lot from EMU. In addition, it will have the effect of reducing the size of the monetary union, thereby reducing the loss of Germany's hegemonial position in the monetary field in Europe.

7. CONCLUSION

In this chapter it was argued, first, that the Maastricht convergence criterion for inflation is too tight. Some EMS countries will experience great difficulties in achieving the required degree of inflation-convergence. In addition, the tight convergence criterion, coupled with the long transition process to EMU, is likely to be counter-productive. It maximizes the likelihood that accidents (re-alignments) will happen on the road to EMU. With each realignment, however, inflation-convergence will be set back. Thus, the long transition to EMU will not make monetary union easier to achieve. On the contrary it will make the transition to EMU crisis-prone. (For a similar conclusion, see Begg *et al.*, 1991.)

Second, we argued that tight convergence of inflation rates is not a technical condition to form a monetary union. Monetary union between countries that have larger differences of inflation than 1.5 per cent per year is possible. The reason is that monetary union is equivalent to monetary reform. The latter abolishes national currencies together with past inflation experiences associated with these currencies, and introduces a new currency which will not be affected by the inflationary experiences of individual countries. There are of course transitional problems of a monetary union that have to be solved. These problems become more important when inflation differentials are high. We have argued, however, that these problems can be dealt with even if the inflation differentials are of the order of magnitude as observed in 1992.

The most important reason why countries have accepted a low-inflation corset during the transition period is a political one. The tight inflation-convergence criterion appears to have been a political condition aimed at convincing the 'anchor country' of the seriousness of the other member countries in making a low-inflation policy their first priority. In addition, the inflation-convergence criterion (together with the other Maastricht norms) will necessarily restrict the size of the monetary union, so that the loss of influence of Germany in European monetary affairs can be limited.

APPENDIX 1

Inflation and Productivity Growth

The effect of differential productivity growth on inflation can be analysed in the framework of the 'Scandinavian' model.

The rate of change in the CPI index in country A (inflation) can be defined as follows:

$$\pi_A = (1 - a)\pi_{T,A} + a\pi_{N,A}, \tag{A.1}$$

where $\pi_{T,A}$ is the rate of change in the price of tradables in country A and $\pi_{N,A}$ is the rate of change of the price of non-tradables in country A; a is the share of non-tradables in the CPI index.

A similar equation can be defined for country B, i.e.

$$\pi_B = (1-a)\pi_{T,B} + a\pi_{N,B}. \tag{A.2}$$

It is assumed here that the share of non-tradables is the same in the two countries.

If countries A and B maintain a fixed exchange rate, the rate of price increases in the tradable-goods sectors must be equal. If this is not the case one country will continuously lose competitiveness and be confronted with increasing current account deficits. Thus

$$\pi_{T,A} = \pi_{T,B}. \tag{A.3}$$

A second equilibrium condition in this model is that the rate of price increases in the traded- and non-traded-goods sectors should be equal to the rate of growth of the unit labour costs. The latter is defined as the difference between the rate of growth of nominal wages and of labour productivity:

$$\pi_{T,A} = w_A - q_A \tag{A.4}$$

$$\pi_{N,A} = w_A - v_A \tag{A.5}$$

where w_A is the rate of growth of nominal wages in country A, assumed to be equal in the traded- and non-traded-goods sectors; q_A is the rate of productivity growth in the traded-goods sector of country A, and v_A is the rate of growth of productivity in the non-traded-goods sector of country A. A similar set of equations can be written for country B, i.e.

$$\pi_{T,B} = w_B - q_B \tag{A.6}$$

$$\pi_{N,B} = w_B - v_B. \tag{A.7}$$

We can now substitute (A.4) and (A.5) into (A.1), and (A.6) and (A.7) into (A.2) to obtain (after rearranging):

$$\pi_A = (1 - a)\pi_{T,A} + a(\pi_{T,A} + q_A - v_A) \tag{A.8}$$

$$\pi_B = (1 - a)\pi_{T,B} + a(\pi_{T,B} + q_B - v_B). \tag{A.9}$$

We now subtract (A.9) from (A.8) and we use (A.3). This yields an expression for the inflation differential:

$$\pi_A - \pi_B = a(q_A - q_B) - a(v_A - v_B). \tag{A.10}$$

If we assume that the rate of productivity growth in the non-tradables in the two countries is identical ($v_A = v_B$) we obtain the expression used in the text:

$$\pi_A - \pi_B = a(q_A - q_B).$$

This says that if country A experiences a higher growth of productivity in its tradable-goods sector than B its inflation rate must exceed country B's inflation rate if the two countries have fixed their exchange rate.

REFERENCES

Artis, Michael (1992). 'Counter-Inflationary Policy in the Framework of the EMS', *CEPR Discussion Paper*, 649 (Mar.).

Balassa, B. (1964). 'Purchasing Power Parity: A Reappraisal', *Journal of Political Economy*, 72: 584–96.

Barro, R., and D. Gordon (1983), Rules, Discretion and Reputation in a Model of Monetary Policy, *Journal of Monetary Economics*, 101/21.

Begg, D., P. Chiappori, F. Giavazzi, C. Mayer, D. Neven, L. Spaventa, X. Vives, and C. Wyplosz (1991), *Monitoring European Integration: The Making of Monetary Union*, CEPR, London.

Danthine, J. P., P. De Grauwe, L. Katseli, and N. Thygesen (1991), 'North/South in the EMS', *CEPS Papers*.

Giavazzi, F., and A. Giovannini (1989), Limiting Exchange Rate Flexibility, MIT Press, Cambridge, Mass.

Giavazzi, F., and L. Spaventa (1990), 'The "New" EMS', in De Grauwe and Papademos, *The EMS in the 1990s*, Longman.

Lambertini, Luisa, Marcus Miller, and Alan Sutherland (1991), Inflation Convergence with Realignments in a Two-Speed Europe, *CEPR Discussion Paper*, 597 (Dec.).

Poloz, Stephen (1990), *Real Exchange Rate Adjustment between Regions in a Common Currency Area*, Bank of Canada.

Walters, A. *Britain's Economic Renaissance*, London.

8

Real Exchange Rates and the Prices of Non-Tradable Goods

STEFANO MICOSSI

GIAN MARIA MILESI-FERRETTI

I. INTRODUCTION

After several years of tranquillity and converging inflation performance across countries, the exchange rate mechanism (ERM) of the European Monetary System came under strong pressure starting in the summer of 1992, and eventually broke down in August 1993 (although formally still in existence with 15 per cent fluctuation bands). In this chapter we attempt to provide a perspective on real exchange rate developments following the inception of the EMS by focusing on some structural determinants of real exchange rates, notably the behaviour of tradables and non-tradables prices and productivity.

In the period between 1979 and 1987, the inflation rates in EMS countries showed remarkable convergence. High inflation countries like Italy were able to reduce considerably the inflation differential *vis-à-vis* more 'virtuous' EMS countries by pegging the nominal exchange rate to the Deutschmark, with occasional realignments that failed to compensate fully for inflation differentials. The following period, known as the 'hard EMS', was characterized by the absence of realignments and by a reduction in nominal interest rate differentials. The reduction of inflation differentials, however, came to a halt and differentials in some cases started to widen again.

Incomplete convergence in inflation rates accompanied by fixed exchange rates led to increasing divergence in price *levels*, as highlighted for example by De Grauwe's chapter in this volume. Real effective exchange rate measures based on aggregate price indices such as CPI or GDP deflator show a substantial appreciation for high-inflation countries, such as Italy and Spain (lower quadrant of Fig. 8.1); while Germany, Belgium, Denmark, and the Netherlands, on the other hand, were able to reverse the large appreciation of the early 1970s and enjoyed a strong competitive position through most of the EMS period, despite sizeable nominal appreciation (Fig. 8.1, upper quadrant). These

This chapter was prepared as part of the EC SPES Research Project 'Controlling Inflation during the Transition to EMU'. Maria Grazia Pazienza, Marco Malgarini, and especially Gianna Bargagli provided excellent research assistance. We thank Paul De Grauwe, Carmen Reinhart, Hossein Samiei, Giuseppe Tullio, Holger Wolf, and in particular José De Gregorio for discussions, clarifications, and comments. The views expressed do not necessarily reflect those of the International Monetary Fund.

facts, and the (sizeable) depreciation of both the lira and peseta after September 1992, suggest that both currencies were 'overvalued'. Overvaluation can only be ascertained relative to some notion of equilibrium real exchange rate: however, in the presence of diverging productivity developments, the equilibrium real exchange rate changes over time, making any assessment of actual developments more difficult.[1] Also, different measures of the real exchange rate seem to lead to different conclusions (compare Fig. 8.1 with Fig. 8.2, where real exchange rates are calculated on the basis of manufactured goods deflators). We have tried to throw some light on these issues by concentrating our attention on the interaction between (various measures of) the real exchange rate and relative prices and productivity developments in manufacturing and services within EC member countries.

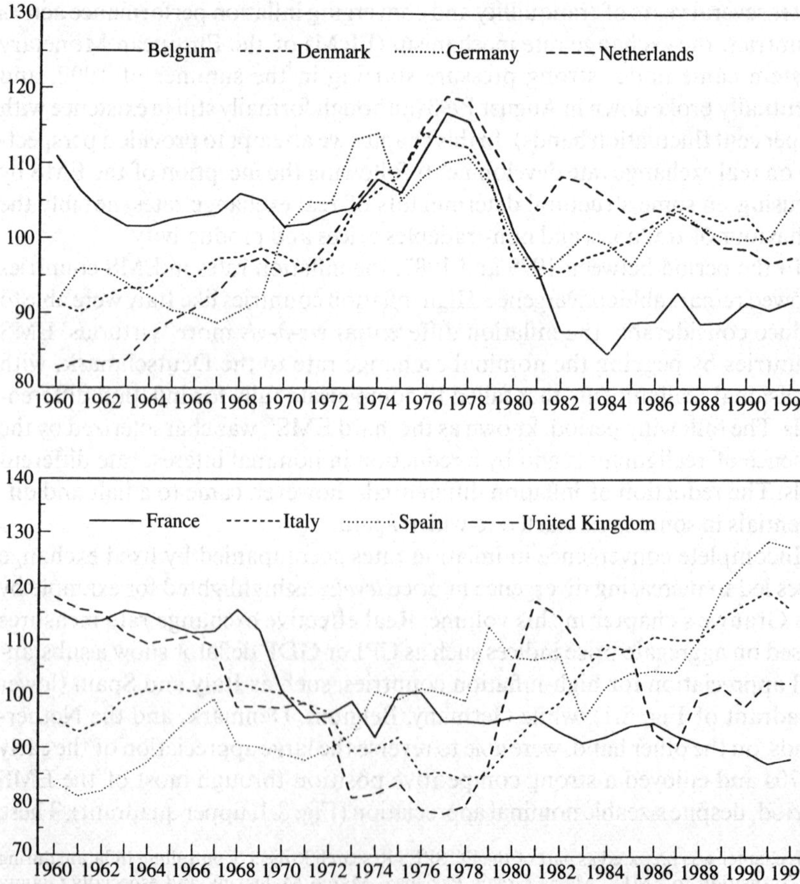

FIG. 8.1. Real effective intra-EC exchange rate (1960–92 average = 100)

[1] Barro (1983) and Bergstrand (1991), among others, focus on structural determinants of real exchange rates.

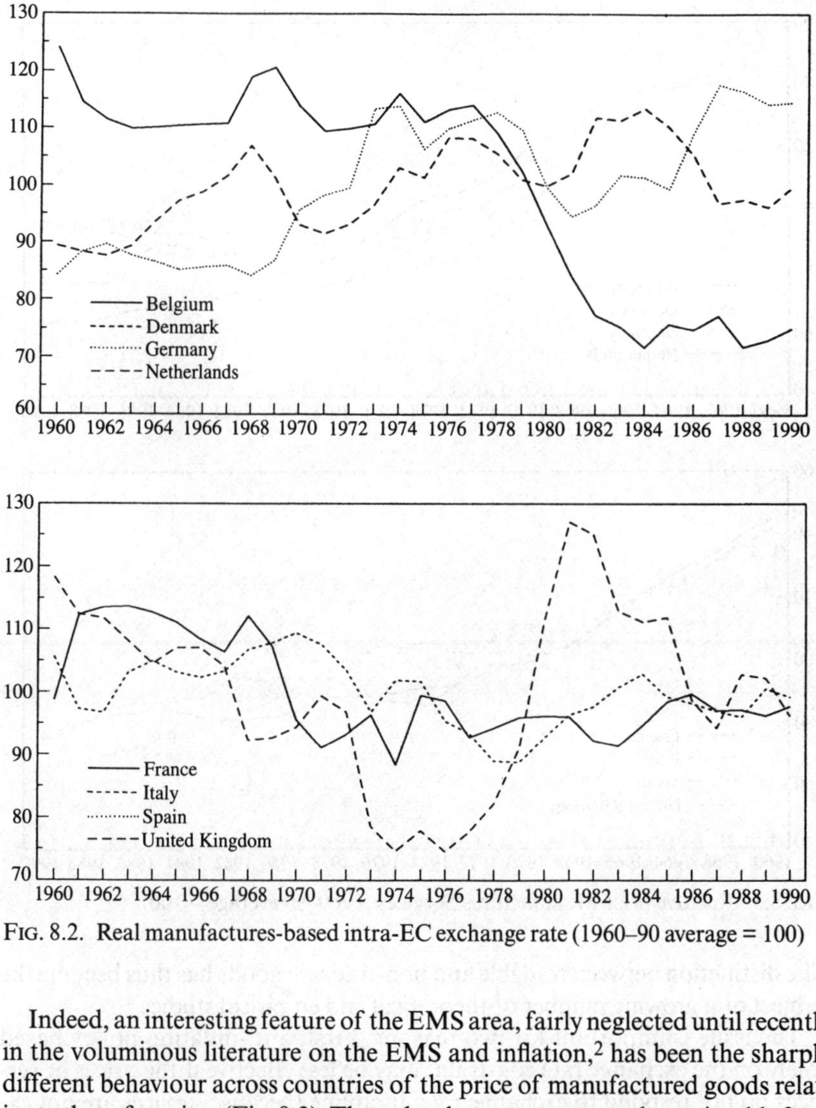

FIG. 8.2. Real manufactures-based intra-EC exchange rate (1960–90 average = 100)

Indeed, an interesting feature of the EMS area, fairly neglected until recently in the voluminous literature on the EMS and inflation,[2] has been the sharply different behaviour across countries of the price of manufactured goods relative to that of services (Fig. 8.3). These developments suggest that a sizeable fraction of the change in intra-European real exchange rates may have been driven by changes in domestic relative prices between tradable and non-tradable goods, rather than by changes in the price of tradable goods across countries.[3]

[2] See e.g. Giavazzi and Giovannini (1989) and the volumes edited by Giavazzi *et al.* (1988) and De Grauwe and Papademos (1990).

[3] Of course, if traded goods are perfect substitutes and there are no trade barriers then any real exchange rate change is necessarily driven by a change in the relative price of traded vs. non-traded goods.

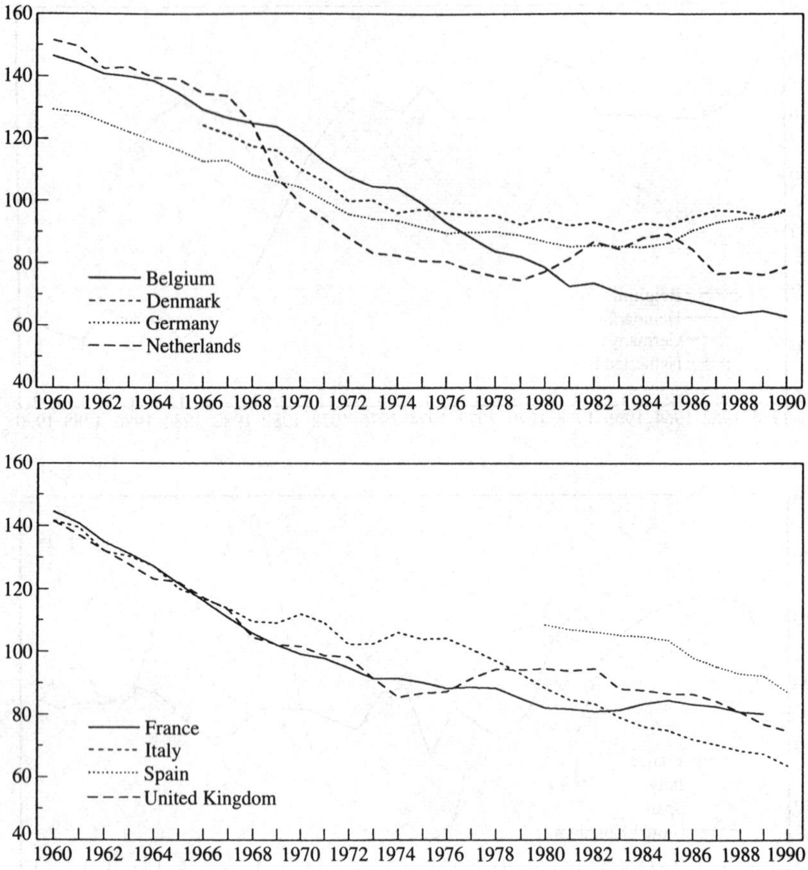

FIG. 8.3. Relative price Manufactures/Services (1960–90 average = 100)

The distinction between tradable and non-tradable goods has thus become the subject of a growing number of theoretical and empirical studies.[4]

The issue is important for two reasons. First, anti-inflation policy based solely on the exchange rate constraint may be less effective if the prices of services do not respond to exchange rate discipline (because services are not exposed to international competition). Second, if wages are equalized across sectors and their rate of increase is determined by productivity increases in manufacturing, then it is possible that productivity increases in manufacturing

[4] Recent papers using two-sector open-economy models to study the dynamics of real exchange rates are Froot and Rogoff (1991), De Gregorio *et al.* (1992), and De Gregorio *et al.* (1993). See also Eichengreen and Wyplosz (1993). The literature on exchange rate-based stabilizations in Latin America has addressed similar questions for a number of years. See e.g. Calvo and Vegh (1991), Kiguel and Liviatan (1992). In that literature the relative price tradables/non-tradables—defined as the real exchange rate—plays a key role.

induced by exchange rate discipline may have inflationary effects on wages and prices in the service sector (where productivity increases are much lower).[5]

This chapter is motivated by the desire to explain observed differences in the evolution of real exchange rate indicators over the years 1960–91 for a group of eight countries: Belgium, Denmark, France, Germany, Italy, the Netherlands, plus Spain and United Kingdom.[6] The EMS period is contrasted with the period 1960–78. The length of the sample allows us to perform a comparison of the pre-EMS and EMS periods, complementing other studies, such as Froot and Rogoff (1991), De Gregorio *et al.* (1993), and De Gregorio *et al.* (1993) that were based on shorter time-series.

The structure of this chapter is as follows. Section 2 presents a simple accounting framework, taken from Marston (1987), that links together several definitions of the real exchange rate; Section 3 identifies some simple 'stylized facts' concerning real exchange rates, productivity, and relative price developments: Section 4 presents empirical evidence on the determinants of real exchange rate behaviour; Section 5 concludes.

2. THE MODEL

We present below a simple accounting model that highlights the role of labour costs and productivity in determining real exchange rates; the model is a simplified version of Marston (1987). All variables are expressed in logarithmic terms. The equation for value added in each sector takes a Cobb–Douglas form, with exogenous technical progress:

$$V^{1} = (1 - c_i)L_i + c_iK^{i} + h^{i}i \qquad i = T, N, \tag{1}$$

where V is value added, K is capital, L is labour, h^i is technical progress in sector i and c_i is the capital share in sector i. The superscripts T and N indicate the traded- and non-traded-goods sector respectively; in what follows we identify traded goods with manufactures and non-traded goods with services.[7] Our analysis will be based on sectoral value added and value-added deflators, therefore excluding the effects of intermediate and imported inputs.[8]

5 The relation between productivity differentials in different sectors and the value of the real exchange rate was studied by Balassa (1964) and Samuelson (1964). During the 1970s the 'Scandinavian model' related inflation developments in a country with an 'imported' and a 'structural' component, where the latter depended on productivity differentials (see Lindbeck 1979). More recent intertemporal two-sector models with utility-maximizing consumers are presented, e.g. in Obstfeld (1992, 1993) and De Gregorio *et al.* (1993). These models show how persistent differentials in the rate of productivity growth between tradable and non-tradable goods can cause a fall over time of the relative price of traded goods.

6 For Spain we lack data on sectoral value-added deflators and on productivity prior to 1980.

7 See the discussion in Section 3.

8 This approach allows a more simplified treatment of the real exchange rate based on an aggregate index. If instead we focused on the consumer price index, we would have to take into account the role of the price of imports of final goods, as well as the role of intermediate and imported inputs in determining the final price of goods. See e.g. Marston (1987) and Lipschitz and McDonald (1992).

Labour productivity H is defined as follows:

$$H^i = V^i - L^i = c_i(K^i - L^i) + h^i t \qquad i = T, N. \tag{2}$$

There are two possible sources of labour productivity growth: one is exogenous technical progress (h^T) and the other is capital-deepening or labour-shedding. Ideally we would like to focus on the behaviour of total factor productivity, as De Gregorio *et al.* (1993) and De Gregorio *et al.* (1993). However, since consistent data on the evolution of the capital stock for the whole sample were not available, we focused instead on labour productivity, following Hsieh (1982) and Marston (1987). Since our empirical analysis is conducted on rates of change of variables, we hope that labour productivity is a reasonable approximation for total factor productivity. Assuming a constant mark-up over labour costs,[9] the relation between value-added deflator, wages, and productivity in each sector is given by:

$$P^i = W^i - H^i \qquad i = T, N. \tag{3}$$

With perfect labour mobility across sectors wages will be equalized, implying that the relative price of tradable goods in terms of non-tradables will depend on the productivity differential between the two sectors:[10]

$$P^T - P^N = H^T - H^N. \tag{4}$$

The aggregate GDP deflator is defined as follows:

$$P^V \equiv \alpha P^N + (1 - \alpha)P^T, \tag{5}$$

where α is the share of tradables in total value added and the superscript V indicates the aggregate value-added deflator.

Given these equations, we can relate the behaviour of various definitions of the real exchange rate to variables such as productivity, wage behaviour, and the relative price of tradable and non-tradable goods. Marston (1987) argues that supply-side effects can be detected by looking at the differential behaviour of various real exchange rate indicators. Consider the real exchange rate based on aggregate GDP and manufacturing deflators. Let X be the nominal exchange rate between the home country and the rest of the world (defined as the foreign currency price of a unit of domestic currency), and $R^i = P^i + X - P^{*i}$ the real exchange rate based the price index i. We can then express the real exchange rate based on the aggregate GDP deflator as follows (a star indicates foreign variables):

[9] Lipschitz and McDonald (1992) adopt a more elaborate model that allows for variability in profit margins. One of the advantages of their approach is that they are able to distinguish between the real exchange rate based on unit labour costs in the tradables sector and the one based on the value-added deflator in the same sector. Using the Marston approach these two measures are equivalent (see below).

[10] A similar relation between the relative price of tradable goods and productivity is derived from a utility-maximizing model in recent papers such as Obstfeld (1993) and De Gregorio *et al.* (1993).

$$R^{V} = (X + P^{T} - P^{T*}) - \alpha (P^{T} - P^{N}) + \alpha^{*} (P^{T*} - P^{N*}). \quad (6)$$

Clearly, when the domestic relative price of manufactured goods falls more than the foreign relative price, the real exchange rate based on GDP deflators will *appreciate* relative to that defined in terms of tradable goods alone.

Because of the assumption of constant mark-ups, the real exchange rate based on the value-added deflator in manufacturing, or services, is equal to the real exchange rate based on unit labour costs in the same sector. Define R^{ULC} as follows:

$$R^{ULC} = (W^{T} + X - W^{T*}) - (H^{T} - H^{T*}). \quad (7)$$

Equation (6) can then be expressed in terms of relative wages and productivity rates of change. Using (6) we obtain:

$$R^{V} = R^{ULC} + \alpha^{*}[(W^{T*} - W^{N*}) - (H^{T*} - H^{N*})] - \alpha[(W^{T} - W^{N}) - (H^{T} - H^{N})]. \quad (8)$$

If wage dynamics are the same in the tradable and non-tradable sectors, because of labour mobility across sectors, equation (8) simplifies to:

$$R^{V} = R^{ULC} + \alpha(H^{T} - H^{N}) - \alpha^{*}(H^{T*} - H^{N*}) \quad (9)$$

That is, if the differential in labour productivity between the tradables and the non-tradables sector is higher at home than abroad, then the real exchange rate based on value-added deflators will appreciate relative to that based on unit labour costs in manufacturing. This happens because a higher productivity differential between traded and non-traded goods causes higher wage and price increases in the non-traded goods sector, and hence an appreciation of R^{V}. Equations (4), (6) and (7) present different definitions of the real exchange rate: the relative GDP deflators and the relative unit labour costs in manufacturing, expressed in common currency, and the relative price of tradables in terms of non-tradables. Together with (8) these relations highlight various factors that can account for the different behaviour of these measures of real exchange rates.

3. STYLIZED FACTS

Before turning to empirical analysis, it is useful to review some stylized facts in the data. As we mentioned, we take manufactured goods, excluding construction, as tradables, and services as non-tradables. This classification is often used in the literature. An alternative approach (e.g. Hsieh, 1982) is to identify some appropriate notion of traded goods and then take the residual value added as non-traded. This approach has the obvious advantage of complete coverage of the value added. We have preferred the former, however, because it allows a more accurate measure of productivity in services, a very important variable in the analysis, and because our approach excludes agricultural prices that are heavily distorted. As stated in the previous section, we have focused on GDP deflators rather than consumer price indices, because the latter are also influenced by import prices.

(*a*) *Relative price tradables/non-tradables.* As can be seen in Table 8.1 and Fig. 8.3, during the 1980s the relative price of manufactures in terms of services fell considerably in Belgium, Italy, Spain, and the UK, while it was stable or rising in Denmark, France, Germany, and the Netherlands. During the 1960s and 1970s, the relative price of manufactured goods in terms of services shows instead a clear declining trend in all countries. The average inflation differential between manufactures and services during the period 1961–80 varies between a minimum of 2 per cent in Germany and a maximum of 3.5 per cent in the Netherlands. This trend stops in 'core' countries during the 1980s (the inflation differential even changes sign in Denmark, Germany, and the Netherlands), while it continues unabated in Italy, Spain, and the United Kingdom.

(*b*) *Productivity.* Data on productivity growth rates across countries and sectors are presented in Table 8.2. In the 1980s, labour-productivity growth in

TABLE 8.1. *Price increases in EC Countries (1960–1990)* (Value added deflators, average yearly percentage changes)

Countries	1961–70	1971–80	1980–90	1987–90
	Total VA deflator			
Belgium	3.4	7.1	4.4	2.8
Denmark	5.9	9.7	5.7	3.6
France	4.4	9.5	6.3	3.0
Germany	3.8	5.2	2.9	2.4
Italy	4.9	15.5	10.1	5.9
Netherlands	5.2	7.6	2.3	1.5
Spain	6.4	15.2	9.5	6.5
United Kingdom	4.2	14.0	6.3	6.3
EC	4.7	11.3	6.1	4.2
Standard dev.	3.8	22.5	25.8	9.3
	VA manufacturing			
Belgium	1.7	3.9	2.7	0.9
Denmark	—	8.1	6.2	4.3
France	3.6	8.5	6.2	2.3
Germany	2.1	4.2	3.1	2.2
Italy	3.1	13.4	7.8	3.7
Netherlands	2.5	5.8	2.5	0.1
Spain	—	—	7.6	4.1
United Kingdom	2.2	13.4	4.8	3.2
	VA services			
Belgium	3.8	8.3	5.0	2.9
Denmark	—	9.8	5.9	3.6
France	5.9	10.4	6.8	3.7
Germany	4.3	6.2	2.0	0.5
Italy	5.6	16.1	11.3	7.0
Netherlands	7.0	8.4	2.3	1.9
Spain	—	16.3	10.0	7.3
United Kingdom	5.6	14.2	7.3	7.0

TABLE 8.2. *Labour productivity (1961–1990)* (average yearly percentage changes)

Countries	1961–70	1971–80	1981–90	1987–90
		Total		
Belgium	4.3	3.2	1.8	2.4
Denmark	3.9	1.6	1.6	1.2
France	4.9	3.2	2.2	2.5
Germany	4.0	2.6	1.7	2.4
Italy	6.1	2.6	1.7	2.6
Netherlands	3.9	2.7	1.4	1.2
Spain	6.7	4.2	1.8	1.2
United Kingdom	2.7	1.7	1.9	0.5
		Manufacturing		
Belgium	5.9	6.4	4.5	4.6
Denmark	—	4.2	0.7	0.3
France	7.1	3.9	2.9	3.3
Germany	4.3	3.2	2.0	2.9
Italy	6.5	4.8	4.1	4.1
Netherlands	6.0	5.4	2.0	1.6
Spain	—	—	2.3	0.7
United Kingdom	3.1	1.4	4.9	3.7
		Services		
Belgium	3.1	1.7	0.9	1.5
Denmark	—	0.4	1.3	0.8
France	2.6	2.0	1.6	1.9
Germany	4.9	1.7	1.9	2.8
Italy	3.7	1.3	0.2	1.6
Netherlands	2.4	1.8	0.9	0.6
Spain	—	—	–0.6	–2.6
United Kingdom	1.4	1.0	1.0	0.3

manufacturing outstripped that of services by more than two and a half percentage points in Belgium, Italy, Spain, and the United Kingdom. In Italy, the average growth rate of productivity in manufacturing was one of the highest among the countries in our sample, while productivity in services was the second lowest. Productivity-growth differentials between manufactured goods and services were much lower (or negative) in Denmark, France, Germany, and the Netherlands. Interestingly, productivity growth in manufacturing slowed down in the 1980s compared with the 1970s for all countries except the United Kingdom. This slow-down is particularly large in Denmark and the Netherlands (more than 3 per cent). These two countries, as well as France, showed rapid productivity growth in manufacturing in the 1960s and 1970s, with large differentials in productivity-growth rates between manufacturing and services.

We must also take into account the possibility that quality changes may not be appropriately accounted for in aggregate price indices, thus underestimating productivity growth.

(*c*) *Real exchange rates*. In the EMS years GDP-deflator-based RERs show depreciation or stability, relative to the 1970s, for the DM-area countries, France, and the United Kingdom, appreciation for Italy and Spain (Fig. 8.1 and Table 8.3). Manufactures-deflator-based RERs, on the other hand, show a strong depreciation for the Belgian franc, appreciation for the Deutschmark (some 9 per cent), relative stability for the other countries, with high variability for the United Kingdom (Fig. 8.2). For most countries, cumulative changes in the manufactures deflator-based RER were smaller than in the total deflator-based RER (Germany and Belgium stand as the exceptions).

(*d*) *Shares in value added and real trade developments*. The observed changes in sector shares in value added and real trade balance can in principle offer a clue as to the real nature of observed changes in real exchange rates: one could argue, for example, that a constant or increasing share of manufacturing could be taken as evidence against overvaluation of a country's currency, and the same would be true for improving trade balances. However, the picture that

TABLE 8.3. *Real exchange rates of EC countries**

Countries	1960–78		1979–92	
	Mean	Coeff. of variation	Mean	Coeff. of variation
		Global		
Belgium	105.3	0.05	92.2	0.10
Denmark	99.5	0.08	100.7	0.05
France	105.2	0.07	92.4	0.05
Germany	100.5	0.08	99.3	0.06
Italy	96.1	0.06	105.7	0.09
Netherlands	97.3	0.13	103.9	0.06
Spain	92.7	0.08	110.7	0.11
United Kingdom	97.9	0.11	103.1	0.08
		Intra-EC		
Belgium	105.7	0.05	91.7	0.07
Denmark	99.8	0.08	100.3	0.04
France	105.5	0.08	92.0	0.03
Germany	99.9	0.09	100.0	0.03
Italy	95.8	0.06	106.1	0.10
Netherlands	97.6	0.13	103.6	0.04
Spain	92.8	0.07	110.5	0.09
United Kingdom	98.4	0.14	102.3	0.09
		Intra-EC, Manufacturing		
Belgium	112.5	0.03	79.3	0.12
France	102.7	0.09	96.1	0.02
Germany	96.7	0.12	106.3	0.08
Italy	101.4	0.05	97.5	0.04
Netherlands	98.1	0.07	103.8	0.06
United Kingdom	94.3	0.14	107.1	0.11

* Exchange rate indices with base 100 = average 1960–92.

emerges from the data is far from clear.[11] The real share of manufacturing in total GDP in 1980–90 rose in Italy and fell in Spain, and both were apparently appreciating and experiencing a large decline in the relative price of manufactured goods. The share also rose in Belgium, where relative prices of manufactures declined, but fell in France (fairly stable real exchange rate and relative price of manufactures), Germany and Denmark (rising relative price of manufactures), and the Netherlands (real depreciation, falling relative price of manufactures after 1983). Germany, on the other hand, shows a large improvement in its trade balance, and so do Belgium, Denmark, and the Netherlands; Italy and Spain show wider deficits.

In sum, while trade balance data would seem to confirm roughly the picture of real exchange rate changes described above, developments in sectoral shares would point to more complex interpretations.

4. EMPIRICAL EVIDENCE

4.1 Real exchange rates based on GDP deflators

We first examine real effective exchange rates constructed using GDP deflators in a group of EC countries. We have used a 'global' exchange rate, constructed with world trade weights, and an 'EC' based on intra-EC trade weights. For reasons of data availability, the countries considered are: Belgium, Denmark, France, Germany, Italy, the Netherlands, Spain, and the United Kingdom. A glance at Fig. 8.1 suggests the existence of a high correlation between real exchange rate movements in Germany and those of the three small economies—Belgium, Denmark, and the Netherlands, also in the period 1960–78.

Table 8.4 presents the correlation matrix between global real exchange rates at yearly frequency, both for the pre-EMS and the EMS period; Spain and the United Kingdom are also included, even though these two countries joined the exchange rate mechanism of the EMS only in 1990. In the pre-EMS period, the French franc and the Italian lira have a high negative correlation with the DM; for the French franc this becomes positive during the EMS period (0.74). For the Italian lira the negative correlation drops from –0.74 to –0.15. The correlation with the German real exchange rate also increases in the EMS period for Belgium, Denmark, and the United Kingdom, while it remained more or less constant for the Netherlands and Spain. The variability of real effective exchange rates at yearly frequency, measured with the coefficient of variation,[12] fell during the EMS period for Denmark, France, Germany, the Netherlands, and the United Kingdom; it increased for Italy, Belgium, and

[11] We computed the share of manufacturing in value added and the trade balance, in current and constant (1985) prices, for the periods 1970–2, 1979–82, and 1989–91. The results are not reported here, but are available from the authors upon request.

[12] We focus on the coefficient of variation, rather than the standard error, because there are differences in the mean of the variables between the two subperiods.

TABLE 8.4. *Real effective exchange rates correlations*

	Belgium	Denmark	France	Germany	Italy	Nether-lands	Spain
1960–78							
Denmark	0.810						
France	–0.487	–0.694					
Germany	0.621	0.813	–0.885				
Italy	–0.874	–0.729	0.538	–0.746			
Netherlands	0.802	0.976	–0.775	0.827	–0.705		
Spain	0.630	0.876	–0.555	0.578	–0.444	0.854	
United Kingdom	–0.655	–0.895	0.797	–0.827	0.629	–0.941	–0.729
1979–92							
Denmark	0.786						
France	0.901	0.575					
Germany	0.900	0.913	0.746				
Italy	–0.407	0.035	–0.563	–0.156			
Netherlands	0.870	0.600	0.869	0.815	–0.671		
Spain	0.508	0.593	0.267	0.571	0.453	0.176	
United Kingdom	–0.183	–0.320	0.313	–0.041	–0.273	0.212	0.187

Spain. The variability of inter-European real exchange rates shows similar behaviour.

We also performed a simple time-series analysis with the purpose of identifying trends and structural breaks in inter-European real exchange rates. For all countries we were unable to reject the null hypothesis that the real exchange rate follows a random walk, using standard Dickey–Fuller and augmented Dickey–Fuller tests. This is a well-known result; one must however take into account that in such a short sample (1960–92) unit root tests have very limited power against alternative hypotheses with highly persistent autoregressive processes.

Visual inspection suggests a change in behaviour since the inception of the EMS in 1979. Following Perron (1989) (see also Campbell and Perron 1991) we allowed for a possible structural break, in the form of a change in the intercept, following the inception of the EMS.[13] At the 5 per cent confidence level, we were able to reject the random-walk hypothesis only for two of the smaller 'core' countries (Belgium and Denmark), and only for the intra-EC real exchange rate.[14] Thus, the evidence of a break based on this simple time-series analysis is weak.

4.2 *Real exchange rates based on manufactured goods' prices*

The analysis of the variability of intra-European real exchange rates based on manufacturing deflators for the pre-EMS and EMS periods yields results

[13] Test statistics and significance levels are tabulated in Perron (1989).

[14] The EMS dummy is generally significant in first-difference regressions. Tests, not reported for reasons of space, are available from the authors.

similar to those described above. Table 8.3 reports means and coefficients of variation for this real exchange rate measure for the periods 1960–78 and 1979–90. Interestingly, we find that in Italy the variability of this real exchange rate measure drops from 5.4 per cent to 3.8 per cent. Only for Belgium there is an increase in the variability of this real exchange rate measure. This suggests that the behaviour of services' prices may account for the increased volatility of the lira real exchange rate during the 1980s. We also performed standard non-stationarity tests, allowing for the possibility of a structural break following the inception of the EMS. The results of the tests, not reported, can be summarized as follows. Only for Belgium can one reject the unit root in favour of a trend-stationary autoregressive specification with a break in 1980. For all the other countries the EMS dummy is insignificant at standard confidence levels. This evidence, admittedly based on tests with low power, seems to suggest that the impact of the EMS has mainly affected the relative price of tradable goods in each country.

4.3 Decomposition of real exchange rate changes

In order to disentangle the impact of changes in the relative price of tradables in each country from that of changes in tradables' prices across countries we have decomposed the changes in the real effective exchange rate (measured with aggregate GDP deflators) during the 1980s into changes in the real exchange rate based on tradable goods' prices and changes in the relative price of tradable goods in the home country and 'abroad', based on equation (6). The results are reported in Table 8.5.[15] The fourth column of the Table ('residual') is the percentage change in the real exchange rate that is accounted for by changes in the relative price of manufactured goods in terms of services at home and abroad.[16] As can be seen by comparing columns 1 and 4, the appreciation of the Italian lira and the Spanish peseta is explained almost entirely by changes in the relative price of manufactured good in terms of services, rather than by changes in the relative price of manufactured goods across countries (RER based on manufactured goods' deflators). The large positive 'residuals' for Belgium and the United Kingdom indicate that for both countries the large depreciation of the real exchange rate based on manufacturing deflators has been mitigated by changes in the relative price of manufactures in terms of services. In Germany the RER based on manufactures' deflators appreciated by over 9 per cent, but this was offset by a sharp fall in the relative price of manufactured goods in terms of services abroad.[17] Overall, the table highlights the importance

[15] One should remember, here, that our definition of tradable goods (manufactured goods) and non-tradable goods (services) is not exhaustive since the sum of the two sectors does not add up to total value added.

[16] The exchange rate index is constructed so that an increase in its value corresponds to an appreciation of the currency.

[17] Giuseppe Tullio suggested to us that the appreciation of the manufactures-deflator-based

TABLE 8.5. *Decomposition of exchange rate changes (1980–1990)* (per centage terms)

	q (1)	e (2)	(p_T/p_T^*) (3)	*residual* (4)	(p_N/p_T) (5)	(p_N^*/p_T^*) (6)
Belgium						
intra-EC	–9.6	–3.2	–18.7	14.9	25.1	8.1
v. DM	–9.8	–21.6	–4.1	20.0	—	–10.0
Denmark						
intra-EC	6.3	–12.1	18.4	2.1	–3.0	9.5
v. DM	5.9	–19.0	34.5	1.0	—	–10.0
France						
intra-EC	–7.1	–16.1	17.1	–5.5	5.9	14.2
v. DM	–4.8	–30.9	35.6	1.6	—	–10.0
Germany						
intra-EC	–0.6	36.3	–19.9	–9.0	–3.0	18.9
v. DM	—	—	—	—	—	
Italy						
intra-EC	28.6	–24.0	37.6	22.9	38.6	3.8
v. DM	25.2	–36.6	55.7	26.8	—	–10.0
Netherlands						
intra-EC	–8.5	20.1	–19.1	–6.4	–1.9	10.2
v. DM	–8.2	–2.9	–5.9	0.5	—	–10.0
Spain						
intra-EC	15.9	–20.9	28.1	14.3	24.6	9.6
v. DM	16.1	–37.5	53.5	21.0	—	–10.0
United Kingdom						
intra-EC	–6.8	–16.1	–0.2	11.3	26.3	9.6
v. DM	–5.6	–31.8	17.7	17.6	—	–10.0

(1) Real exchange rate based on total value added deflator.
(2) Nominal exchange rate.
(3) Relative deflator of manufacturing.
(4) [1 + (1)/100]/{ [1 + (2)/100}*[1 + (3)/100] } – 1
(5) Relative deflator: non-tradables versus tradables, domestic.
(6) Relative deflator: non-tradables versus tradables, foreign.
Source: OECD.

of domestic relative price developments for the evolution of real exchange rates. In the following section we focus directly on the relative price of traded goods and on productivity.

4.4. The relative price of tradable goods

It appears that a main reason of divergence between manufactures-deflator-based and GDP-deflator-based real exchange rate is the behaviour of the

RER for Germany in the 1980s may be in part caused by quality changes, especially for capital goods.

relative price of tradables vs. non-tradables.[18] For this reason, we first performed a simple time-series analysis of the relative price of tradable goods: for the whole sample (1961–90), one cannot reject the null hypothesis that the relative price p^T/p^N follows a random walk with a negative drift. Since the level series shows non-stationarity, we focused our attention on rates of change in this relative price over time.

According to equation (5), differences in productivity growth between the tradables and non-tradables sector will cause changes in the relative price of tradable goods. Following De Gregorio *et al.* (1993), we took into account two additional variables that may affect the behaviour of the relative price of tradable goods, namely the change in (GDP deflator) inflation and the GDP growth rate. The former variable is there to capture possible inertial factors that may cause inflation to decelerate more slowly in the non-tradables sector during a disinflation; it may also account for some of the effects of oil shocks—an increase in the price of oil raises overall inflation but has a stronger impact on the price of tradable goods. More generally, this variable can capture cyclical influences on the behaviour of the relative price of tradable goods.[19] As for the GDP growth rate, if the elasticity of services' consumption with respect to income is larger than one, then high-income growth would be associated with a more than proportional increase in the demand for non-tradable goods, thus causing an increase in their relative price.[20]

A shortcoming with using these variables is that they can hardly be taken as exogenous; on the other hand, we lacked appropriate instruments for instrumental variable correction. As these countries are relatively similar and highly integrated, it is possible that exogenous shocks hitting the EC may be responsible for common changes in the relative price of tradables. We ended up estimating single-country regressions with seemingly unrelated regressions (SUR), to allow for the covariance between error terms in the relative price equations. For each country, the regression equation is:

$$(\hat{p}^T_{it} - \hat{p}^N_{it}) = \beta_{0i}(\hat{H}^T_{it} - \hat{H}^N_{it}) + \beta_{1i}EMS + \beta_{2i}(\hat{p}^Y_{it} - \hat{p}^Y_{i,t-1}) + \beta_{3i}GROWTH_{it} + \varepsilon_{it}. \tag{10}$$

The variable EMS takes value equal to unity in the years 1979–90, and is introduced in order to capture potential effects of the nominal exchange rate regime on relative price developments. According to our simple accounting framework, the coefficient β_{0i} should be negative and equal to unity in absolute value. If inertial factors are present in the determination of non-tradables' prices the coefficient β_{2i} should have a positive sign; if the elasticity of demand for

18 See also Kravis and Lipsey (1988), and De Gregorio *et al.* evidence on OECD countries.

19 The latter interpretation is consistent with Sommariva and Tullio (1987).

20 Froot and Rogoff (1991) argue that government spending is an important determinant of the relative price of tradable goods since it falls mainly on non-tradable goods, and present some empirical evidence in support of their view. De Gregorio *et al.* (1993) find instead little evidence of an impact of government spending on the relative price of tradables. See also Dornbusch (1991).

TABLE 8.6. *Determinants of relative price changes. Dependent variable: Relative price of manufactures in terms of services (Rates of change) 1966–1990, seemingly unrelated regressions* (t-statistics in parentheses)

	Constant		Prod. diff.		EMS		Inflation		Growth		$\bar{R}^2$
Belgium	−2.13	(−2.32)**	−0.33	(−2.33)**	1.15	(1.35)					0.07
	−2.65	(−3.21)**	−0.22	(−1.62)	1.21	(1.59)	0.66	(3.72)**			0.25
	−3.93	(−4.13)**	−0.17	(−1.36)	1.70	(2.24)**	0.73	(4.37)**	0.29	(1.77)*	0.28
Denmark	−1.35	(−2.14)**	−0.26	(−2.46)**	1.54	(1.90)*					0.35
	−1.26	(−2.00)**	−0.26	(−2.46)**	1.36	(1.66)*	−0.13	(−0.55)			0.32
	−0.77	(−0.81)	−0.41	(−3.86)**	0.32	(0.37)	−0.30	(−1.36)	−0.51	(−2.70)**	0.40
France	−1.74	(−3.67)**	−0.30	(−2.73)**	2.00	(3.73)**					0.30
	−1.41	(−2.70)**	−0.35	(−2.64)**	1.18	(1.83)*	−0.289	(−1.41)			0.35
	−0.77	(−1.18)	−0.32	(−1.97)**	0.89	(1.41)	−0.238	(−1.07)	−0.19	(−0.95)	0.33
Germany	−1.64	(−3.15)**	−0.17	(−1.39)	2.26	(3.18)**					0.32
	−1.41	(−2.70)**	−0.31	(−2.48)**	2.01	(2.84)**	−0.22	(−0.90)			0.27
	−1.46	(−2.09)**	−0.37	(−2.45)**	1.95	(2.74)**	−0.20	(−0.68)	0.04	(0.27)	0.23
Italy	−1.65	(−2.27)**	0.01	(0.10)	−1.83	(−2.12)**					0.09
	−1.85	(−2.60)**	0.01	(0.08)	−1.51	(−1.77)*	0.29	(2.00)**			0.16
	−1.11	(−0.27)	0.14	(0.90)	−1.98	(−2.14)**	0.41	(2.57)**	−0.30	(−1.27)	0.08
Netherlands	−2.50	(−1.41)	−0.45	(−1.69)*	3.26	(1.67)*					0.27
	−2.53	(−1.44)	−0.46	(−1.70)*	3.35	(1.70)*	0.29	(0.04)			0.23
	0.87	(−0.50)	0.57	(0.21)	2.17	(1.31)	0.49	(1.03)	−1.31	(−3.74)**	0.43
UK	−1.02	(−1.54)	−0.43	(−3.02)**							0.16
	−1.54	(0.91)	−0.65	(−4.22)**			−0.41	(−3.49)**			0.30
	0.23	(0.31)	−0.57	(−3.26)**			−0.42	(−3.40)**	−0.40	(−1.73)*	0.24

* Significant at the 10% confidence level.
** Significant at the 5% confidence level.

non-tradables with respect to income is larger than one, we would expect the coefficient β_{3i} to be negative.

The results are presented in Table 8.6.[21] The coefficient of the productivity differential is significant for most countries and has the right sign. It is, however, significantly smaller than one: indeed, it is higher than 0.5 only for the United Kingdom. For Italy and Belgium we find that the coefficient of the change in the inflation rate is significant and has a positive sign: this means that indeed when inflation slows down (accelerates) the inflation differential between the two sectors widens (shrinks). The coefficient is insignificant for Denmark, France, Germany, and the Netherlands, and has a negative sign for the United Kingdom.

Higher growth rates are associated with a widening inflation differential between tradable and non-tradable goods in Belgium, Denmark, and especially the Netherlands. The EMS dummy is significant and positive for Belgium, Germany, and France. In this last case, the dummy takes the value of one from 1983 onwards, which implies that the rate of decline of the relative price of tradable goods slowed during the EMS period. There is instead some evidence of an *acceleration* in the decline of the relative price of tradable goods in Italy, while for the remaining countries the dummy is insignificant. The country-specific constants are significant and negative for Belgium, Germany, and Italy, indicating a trend depreciation which is unaccounted for by productivity developments.

Overall, the empirical evidence confirms the importance of productivity differentials in explaining the behaviour of the relative price of traded goods. At yearly frequency, however, productivity differentials are not reflected one-to-one into changes in the relative price of tradable goods, as our accounting model would suggest. Indeed, if we constrain the coefficient on productivity-growth differentials to be equal across countries, it takes the value 0.26 and is highly significant (regression not reported). Furthermore, for some countries there is a significant drift term in the relative price of tradable goods that is unrelated to productivity. One possible explanation is that our results are contaminated by short-run demand effects, not captured by the growth and change in inflation variables.

In order to focus more clearly on the long-run determinants of the relative price of tradable goods we also plotted the (average) inflation and productivity growth differentials between manufactured goods and services over ten year periods (1961–70, 1971–80, and 1981–90; see Fig. 8.4); the 45-degree line is also shown in the figure. The scatter plot seems to show a high correlation between inflation and productivity differentials over the long term. In the case of Italy, for example, the average productivity-growth differential over each decade is very close to the average inflation differential, even though at yearly frequency productivity growth differentials do not 'explain' inflation differentials very

[21] The SURs were also performed for a longer time-period (1961–90) excluding Denmark (for which productivity data are available starting in 1966). Results were in line with those presented in Table 8.6.

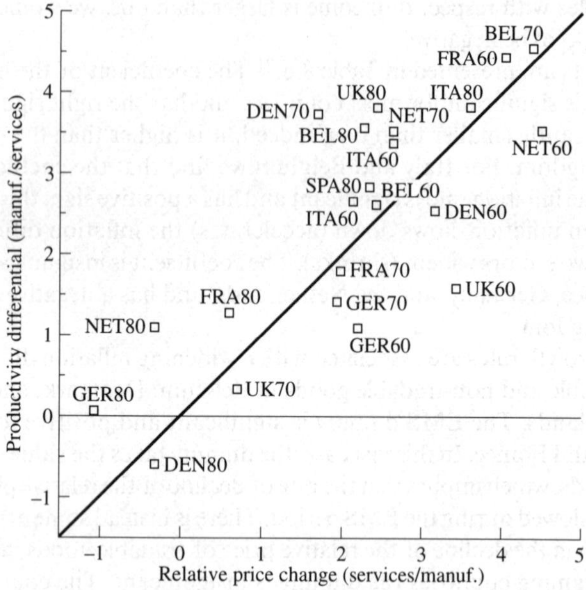

FIG. 8.4. Relative price and productivity (average change 1961–70, 1971–80, 1981–90)

well. Using pooled data on decade-long averages, we regressed the average change in the relative price of traded goods on the average productivity differential, average growth rates, and a dummy for the 1980s. The results were as follows (t-statistics in parentheses):

$$\hat{p}^{\mathrm{T}}_{it} - \hat{p}^{\mathrm{N}}_{it} = \underset{(-5.4)}{-0.7}(\hat{H}^{\mathrm{T}}_{it} - \hat{H}^{\mathrm{N}}_{it}) - \underset{(-2.36)}{0.23}\, GROWTH + \underset{(2.36)}{0.706}\, DUM80 \qquad (11)$$
$$R^2 = 0.76$$

As can be seen, the coefficient of productivity differentials is higher than in the SURs; also, the coefficient on growth is significant, and so is the dummy for the 1980s, indicating a slow-down or reversal in the decline of the relative price of tradable goods. Analogous results are obtained if one replaces the 1980's dummy with an EMS dummy.[22] Overall, the evidence is consistent with a large long-run impact of productivity differentials on sectoral inflation differentials. There is also some evidence that countries that grow faster tend to have higher intersectoral inflation differentials, and that the 1980s were characterized by a reduction in inflation differentials between sectors, even after controlling for productivity developments and growth.[23]

[22] The difference between the two dummies is the value of the coefficient for Spain and the UK, which did not belong to the EMS until 1990. Focusing on a larger sample of countries may allow to establish whether the change in relative price developments during the last decade is exclusively a feature of EMS countries.

[23] De Gregorio *et al.* (1993), using a sample with more countries, find that the average productivity growth differential over the period 1970–85 has a coefficient insignificantly different from unity in a cross-section regression. They also find that growth is insignificant.

4.5 Unit labour costs and productivity differentials

The evidence in the previous sections seems to confirm that relative price changes and productivity differentials can account for a good deal of the observed divergence between different real exchange rate measures. We now want to examine the behaviour of the real exchange rate based on unit labour costs in manufacturing. For Italy, this measure of the real exchange rate shows a less pronounced appreciation than the real exchange rate based on the aggregate GDP deflator. Our theoretical framework of Section 2 suggests that productivity differentials between tradables and non-tradables may account for this difference in behaviour. For each country, we regressed the change in the real exchange rate measured with the aggregate GDP deflators on the change of the real exchange rate measured with unit labour costs in manufacturing and on the productivity growth differential between sectors at home and 'abroad':

$$\hat{R}^{V}_{it} = \beta_{0i}\,\hat{R}^{ULC}_{it} + \beta_{1i}(\hat{H}^{T}_{it} - \hat{H}^{N}_{it}) + \beta_{2i}(\hat{H}^{T}_{it} - \hat{H}^{N}_{it}). \quad (12)$$

With this regression we try to determine what fraction of the difference between the dynamic behaviour of R^{V} and R^{ULC} can be 'explained' by productivity differentials. A similar approach was followed by earlier studies on the impact of productivity differentials and relative price changes on real exchange rate behaviour, such as Hsieh (1982) and Marston (1987).[24] The productivity differentials for the 'foreign' country were constructed with the same weights used for the construction of the real exchange rate. The sample we consider is shorter (1970–90) because of data availability. Our simple model would imply that β_{0i} is equal to unity and that the coefficients on the productivity differentials, in absolute terms, are equal to the shares of non-tradable goods in value added (see equation (9)).

The results are presented in Table 8.7; for reference, Table 8.2 shows labour-productivity growth rates in the manufactures and services sectors. The point estimate for the coefficient β_{0i} is smaller than one for all countries, consistently with the results obtained in the studies by Hsieh and Marston. A larger differential in productivity growth rates between manufactures and services should cause the real exchange rate based on GDP deflators to appreciate with respect to the one based on unit labour costs in manufacturing because it raises wage inflation in the non-tradable goods sector. For most countries, results are consistent with the theory. The exception is Denmark, where productivity differentials do not explain the different behaviour of the two deflators. Overall, Table 8.7 highlights the important role of productivity developments in explaining divergences between different real exchange rate indicators.

24 Hsieh defines non-tradables as the GDP complement to manufacturing.

TABLE 8.7. *Real Exchange Rate Measures and Productivity Differentials (1970–1990) Dependent variable: Real effective exchange rate* (Rate of change) (GDP deflators, EC weights)*

	R^{ULC}	Prod. differ.	For. prod. differ.	R^2
Belgium	0.698 (11.67)	0.40 (3.02)	–0.53 (–2.09)	0.89
Denmark	0.561 (5.17)	0.10 (0.73)	0.29 (1.60)	0.76
France	0.751 (9.98)	0.29 (1.24)	–0.24 (–1.47)	0.86
Germany	0.744 (10.80)	0.60 (3.52)	–0.60 (–3.90)	0.88
Italy	0.717 (8.88)	0.76 (6.12)	–1.10 (–4.42)	0.85
Netherlands	0.693 (7.18)	0.51 (3.22)	–0.05 (0.84)	0.78
United Kingdom	0.936 (12.90)	0.62 (2.67)	–0.62 (–2.30)	0.92

* Ordinary Least Squares, *t*-Statistics in parentheses.

5. CONCLUDING REMARKS

This chapter has highlighted some interesting facts in the behaviour of various real exchange rate indicators in countries belonging to the European Community, and provided some evidence on the role of productivity in driving real exchange rate developments in EEC countries, especially in the longer run. Differences in productivity growth rates between manufactures and services and between countries help explain real exchange rate behaviour and account for the 'puzzle' of the different behaviour of different real exchange rate measures. The behaviour of relative prices seems to have been affected by the exchange rate regime, at least in some of the countries, although the channel through which this occurred is unclear. We also provided some evidence of inertial factors in the non-traded-goods sector (widening inflation differential between sectors when inflation falls and vice versa) in Belgium and in Italy.

Regarding productivity developments, we are unable to infer whether productivity growth was spurred by the exchange rate regime (the increases in productivity in the tradables sector were dictated by the need to remain competitive in the absence of any accommodation of higher inflation through devaluation) or whether productivity growth caused the appreciation of the real exchange rate, regardless of the exchange rate regime. In other words, an alternative explanation of our finding is that the discipline provided by a (semi-)fixed exchange rate has forced the manufacturing sectors of weak-currency countries into large restructuring and productivity increases. The fact that productivity growth in manufacturing in Italy did not accelerate during the EMS period (although productivity *differentials* widened) may be interpreted as supporting the 'productivity to real exchange rate' nexus. However, the 1980s were characterized by a generalized decline in productivity growth in industrialized economies. The widening of the productivity differential between tradables and non-tradables in Italy may also suggest that the exchange rate regime and the lira's appreciation have raised productivity in the manufacturing sector.[25]

[25] We are grateful to Paul De Grauwe for this suggestion.

APPENDIX: *Data Sources and Definitions*

Gross Domestic Product: OECD, National Income Accounts
Value added and deflators, manufacturing and services: OECD, National Income Accounts
Total employment, manufacturing and services: OECD, National Income Accounts
Total income, manufacturing and services: OECD, National Income Accounts
Exchange rates: IMF, International Finance Statistics
Exports and imports: IMF, International Finance Statistics

'Services' defined as 'Market Services' (excluding public administration)
'Manufacturing' defined as industry minus construction
'Unit labour costs in manufacturing' defined as income per worker over unit of output per worker in the manufacturing sector
The OECD series have been integrated with elaborations by the Centro Studi Confindustria, Rome

BIBLIOGRAPHY

Alogoskoufis, G. (1990), 'Traded Goods, Competitiveness and Aggregate Fluctuations in the United Kingdom', *Economic Journal*, 100.

Balassa, B. (1964), 'The Purchasing Power Parity Doctrine: A Reappraisal', *Journal of Political Economy*, 72 (Dec.): 584–96.

Barro, R. J. (1983), 'Real Determinants of Real Exchange Rates', mimeo, University of Chicago.

Bergstrand, J. H. (1991), 'Structural Determinants of Real Exchange Rates and National Price Levels: Some Empirical Evidence', *American Economic Review*, 81 (Mar.): 325–34.

Calvo, G., and C. Vegh (1991), 'Exchange Rate-Based Stabilization: The Dynamics of Non-Credible Policy', mimeo, International Monetary Fund.

Campbell, J. Y., and P. Perron (1991), 'Pitfalls and Opportunities: What Macroeconomists Should Know About Unit Roots', *NBER Macroeconomics Annual*, 6.

De Gregorio, J., A. Giovannini, and T. Krueger (1993), 'The Boom of Non-Tradeable Goods Prices in Europe: Evidence and Interpretation', *IMF Working Paper*, 93/45.

—— ——, and H. Wolf (1993), 'International Evidence on Tradables and Non Tradables Inflation', *NBER Working Paper*, 4438 (Aug.), forthcoming, *European Economic Review*.

De Grauwe, P. (1992), 'Inflation Convergence during the Transition to EMU', *CEPR Discussion Paper*, 658, and Ch. 7 in this volume.

—— and L. Papademos (eds.) (1990), *The European Monetary System in the 1990s*, Longman for CEPS, London.

Dornbusch, R. (1989), 'Real Exchange Rates and Macroeconomics: A Selective Survey', *Scandinavian Journal of Economics*, 91/2.

Dornbusch, R. (1991), 'Comment to Froot and Rogoff', *NBER Macroeconomics Annual*, 6: 317–22.

Eichengreen, B., and C. Wyplosz (1993), 'The Unstable EMS', *Brookings Papers on Economic Activity*, 1.

Froot, K., and K. Rogoff (1991), 'The EMS, The EMU and the Transition to a Common Currency', *NBER Macroeconomics Annual*, 6: 269–317.

Giavazzi, F., S. Micossi, and M. Miller (eds.) (1988), *The European Monetary System*, Cambridge University Press.

Giavazzi, F., and L. Spaventa (1990), 'The "New" EMS', in De Grauwe and Papademos (1990).

Hsieh, D. A. (1982), 'The Determination of the Real Exchange Rate: The Productivity Approach', *Journal of International Economics* 12: 355–62.

Kiguel, M., and N. Liviatan (1992), 'The Business Cycle Associated with Exchange Rate-Based Stabilizations', *World Bank Economic Review*, 6.

Kiyotaki, N. (1991), 'Comment to Froot and Rogoff', *NBER Macroeconomics Annual.*

Kravis, I. B., and R. E. Lipsey (1987), 'The Assessment of National Price Levels', in S. W. Arndt and J. D. Richardson (eds.), *Real-Financial Linkages among Open Economies*, Cambridge, Mass., MIT Press.

—— —— (1988), 'National Price Levels and the Prices of Tradables and Non Tradables', *American Economic Review*, 78/2.

Lindbeck, A. (1979), 'Imported and Structural Inflation and Aggregate Demand: The Scandinavian Model Reconstructed', in A. Lindbeck (ed.), *Inflation and Employment in Open Economies*, North-Holland.

Lipschitz, L., and D. McDonald (1992), 'Real Exchange Rates and Competitiveness: A Clarification of Concepts, and Some Measurements for Europe', *Empirica*, 19/1: 37–69.

Marston, R. (1987), 'Real Exchange Rates and Productivity Growth in the United States and Japan', in S. W. Arndt and J. D. Richardson (eds.), *Real-Financial Linkages Among Open Economies*, Cambridge, Mass., MIT Press.

Obstfeld, M. (1992), 'Modeling Trending Real Exchange Rates', mimeo, University of California at Berkeley.

—— (1993), 'The Adjustment Mechanism', in M. Bordo and B. Eichengreen (eds.), *A Retrospective of the Bretton Woods System*, Chicago University Press for NBER.

Perron, P. (1989), 'The Great Crash, the Oil Price Shock and the Unit Root Hypothesis', *Econometrica* 57 (Nov.): 1361–1401.

Rogoff, K. (1992), 'Traded Goods Consumption Smoothing and the Random Walk Behavior of the Real Exchange Rate', *NBER Working Paper*, 4119.

Samuelson, P. (1964), 'Theoretical Notes on Trade Problems', *Review of Economics and Statistics* 46 (Mar.): 145–54.

Sommariva, A., and G. Tullio (1987), 'A Note on the Real Exchange Rate, Differential Productivity Growth and Protectionism in Gold Standard Germany, 1878–1913', *Weltwirtschaftliches Archiv* 123/2: 354–62.

9

Another Look at the 'EMS Effect' in European Labour Markets

MICHAEL J. ARTIS
PAUL ORMEROD

1. INTRODUCTION

This chapter follows in a line of previous studies of the behaviour of wages and prices in the European Monetary System (see e.g. Artis and Ormerod, 1991, Blackburn *et al.*, 1992, Bleaney and Mizen, 1995). An obvious source for hypothesis-testing in this context has been provided by the 'credibility' argument that the EMS provided a means for countries to 'import' the counter-inflationary reputation of the Bundesbank. The view that non-German countries could find a benefit in obliging themselves to target the exchange rate of their currency against the DM and, by thus 'tying their hands', deny themselves the evanescent employment benefits of discretion in favour of the long-run advantage of lower inflation, was set out most famously by Giavazzi and Pagano (1988).

This view of the rationale of the system, if correct, would seem to imply that it should be possible to detect an 'EMS effect' in European labour markets. The benefit of enhanced credibility should in principle be apparent in a reduction in the unemployment cost of reducing inflation within the EMS as compared with the alternative of disinflation outside that framework. In more detail, the hypothesis can be held to suggest, first, that the credibility of the exchange rate peg should make for a detectable influence of German inflation expectations upon expectations in other ERM countries and, second, that through this mechanism and/or another (change in institutions), the unemployment and output cost of disinflation should be reduced below what would otherwise have happened. On this interpretation, then, it is clearly not enough to show, simply, that inflation fell inside the EMS; not only would this be compatible with a hypothesis of global disinflation, implying nothing special about disinflation inside the EMS; even had inflation not fallen (as in fact it did) throughout the industrialized world at the same time as it fell within the EMS, this would not be evidence of an EMS effect in the sense defined since it says nothing about the differential cost of the achievement.

2. PREVIOUS INVESTIGATIONS

A number of existing papers have attempted to provide estimates of the two components of an EMS effect: Artis and Nachane (1990) *inter alia* put forward evidence based on augmented autoregressions of prices to suggest that German inflation expectations may have become more important, or important where they were not before the inception of the EMS, in influencing inflation expectations elsewhere in Europe. Their data period expired in 1985, but a recent exercise conducted in similar vein on a later data-set by Bleaney and Mizen (1995) reached broadly similar conclusions. Meanwhile, investigations of the credibility effect of the EMS approached from the financial aspect and using UIP-related criteria, such as the study by Blackburn *et al.* (1991), have also concluded that the evidence supported the view that the EMS 'helped the inflation-prone countries acquire anti-inflationary credibility'. At the same time, investigators have set out to examine whether there was evidence in the labour markets of an EMS effect. Artis and Ormerod (1991) estimated wage equations for the leading ERM countries which incorporated the 'expectations effect' by instrumenting inflation expectations as dependent *inter alia* upon German inflation and also searched for evidence of structural change. However, they found that whilst the estimated wage equations gave some evidence of undergoing structural change at some point in the 'EMS period' (i.e. after 1979), the later wage equations were not greatly different from those estimated for the earlier periods whilst point estimates of 'real wage rigidity' and 'real wage inflexibility' gave disappointingly non-uniform evidence of moving in the 'right' direction. Wage rigidity was defined in terms of the increase in unemployment required to cancel a one-point rise in expected inflation, inflexibility as the increase in unemployment required to cancel the autonomous rise in wages associated with the passage of time. A reduction in wage rigidity and inflexibility as defined would usually be regarded as indicating a desirable development. They noted that unemployment has risen in all the countries concerned over their estimation period (to 1989). Anderton and Barrell in a series of papers (of which 1995 is a good example) studied the stability of wage-determination relationships in ten European countries using carefully constructed wage-compensation data; they also benefited from their own earlier study of institutional change (Anderton *et al.*, 1992; Anderton and Barrell, 1993) in the labour markets of European countries. Their conclusion was that, with the exception of Italy, there was not a great deal of evidence of EMS-inspired structural change in their relationships: 'our empirical work indicates that the ERM may have provided some pressure towards more symmetric responses to shocks, but the changes have not been great' (Anderton and Barrell, 1995, 60).

Investigators who have used a reduced-form approach to the problem have come up with results which they find more reassuring. First in this line was the paper by Giavazzi and Giovannini (1988), which fitted a VAR to ERM country data (and to the UK) for the pre-ERM period and then used the system to forecast through the subsequent ERM experience. Overprediction of inflation for this period was interpreted as evidence of a 'structural break' or 'ERM regime shift'. The results were found suggestive of such a shift in that for every country (except Germany) inflation was overpredicted in the ERM period, in most cases, only after three years or so—but this seemed consistent with the known facts of institutional change and the decisive reversal of previous policies (France being the most notable case). A similar result was also found for the UK, presumably a reflection of the 'Thatcher effect'. A more recent example of the reduced-form approach is to be found in Bini-Smaghi (1995) where a cross-country macro-relationship (basically an inverted money-demand relationship with inflation on the left-hand side) is estimated over twenty-one OECD countries with dummies entered for ERM membership (with variations to test for narrow-band membership and informal membership). This exercise produced a string of significant *t*-values on the dummy variables suggestive of 'ERM added value'. In the present volume, De Jong (chapter 10) finds evidencc of a credibility effect in prices for Italy, France, and the UK. Finally, mention should be made of single-country studies that support the presence of an ERM effect. Of these, those by Kremers (1990) for Ireland and by Gressani *et al.* (1988) for Italy are among the most notable, whilst in chapter 2 of this volume, Artus and Salomon report favourable results also for France.

It has become apparent that even if the basic inspiration of the credibility model is correct, instrumenting an appropriate approach is not straightforward. Three problems, in particular, may be singled out. First, even the most determined advocate of the 'credibility' hypothesis would not want to maintain that credibility comes easily; it has to be earned. Hence there will be a period, of unknown length, during which the disinflation effort will exhibit no EMS effect; dating the length of time before a credibility effect can be discerned must be part of the exercise and an obvious problem is that the data may allow the investigator too much latitude. Second, the modelling of wage behaviour customarily involves instrumenting expectations: in this case the underlying hypothesis provides a strong suggestion that the key factor will be expectations of inflation in Germany. Hence a successful instrumenting of the credibility-augmented wage equation will involve some transformation of German inflation on the right-hand side. However, since we know to begin with that over time inflation did fall in the EMS towards the lower levels enjoyed by Germany, it is a likely conclusion that over time it may look as though inflation in countries outside Germany becomes more like inflation inside Germany. In itself, this does not 'prove' the credibility hypothesis. Third, we have to be aware that in trying to detect an EMS effect we may in effect be trying to make a marginal inference about wage behaviour in a context where it is next to impossible to control properly for the impact of structural change (*not* related to the EMS) and other factors.

Finally, of course, we have to recognize that the definition of the EMS effect that investigators have been seeking to discover or perhaps to parameterize may be the wrong one. Political economy considerations could equally as well argue that the EMS effect lay in the fact that the presence of the EMS enabled central banks and governments to determine on a realizable path of disinflation, so that rather than the EMS effect taking the form of a reduction in the unemployment and output cost of disinflation, it should rather be defined as a reduction in the political cost of disinflation—as allowing disinflation to occur—rather than reducing its economic cost.

All these considerations are sufficient warning that the likelihood of obtaining clear-cut results for the credibility version of the EMS effect is not high. Previous papers in the field (including our own) can perhaps be faulted for not showing sufficient awareness of some of these qualifications, just as they may for not perceiving that the critical cost to be lowered may have been a political one.

The rest of this chapter is given over to a further attempt to model the wage–price process in some ERM countries in a way that separates out the expectations and the structural change effects.

NEW ESTIMATES OF THE EMS EFFECT

The sample

The starting-point for the work reported in this section is the analysis reported in Artis and Ormerod (1991). The estimation period used in that paper expired in 1989; in the present analysis the period has been extended to the end of 1991, six months before the first of the speculative storms that was to sweep the EMS. Just as in the 1991 paper the estimation process here is a two-stage process. In the wage formation equation that constitutes the second stage of this process, inflation expectations have a key role to play. The first stage is the modelling of those expectations. Our starting-point is the assertion that AR processes provide a fairly robust means of forecasting phenomena like inflation; specifically, in our case, the basic forecasting tool which can be taken as an 'as if' expectations generator is an AR process of up to order (4). For each country we then examine whether terms in German inflation serve to 'knock out' some of the lagged own-inflation terms whilst satisfying the usual battery of diagnostic tests. Only three non-German countries are represented in the estimation: France, Belgium, and the Netherlands. Other countries were excluded for reasons of data (un)availability.

Inflation expectations

In the 1991 paper, there seemed to be quite good evidence that with the passage of time the influence of German inflation on expectations of 'own'-country inflation became stronger through the EMS period, supporting the basic credibility hypothesis outlined above (but with the qualifications mentioned there too). This finding has been replicated for a more up-to-date data-set and with a different range of auxiliary variables by Bleaney and Mizen (1995). However, our own replication has resulted in a weakening of that evidence. Specifically, in the earlier exercise, our 'pre-EMS' periods included the oil shock years. In trials for the present exercise, the inclusion of these years was found to bias the results in various ways. Now, our pre-EMS period starts in 1975 and ends in the first quarter of 1983 (the basic data are for consumer prices, quarterly): there is quite good evidence that 1983 marked a watershed in the counter-inflationary evolution of the EMS, so our 'EMS period' runs from 1983 (2) to 1991 (4). Tables 9.1–4 provide the main results; the estimation started with an AR(4), testing down to eliminate insignificant contributions as terms in German inflation were added in. Inflation is measured as the fourth log-difference of consumer prices. The tables show the coefficient estimates, together with their *t*-values and various diagnostics based on output from PC-Give; the test statistics are distributed as χ^2 and are below the corresponding critical values in every case. The symbols are obvious: thus Δ_4l fp, for example, indicates the fourth log-difference of French prices, Δ_4l bp the fourth log difference of Belgian prices etc.

Turning now to the results, we can see that for *France* (Table 9.1), the estimates suggest that German inflation was a significant contributor to French inflation expectations (as we shall call the fitted values of this series) in the pre-EMS period as well as in the EMS period itself, with only a marginal strengthening (on the point estimates) in the total effect between the two periods. For both *Belgium* and the *Netherlands* (Tables 9.2 and 9.3 respectively) information about German inflation was already important before the formation of the EMS—not surprisingly given the links through trade between the countries and the fact that both were participants in the pre-EMS exchange rate arrangements, the Snake. There is not a great deal of difference in the weight of the German contribution between the two periods (if anything, on the point estimates there is a slight reduction in effect).[1] Table 9.4 provides estimates for Germany based on the same procedure, with a break point at 1983 (1); as can be seen, the form of the equation and the coefficient estimates are almost exactly the same in the two periods. This steadiness is of course desirable in the anchor country of the system. The next step is to incorporate the fitted values from these inflation equations as expectation terms in wage formation relationships.[2]

[1] Constant terms, suppressed from the display, were included in the estimation, which was therefore unrestricted.

[2] Strictly speaking, it would be preferable to instrument the expectations term with one-step-ahead forecasts from a rolling or recursive regression so as to minimize reliance on information that could not have been available in real time. When this was done in earlier work, however, it was not found to make a great difference and in view of the somewhat cumbersome procedure involved it was not pursued on this occasion.

TABLE 9.1. *The German content of inflation predictors: France*

Pre-EMS: 1975(1)–1983(1)			EMS: 1983(2)–1991(4)		
$\Delta_4 lfp(-1)$	0.770	(8.4)	$\Delta_4 lfp(-1)$	0.888	(16.4)
			$\Delta_4 lfp(-4)$	–0.479	(5.0)
$\Delta_4 lfg(-1)$	0.475	(3.2)	$\Delta_4 lfp(-5)$	0.469	(5.7)
$\Delta_4 lfg(-4)$	–0.526	(5.8)	$\Delta_4 lfg(-1)$	0.072	(1.5)
			*DF*1	–0.008	(5.5)
R^2	0.905			0.986	
SE(x 10^3)	5.432			2.761	
ξ^2 ()					
Autocorrelation (3)	0.470			4.072	
ARCH (3)	3.464			5.940	
Normality (2)	0.800			0.157	
Heteroskedasticity (6)	4.718		(9)	15.617	

Notes: *t*-values are shown in parentheses. The constants are suppressed from the display. *DF*1 is a dummy variable taking the value unity in the quarter 1983(3)–1986(2) inclusive.

TABLE 9.2. *The German content of inflation predictors: Belgium*

Pre-EMS: 1975(1)–1983(1)			1983(2)–1991(4)		
$\Delta_4 lbp(-1)$	1.550	(9.2)	$\Delta_4 lbp(-1)$	0.937	(9.0)
$\Delta_4 lbp(-2)$	–0.251	(2.1)	$\Delta_4 lbp(-4)$	–0.487	(2.3)
			$\Delta_4 lbp(-5)$	0.385	(2.7)
$\Delta_4 lgp(2)$	0.594	(3.4)	$\Delta_4 lgp(-1)$	0.369	(1.7)
$\Delta_4 lgp(-4)$	0.147	(0.8)	$\Delta_4 lgp(-3)$	0.214	(1.6)
R^2	0.969			0.951	
SE(x 10^3)	4.656			4.831	
ξ^2 ()					
Autocorrelation (3)	5.159			8.755	
ARCH (3)	0.595			0.954	
Normality (2)	1.178			1.701	
Heteroskedasticity (8)	6.330		(10)	6.256	

Note: *t*-values are shown in parentheses. The constants are supressed from the display.

Wage relationships

A general form for the wage-determination process which can be viewed as an error-correction model in the real wage or alternatively as a hybrid augmented Phillips curve/real wage resistance process is as follows:

$$\Delta_4 lw = \alpha + \beta_1 \Delta_4 lw_{-1} + \beta_2 E\Delta_4 lp + \beta_3 XD + \beta_4 l(w/p)_{-i} + \beta_5 D_i + \beta_6 t.$$

Here, the left-hand side term is a four-quarter overlapping rate of change of wages in manufacturing (measured as the four-quarter log-difference); the first term on the right-hand side after the constant is the inertia term and the next the expected rate of inflation, instrumented as the fitted value of the appropriate

TABLE 9.3. *The German content of inflation predictors: The Netherlands*

Pre-EMS: 1975(1)–1983(1)		EMS: 1983(2)–1991(4)		
$\Delta_4 lnp(-1)$	1.013	$\Delta_4 lnp(-1)$	0.820	(7.3)
$\Delta_4 lgp(-1)$	0.626	$\Delta_4 lgp(-1)$	0.662	(3.5)
$\Delta_4 lgp(-3)$	0.566	$\Delta_4 lgp(-3)$	0.219	(1.8)
R^2	0.947		0.910	
SE(x 10^3)	4.810		4.756	
ξ^2 ()				
Autocorrelation (3)	2.700		1.351	
ARCH (3)	2.345		1.378	
Normality (2)	0.072		1.608	
Heteroskedasticity (8)	10.000	(6)	2.362	

Note: *t*-values are shown in parentheses. The constants are suppressed from the display.

TABLE 9.4. *German inflation*

Pre-EMS: 1975(1)–1983(1)		EMS: 1983(2)–1991(4)		
$\Delta_4 lgp(-1)$	1.370	$\Delta_4 lgp(-1)$	1.320	(8.4)
$\Delta_4 lgp(-2)$	–0.497	$\Delta_4 lgp(-2)$	–0.423	(2.8)
R^2	0.878		0.882	
SE(x 10^3)	4.367		4.61	
ξ^2 ()				
Autocorrelation (3)	1.909		4.704	
ARCH (3)	3.440		1.031	
Normality (2)	0.420		0.033	
Heteroskedasticity (4)	2.450	(4)	1.931	

Note: *t*-values are shown in parentheses. The constants are suppressed from the display.

inflation equation (see Tables 9.1–4); *XD* is a vector of excess demand terms, in practice proxied by the level and/or rate of change of unemployment or a transformation thereof. The fifth is the error-correction term, the lagged real wage; in estimation, the lag *i* is consistently estimated at 4; *D* is a dummy variable and *t* is a time trend.

The estimation procedure used the framework provided by this equation to find well-fitting equations passing the diagnostic tests with dummy variables inserted where both the data and outside information appeared to provide a justification. Turning now to the results, those for *France* do not provide strong evidence of a change in structure although it is true that there is a big increase in the strength of the error-correction term and a fall in the value of the trend, with a cubic term in the change in unemployment proving necessary to preserve good diagnostics. On the whole, the estimates suggest support for the verdict of

Barrell *et al.* (1992) that 'there appears to be little evidence of systematic structural change in French labour markets'. The sample separation date, on the other hand, was heavily influenced by the knowledge that the Mitterand U-turn was a significant and influential policy change. As we have already seen, there is slight evidence of a change in the expectations-formation process. To the extent that French wage inflation (Table 9.5) has moderated, it is clear that the right-hand side excess demand (unemployment) argument must have played a major role. In *Belgium* (Table 9.6), on the other hand, the end of the first subperiod is marked by the beginnings of drastic reforms (the elimination of indexation) as indicated by the necessity for the dummy variable, whilst in 1983 a 'competitiveness' norm was introduced to limit wage growth (see Barrell *et al.*, 1992)—this may account for the change in structure between the two periods and the sharp fall in the value of the trend term. In the case of the *Netherlands* (Table 9.7), on the other hand, there is much stronger evidence of relative stability. The coefficient on the inflation-expectations term is notably much less than in the case of either France or Belgium, putting the Netherlands closer to the German camp in this respect. Otherwise, as in all cases, the error-correction term is significantly negative, as theory requires and unemployment exerts a dampening influence on wage developments. Here again our results confirm those of Barrell *et al.* in suggesting little evidence of any structural change in Dutch labour markets. Table 9.8, finally, pertains to Germany. Aside from the need to incorporate a dummy variable for one quarter in the second subperiod (for 1986 (2)) these estimates also suggest relative stability. As in the case of other investigators (e.g. Barrell *et al.*, 1992) the results give no room to an inflation-expectations term. On the other hand, the error-correction term, a trend term, and unemployment are all highly significant, the significance of the first of these implying no long-run money illusion in spite of the absence of a significant expectations effect.

TABLE 9.5. *Wage determination in France*

Pre-EMS: 1975(1)–1983(1)			EMS: 1983(2)–1991(4)		
$\Delta_4 lfw(-1)$	0.236	(1.6)		0.266	(3.5)
fpe	0.642	(5.9)		0.699	(8.2)
lfrw(–4)	–0.415	(3.0)		–0.851	(7.2)
trend	0.002	(2.5)		0.001	(6.9)
lfu(–4)	–0.018	(2.5)	$(\Delta_4 lu)^3_{-2}$	–2.217	(2.6)
R^2	0.873			0.985	
ξ^2 ( )					
Autocorrelation (3)	4.552			2.853	
ARCH (3)	6.315			5.694	
Normality (2)	1.278			0.446	
Heteroskedasticity (10)	14.26		(10)	19.089	

Note: *t*-values are shown in parentheses. The constants are suppressed from the display.

TABLE 9.6. *Wage determination in Belgium*

Pre-EMS: 1975(1)–1983(1)			EMS: 1983(2)–1991(4)		
bpe	0.545	(2.1)		1.035	(5.1)
lbrw(–4)	–0.300	(1.4)			
trend	0.003	(2.2)		0.001	(5.7)
lbu(–4)	–0.099	(2.8)			
*D*1	–0.009	(0.5)	$(\Delta_4 lu)^3_{-1}$	–6.241	(2.9)
R^2	0.839			0.710	
ξ^2 ( )					
Autocorrelation (3)	1.141			4.934	
ARCH (3)	0.705			1.255	
Normality (2)	0.145			0.005	
Heteroskedasticity (10)	12.926		(6)	4.473	

Note: *t*-values are shown in parentheses. The constants are suppressed from the display. *D*1 is a dummy variable taking the value of unity for the quarter 1982(3)–1983(1).

TABLE 9.7. *Wage determination in The Netherlands*

Pre-EMS: 1975(1)–1983(1)			EMS: 1983(2)–1991(4)		
$\Delta_4 lnw(-1)$	0.470	(4.2)		0.384	(3.2)
npe	0.519	(2.9)		0.265	(3.0)
lnrw(–4)	–0.500	(4.3)		–0.517	(4.3)
trend	0.001	(0.8)		0.001	(4.7)
lnu(–4)	–0.021	(1.7)		–0.012	(0.9)
$\Delta_4 lnu$	–0.049	(2.6)			
R^2	0.927			0.777	
ξ^2 ( )					
Autocorrelation (3)	2.783			6.189	
ARCH (3)	4.946			1.092	
Normality (2)	0.986			1.270	
Heteroskedasticity (12)	16.038		(10)	14.634	

Note: *t*-values are shown in parentheses. The constants are suppressed from the display.

TABLE 9.8. *Wage determination in Germany*

Pre-EMS: 1975(1)–1983(1)			1983(2)–1991(4)		
lgrw(–4)	–0.870	(6.14)		–0.434	(7.1)
trend	0.004	(4.89)		0.004	(8.8)
lgu(–4)	–0.067	(5.89)		–0.053	(4.6)
$\Delta l_4 gu$	–0.041	(3.71)		0.043	(2.1)
			*D*1	–0.023	(4.5)
R^2	0.789			0.870	
χ^2 ( )					
Autocorrelation (3)	1.757			1.497	
ARCH (3)	5.119			2.840	
Normality (2)	0.017			0.406	
Heteroskedasticity (8)	9.018		(9)	4.534	

Note: *t*-values are shown in parentheses. The constants are suppressed from the display.

CONCLUSIONS

In this chapter we have sought to look for evidence of an EMS effect in the labour markets of France, Belgium, and the Netherlands on an extended data period. The effect sought could be expected to be mediated through a growing influence of German experience upon the inflation-expectations generating process and through changes in labour market structures. Otherwise, to the extent that convergence has occurred in nominal wage growth it would have to be to the evolution of the arguments of the excess demand for labour function that one would have to look for an explanation. The extent of unemployment in Europe is mute witness to the price that has been paid for convergence on the lower rates of inflation traditionally enjoyed in Germany. Our investigations do not yield as much evidence of an EMS effect (above the political conviction that this price should be paid) as might be hoped—though the exclusion of Italy from the sample (given the favourable findings of others) may have produced a 'pessimistic' bias. In our sample there is no very clear evidence overall that expectations have been influenced increasingly by German experience and only some evidence overall (though notably, quite a lot for Belgium) that EMS pressures forced structural change in labour markets.

REFERENCES

Anderton, R., and Barrell, R. (1993). 'The ERM and Structural Change in European Labour Markets: A Study of 10 countries', *National Institute Discussion Paper, 40.*, National Institute of Economic and Social Research, London.

—— —— (1995). 'The ERM and Structural Change in European Labour Markets', *Weltwirtschaftliches Archiv*, 131/1: 47–66.

—— —— and J. McHugh (1992). 'Nominal Convergence in European Wage Behaviour: Achievements and Explanations', in R. Barrell (ed.), *Economic Convergence and Monetary Union in Europe*, Sage Publications.

Artis, M. J., and P. Ormerod (1991). 'Is there an "EMS effect" in European Labour Markets?', *CEPR Discussion Papers, 598* (Dec.), repr. with addenda in C. Johnson and S. Collignon (eds.), *The Monetary Economics of Europe*, Pinter, 1994.

Bleaney, M., and P. Mizen (1995). 'Credibility and Disinflation in the European Monetary System', mimeo, University of Nottingham.

Bini Smaghi, L. (1994). 'EMS Discipline: Did It Contribute to Inflation Convergence?', *Banca Nazionale Quarterly Review*.

Blackburn, K., Mongiardino, A., and M. Sola (1992). 'Was there an "EMS Effect" in the European Disinflation?', mimeo, University of Southampton.

Giavazzi, F., and A. Giovannini (1988). 'The Role of the Exchange Rate Regime in a Disinflation: Empirical Evidence on the EMS', in F. Giavazzi, S. Micossi, and M. Miller (eds.), *The European Monetary System*, Cambridge University Press.

—— and M. Pagano (1988). 'The Advantage of Tying One's Hands', *European Economic Review*, 32: 1055–82.

Gressani, D., Guiso, L., and I. Visco (1988). 'Disinflation in Italy: An Analysis with the Econometric Model of the Banca d'Italia', *Journal of Policy Modeling*, 8: 163–203.

Kremers, J. J. M., (1990). 'Gaining Policy Credibility for a Disinflation', *IMF Staff Papers*, 37 (Mar.), 116–145.

10

Expectations of Selling-Prices in the EMS

EELKE DE JONG

I. INTRODUCTION

Irrevocably fixed exchange rates form an important element of the proposal for establishing an Economic and Monetary Union (EMU) in Europe. A prerequisite for a sustainable system of fixed exchange rates or an area with a common currency is that the differences between the inflation rates in the member countries remain rather small. In case the inflation rates of two countries differ substantially, the country with the highest inflation rate experiences a worsening of its competitiveness and a decline of its production and employment. Since the exchange rate cannot be used for improving the country's competitiveness, the relative price of its output has to decline so that the inflation rates of the two countries converge.

Although in principle the inflation rates can converge to any level, both academics and policy-makers agree that a low rate (zero or slightly above zero) is to be preferred to a high one. The reason for this preference is that there are many costs of inflation. Types of costs of inflation are: menu costs, the decrease in real money balances, and the worsening of the operation of the price system.[1] The consequence of a decrease in the real value of money balances is that people will seek to make less use of money, and this has implications for their holdings of other assets. Higher inflation rates are thought to undermine the operation of the price system because one fears that higher inflation rates will generate greater uncertainty about inflation or greater variability in relative prices.

Since the beginning of the 1980s the inflation rates in the member countries of the European Monetary System (EMS) satisfy the two conditions mentioned above; they converged and declined to the lower rates (see e.g. Ungerer *et al.*, 1990; De Grauwe, 1989*a*). At several places in the Maastricht Agreement the text shows that the heads of state of the EEC want to guarantee that in the

Financial support by the European Commission (SPES-Project no. CT91-0053) is gratefully acknowledged. I thank Peter Wesselius for research assistance, Marleen Smit and Josphine Ruitenberg for accurate secretarial assistance, Giuseppe Tullio and colleagues of the Department of Macroeconomics of the University of Amsterdam, for their comments on an earlier version, and the European Commission for providing the survey data.

[1] See Driffill *et al.* (1990) for a survey of the theoretical and empirical literature on the costs of inflation, and the EEC (1990, ch. 4) for a brief survey of the benefits of stable prices.

future EMU these two criteria still will be met. Hence, 'the primary objective of the European System of Central Banks shall be to maintain price stability' (Article 105). Price stability is also one of the convergence criteria on the achievement of economic and monetary union. The text of the treaty states that this criterion 'shall mean that a Member State has a price performance that is sustainable and an average inflation, observed over a period of one year before the examination, that does not exceed that of at most the three best performing Member States by more than 1½ percentage points. Inflation shall be measured by means of the consumer price index (CPI) on a comparable basis, taking into account differences in national definitions.' (Article 1 of the Protocol on the convergence criteria as mentioned in Article 109 F of the treaty.)

In order to obtain the goal of sustainable price stability within the EMU, the high-inflation countries that are or will become members have to implement a disinflationary policy. As is well known, the costs of such a disinflationary policy are reduced if the private sector regards this policy shift to be credible. Credible policy changes will lead to structural changes in price expectations. Expectations are becoming more forward-looking than backward-looking (Chadha *et al.*, 1992; and Sachs and Wyplosz, 1986), and in case the anti-inflationary policy consists of pegging the exchange rate to that of a low-inflation country, the influence of (expected) changes in this anchor country on inflationary expectations will increase (see Giavazzi and Giovannini, 1988, 1989, for a formal derivation). For the EMS this implies that the effect of German variables is expected to rise. If the Exchange Rate Mechanism (ERM) of the European Monetary System is credible, it will constrain the economic policy of individual countries. As a consequence domestic factors will become less and common factors more important for explaining (expected) inflation. Hence, the expected inflation rates will move towards a common level and will become more correlated across countries.[2]

The aim of the present chapter is to investigate whether the membership of the ERM has affected inflationary expectations and, hence, has fascilitated the disinflation process in the EMS countries. With a view towards servicing this goal the performance of inflationary expectations in EEC countries during the 1970s and 1980s is studied. In particular, attention is paid to the EMS's influence on the inflationary expectations in some countries. There are some papers that deal with the EMS's effect on inflation and inflationary expectations (e.g. Artis and Ormerod, 1991; Christensen, 1987*a*, *b*; Giavazzi and Giovannini, 1988, 1989; Kremers, 1990; Papi, 1991). A drawback of many of these papers[3] is that the time-series of expected inflation is obtained in a more or less mechanical way. As a consequence, a structural break can represent a change in the expectation formation but it can also be a result of an inaccurate expectation proxy (see e.g. De Jong, 1991, ch. 3 for criteria on expectation proxies). In

2 An investigation of these correlations can be found in Batchelor (1982: 21–4).

3 The only exception is Papi (1991)

this chapter I circumvent this problem by using survey data regularly published by the European Commission.

The set-up of the chapter is the following. The next section briefly reviews the literature on the role of inflationary expectations in the disinflation process. Section 3 reviews empirical studies of the influence of the EMS on inflationary expectations. A preliminary investigation of the expected prices is presented in Section 4. Section 5 discusses the form of the expectations-generating function and the tests used for detecting the influence of the EMS on the expectations. The empirical results of these tests are presented in Section 6. The final section contains the conclusions.

2. DISINFLATION POLICY, INFLATIONARY EXPECTATIONS, AND THE EXCHANGE RATE MECHANISM

As stated above, high-inflation countries that will become or will remain a member of the Exchange Rate Mechanism (ERM) or of the EMU will have to implement a disinflation policy. As goods and labour markets do not clear instantaneously, such a policy will be accompanied by a period of economic slack. Broadly speaking, the severness of this period of lower economic activity can be reduced in two ways. The flexibility in the labour and goods markets can be increased, so that the rate of inflation becomes more responsive to the unemployment. This mechanism is studied in Artis and Ormerod (1991). In the present chapter we concentrate on the second way of reducing the costs of disinflation, which is that the policy affects the expected inflation rate. In case the policy is credible, the expectations should become more forward-looking and more responsive to the announced policy regime.

As in Papi (1991) the theoretical studies on the role of expectations in disinflation policy are grouped in three categories, namely the disinflation literature, the game-theoretic approach, and the Walters' critique on the EMS. In the disinflation literature attention is focused on the sacrifice ratio.[4] The authorities implement a contractionary policy in order to reduce inflation, the result is a reduction in output. This reduction in output will be smaller if the policy is credible and the private agents expect a lower inflation rate.

Theoretical studies on the disinflation policy in the EMS often make use of the game-theoretical model inspired by Barro and Gordon (1983). In this model the policy-makers strive for a low inflation rate and a high rate of employment. The policy-makers have an incentive to create surprise inflation in order to boost employment. Since the private agents are aware of this incentive, they don't trust a policy-maker's announcement of a disinflation policy. Instead they expect that there is a chance that policy-makers will renege. As a result, the economy reaches an equilibrium in which the expected inflation is rather high,

[4] The sacrifice ratio is defined as the percentage points of GDP which have to be forgone in order to obtain 1 percentage point reduction in inflation.

and policy-makers have little room for implementing an expansionary policy. Various methods have been proposed for solving this time inconsistency of a disinflation policy so that the latter becomes credible. Possible solutions are: the appointment of a conservative central banker, the implementation of a rule instead of a discrete policy, reputation, and bonding. In the case of bonding, the government arrives at a consistent solution by posting a bond that penalizes it for not carrying out the first-best outcome (see e.g. Blanchard and Fischer, 1989: 599–600). Entering an exchange rate arrangement such as the ERM can be regarded as a form of acquiring credibility by means of adopting a rule instead of discretionary policy. In addition the ERM is an international agreement (contract) which authorities can only dispose of at great political costs. So it can also be considered as a form of bonding. Then the bond is the loss of political reputation (voters) in case the authorities cancel the agreement. So the government can increase its credibility by tying its hands (Giavazzi and Pagano, 1988).

Inflationary expectations play an important role in Walters' critique on the functioning of the ERM. He argues that since the abolition of capital controls in most member countries of the ERM, perfect capital mobility will equalize nominal interest rates in ERM countries. This implies that in the high-inflation countries the nominal interest rate will decline. In his opinion the expected inflation will remain high in these countries, so that the real interest rate will decrease, which will boost the economy and lead to an appreciation of the currency until the exchange rate hits its intervention margin. An effective intervention in the foreign exchange market will raise the domestic money supply, which in its turn will generate inflation. Summarizing, according Walters the 'new' ERM (fixed exchange rates and perfect capital mobility) is inconsistent, in that inflation will rise in high-inflation countries. As has been argued by Miller and Sutherland (1990), Walters implicitly assumes that the inflation expectations in financial markets differ from those in goods and labour markets. If the economic agents in the latter markets also expect a lower inflation rate, then the real interest rate doesn't change and there is no expansionary effect and as a consequence no inflationary impulse. Another critique of Walters' critique is that he assumes that the investors do not expect a realignment of the exchange rates. This assumption might be realistic for the first months after the realignment. Thereafter it becomes unrealistic. Since capital flows in and the domestic money stock increases, the economic agents will expect that the currency will be devalued in the months ahead. Hence, capital inflows stop and/or nominal interest rates increase, so that Walters' critique is only relevant for the short period just after the realignment.

Before ending this section it should be stressed that in the preceding paragraphs we have paid attention to the credibility of an announced change in policy and not to the possible disciplinary effects of such a policy. In case economic agents regard the entry of a currency to the ERM as credible, they expect a lower inflation rate although the monetary instruments (discount rate and money growth) have not yet changed. In other words it is expected that in the future the membership of the ERM will work as a disciplinary device. At that time private agents will expect a low inflation rate because the policy, in particular monetary policy, will have changed as a result of the discipline imposed by the exchange rate arrangement. The credibility effect comes to the fore at the time of the announcement of the policy change, so before the actual change of the policy. It is generally expected to be of a temporary nature. The disciplinary effects come gradually and will last as long as the authorities adhere to the constraints on economic policy resulting from the membership of the fixed exchange rate mechanism.

3. EMPIRICAL STUDIES ON THE ROLE OF INFLATIONARY EXPECTATIONS IN THE ERM

By now, various studies have been published in which the effect of ERM on inflationary policies is studied. Mostly these studies investigate whether there is a credibility effect.[5] Two main approaches are distinguished, namely the indirect and the direct approach. The studies belonging to the indirect approach restrict themselves to the effects of a credible policy compared with one that is not. No attempt is made to derive a proxy of inflationary expectations. The direct approaches derive a proxy of the inflationary expectations.

Studies belonging to the indirect approach are Egebo and Englander (1992), De Grauwe (1989*a*), and Giovazzi and Giovannini (1988) in which one seeks structural changes in the sacrifice ratio of European countries. A disadvantage of this approach is that a shift of the sacrifice ratio can be caused by a change in the expectations (credibility) or by a change in the functioning of labour markets. Hence the method does not enable one to distinguish the two effects from each other. Another indirect approach concentrates on the interest differentials between Germany and a member country (see e.g. Anderson and Risager 1988; Egebo and Englander, 1992; and Mohlo, 1991). In case the gap between the interest rate in Germany and the corresponding rate in another ERM country closes, then this can be interpreted as a convergence of the inflationary expectations in both countries. However, movements in this interest rate differential can also be explained by other circumstances, such as the thinness of the market (In 't Veld, 1992: 158, n. 1), the announcement of the introduction (or postponement) of a source tax, and the dynamics of public debt. Summarizing, the indirect methods share the disadvantage that the phenomenon studied can always be explained by at least two variables. Increased credibility of the disinflation policy is just one of these possible explanations.

In principle, the drawbacks of the indirect approaches can be circumvented by studying (a proxy of) the expected inflation. A problem with this direct

[5] Egebo and Englander (1992) and Papi (1991) contain a review of these studies.

approach is that expectations are unobservable and one therefore has to make use of proxies. Most proxies used are derived from the history of the prices, for example by means of Vector Autoregression (VAR). This method is used in Artis and Ormerod (1991), Giavazzia and Giovannini (1988, 1989), and Collins (1988). Another proxy is the so-called McCallum proxy of rational expectations used in Kremers (1990). According to this approach of rational expectations, the expected inflation is equal to the actual inflation up to a disturbance term, which has a zero mean. Kalman filters have also been used for deriving inflationary expectations (see Weber, 1991). An important drawback of all these proxies is that they are based on the history of the variables concerned. Hence, these proxies do not incorporate the effects of an announcement of a switch in policy regime. However, these are the very effects which can reflect a change in the authorities' credibility. As a consequence, the proxies mentioned above are not useful for studying the question whether the ERM has served as a credibility bonus to some of its members.

In order to study this issue, use should be made of a more direct proxy of inflation expectations, ideally one based on questionnaires.[6] To the best of my knowledge Papi (1991) is the only study which makes use of opinion surveys on inflation for studying credibility effects of the ERM.[7] She uses the inflation expectations from the *Mondo Economico Survey* for investigating credibility effects of the ERM on the expected inflation in Italy. In the present study I will also make use of survey data on inflation expectations. These data are opinions of producers from various European countries on their expected selling-prices and are regularly published by the European Commission.[8] Of course the methods used for acquiring this information on opinions can always be criticized. Does the sample represent the population? Are there no structural differences between the people interviewed in this period and those interviewed in previous periods? Notwithstanding the validity of these questions, I think that it is the best available data-set that can be used for analysing the credibility effects of the ERM. As far as I know the data-set used in this study is the only one which is available for various European countries. An important additional advantage is that the questionnaire is the same for all countries, so that in this respect the results in the various countries are consistent.

6 See also Malinvaud's arguments in favour of direct methods like opinion surveys and the financial press in the general discussion of Weber's paper, p. 94.

7 In a study on a related subject Collins and Giavazzi (1992) also use opinion surveys.

8 The Maastricht Treaty mentions the Consumer Price Index as a measure for inflation (see the Introduction), so that the use of expectations of consumer prices seems to be more appropriate than those of selling-prices. However, the time-series of the former expectations are shorter and there are some methodological problems with these data (see Simmons and Weiserbs, 1992), so that a more detailed study of these series is required before they can be used. In this study, therefore, I restrict the analysis to the expected selling-prices.

4. MAIN CHARACTERISTICS OF SELLING-PRICE EXPECTATIONS

The time-series of expected percentage changes in selling-prices in manufacturing are derived from the responses to the question: Do you expect that the selling-price during the months ahead will go up, unchange, or go down? From January 1968 onwards these questionnaires have been organized monthly in Germany, Belgium, France, and Italy. Ireland started in 1975 and the United Kingdom in 1976. The starting-date for the organization of this questionnaire in the other countries of the European Community is in the 1980s or even in the 1990s. In this study I investigate the time-series of Germany, Belgium, France, Italy, and the United Kingdom. For these countries the time-series is long enough to allow for an investigation of the possible effects of the European Exchange Rate Mechanism on the expectations. The times-series of Ireland is also of sufficient length. However, no other chapter in this volume deals with the effects of the ERM on Ireland, and therefore this country is excluded from the analysis. Note that the answers to the questions are qualitative and should thus be transformed into a quantitative measure in order to be comparable with the actual change of prices. Details of the method used for deriving the quantitative series from the qualitative ones are presented in Appendix 1.

4.1 A comparison with the expected change in German selling-prices

Whereas in the 1970s the levels of expected inflation in the individual countries are quite different, they are more or less the same at the end of the 1980s. The German level appears to be the lowest in most periods. The econometric analysis, to be presented in the following sections, is based on the assumption that if the ERM is credible, the German price changes form the anchor. I therefore compare the expectations in the other countries with that in Germany, which very often is regarded to be the anchor of the ERM.

The inflationary expectations of the Belgian producers fluctuate around the German level (Fig. 10.1(*a*)). This suggests that the producers' expectations had already converged before the founding of the EMS in 1979. From 1982 to 1984 the expected selling-price was on average higher than the German one, whereas the opposite holds for the years before and after this period. This suggests that during the early years of the EMS the system wasn't binding according to the producers interviewed. It is not until 1986 that the average of the differences is equal to that in 1981. This suggests that the Belgian authorities lost credibility in 1982 and 1983, and that it took two years before they regained it.

From 1974 to approximately 1983 the French producers' inflationary expectations were definitely higher than those of their German colleagues, whereas from 1987 onwards they were more or less equal to each other (Fig. 10.1(*b*)). From the first quarter of 1983, the French expectations gradually converged

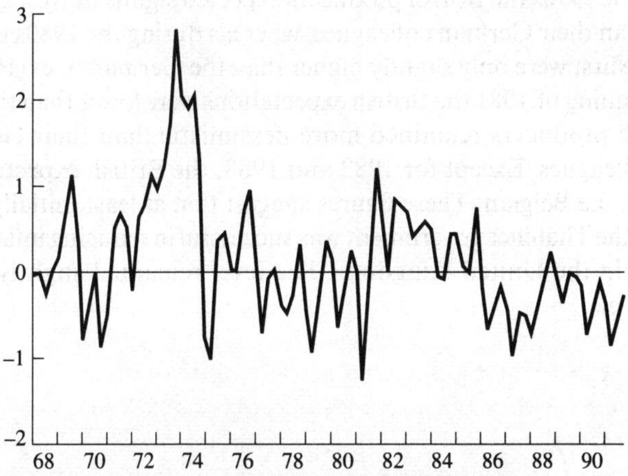

FIG. 10.1a. Difference between expected selling-prices in Belgium and Germany (% per quarter)

towards the German level. From 1986 onwards the French expected increase in selling-prices was smaller than the German ones.

At first sight the differences between the expectations of Italian and German producers look quite similar to that of the difference between French and German producers (Fig. 10.1(*b*)). As with the French series, until 1983 the Italian level was higher than the German and after 1986 they were more or less the same. There were, however, two important differences between the French and Italian time-series. First, the Italian figures remain higher than the French (and German) series. Secondly, the convergence to the new level doesn't occur as gradually as in the French case, but rather suddenly at the end of 1985.

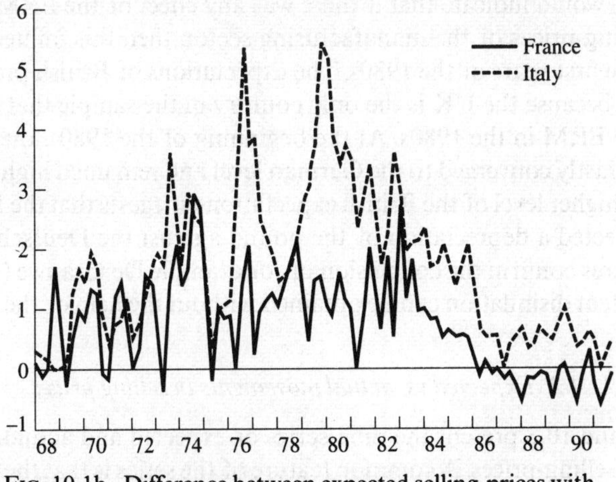

FIG. 10.1b. Difference between expected selling-prices with Germany: France and Italy (% per quarter)

During the 1970s the British producers expected significantly higher rates of inflation than their German colleagues, whereas during the 1980s the expectations of the first were only slightly higher than the German ones (Fig. 10.1*c*)). At the beginning of 1981 the British expectations were lower than the German. The British producers remained more pessimistic than their German and Belgian colleagues. Except for 1982 and 1983, the British expectations were higher than the Belgian. These figures suggest that at least initially the shock therapy of the Thatcher government was successful in reducing inflationary expectations in the United Kingdom. The level remained slightly above the German level.

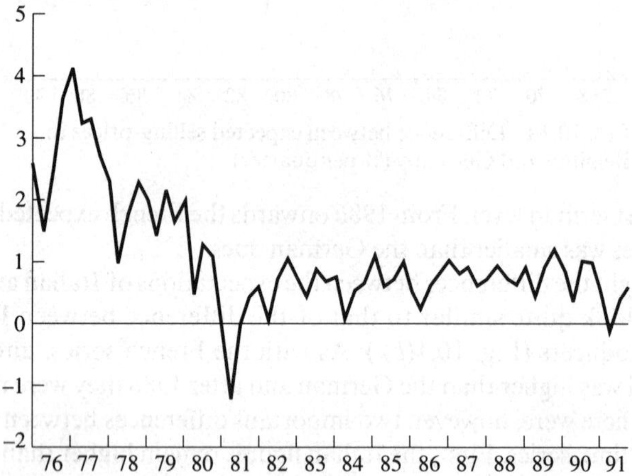

FIG. 10.1c. Difference between expected selling-prices in the UK and Germany (% per quarter)

Fig. 10.1 would indicate that if there was any effect of the ERM on the expected selling-prices of the manufacturing sector, then this influence did not occur in the first years of the 1980s. The expectations of British producers are interesting because the UK is the only country in the sample that did not belong to the ERM in the 1980s. At the beginning of the 1980s, the British expectations fastly converged to the German level and remained higher than this level. This higher level of the British expectations suggests that the British producers expected a depreciation of the pound against the Deutschmark. The British figures confirm the conclusion of for example De Grauwe (1989*a*) that to some extent disinflation can be obtained without the help of the ERM.

4.2 Expected vs. actual movements in selling prices

Figs. 10.2 and 10.3 present the time-series of expected and actual percentage changes in selling-prices. A common feature of the series is that the variance of the time-series of the expected percentage change of the selling-prices is less

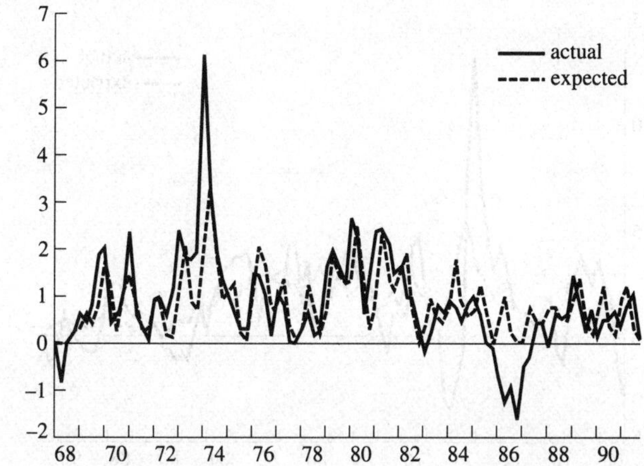

FIG. 10.2a. Germany: Actual and expected selling-prices (% per quarter)

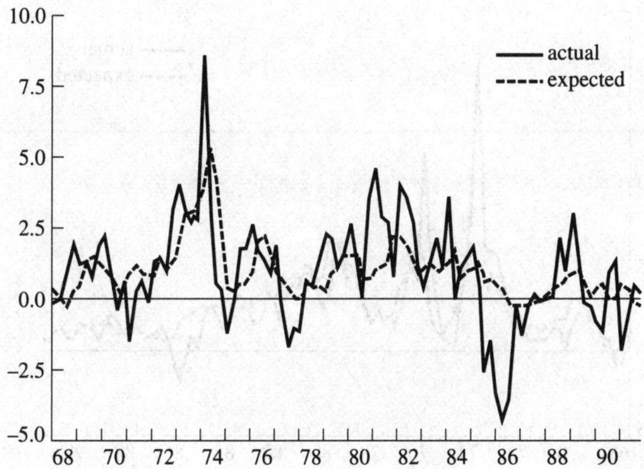

FIG. 10.2b. Belgium: Actual and expected selling-prices (% per quarter)

than that of the actual percentage change in selling-prices. Similar results are found in other studies (see e.g. Pesaran 1987: 227–233).

Sharp increases in actual prices are incorporated with a lag of one period in the expected price changes. A good example of such a high rise in prices is the first oil shock. In such situations people seem to report their opinion on the recent price changes as their expectation for the future.

The economic agents almost never expect a decline in prices. As a consequence, for Germany, Belgium, and to a lesser extent for France and Italy, the expected price changes overpredict the actual ones in 1985 and 1986. During these two years the producer prices declined due to the sharp depreciation of the US dollar. A consequence of this behaviour is that the correlation between

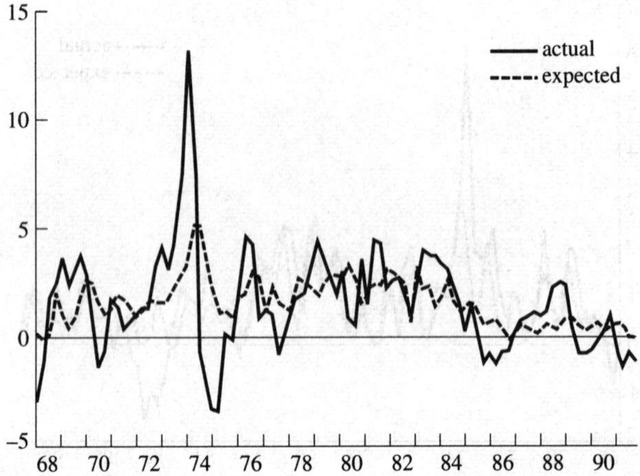

FIG. 10.2c. France: Actual and expected selling-prices (% per quarter)

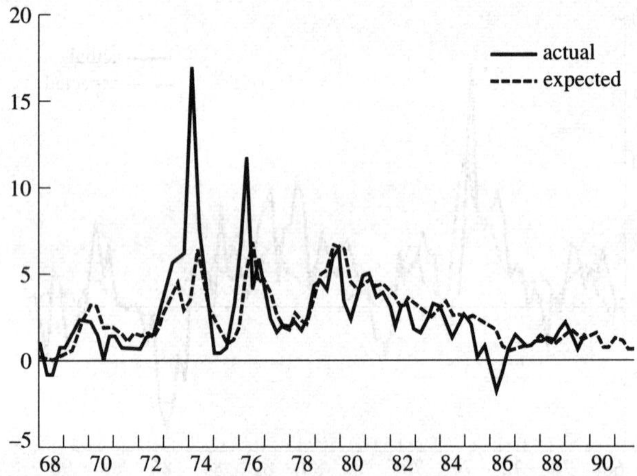

FIG. 10.3a. Italy: Actual and expected selling-prices (% per quarter)

the expected and actual price changes is higher in countries where there are almost no decreases in selling-prices. The best example of such a country is the United Kingdom (see Fig. 10.3(*b*) and Table 10.1)

5. THE EXPECTATIONS-GENERATING FUNCTION AND THE TESTS

Several studies use expectations-generating functions for the evaluation of the effect of the EMS on inflationary expectations. The function used in Papi (1991) is of the adaptive regressive type and contains as explanatory variables lagged values of actual inflation, long-run, or normal inflation (a moving

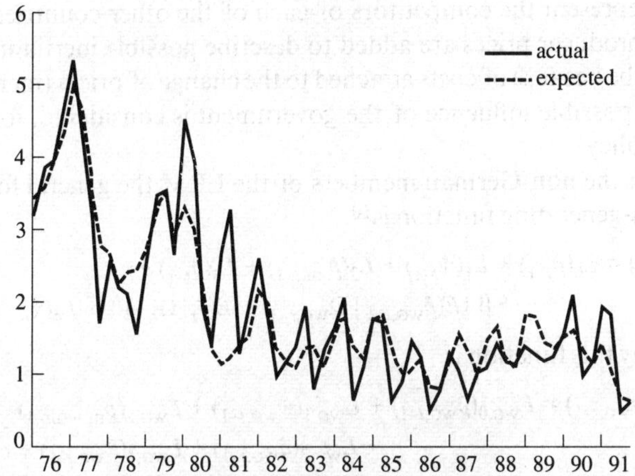

FIG. 10.3b. UK: Actual and expected selling-prices (% per quarter)

TABLE 10.1. *Correlation between actual and expected per centage changes in selling prices*

	1968(1)–1991(4)	1976(1)–1991(4)
Germany	0.44	0.61
Belgium	0.54	0.51
France	0.36	0.61
Italy[a]	0.73	0.69
United Kingdom		0.88[b]

[a] The time-series of actual prices stops in 1989(4). See International Monetary Fund, *International Financial Statistics*.
[b] Survey data start in 1976(1)

average of twenty-eight terms), lagged differences between expected inflation and long-run or normal inflation, and two terms reflecting that the speed of adjustment depends upon the state of the economy (approximated by the index of capacity utilization) and uncertainty. A disadvantage of the relation used in Papi (1990) is that especially the long-term (normal) rate of inflation is mechanically determined. The function used in this study is therefore more related to those used in some other studies, such as Barrel *et al.* (1990), Kremers (1990), and Giavazzi and Giovannini (1988), who use expectations-generating functions which incorporate cost terms such as wages (unit labour costs) and import prices.

The expected selling-prices are supposed to be of the bounded rationality type (Pesaran, 1987, p. 35). Producers base their selling-prices on recent developments in production costs, wages, and import prices. In order to make a profit, they add a mark-up to these costs. The level of this mark-up depends on the rate of capacity utilization and the expected behaviour of competitors. It is supposed that Germany is the dominant partner, so that the German producers represent the competitors of each of the other countries.[9] Lagged changes in producer prices are added to describe possible inertia in the price setting (maybe because of costs attached to the change of prices (menu costs)). Finally, the possible influence of the government is considered, for example monetary policy.

Hence, for the non-German members of the ERM the general form of the expectations-generating function is[10]

$$E(\mathring{p}_t \mid \Omega_{t-1}) = L_0(\mathring{p}_{t-1}) + L_1(\mathring{w}_{t-1}) + L_2(\mathring{p}_{\mathrm{m},t-1}) + L_3(\mathring{q}_{t-1}) + \\ + \beta\,\{E(\mathring{p}_{\mathrm{WG},t-1} \mid \Omega_{\mathrm{WG},t-2}) + E(\mathring{e}_t \mid \Omega_{t-1})\} + L_4(\mathring{x}_{t-1}) + c. \quad (1)$$

For Germany this function is

$$E(\mathring{p}_{\mathrm{WG},t} \mid \Omega_{\mathrm{WG},t-1}) = L_{\mathrm{WG},0}(\mathring{p}_{\mathrm{WG},t-1}) + L_{\mathrm{WG},1}(\mathring{w}_{\mathrm{WG},t-1}) + L_{\mathrm{WG},2}(\mathring{p}_{\mathrm{m,WG},t-1}) \\ + L_{\mathrm{WG},3}(\mathring{q}_{\mathrm{WG},t-1}) + L_{\mathrm{WG},4}(\mathring{x}_{\mathrm{WG},t-1}) + c_{\mathrm{WG}}, \quad (2)$$

where

L_i, $1 = 0, \ldots, 4$ are polynomials, e.g. $L_0(\mathring{p}_{t-1}) = \alpha_{01}\,\mathring{p}_{t-1} + \alpha_{02}\,\mathring{p}_{t-2} + \ldots + \alpha_{0n}\,\mathring{p}_{t-n}$ (the lag length, n, can be different for each polynomial)

Ω_{t-1}: the set of information available at time $t-1$

$\mathring{p}_t$: percentage change of the selling price

$\mathring{e}_t$: percentage change of the exchange rate measured as the amount of domestic currency per unit of foreign currency

$E(\mathring{p}_t \mid \Omega_{t-1})$: the expectation of $\mathring{p}_t$ conditional upon the information set Ω_{t-1}

$E(\mathring{e}_t \mid \Omega_{t-1})$: the expectation of $\mathring{e}_t$ conditional upon the information set Ω_{t-1}

$\mathring{w}_{t-1}$: percentage change in labour costs (wages)

$\mathring{p}_{\mathrm{m},t-1}$: percentage change of import prices

$\mathring{q}_{t-1}$: percentage change of rate of capacity utilization

$\mathring{x}_{t-1}$: influence of the government (in the empirical part this is the percentage change in money).

The subscript WG refers to Germany.

The membership of the EMS can affect the expected inflation formula in two ways. First, a credible shift to a system of lower inflation will lead to a lower constant term. Second, membership of the ERM and especially the expectations of the producers with respect to the functioning of this mechanism will determine the expected depreciation of the country's currency *vis-à-vis* the Deutschmark. Two regimes are distinguished: an incredible and a credible one.

[9] Several empirical studies reveal that Germany dominates the European Monetary System (see e.g. Herz and Röger, 1992).

[10] Barrell *et al.* (1990) use both the percentage change and the level of the rate of capacity utilization, whereas Papi (1991) uses the level of the rate of capacity utilization. I have chosen the percentage change because this time-series is stationary for all countries concerned, whereas the time-series of the level is only stationary for France and Germany (results can be obtained from the author).

In the incredible exchange rate system, the parity rates are periodically revised so that a devaluation of the soft currency more or less compensates the worsening of its competitive position since the last realignment. In order to illustrate the effects of such a policy on the expectations, let us assume, for simplicity, that the realignments perfectly compensate the cumulative difference in the costs between the country concerned and Germany. If this compensation is made effective every period, then the expected change in the exchange rate is

$$E(\mathring{e}_t \mid \Omega_{t-1}) = L_1(\mathring{w}_{t-1}) + L_2(\mathring{p}_{\mathrm{m},t-1}) - \{L_{\mathrm{WG},1}(\mathring{w}_{t-1,\mathrm{WG}}) + L_{\mathrm{WG},2}(\mathring{p}_{\mathrm{m,WG},t-1})\}. \quad (3)$$

Substituting the relations (2) and (3) into the expectations-generating functions of (1) yields

$$\begin{aligned} E(\mathring{p}_t \mid \Omega_{t-1}) = L_0(\mathring{p}_{t}-1) &+ L_1(\mathring{w}_{t-1}) + L_2(\mathring{p}_{\mathrm{m},t-1}) + L_3(\mathring{q}_{t-1}) \\ &+ \beta\,\{L_{\mathrm{WG},0}(\mathring{p}_{\mathrm{WG},t-1}) + L_{\mathrm{WG},1}(\mathring{w}_{\mathrm{WG},t-1}) + L_{\mathrm{WG},2}(\mathring{p}_{\mathrm{m,WG},t-1}) \\ &+ L_{\mathrm{WG},3}(\mathring{q}_{\mathrm{WG},t-1}) \\ &+ L_{\mathrm{WG},4}(\mathring{x}_{\mathrm{WG},t-1}) + L_1(\mathring{w}_{t-1}) + L_2(\mathring{p}_{\mathrm{m},t-1}) \\ &- \{L_{1,\mathrm{WG}}(\mathring{w}_{t-1,\mathrm{WG}}) \\ &+ L_{\mathrm{WG},2}(\mathring{p}_{\mathrm{m,WG},t-1})\} + c_{\mathrm{WG}}\} + L_4(\mathring{x}_{t-1}) + c. \quad (4) \end{aligned}$$

Rearranging terms leads to

$$\begin{aligned} E(\mathring{p}_t \mid \Omega_{t-1}) = L_0(\mathring{p}_{t-1}) &+ (1+\beta)\,L_1(\mathring{w}_{t-1}) + (1+\beta)\,L_2(\mathring{p}_{\mathrm{m},t-1}) + L_3(\mathring{q}_{t-1}) \\ &+ \beta\,\{L_{\mathrm{WG},0}(\mathring{p}_{\mathrm{WG},t-1}) + L_{\mathrm{WG},3}(\mathring{q}_{\mathrm{WG},t-1}) \\ &+ L_{\mathrm{WG},4}(\mathring{x}_{\mathrm{WG},t-1}) + c_{\mathrm{WG}}\} + L_4(\mathring{x}_{t-1}) + c. \quad (5) \end{aligned}$$

Comparing this relation with (1) reveals that under this incredible exchange rate regime, the domestic cost components are more important and the German variables are less important than in the original relation (1). On the other hand, when the commitment of a fixed exchange rate *vis-à-vis* the Deutschmark is credible, the expected depreciation of the exchange rate will be zero, and thus does not compensate the different developments in the two countries. As a consequence, the influence of the domestic (German) variables is less (greater) than under the incredible regime.

In the empirical part the following relation is estimated[11]

$$\begin{aligned} E(\mathring{p}_t \mid \Omega_{t-1}) = L_0(\mathring{p}_{t-1}) &+ L_1(\mathring{w}_{t-1}) + L_2(\mathring{p}_{\cdot\mathrm{m},t-1}) + L_3(\mathring{q}_{t-1}) \\ &+ \beta\,E(\mathring{p}_{\mathrm{WG},t-1} \mid \Omega_{\mathrm{WG},t-2}) + L_4(\mathring{x}_{t-1}) + c + \mu_t, \quad (6) \end{aligned}$$

where μ_t is a disturbance term. A credible change to a regime of fixed exchange rates, such as the ERM, is reflected in smaller coefficients of the domestic variables and a greater influence of the expected percentage change in the German

[11] Note that this relation of the producers' expectation of price changes does not contain tax variables. The reason for this is that although indirect taxes appear to be relevant for explaining consumer prices, they are not for explaining producer prices. See e.g. Barrel *et al.* (1990), who estimate equations for both consumer prices and producer prices.

selling-price. A credible shift can also be reflected by a smaller constant term (see e.g. Papi, 1991, p. 31).

Above, the expectations-generating functions are derived from an information-set that contains the German expected selling-prices lagged one period. This choice is based on the assumptions that there is a time-lag between the formation of the expectation and its publication, and that the producer doesn't know his competitors' expectation prior to the date of its publication. Kremers (1990) assumes that in period t–1 the producers know the competitors' expectation for the next period. This implies that Kremers thinks that a producer knows the expectations of his competitors at the time of the formation of this expectation. Kremers might be correct in cases where there are rather intensive connections between the two. A reason why in this study the present expectation of the German producers might influence the present expectations of the producers in the other countries is that the expectations are published monthly whereas quarterly data are used for estimating the expectations-generating functions. In the regression analysis I start with a specification containing the expected German selling-prices lagged one period and thereafter investigate whether the unlagged variable would have led to more plausible results.

If the present expectation of the German producers enters the equation, the Ordinary Least Squares (OLS) estimates would be inconsistent. The Instrumental Variables (IV) method is an often used technique for solving this problem. Since it is a limited information method it is more robust to specification errors than a full information method (Pesaran, 1987: 162). Under the usual assumptions the IV estimates are consistent and asymptotically efficient (Bowden and Turkington, 1984: 110–11). It is a two-step method. In the first step the endogenous variable, the expected German selling-prices in this case, is regressed upon a set of variables, the instrumental variables, which are uncorrelated with the disturbance term of the expectations-generating function. In finite samples the efficiency of the estimates will be enhanced by selecting the instrumental variables as closely correlated as possible with the endogenous variable. The variables in the expectations-generating function of the German selling-prices fulfil this requirement (see also De Jong, 1991: 75–7). In the second step of the IV method the fitted values of the German expectations-generating function are substituted in the regression of the expectations-generating function of the other members of the EMS.

The first test on the possible effects of a country's membership of the ERM on inflationary expectations consists of the estimation of relation (6) for the pre-EMS period. Then the out-of-sample forecasting performance of this relation is investigated for the EMS period. If the relation consistently overestimates the actual expectations then we conclude that the ERM has increased the credibility of the country's anti-inflationary policy. The second test compares the estimated coefficient of the expected German selling-price and the constant term in a relation estimated for the pre-EMS period with those obtained from estimating the equation for the EMS period. A credible ERM membership would increase the coefficient of the former and would decrease the constant term. In addition the domestic variables would become less important. The third test comprises the estimation for the entire period (or a period that is as long as possible) and applies recursive regression for an investigation of the coefficient of the expected German prices and of the constant term.

6. EMPIRICAL RESULTS

6.1 Germany

Whereas the other members of the Exchange Rate Mechanism (ERM) can benefit from the credibility of the anti-inflationary policy of the Deutsche Bundesbank, it is less clear what the benefits are for Germany. It even can be and is argued that the Bundesbank will lose part of its credibility as long as one expects that some of the other ERM members are not always prepared to follow the German restrictive monetary policy. Then, at times these members will put pressure on the Bundesbank to loosen its strict monetary policy. The ERM will reduce the Germans' disinflationary credibility as long as the economic agents think that there is a chance that the Bundesbank will (partly) give way to these pleas for a more expansionary policy. In the regression analysis, a loss of credibility comes to the fore in the following ways (a) the forecasts for the EMS period based on the regression of the pre-EMS period are lower than the actual expected rate of inflation and (b) the constant term in the regression of the entire period and that in the regression of the EMS period is higher than the intercept in a regression of the pre-EMS period.

During the 1970s, the expected percentage change in German selling-prices are determined by lagged changes in producer prices, in money, and in the rate of capacity utilization (Table 10.2, col. 1). In addition a dummy for the second and third quarter of 1976 is included in the regression. The residuals are normally distributed and do not contain autocorrelation of the first order. The hypothesis of autocorrelation of the fourth order cannot be rejected.

The forecasts do not show any bias during the first years of the EMS period (graphs can be obtained from the author). Significant forecast errors occur in 1984 and during the period 1986 and 1987. I do not know of an event that can explain the forecast errors in 1984. The second period is characterized by a decline in the selling-prices. During this period expectations based on the relation for the pre-EMS period are lower than the actual inflationary expectations. The forecasts follow the pattern of the actual percentage change of selling-prices better than the expected percentage change. As has been illustrated in Section 4.2 in all EMS countries the expected selling-prices during this period are higher than the realized prices. Hence these results do not indicate a change in the credibility of the German policy, but should be ascribed to a common factor, namely the deflationary effect of the depreciation of the dollar.

TABLE 10.2. *Regression of the expected percentage change of the German selling prices*

Variables	Period 1968(1)–1978(4)	Period 1968(1)–1989(4)	
$\mathring{p}_{t-1}$	0.514	0.449	0.536[a]
	(9.56)	(10.24)	(13.47)
$\mathring{p}_{t-4}$	0.252	0.127	0.244[a]
	(4.10)	(2.81)	(5.82)
$\mathring{q}_{t-1}$	0.134	0.062	0.131[a]
	(2.95)	(2.95)	(5.84)
$\mathring{q}_{t-4}$	0.051	0.038	0.054[a]
	(2.05)	(2.06)	(3.00)
$\mathring{m}1_{t-2}$	0.049	0.027	0.038[a]
	(2.69)	(2.90)	(4.01)
C	–0.084	0.282	–0.22[a]
	(0.69)	(4.37)	(0.297)
$D76Q23$	0.733	0.684	0.660[a]
	(2.75)	(2.38)	(2.89)
$\mathring{p}_{t-1}$			0.296[b]
			(3.4)
$S2$			0.646[b]
			(4.38)
$DUMWG$			0.445[b]
			(4.22)
R^2 (adj.)	0.78	0.66	0.79
SE	0.35	0.39	0.31
LM (1)	0.09	3.41	0.10
LM (4)	2.12*	11.00***	3.38***
Q (4)	9.04**	35.15***	13.65***
SK	–0.05	0.08	–.07
K	2.22	1.90	2.56
JB	1.13	4.53*	0.79
ARCH (2)	0.95	0.19	0.90

[a] 1968(1)–1983(4).
[b] 1984(1)–1989(4)

Notes: *, **, or *** show that the corresponding null hypothesis can be rejected at the 0.1, 0.05, or 0.01 level, respectively. The numbers in parentheses are the absolute values of the *t*-statistics of the estimated parameters. Besides the standard error of regression (SE), I use as criteria for evaluating the estimated equations, the Langrange-Multiplier test for autocorrelation of order one (LM(1)) and up to order four (LM(4)), as well as the Box-Pierce Portmanteau statistic with 4 lags (Q(4)), a test for autoregressive conditional heteroskedasticity in the residuals up to order two (ARCH(2)), and the Jarque-Bera test for normality of the residuals (JB). Additionally I present the skewness (SK) and the kurtosis (K).

All coefficients remain significant at the 5 per cent level if the relation is estimated for the period 1968(1) to 1989(4). The sample period for estimating the equation stops in 1989(4) in order to circumvent possible influences due to the reunification of Germany. The quality of the disturbance terms worsens considerably, however (Table 10.2, col. 2). The hypothesis of no autocorrelation of the first order and of normality are rejected at the 10 per cent level, whereas the hypothesis of no autocorrelation of the fourth order even has to be rejected at a level of 1 per cent. The CUSUM of squares suggests that there is a structural change at the end of 1985. The recursive estimate of the intercept increases at the end of 1984 and during 1987. As mentioned above it is not certain whether these increases indicate a worsening of the German credibility or whether they should be ascribed to movements in the US dollar.

It appeared that the correlation between the expected inflation on the one hand and the actual or forecasted inflation—the latter based on a pre-EMS relation—on the other hand worsens considerably if the latter two time-series show a decline in the inflation rate. At these times the expected inflation is low but still positive. This suggests that the lower bound of the producers' inflationary expectations is equal to zero: declining prices and stable prices have the same effect on the expectations. Therefore I have also estimated relations in which the negative price changes are replaced by zero. Furthermore, I assume that the declining prices in 1985 and 1986 result from the depreciating dollar. The estimated relation for the pre-EMS period (Table 10.3, col. 1) differs from the previous specification in that the coefficient of capacity utilization (lagged four quarters) becomes insignificant and is therefore deleted from the equation. The characteristics of the disturbance terms are even better than those of the original relation; no test statistic indicates any more the existence of autocorrelation of the fourth order. Now the forecasts of the equation are much closer to the time-series of expected price changes than in the original relation. During 1987 and 1988 the forecasts are lower than the expected percentage change in prices. If the assumption is correct that the effect of the declining value of the dollar is captured by the redefinition of the variables, then this difference between forecasts and expectations indicates that during this period the German authorities lost some of their disinflationary credibility. The estimates for the entire period (the second column of Table 10.3) are slightly better than the original relation (the second column of Table 10.2). The constant term is higher than that in the equation for the pre-EMS period. This once again is an indication that the credibility of the German anti-inflationary policy was lower in the EMS period than it was in the 1970s. The recursive estimates of the intercept reaffirm this conclusion and suggest that worsening of the credibility took place in 1984. The CUSUM of squares indicates that there is a structural break in 1984 I. The Chow break points test is $F = 2.86$ and $P = 0.02$ and hence reaffirms the impression of a structural break.[12]

The correlation between the percentage changes in the selling-prices and those of the import prices is rather high. The influence of lagged selling-prices on the expected future selling-prices appears to be more significant than the

[12] The CUSUM of squares does not indicate a structural change if the dummy variable *D76Q23* is deleted from the relation. The Chow test is based on the relation without this dummy variable.

effect of lagged import prices on these expectations. Due to the high correlation between the two variables, the lagged import prices are not included in the ultimately selected relation. In order to investigate the robustness of the results I have also estimated an equation in which the lagged producer prices are replaced by the lagged import prices. The quality of the estimated relation is for the 1970s slightly less than the corresponding relation with lagged producer prices (compare column one of Table 10.4 with that of Table 10.3). The quality of the estimated relation for the entire period is much worse (see column two of Tables 10.4 and 10.3). Now the disturbances are no longer normally distributed. The estimated intercept is greater for the entire period than for the pre-EMS period. Hence, the conclusion that the German anti-inflationary credibility decreased during the EMS period is robust to this change in the specification. The recursive estimates (not shown) suggest that this worsening

TABLE 10.3. *Regression of the expected percentage change of the German selling prices (only non-negative changes in prices)*

Variables	Period 1968(1)–1978(4)	Period 1968(1)–1989(4)	
$\mathring{p}_{t-1}$	0.534	0.530	0.563[a]
	(9.40)	(11.96)	(13.49)
$\mathring{p}_{t-4}$	0.203	0.145	0.214[a]
	(3.44)	(3.22)	(4.96)
$\mathring{q}_{t-1}$	0.094	0.064	0.107[a]
	(2.15)	(3.31)	(4.78)
$\mathring{m}1_{t-2}$	0.045	0.027	0.040[a]
	(2.39)	(3.18)	(4.09)
C	−.066	0.145	−.048[a]
	(0.51)	(2.15)	(0.60)
$D76Q23$	0.770	0.669	0.680[a]
	(2.77)	(2.48)	(2.85)
$\mathring{p}_{t-1}$			0.595[b]
			(3.50)
$S2$			0.588[b]
			(3.76)
$DUMWG$			0.289[b]
			(2.26)
R^2 (adj.)	0.75	0.71	0.77
SE	0.36	0.37	0.32
LM (1)	0.26	1.40	0.30
LM (4)	1.18	9.32***	2.71**
Q (4)	5.01	32.05***	10.33**
SK	0.00	−.03	−.11
K	2.25	2.12	2.71
JB	1.04	2.87	0.49
ARCH (2)	1.35	1.42	0.96

[a] 1968(1)–1983(4).
[b] 1968(1)–1989(4).

TABLE 10.4. *Regression of the expected percentage change of the German selling prices (only non-negative changes in prices, no lagged selling prices)*

Variables	Period 1968(1)–1978(4)	Period 1968(1)–1989(4)
$\mathring{w}_{1,t-1}$	0.134	0.098
	(3.36)	(2.92)
$\mathring{p}_{m,t-1}$	0.112	0.158
	(4.83)	(7.95)
$\mathring{p}_{m,t-2}$	0.089	0.053
	(3.71)	(2.62)
$\mathring{q}_{t-4}$	0.069	0.022
	(2.32)	(1.16)
C	0.148	0.333
	(1.50)	(4.46)
*S*1	0.550	0.194
	(3.07)	(1.78)
*D*76*Q*23	1.371	1.201
	(4.75)	(3.83)
R^2 (adj.)	0.73	0.59
SE	0.39	0.43
LM (1)	1.23	2.24
LM (4)	1.95	8.49***
Q (4)	5.70	30.06***
SK	0.46	0.68
K	3.05	3.33
JB	1.54	7.26**
ARCH (2)	0.08	0.25

already appeared in 1982. Since the quality of the regression is worse than that of the regression with lagged producer prices, I ascribe more worth to the estimated relation of the latter, and thus assume that the structural change occurred in 1984.

The last columns of Tables 10.2 and 10.3 contain the estimates of a relation which explicitly takes the structural break at 1984(1) into account. Two subperiods are distinguished, viz. 1968(1)–1983(4) and 1984(1)–1989(4). It is assumed that in principle the specification of the first two columns holds for both subperiods but that the coefficients of the variables can be different in each subperiod. Therefore each variable enters the relation twice, one time multiplied by (1.0 – *DUMWG*) and one time multiplied by *DUMWG*. The dummy variable *DUMWG* is 1.0 in 1984(1)–1989(4) and zero elsewhere. Starting with this specification, the statistically insignificant variables are deleted from the relation. The ultimately selected relation is presented in the last column of the tables.

Once again the quality of the residuals is slightly better for the relation which considers non-negative price changes only than for the original relation. The conclusion with regard to the possible effect of the EMS does not depend upon the specification used. In both relations the coefficient of *DUMWG* is positive and significantly different from zero. This indicates that during the EMS period the credibility of the German disinflationary policy declined. Note that if the non-negative price changes are considered, this coefficient is smaller and less significant than in the original specification, which reflects the fact that the expectations remain positive if the actual prices decline.

6.2 *Belgium*

For Belgium no plausible estimates were obtained for relations that contain the expected German selling-prices lagged one quarter. This variable therefore has been replaced by the fitted values of the German expectations-generating function (Table 10.3, col. 2). The equation is extended with a dummy variable representing the effects of the first oil crisis. It is not-zero in the fourth quarter of 1973 and in the first quarter of 1974. Other explanatory variables of the pre-EMS period are: lags of the percentage change in producer prices, import prices, and money supply (Table 10.5, col. 1). The fit of this relation is very good (R^2(adj.) = 0.86) and the disturbances do not contain autocorrelation or heteroscedasticity and are normally distributed. For the years 1979 to 1981 the forecasts of this relation are higher than the actual expectations. This might indicate that the EMS has increased the producers' belief in the Belgian anti-inflationary policy.

The disturbance terms of the estimated relation for the entire period are autocorrelated (Table 10.5, col. 2). The coefficient of the expected German selling-prices and the constant term are slightly higher than in the relation estimated for the 1970s. The estimates of the expected German selling-prices reaffirm the conclusion that the Belgian membership of the ERM increased the credibility of the disinflation policy. The estimates of the intercept, however, point into the opposite direction. The recursive estimates of these two coefficients also raise doubts about the implicit assumption that the differences between the two periods can be ascribed to the effect of the EMS. The intercept is more or less stable until the end of 1982. At that time it increases sharply and decreases after 1986. The coefficient of the expected German selling-prices is smaller during the first years of the EMS than it was in the mid-1970s. This suggests that in the first years of the EMS, this system didn't function as a reliable device for reducing inflationary expectations. In my view the estimated results correspond with the observation that during the 1970s the Belgian franc was one of the few European currencies that was able to remain a member of the snake arrangement. During the first years of the functioning of the EMS, the Belgian franc was very often one of the currencies that was under heavy pressure (see Ungerer *et al.* 1990: 50–2). On 22 February 1982 the Belgian franc was devalued by 8.5 per cent. The recursive estimates suggest that with a lag of slightly more than half a year, this led to an increase in expected inflation, whereas on the other hand the domestic selling-prices were expected to be more

TABLE 10.5. *Regression of the expected percentage change of the Belgian selling prices*

Variables	Period 1968(1)–1978(4)	Period 1968(1)–1989(4)		
$E(\mathring{p}_{WG,t})$	0.823	0.935	0.740[a]	0.523[a]
	(4.91)	(6.89)	(4.67)	(4.27)
$\mathring{p}_{t-1}$	0.165	0.141	0.176[a]	
	(2.39)	(2.61)	(2.65)	
$\mathring{p}_{m,t-1}$	0.098	0.020	0.097[a]	0.103[a]
	(2.46)	(0.63)	(2.69)	(3.48)
$\mathring{q}_{t-3}$	0.104	0.079	0.088[a]	
	(2.64)	(2.38)	(2.38)	
$\mathring{m}1_{t-1}$	0.049	0.036	0.047[a]	
	(2.37)	(2.16)	(2.31)	
$\mathring{m}1_{t-2}$	0.111	0.076	0.108[a]	
	(4.14)	(3.94)	(4.39)	
$\mathring{m}1_{t-3}$	0.046	0.057	0.050[a]	
	(2.24)	(3.37)	(2.40)	
D7374	1.518	1.742	1.595[a]	0.820
	(4.31)	(4.61)	(4.56)	(2.27)
C	–.289	–.243	–.271	0.526[b]
	(1.70)	(1.77)	(1.68)	(2.67)
$E(\mathring{p}_{WG,t})$			0.531[b]	0.460[b]
			(2.96)	(4.03)
$\mathring{p}_{t-1}$			0.151	
			(3.32)	
$\mathring{q}_{t-1}$			0.119	
			(2.23)	
DUMBL			0.524[b]	
			(2.42)	
ρ				0.747
				(9.99)
R^2 (adj.)	0.86	0.74	0.79	0.82
SE	0.46	0.51	0.46	0.43
LM (1)	0.00	6.34**	6.19**	1.29
LM (4)	0.54	2.70**	1.63	0.37
Q (4)	2.05	8.84*	8.26*	1.35
SK	–.04	0.02	0.03	–.51
K	3.18	3.89	3.10	4.75
JB	0.07	2.92	0.05	14.97***
ARCH (2)	0.74	0.98	1.29	0.04

[a] 1968(1)–1979(4).
[b] 1980(1)–1989(4).

determined by the German ones. The coefficient of the expected German selling-prices increased gradually in 1985 and 1986. As argued before, this might indicate that the producers were not aware of the price-reducing effects of the declining dollar.

In order to investigate the effect of price reductions (assumed to be induced by an appreciating exchange rate of the Belgian franc) on the expectations, I have also run regressions in which the negative percentage changes in prices are replaced by zero (see the discussion in Section 6.1). The fit of the equation is good, although the *ARCH(2)* statistic indicates that there is heteroscedasticity (Table 10.6, col. 1). In 1979, 1981, 1986, and 1987 the forecasted values are higher than the expected price changes. Since by assumption this difference no longer can be ascribed to the deflationary influence of exchange rate movements, the forecast errors suggest that during these periods the EMS increased the credibility of the Belgian anti-inflation policy.

The estimated coefficients of the expected German selling-prices for the pre-EMS and EMS period (Table 10.6, col. 2) reaffirm this impression. Once again the intercept suggests the opposite. The recursive estimate of the coefficient of the expected German selling-prices declines in 1979(4) and increases at the end of 1982. Thereafter this coefficient remains stable. Thus, in contrast to the corresponding recursive coefficient in the original relation, there are no signs of an improved credibility after the beginning of 1983. The time-series of the recursive estimate of the constant term is almost exactly equal to that of the original relation, and this suggests a worsening of credibility in 1983 and an improvement in 1986–7.

The Chow test on structural breaks suggests for both relations a structural change in 1979(4) (Chow test $F = 3.53$, $P = 0.00$). The relations are therefore re-estimated for the period 1968(1)–1989(4), where the coefficients are allowed to have different values in each subperiod. Since the residuals of the estimated relations show some form of autocorrelation (col. 3 of Tables 10.5 and 10.6) I have also estimated the relations with correction for autocorrelation (col. 4 of Tables 10.5 and 10.6). Now there are more indications that the credibility worsened than that it improved during the EMS period; the coefficient of the expected German selling-prices is mostly smaller in the EMS period than it was before, and the intercept increased during this period.

To summarize, the various tests give opposite signs with regard to the effect of the Belgian membership of the EMS on its anti-inflationary credibility. Hence it is not possible to derive unambiguous conclusions as to the effect of this membership on Belgian credibility. In fact during the 1970s the Belgian franc was already a member of a fixed exchange rate regime (the snake arrangement).

6.3 France

The preferred relation for explaining the expected selling-price inflation in France during the pre-EMS period is presented in the first column of Table 10.7. Except for the capacity term all variables in equation (6) appear to be relevant. The various statistics indicate that the disturbance terms are not autocorrelated nor heteroscedastic, and that they are normally distributed.

TABLE 10.6. *Regression of the expected percentage change of the Belgian selling prices (non-negative price changes only)*

Variables	Period 1968(1)–1978(4)	Period 1968(1)–1989(4)	Period 1968(1)–1989(4)	
$E(\mathring{p}_{WG,t})$	0.676	0.772	0.604[a]	
	(3.85)	(4.94)	(3.60)	
$\mathring{p}_{t-1}$	0.249	0.219	0.260[a]	0.235[a]
	(3.00)	(3.30)	(3.30)	(3.77)
$\mathring{p}_{m,t-1}$	0.100	0.041	0.101[a]	0.126[a]
	(2.06)	(1.05)	(2.31)	(3.34)
$\mathring{q}_{t-3}$	0.122	0.094	0.105[a]	
	(3.25)	(2.85)	(2.93)	
$\mathring{m}1_{t-1}$	0.048	0.032	0.047[a]	
	(2.37)	(1.90)	(2.35)	
$\mathring{m}1_{t-2}$	0.110	0.065	0.107[a]	
	(4.45)	(3.35)	(4.39)	
$\mathring{m}1_{t-3}$	0.040	0.052	0.044[a]	
	(2.01)	(3.15)	(2.18)	
D7374	1.535	1.736	1.600[a]	1.043
	(4.43)	(4.58)	(4.60)	(2.87)
C	–.318	–.269	–.313	0.577
	(1.99)	(2.06)	(2.03)	(3.29)
$E(\mathring{p}_{WG,t})$			0.505[b]	0.430
			(2.50)	(3.70)
$\mathring{p}_{t-1}$			0.226[b]	
			(2.97)	
$\mathring{q}_{t-3}$			0.150[b]	
			(2.77)	
DUMBL			0.414[b]	
			(2.00)	
ρ				0.720
				(9.46)
R^2 (adj.)	0.87	0.74	0.80	0.82
SE	0.45	0.51	0.46	0.43
LM (1)	0.00	3.04*	4.65**	1.14
LM (4)	0.53	2.29*	1.29	0.45
Q (4)	2.04	7.19	5.45	1.76
SK	0.23	0.25	0.36	0.19
K	2.27	3.62	3.18	3.24
JB	0.54	2.36	1.99	0.76
ARCH(2)	3.75**	0.34	1.29	0.44

[a] 1968(1)–1979(4)
[b] 1980(1)–1989(4)

This equation has been used for calculating the one-period ahead predictions for the period 1979 to 1990. Until 1986 the predictions of this equation are not systematically biased. After 1986(3) the relation systematically over-predicts the actual expected percentage change in the selling-prices. As for Germany and Belgium a further analysis is warranted in order to be sure that this effect can be ascribed to the functioning of the EMS and not to the disinflationary impact of the declining value of the US dollar (see below).

The relation has been re-estimated for the period 1968(2)–1989(4) (Table 10.7, col. 2). This extension of the estimation period worsens the estimates in that the coefficients of the unit labour costs, the seasonal dummy, and the intercept become insignificant, and the disturbance terms are no longer normally distributed and show autocorrelation of the fourth order. The recursive estimate of the expected German selling-prices indicates that the coefficient changes after 1986. The recursive estimate of the constant term suggests a change in 1983.

The CUSUM of squares suggests that there are structural changes in the relation in 1976 and 1983. The Chow break-point statistics (bottom of Table 10.7)

TABLE 10.7. *Regression of the expected percentage change of the French selling prices*

Variables	Period	Period	Period
	1968(2)–1978(4)	1968(2)–1989(4)	1968(2)–1989(4)
$E(\mathring{p}_{WG,t-1}$	0.638	0.770	0.588[a]
	(5.37)	(5.90)	(5.92)
$\mathring{p}_{t-1}$	0.203	0.192	0.199[a]
	(8.32)	(6.51)	(8.07)
$\mathring{w}_{1,t-2}$	0.032	0.017	0.015[a]
	(3.71)	(1.74)	(3.45)
$\mathring{w}_{1,t-3}$	0.016	0.015	
	(2.40)	(1.78)	
$\mathring{w}_{1,t-3}$	0.059	0.054	0.060[a]
	(3.57)	(2.94)	(3.98)
$\mathring{m}1_{t-1}$	0.056	0.056	
	(3.46)	(2.78)	
$\mathring{m}1_{t-2}$	0.060	0.068	0.062[a]
	(3.76)	(3.43)	(4.30)
C	0.570	0.240	0.722
	(4.09)	(1.58)	(6.18)
$S1$	–.781	–0.181	
	(2.69)	(0.56)	
$E(\mathring{p}_{WG,t-1})$			0.752[b]
			(2.72)
$\mathring{p}_{t-1}$			0.177[b]
			(2.66)
$\mathring{m}1_{t-1}$			0.082[b]
			(2.44)
$\mathring{m}1_{t-2}$			0.115[b]
			(3.23)
DUMFR			–.942
			(3.34)
*D*8283			1.625
			(5.09)

TABLE 10.7. (*cont.*)

Variables	Period 1968(2)–1978(4)	Period 1968(2)–1989(4)	Period 1968(2)–1989(4)
R^2 (adj)	0.87	0.71	0.83
SE	0.40	0.56	0.45
LM(1)	1.21	0.15	0.03
LM(4)	0.59	2.45*	0.88
Q (4)	2.04	8.26*	3.52
SK	0.31	0.26	–.01
K	2.53	4.21	3.34
JB	1.09	6.32**	0.43
ARCH (2)	0.38	2.32	0.07

[a] 1968(2)–1983(3)
[b] 1983(4)–1989(4)

CHOW test for structural breaks:

Break points	F	P
1976(4) and 1983(4)	3.01	0.00
1976(4)	1.52	0.16
1983(4)	3.18	0.00

accept the joined hypothesis of structural changes in 1976(4) and 1983(4). The statistic for each of these points reaffirms that there is a break in 1983(4), but rejects the structural change in 1976(4) (bottom Table 10.7). The relation is therefore re-estimated for the entire period where the coefficients are allowed to change in 1983(4). Some coefficients that were significant in the previous estimate become insignificant, the corresponding variables are therefore deleted from the regression. A dummy variable, *D8283*, representing outliers in 1982(4) and 1983(1) is added to the relation. The resulting equation is quite satisfactory (col. 3 of Table 10.7). The disturbance terms meet all relevant statistics. The coefficient of the expected selling-price in Germany and the intercept once again suggest that the credibility of French disinflationary policy increased during the EMS period. According to the tests on structural changes, this improvement of the credibility occurred at the end of 1983. That is about six months after the realignment of March 1983. This realignment was supported by a package of measures aimed at reducing inflation and budget deficits. The present estimates show that the peg of the French franc to the Deutschmark became credible after these measures were implemented.

The results of the analysis that considers only non-negative price changes differ only slightly from the previous ones and are therefore not presented. All measures for estimating the change in credibility during the EMS period reaffirm the conclusions stated above, namely that credibility in French disinflation policy improved after 1983(3).

6.4 Italy

The impact of the two increases in oil prices on the expected (and actual) change in the Italian selling-price was greater than on the expected selling-prices in other countries. In addition, the huge depreciation of the Italian lira at the beginning of 1976 caused a sharp increase in the (expected) selling-prices. Hence during a period of about seven years, 1973 to 1980, three huge exogenous shocks dominated the development of the (expected) producer prices.

The effects of all three shocks led to an increase in the price of imported goods and were then almost immediately felt in the higher price of products. As a consequence the percentage change in the import prices and in producer prices is highly correlated. The inclusion of both time-series in a regression leads to multicollinearity and thus to spurious results. I therefore decided to estimate two sets of relations: those including lagged producer prices and those containing lagged percentage changes of import prices. The differences between the two sets of estimated regressions appeared to be very small: the same regressors are significant and the statistics indicate the same periods in which the estimated relation shows a structural change. From a statistical point of view, in most cases the regressions with lagged percentage changes in producer prices were slightly better than those with the lagged import prices. Therefore, I report only the results obtained by regressions with lagged producer prices.

During the 1970s the expected percentage change in producer prices appears to be explained by the lagged percentage change in the producer prices, the rate of capacity utilization, the intercept, a seasonal dummy, and dummy variables representing the first oil shock (*D74Q12*), and the sharp fall of the lira in 1976 (*D76Q23*). The disturbance terms of this relation meet all test statistics (Table 10.8, col. 1). From 1979 to 1984, the forecasts of this relation are lower than the actual expectation, whereas the reverse holds for 1986 to 1990. This suggests that during the first five years of its operation the ERM did not increase the credibility of the Italian monetary authorities. It might be that the difference between the forecasts and the actual expectations for the second half of the 1980s indicate that by 1985 the credibility of the Italian disinflation policy had increased. These differences might also reflect the effect of dollar movements.

The coefficients of $\mathring{p}_{t-1}$, *D74Q12* and the constant term remain significant if the previous relation is estimated for the entire period. However, the quality of the disturbance terms deteriorates considerably (Table 10.8, col. 2). Adding a dummy variable for the effects of the second increase in oil prices improves the quality of the disturbance terms, but they remain autocorrelated and heteroscedastic (col. 3 of the same table). In both equations the intercept is slightly smaller than in the pre-EMS relation. This might point at improved credibility of the Italian monetary policy. However, in my view the quality of the last two equations is so bad that they are not useful for an analysis of the change in credibility by means of recursive regression. According to Chow

TABLE 10.8. *Regression of the expected percentage change of the Italian selling prices*

Variables	Period				
	1969(4)–1978(4)	1969(4)–1989(4)	1969(4)–1989(4)	1979(1)–1989(4)	1979(1)–1989(4)
$E(\mathring{p}_{\mathrm{WG},t-1})$				0.803	0.806[a]
				(4.38)	(4.32)
$E(\mathring{p}_{\mathrm{WG},t-1})$					0.841[b]
					(3.29)
$\mathring{p}_{t-1}$	0.405	0.578	0.534	0.526	0.529
	(11.77)	(12.39)	(14.41)	(10.11)	(9.64)
$\mathring{p}_{t-2}$				–.302	–.306
				(3.47)	(3.39)
$\mathring{p}_{t-3}$				0.274	0.277
				(6.02)	(5.77)
q_{t-3}	0.113	0.070	0.074		
	(4.06)	(1.86)	(2.14)		
$\mathring{w}_{1,t-3}$				0.127	0.127
				(5.19)	(5.10)
$0.25\,\Sigma_{i=1}^{4}\,\mathring{m}1_{t-i}$				0.569	0.572
				(9.61)	(9.13)
D74Q12	–1.517	–3.196	–2.725		
	(3.13)	(4.20)	(4.21)		
D76Q23	0.970	–.467			
	(2.29)	(0.68)			
D7980			2.650		
			(4.89)		
D79Q4				1.166	1.159
				(3.58)	(3.49)
C	1.501	1.309	1.342	–1.00	–1.025
	(12.32)	(8.84)	(10.68)	(5.29)	(4.46)
S3				–.651	–.661
				(3.74)	(3.62)
R^2 (adj.)	0.89	0.71	0.76	0.97	0.97
SE	0.49	0.86	0.75	0.30	0.30
LM(1)	1.58	41.88***	27.84***	0.91	0.88
LM(4)	1.00	15.71***	11.66***	1.27	1.30
Q (4)	4.16	75.91***	63.11***	4.82	4.83
SK	0.48	0.51	0.08	0.27	0.26
K	2.19	3.96	2.44	3.73	3.75
JB	2.41	6.56***	1.15	1.52	1.53
ARCH (2)	2.34	11.09***	10.65***	0.47	0.50

[a] 1979(1)–1985(2)
[b] 1985(3)–1989(4)

break point tests it is most likely that a structural change occurred in the first quarter of 1979, although the statistics do not exclude the possibility of a break later in 1979.[13] Therefore, I have re-specified the expectations-generating

[13] These tests are calculated for the original relation excluding the two dummy variables. The test values (F-test) are: 19.05 for a break in 1979(1); 18.45 for a break in 1979(2); 15.75 for a break in 1979(3); and 13.40 for a break in 1979(4). The *P* value is zero for all these tests

function for the EMS period, starting in 1979(1). The disturbance terms of this relation meet all criteria (Table 10.8, col. 4). Contrary to the previous specification, the German expectations of selling-prices enter the equation with a significant coefficient. The recursive estimates of this coefficient reaffirm the impression of an improvement in the credibility at the end of 1985. The recursive estimate of the intercept shows a gradual decline in the 1980s. In order to determine the exact period in which the change occurs and the level of significance of the change, the relation has been re-estimated where the coefficient of $E(\mathring{p}_{WG,t-1})$ is allowed to change in a quarter of 1985. The greatest difference between the coefficient before and after the break is obtained if it is assumed that the change occurs in 1985(3). Then the coefficient in the second subperiod is 0.041 greater than that of the first subperiod (see Table 10.8, column 5), which is not statistically significant. The test statistics of the hypothesis of equal coefficients are: $F = 0.05$ and $P = 0.83$.

Once again relations are estimated that contain non-negative changes in inflation rates only, in order to investigate whether erroneously the disinflationary effect of the dollar is ascribed to the working of the EMS. The estimates (which can be obtained from the author) show much similarity with those of Table 10.8. The German expectations do not enter the relation with a significant coefficient for the pre-EMS period, whereas it is included in that of the EMS period. Lagged producer prices and percentage changes of the rate of capacity utilization are significant for the 1970s. The forecasts are lower than the actual expectations during the first years of the EMS, whereas the opposite holds for 1986 onwards. Once again, the recursive estimate of the coefficient of German expectations (lagged one quarter) slightly increases at the end of 1985, whereas the recursive estimate of the intercept decreases slightly after 1986. Estimates of the relation in which the coefficient of German expectations can change show again the greatest difference between the coefficient before and after the break when the break occurs in 1985(3). The difference between the coefficients before and after the break is now 0.07, which is insignificant. The test statistics of the hypothesis of equal coefficients are: $F = 0.20$, $P = 0.66$.

In sum, there is a structural change in the expectations-generating function in 1979. The expected German selling-prices, which were not significant in the relation for the 1970s, become relevant for the expectations-formation by the Italian producers. This increase in importance of German variables indicates that economic agents immediately were aware of the constraints which the EMS would impose on domestic policy. In fact they were right in that as from July 1981 the Italian central bank was no longer required to buy unsold Treasury bills (OECD, 1982: 42). The forecasts and the recursive estimates of the coefficient of the German expectations suggest that there is a further improvement in Italian anti-inflationary credibility in 1985. This might reflect the agents' confidence in the measures taken to reduce inflation in Italy. Examples of these measures are those adopted in early 1984 to mitigate the effects of the sliding wage-scale ('scala mobile') and the tight monetary policy in 1984 (see

OECD, 1985). Tests of a structural change of the last coefficient indicate, however, that this change is not statistically significant.

In large, our results correspond with those in Papi (1991), who uses another data-set of expectations and another specification of the expectations-generating function. A common factor of the present study and Papi's study is that the expectations of more or less informed agents are analysed. She also finds a structural decline in expected inflation in 1979, and although in her analysis there are some changes in the coefficients for later periods, as in the present study, these changes appear to be insignificant.

6.5 United Kingdom

For the United Kingdom the time-series of expected selling-prices start in 1976(1). In October 1990 the pound sterling entered the Exchange Rate Mechanism of the EMS. From about June 1990 onwards, there were already rumours about a possible entrance of the pound sterling into the ERM. Therefore, I selected the period ending in 1990(2) as the sterling's pre-ERM period. Some regressions were run for the period 1976(1) to 1990(2). The results of these regressions were very bad: the expected German price changes had significantly a negative sign and the disturbance was highly correlated. The plot of the differences between the expected price changes in the United Kingdom and Germany (Fig. 10.1*c*)) suggests that this bad performance of the relation might indicate that there is a structural change in the relation in the beginning of the 1980s. Chow break point tests reaffirm this suggestion. The highest value of the break-point statistic is obtained for 1980(3) ($F = 13.28$, $P = 0.0$). I therefore decided to estimate a relation for the period 1980(3)–1990(2).

The selected relation for the period 1980(3)–1990(2) shows that during the 1980s the expected changes in German selling-prices had a significant impact on the expectations of their British colleagues (Table 10.9, col. 1), although the German influence on British expectations (0.348) is smaller than that on the Belgian (0.531), French (0.752), and Italian (0.641) expectations. The coefficient of the producers' prices (lagged four periods) appears to be significant and negative. Deleting of this term leads to a high order of autocorrelation. Maybe this negative coefficient can be ascribed to the rather strong seasonal pattern in the time-series of expected selling-prices in the United Kingdom. The test statistics indicate that there is no autocorrelation of the first and fourth order in the disturbance terms, and that these are normally distributed. The hypothesis of no heteroscedasticity can, however, not be rejected. The forecasts for the period 1990(3) to 1991(2) are for 1991 higher than the actual expectations. For the United Kingdom the EMS period is too short to be used for estimating a relation. This also explains why the equation estimated for the entire period does not differ much from that of the pre-ERM period (Table 10.9 cols. 2 and 1, respectively). The Chow forecast test does indicate that the there is a structural change starting in 1990(3) (see bottom of Table 10.9).

TABLE 10.9. *Regression of the expected percentage change of the selling prices in the United Kingdom*

Variables	Period 1980(3)–1990(2)	Period 1980(3)–1991(2)
$E(\mathring{p}_{WG,t-1})$	0.348	0.330
	(5.09)	(4.67)
$\mathring{p}_{t-4}$	–.109	–.111
	(2.33)	(2.24)
$\mathring{w}_{1,t-1}$	0.058	0.059
	(2.85)	(2.78)
$\mathring{p}_{m,t-2}$	0.062	0.061
	(4.01)	(3.84)
C	0.881	0.909
	(11.06)	(11.16)
$S1$	0.546	0.539
	(5.45)	(5.31)
$S2$	0.559	0.495
	(6.24)	(5.41)
R^2 (adj.)	0.71	0.64
SE	0.19	0.20
LM(1)	0.04	0.07
LM(4)	0.12	0.29
Q (4)	0.65	1.09
SK	–.19	–.49
K	2.23	2.98
JB	1.24	1.78
ARCH (2)	2.95*	1.49

Note: Chow (forecast 1990(3)) F = 2.28, P = 0.08.

The forecast errors and Chow forecast test suggest that the entry of the pound sterling did reduce inflationary expectations in the United Kingdom. This result contrasts with that drawn from the forecasted values of the expectations of the other countries for which I could not find an immediate reduction in the expected inflation.[14] In my view the difference between the results for the United Kingdom, which entered the ERM in 1990, and those initial members of the ERM can be ascribed to the fact that in the first years of the EMS one was very sceptical on the sustainability of the system. Gradually, however, the monetary authorities obtained credibility for their policy of using the EMS as a disinflationary mechanism (see for example our results for France). At the beginning of the 1990s the EMS had established a reputation as a credible anti-inflation mechanism.

7. CONCLUSIONS

In this chapter I have investigated whether the membership of the EMS and in particular of its Exchange Rate Mechanism has reduced the inflationary

[14] Note that introduction of the EMS led to a greater influence of German expectations on Italian expectations. This is also a test of the influence of the EMS.

expectations in European countries. In contrast to the majority of papers on this subject, use has been made of a direct measure of inflationary expectations, namely the producers' expectations on selling-prices for the months ahead. An additional advantage of these data is that the questionnaire is the same for all countries concerned so that no differences between countries can be ascribed to differences in the data collection. Forecast errors, recursive regressions, and tests on structural changes (CUSUM of squares and Chow tests) are used for detecting the influence of the countries' membership of the ERM on inflationary expectations.

The results suggest that the EMS has led to an increase in inflationary expectations in Germany. Hence, it is likely that at times producers thought that the Bundesbank would (partly) give way to the pleas of ERM members with higher inflation rates to loosen its strict restrictive monetary policy. The expectation of an increase in inflation might also reflect the confidence of the agents in fixed exchange rates. Then they expect that higher foreign prices will give rise to higher German prices because there will be no compensating appreciation of the Deutschmark. For Belgium the results are inconclusive: some tests indicate an improvement in credibility while others point in the opposite direction. The graph of the difference between the Belgian and German expected selling-price suggests that this result is due to the fact that during the period 1980–4 Belgian producers expected higher price increases than their German colleagues, whereas the opposite holds for the years before and after this period. Hence, credibility in the Belgian anti-inflationary policy was low during the first years of the EMS. The credibility of French monetary policy increased at the end of 1983, about six months after the realignment of March 1983. This realignment was supported by a package of restrictive measures in budgetary and monetary policy. For Italy a structural break occurred in 1979. Whereas before 1979 German expectations did not influence Italian expectations, German expectations are significant explanatory variables during the EMS period. This is a sign that the agents were aware of the constraints the EMS would impose on Italian policy. The pound sterling's entry into the ERM appears to have increased the credibility of British anti-inflationary policy in 1991. This result suggests that at the beginning of the 1990s the EMS had established a reputation as a credible anti-inflation mechanism.

APPENDIX 1.

Deriving Inflationary Expectations

The time-series of expected selling-prices in manufacturing are derived from a monthly survey by the national bureaux of statistics of member countries. The respondents were asked whether they expected that in the months ahead the selling-prices would: (a) go up, (b) unchange, or (c) go down. For each country the answers on these questions are summarized in the following statistics.

$_tR^e_{t+1}$: proportion of firms that at time t expect a rice in their price from t to t+1
$_tF^e_{t+1}$: proportion of firms that at time t expect a fall in their price from t to t+1
$_tN^e_{t+1}$: neutral
$_tB^e_{t+1}$: $tR^e_{t+1} - {}_tF^e_{t+1}$ balance statistic.

The European Commission regularly publishes the balances $_tB^e_{t+1}$.

These qualitative data are converted into quantitative data by means of the probability method.[15] Important assumptions of this method are that 'except for a finite number of parameters, the form of the subjective probability distribution of the respondents over future changes in the variable in question is the same' and 'an expected change will be reported only when respondents expect the variable in question to change by more than a certain threshold value' (Pesaran, 1987: 211). Various variants of the probability method are available. The main differences between these variants concern the assumption with regard to the probability distribution and the characteristics of the indifference interval. The probability distributions that have been used are the uniform, logistic, and normal distribution. The indifference interval can be assumed to be symmetrical or asymmetrical with respect to the origin, and its boundaries can be assumed to be constant or variable.

Assume that the distribution is uniform with a constant range $2q$ and that the indifference interval is symmetrical. In this case the estimate of the expected inflation, $_t\pi^e_{t+1}$, is:

$$_t\pi^e_{t+1} = q\, {}_tB^e_{t+1}. \tag{A1.1}$$

Relaxing the assumption of a symmetrical indifference interval yields:

$$_t\pi^e_{t+1} = \alpha\, {}_tR^e_{t+1} - \beta\, {}_tF^e_{t+1}, \tag{A1.2}$$

where

$$\alpha = \frac{2q\,(q-a)}{2q-a-b}, \beta = \frac{2q\,(q-b)}{2q-a-b}.$$

In both cases the variance of the expected inflation is constant, which implies that it is assumed that the uncertainty of the expectations does not change.

The variance of the expectations is time-variant if the range of the uniform distribution varies with time and the indifference interval is assumed to be symmetrical (Visco, 1984: 69–71). In this case the formula of expected inflation is:

15 See Pesaran (1987): 211–24, and Visco (1984): 21–8 and 65–74 for a description and assessment of this method.

$$ {}_t\pi^e_{t+1} = c\,({}_tB^e_{t+1} / {}_tN^e_{t+1}) = c\,{}_td^e_{t+1}, \tag{A1.3}$$

where

$$ {}_tN^e_{t+1} = 1 - {}_tF^e_{t+1} - {}_tR^e_{t+1}.$$

Under an asymmetric indifference interval the conversion formula is:

$$ {}_t\pi^e_{t+1} = \alpha\, X^e_{1,t+1} - \beta\, X^e_{2,t+1}, \tag{A1.4}$$

where

$$X^e_{1,t+1} = \frac{(1 - 2\,{}_tN^e_{t+1})\,{}_tR^e_{t+1} - {}_tF^e_{t+1}}{2\,{}_tN^e_{t+1}\,(1 - N^e_{t+1})}$$

$$X^e_{2,t+1} = \frac{(1 - 2\,N^e_{t+1})\,{}_tF^e_{t+1} - {}_tR^e_{t+1}}{2\,{}_tN^e_{t+1}\,(1 - N^e_{t+1})}$$

All four conversion formulas presented above assume a uniform distribution.

Where the distribution is normal, the indifference interval is symmetric and its boundaries fixed, the conversion formula becomes:

$$ {}_t\pi^e_{t+1} = c\,{}_td^e_{t+1}, \tag{A1.5}$$

where

$${}_td^e_{t+1} = \frac{{}_tf^e_{t+1} + {}_tr^e_{t+1}}{{}_tf^e_{t+1} - {}_tr^e_{t+1}}$$

$${}_tf^e_{t+1} = \phi^{-1}\,({}_tF^e_{t+1})$$

$${}_tr^e_{t+1} = \phi^{-1}\,(1 - {}_tR^e_{t+1}).$$

(ϕ Cumulative distribution of standard normal variable)

Assuming a logistic distribution instead of a normal one leads to the following variant:

$${}_tf^e_{t+1} = \log \frac{1 - {}_tF^e_{t+1}}{{}_tF^e_{t+1}}$$

$${}_tr^e_{t+1} = \log \frac{{}_tR^e_{t+1}}{1.0 - {}_tR^e_{t+1}}$$

In order to be able to estimate the scaling parameters in the equations, it is assumed that the expectations are unbiased on average. Then an estimate of the parameter in (A1.5) is:

$$\hat{c} = \Sigma\,\pi_t / \Sigma\,{}_{t-1}d^e_t. \tag{A1.6}$$

The coefficients α and β in formulas (A1.2) and (A1.4) are estimated by means of Ordinary Least Squares.

The various methods for deriving expected price changes yield almost identical time-series. The correlation coefficients between the various proxies range from 0.91 to 0.999. Especially, the time-series derived from the balances only is highly correlated with that derived under the assumption of a normal or a logistic distribution (see Wolters and Lankers, 1989, for similar results). These three proxies are based on the assumption of a symmetrical indifference interval.

The expectations derived from the uniform distribution with a range that varies with time fluctuate more than the others. Especially the two increases in oil prices, 1973/4 and 1979, have a greater impact on these two expectation proxies that on the others. In general this implies that these two series are better forecasts of the actual rise in producer prices than the other proxies. One exception, however, is the effect of the second oil shock on price increases in Italy. Then, the formulas (A1.3) and (A1.4) overpredict the actual price increase.

As is well known (Pesaran 1987: 120 and Visco 1984: 67) for continuous probability distributions, the probability method breaks down whenever the percentage of respondents reporting a rise (or a fall) in prices is equal to zero. In our sample the percentage of respondents reporting a fall is zero in France in 1973(3) and 1974(1) and in Italy during the period 1974(1)–1974(2). Hence, during these periods, the formulas based on the normal and logistic probability distribution are not applicable. Therefore, in the regressions explaining the expectation formation use will be made of the proxies derived from the uniform distribution.

The assumptions underlying formula (A1.4) are less restrictive than those of the other proxies based on uniform distribution. This time-series also shows the highest correlation with the actual time-series. The analysis is therefore based on the time-series of expected percentage changes in selling-prices derived under the assumptions of uniform probability distribution with time-varying range and an asymmetrical indifference interval.

APPENDIX 2.

Data Sources

Two main sources have been used, namely the *Main Economic Indicators* (*MEI*) published by the Organization for Economic Co-operation and Development and the *International Financial Statistics* (*IFS*) published by the International Monetary Fund.

q:	For the United Kingdom this series is the percentage of firms operating at full capacity: manufacturing. For the other countries it is the rate of capacity utilization. *Source:* OECD,*MEI*
D7374:	Dummy variable which is 1 in 1973(4) and in 1974(1) and zero elsewhere.
D76Q23:	Dummy variable which is 1 in 1976(2) and (3), and in 1976 (3) and zero elsewhere.
D74Q12:	Dummy variable which is 1 in 1974(1) and 1974(2) and zero elsewhere
D76Q2:	Dummy variable which is 1 in 1976(2) and zero elsewhere
D7980:	Dummy variable which is 1 in 1979(4) and 1980(1) and zero elsewhere
D79Q4:	Dummy variable which is 1 in 1979 (4) and zero elsewhere
DUMBL:	Dummy variable which is 1 from 1980(1) onwards and zero in the periods before
DUMFR:	Dummy variable which is 1 from 1983(4) onwards and zero in the periods before
DUMWG:	Dummy variable which is 1 in 1984(1) onwards and zero in the periods before
m:	Money (national definitions): *IFS* line 59mc. This series has been used for the United Kingdom because the M1 series contains some changes in the definition
*m*1:	Money. *Source*: *IFS*, line 34
*m*2:	Money (broad definition) consisting of money (*IFS*, line 34) and quasi-money (*IFS*, line 35).
p_{m}:	Unit value of imports. *Source*: *IFS*, line 75
$E(p)$:	Expected selling price
p:	Producer prices (*IFS*, line 63). The German series refers to the prices of industrial products. For France this is the time-series of prices of industrial goods for the period up to 1985. Starting with 1986(1) it is the price of intermediate industrial goods. The Italian series is the wholesale prices and stops in 1989(4). The Belgian series has been corrected for a break in 1980(1)
*S*1, *S*2, *S*3, *S*4:	Seasonal dummies
w_1:	Unit labour costs. For Belgium, Germany, the Netherlands, and the United Kingdom the unit labour costs from the databank of the *MEI*. The times-series of France and Italy are from the National Accounts
w:	Wages. *Source*: *IFS*, line 65. For Belgium and Germany it is a series of hourly earnings. French time-series includes wages and other labour costs established by law or contracts. The Italian series is an index of contractual wages per worker.

The subscript WG refers to West Germany

REFERENCES

Agénor, P-R, and M. P. Taylor (1992). 'Testing for Credibility Effects', *IMF Staff Papers*, 39/3: 545–571.

Anderson, T. M., and O. Risager (1988). 'Stabilisation Policies, Credibility, and Interest Rate Determination in a Small Open Economy', *European Economic Review*, 32. 669–679.

Argy, V. (1990). 'Choice of the Exchange Rate Regime for a Smaller Economy: A Survey of Some Key Issues', in V. Argy and P. De Grauwe (eds.), *Choosing an Exchange Rate Regime: The Challenge for Smaller Industrial Countries*, IMF: 6–81.

Artis, M., and D. Nachane (1990). 'Wages and Prices in Europe: A Test of the German Leadership Thesis', *Weltwirtschaftliches Archiv*, 126: 59–77.

—— and P. Ormerod (1991). 'Is there an "EMS effect" in European Labour Markets?', CEPR Discussion Papers, 598 (Dec.), repr. with addenda in C. Johnson and S. Collignon (eds.) *The Monetary Economics of Europe*, Pinter, 1994.

Artus, J. R., and A. K. McGuirk (1981). 'A Revised Version of the Multilateral Exchange Rate Model, *IMF Staff Papers*, 28/2: 275–309.

Barrell, R., J. Darby, and C. Donaldson (1990). 'Structural Stability in European Wage and Price Systems', *National Institute Discussion Paper*, 188.

Barro, R. J. and C. Gordon (1983). 'A Positive Theory of Monetary Policy in a Natural Rate Model', *Journal of Political Economy*, 91/4: 589–610.

Batchelor, R. A. (1981), 'Aggregate Expectations Under the Stable Laws', *Journal of Econometrics*, 16: 199–210.

Blanchard, O. J., and S. Fischer (1989). *Lectures on Macroeconomics*, MIT Press, Cambridge, Mass.

Bowden, R. J., and D. A. Turkington (1984). *Instrumental Variables*, Cambridge University Press, Cambridge.

Chadha, B. P. Masson, and G. Meredith (1992). 'Models of Inflation and the Costs of Disinflation', *IMF Staff Papers* 39/2: 395–431.

Christensen, M. (1987*a*). 'Disinflation, Credibility and Price Inertia: A Danish Exposition', *Applied Economics*, 19: 1353–66.

—— (1987*b*). 'On Interest-Rate Determination, Testing for Policy Credibility, and the relevance of the Lucas Critique: Some Danish Experiences', *European Journal of Political Economy*, 3/3: 369–88.

Collins, S. M. (1988). 'Inflation and the European Monetary System', in F. Giavazzi, S. Micossi, and M. Miller, (eds.), *The European Monetary System*, Cambridge University Press: 112–36.

—— and F. Giavazzi (1992). 'Attitudes Towards Inflation and the Viability of Fixed Exchange Rates: Evidence from the EMS, *NBER Working Papers*, 4057.

De Grauwe, P. (1989*a*). 'The Cost of Disinflation and the European Monetary System', Centrum voor Economische Studiën, Katholieke Universiteit Leuven, Discussion Paper, 60.

—— (1989*b*). *International Money: Post-War Trends and Theories*, Clarendon Press, Oxford.

De Jong, E. (1991). 'Exchange Rate Determination and Optimal Economic Policy under Various Exchange Rate Regimes', *Lecture Notes in Economics and Mathematical Systems*, 359, Springer-Verlag, Heidelberg.

Driffill, J., G. E. Mizon, and A. Ulph (1990). 'Costs of Inflation', in B. M. Friedman and F. H. Hahn (eds.), *Handbook of Monetary Economics*, ii: 1013–66.

EEC (1990). 'One Market, One Money', *European Economy*, 44.

Egebo, T., and A. S. Englander (1992). 'Institutional Commitments and Policy Credibility: A Critical Survey and Empirical Evidence from the ERM', *OECD Economic Studies*, 18: 45–84.

Englander, A. S., and T. Egebo (1992). 'Adjustment under Fixed Exchange Rates: Application to the European Monetary System', *OECD Working Papers*, 117.

Ericsson, N. R., J. Campos, and H.-A. Tran (1991). 'PC-GIVE and Hendry's Econometric Methodology', Board of the Governors of the Federal Reserve System, *International Finance Discussion Papers*, 406.

Fratianni, M., and J. von Hagen (1990). 'Credibility and Assymetries in the EMS', in V. Argy and P. De Grauwe (eds.), *Choosing an Exchange Rate Regime: The Challenge for Smaller Industrial Countries*, IMF, Washington, DC: 285–315.

Giavazzi F., and A. Giovannini (1988). 'The Role of the Exchange-Rate Regime in a Disinflation: Empirical Evidence on the European Monetary System', in F. Giavazzi, S. Micossi, and M. Miller (eds.), *The European Monetary System*, Cambridge University Press: 85–107.

—— —— (1989). *Limiting Exchange Rate Flexibility: The European Monetary System*, MIT Press, Cambridge, Mass.

—— and M. Pagano (1988). 'The Advantage of Tying One's Hands', *European Economic Review*, 32: 1055–82.

Gramlich, E. M. (1983). 'Models of Inflation Expectations Formation: A Comparison of Household and Economic Forecasts', *Journal of Money Credit and Banking*, 15/2: 155–73.

Harvey, A. (1990). *The Econometric Analysis of Time Series*, 2nd edn., Philip Allan, New York.

Herz, B., and W. Röger (1992). 'The EMS is a Greater Deutschmark Area', *European Economic Review*, 36/7: 1413–25.

In 't Veld, J. W. (1992). 'The Diverse Experience of The Netherlands, Belgium and Denmark in the ERM', in R. Barrell (ed), *Economic Convergence and Monetary Union in Europe*, SAGE Publications, London: 154–73.

Kremers, J. J. M. (1990). 'Gaining Policy Credibility for a Disinflation: Irelands' Experience in the EMS', *International Monetary Fund Staff Papers*, 37/1: 116–45.

Miller, M., and A. Sutherland (1991). 'The Walters' Critique of the EMS: A Case of Inconsistent Expectations?', *The Manchester School*, 59 (Supple): 33–7.

Mohlo, L. (1991). 'The Italian Lira in the Narrow ERM Band: The Challenge of Credibility', *IMF Working Paper*, WP/91/19.

Organization for Economic Co-operation and Development (1982) *Italy, OECD Economic Surveys 1982–1983*.

—— (1985) *Italy, OECD Economic Surveys 1984–1985*.

Papi, L. (1991). 'The Exchange Rate Mechanism and Inflation Performance: A Survey and Some Empirical Evidence for Italy', mimeo, Warwick University.

Pesaran, H. M. (1987). *The Limits to Rational Expectations*, Blackwell, Oxford.

Sachs, J., and C. Wyplosz (1986). 'The Economic Consequences of President Mitterand', *Economic Policy*, 2: 261–323.

Simmons, P. and D. Weiserbs (1992), 'Consumer Price Perceptions and Expectations', *Oxford Economic Papers*, 44: 35–50.

Thygesen, N. (1988). 'Introduction', in F. Giavazzi, S. Micossi, and M. Miller (eds.), *The European Monetary System*, Cambridge University Press, 1–20.
Ungerer, H., J. J. Hauvonen, A. Lopez-Claros, and T. Mayer (1990), 'The European Monetary System: Developments and Perspectives', *IMF Occasional Paper*, 73.
Visco, I. (1984). *Price Expectations in Rising Inflation*, North-Holland, Amsterdam.
Walters, A. (1986). *Britain's Economic Renaissance: Margaret Thatcher's Reforms 1979–1984*, OUP.
Weber (1991). 'EMS Credibility', *Economic Policy*, 12: 58–102.
Wolters, J., and F. Lankes (1989). 'Das Ifo-Geschäftsklima als Kunjunkturindikator: Empirische Ergebnisse für die Verbrauchs- und Investionsgüterindustrie für 1975–1986', *IFO-Studien*, 35/2–4: 198–209.

11

Determination of Long-Term Interest Rates in the EMS

GEBHARD KIRCHGÄSSNER
JÜRGEN WOLTERS

I. INTRODUCTION

One of the entry conditions which prospective European Monetary Union (EMU) members have to fulfil according to the Maastricht agreement is the convergence of long-term interest rate levels. The convergence criterium says that the average long-term interest rate of a country must not exceed by more than 2 percentage points the levels of the three lowest long-term interest rates. Long-term interest rates are taken as an indicator of the durability of convergence. They reflect expected inflation and risk premia. Therefore, in the absence of risk premia real long-term interest rates should equalize if capital markets are perfect and integrated. Moreover, if the bands become very small and realignments are ruled out in the established exchange rate mechanism, this results in a credible commitment to a fixed exchange rate system.[1] In this case nominal interest rates converge and if Germany dominates the other EMS members, monetary policy for all EMS members is set by the German Bundesbank.[2]

In this chapter we are going to describe and explain the development of long-term interest rates in Europe in relation to the German long-term interest rate during the period from January 1980 to December 1991. We present results for Belgium, Denmark, France, Italy, Ireland, and the Netherlands as members of the exchange rate mechanism as well as for the United Kingdom. There already exist papers dealing with the explanation of long-term interest rates in Europe as, for example, Artus *et al.* (1991), Bruneau and Nicolai (1991), or Kneeshaw and Van den Bergh (1985). But these papers generally examine two different aspects: either they treat only the relation between France and Germany (Artus *et al.*, 1991 and Bruneau and Nicolai, 1991) or they investigate only relations

Paper presented at the Seminar of the Europa-Institut, Universität des Saarlandes, 2 July 1993 and at the Congress of the European Economic Association, Helsinki, 27–9 August, 1993; Revised version, September 1993. We gratefully acknowledge financial support from the EC, No. SPES-CT91-0053. We thank P. De Grauwe, B. Lucke, and G. Tullio for helpful suggestions and comments on an earlier version of this chapter.

[1] See e.g. Currie *et al.* (1992).

[2] For a discussion of German dominance in the EMS see e.g. Kirchgässner and Wolters (1993).

in changes of interest rates as Kneeshaw and Van den Bergh (1985) did. From a methodological point of view we, explicitly, take into account the non-stationarity of interest rates and try to model these in an adequate way. Therefore, we analyse the co-integration properties according to Engle and Granger (1987) and estimate error-correction models. This gives empirical information about the adjustment processes as well as the relations in levels. Especially, the level relations are important for the judgement of the convergence behaviour of long-term interest rates within Europe.

The chapter is organized in the following way. First, we present some descriptive measures of convergence. Then in Section 3 we discuss the time-series properties of interest and inflation rates. In Section 4 our theoretical and methodological approaches are presented, followed in Section 5 by the empirical results for the different countries. In Section 6 we compare the long-term relations and in Section 7 we present simulations for the year 1992. Our conclusions are summarized in Section 8.

2. DESCRIPTIVE MEASURES OF CONVERGENCE

As far as the level of long-term interest rates is concerned, one very simple and straightforward measure of convergence is the nominal interest rate differential between Germany and the other European countries.[3] Looking at Fig. 11.1 we see a more or less declining differential for Belgium, France, and Italy since 1982–3. At the end of 1991 the Belgian and French rates reached about the

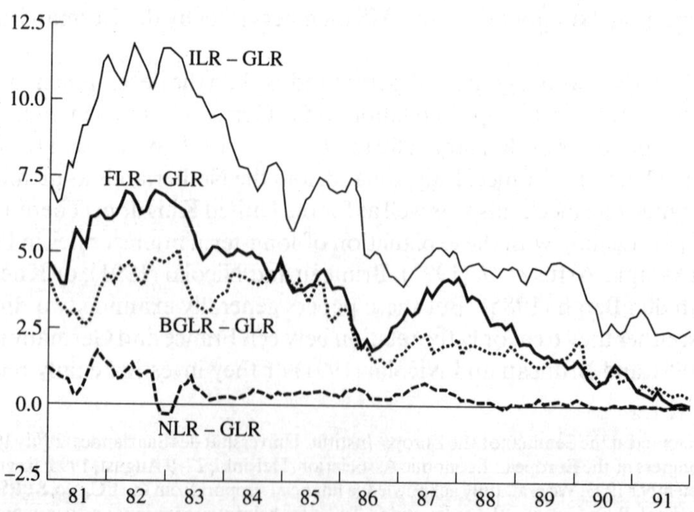

FIG. 11.1. Nominal interest rate differentials

[3] For the description and sources of data see the Appendix.

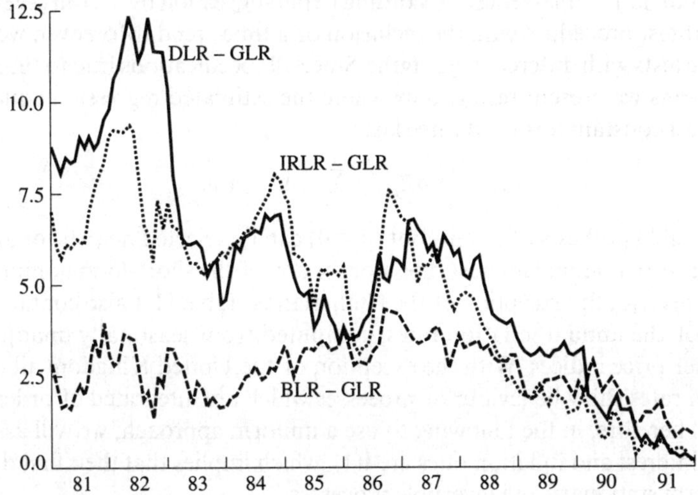

FIG. 11.2. Nominal interest rate differentials

same level as the German rate. The difference between the Italian and German rates stays at about 3 percentage points. For Ireland and Denmark (see Fig. 11.2) the interest rate differentials declined between 1982 and 1991, but they show three distinct peaks. At the end of 1991 both differentials nearly vanished. The difference in the long-term interest rate levels between the Netherlands and Germany, which is very small, vanishes totally as of 1988. During the whole period UK long-term interest rates are about 2–3 percentage points higher than German rates.

High interest rate differentials can be seen as an indicator of the persistence of devaluation expectations and, therefore, as a lack of credibility of the established exchange rate agreements. Apparently there are no credibility problems between the Netherlands and Germany. A lot of credibility has been gained for all other countries except Italy and the United Kingdom. For both countries the mechanism does not seem credible, and devaluation expectations persist. Nevertheless, the interest rate criterium had been met by all countries except Italy by the end of 1991.

3. TIME-SERIES BEHAVIOUR

In this part we investigate the stationarity properties of interest rates, inflation rates, and interest rate differentials, and test for bivariate co-integration between short- and long-term interest rates as well as between European long-term interest rates vs. the German long-term interest rate.

We apply the augmented Dickey–Fuller test to find the order of integration for the individual time-series.[4] According to the suggestion by Perron (1988) we start our test procedure with the inclusion of a time-trend. Moreover, we perform the tests with different lag lengths. Since all specifications lead to the same conclusions we present results only where the estimated regression equation contains a constant term and three lags:

$$\Delta X_t = c + \rho X_{t-1} + \sum_{i=1}^{3} a_i \Delta X_{t-i} + u_t. \tag{1}$$

The null hypothesis of a unit root ($\rho = 0$) can be rejected neither for any of the long-term nominal interest rates nor for any of the short-term nominal interest rates with the exception of the Netherlands. Table 11.1 also contains the results of the annual inflation rates, computed from seasonally unadjusted consumer price indices. With the exception of the United Kingdom all other inflation rates show behaviour of processes which are integrated of order one (I(1)). Therefore, in the following to use a uniform approach, we will assume that all interest and inflation rates are I(1), which implies that their first differences form stationary and invertible processes.

TABLE 11.1. *Unit root tests for interest and inflation rates. Augmented Dickey-Fuller test with constant term and 3 lags* (Sample period 1980(1)–1991(12))

	$[\hat{t}]$		$[\hat{t}]$		$[\hat{t}]$
BLR	–1.85	BSR	–2.54	INFB	–4.80**
BGLR	–0.94	BGSR	–1.71	INFBG	–0.66
DLR	–1.08	—	—	INFD	–1.19
FLR	–1.03	FSR	–1.86	INFF	–1.72
GLR	–1.55	GSR	–1.47	INFG	–1.53
ILR	–0.86	ISR	–1.01	INFI	–1.51
IRLR	–1.29	IRSR	–2.28	INFIR	–0.95
NLR[a]	–1.78	NSR	–3.42*	INFN	–1.17

*,** The null hypothesis of a unit root can be rejected at the 0.05, or 0.01 level, respectively.

[a] Sample period 1981(1)–1991(12).

The spreads between the national long- and short-term interest rates also show I(1) behaviour except for Belgium, France, and Ireland (see Table 11.2). This result is confirmed in Table 11.3. Here the outcomes of the co-integrating regressions

$$XLR_t = \alpha + \beta\, XSR_t + u_t, \qquad X \varepsilon \{B, BG, F, G, I, IR, N\} \tag{2}$$

are presented together with the results of the augmented Dickey–Fuller co-integration tests. The null hypothesis of no co-integration is only rejected for

[4] See e.g. Dickey *et al.* (1986). We do not apply the non-parametric approach by Phillips and Perron (1988), since Schwert (1989) has shown in a Monte Carlo study that this approach has drawbacks when the MA-process has first-order negative autocorrelation.

TABLE 11.2. *Unit root tests for long-short spread and for long-term nominal interest rate differentials. Augmented Dickey-Fuller test with constant term and 3 lags* (Sample period 1980(1)–1991(12))

	$[\hat{t}]$		$[\hat{t}]$
BLR–BSR	–2.46	BLR–GLR	–2.38
BGLR–BGSR	–3.27*	BGLR–GLR	–0.74
—	—	DLR–GLR	–1.02
FLR–FSR	–3.00*	FLR–GLR	–0.40
GLR–GSR	–1.52	—	—
ILR–ISR	–1.91	ILR–GLR	–0.74
IRLR–IRSR	–3.50**	IRLR–GLR	–1.20
NLR–NSR[a]	–1.77	NLR–GLR[a]	–3.63**

*,** The null hypothesis of a unit root can be rejected at the 0.05, or 0.01 level, respectively.
[a] Sample period 1981(1)–1991(12).

TABLE 11.3. *Cointegration tests for long- and short-run interest rates. Augmented Dickey-Fuller test with 3 lags* (Sample period 1980(1)–1991(12))

$XLR = \alpha + \beta\, XSR + u,\ X \varepsilon \{B, BG, F, G, I, IR, N\}$		
	$[\hat{\beta}]$	$[\hat{t}]$
United Kingdom	0.36	–1.83
Belgium	0.68	–3.85*
France	0.97	–2.84
Germany	0.54	–2.31
Italy	1.07	–2.47
Ireland	0.94	–3.15(*)
Netherlands[a]	0.70	–1.66

(*), * The null hypothesis of no cointegration can be rejected at the 0.1, or 0.05 level, respectively.
[a] Sample period 1981(1)–1991(12).

Belgium on the 5 per cent and for Ireland on the 10 per cent level. According to these findings no relations in levels between domestic short- and long-term interest rates seem to exist in most European countries. Level developments in money and bond markets seem to be separated.

Nominal long-term interest rate differentials show non-stationary behaviour with the exception of the relation between the Netherlands and Germany (see Table 11.2). In Table 11.4 the results of the corresponding bivariate cointegration tests are shown for the periods from 1980 to 1991 and 1983 to 1991. The following regressions are run:

$$XLR_t = \alpha + \beta\, GLR_t + u_t,\ X \varepsilon \{B, BG, D, F, I, IR, N\} \qquad (3)$$

Again the convergence of Dutch and German long-term interest rates is confirmed. For 1983 to 1991 the British and the German long-term rates seem

TABLE 11.4. *Cointegration tests for long-run nominal interest rate differentials. Augmented Dickey-Fuller test with 3 lags*

$XLR = \alpha + \beta\, GLR + u,\ X \varepsilon \{B, BG, D, F, I, IR, N\}$

	1980(1)–1991(12)		1983(1)–1991(12)	
	$[\hat{\beta}]$	$[\hat{t}]$	$[\hat{\beta}]$	$[\hat{t}]$
United Kingdom	0.75	–2.78	0.44	–3.40*
Belgium	1.16	–0.87	0.87	–1.21
Denmark	1.60	–1.10	0.08	–1.01
France	1.28	–0.51	0.59	–1.92
Italy	1.59	–1.09	0.83	–2.12
Ireland	1.18	–0.88	0.11	–1.53
Netherlands	1.08[a]	–3.44*	0.91	–3.93*

* The null hypothesis of no cointegration can be rejected at the 0.05 level.

[a] Sample period 1981(1)–1991(12).

to be co-integrated. If two interest rates have converged and they stay in this situation, then we should find co-integration behaviour with $\alpha = 0$ and $\beta = 1$. This is more or less the case for the Netherlands, but not for the United Kingdom.

We can sum up so far: during the period from 1980 to 1991 the development of the long-run interest rates can be characterized by diminishing differentials to the German rate. It seems that convergence was reached at the end of 1991. Only for the Netherlands was the convergence process reached by the beginning of the 1980s and a one-to-one relationship has existed since then.

4. THEORETICAL AND METHODOLOGICAL APPROACH

Often two different hypotheses are used to explain the movements of nominal long-term interest rates. In the context of a closed economy long-term interest rates are explained with the help of the expectations hypothesis of the term structure. Assuming adaptive expectations leads to the model developed by Modigliani and Sutch (1966), whereas in the Campbell and Shiller (1987) model rational expectations are supposed. The Modigliani and Sutch approach presupposes that level relations between short- and long-term interest rates exist. In the Campbell and Shiller model the spread between long- and short-term rates has to be stationary. As we have seen before, in our data-set, these requirements are not fulfilled in most European countries.

Since we are more interested in international linkages, we concentrate on the uncovered interest rate parity (UIP) hypothesis as a possible explanation for the development of long-term interest rates.

The validity of UIP demands rather strong assumptions.[5] Capital has to be perfectly mobile, domestic and foreign bonds are perfect substitutes implying the absence of transaction costs, no differences exist in national tax systems, and no risk premia in forward markets, which are additionally regarded as efficient. Under these conditions in a linearized form[6] nominal interest rate differentials equal the expected change in the exchange rate over the holding period *n*:

$$R_t - R_t^* = E_t(e_{t+n}) - e_t, \tag{4}$$

with

- R_t: domestic *n* period nominal interest rate at period *t*,
- R_t^*: foreign *n* period nominal interest rate at period *t*,
- e_t: logarithm of the exchange rate denominated as the domestic price of the foreign currency,
- $E_t(\cdot)$: conditional expectation given all information available up to time-period *t*.

For a small country participating in a fixed exchange rate regime UIP has strong implications. If there are no realignment expectations, then the domestic interest rate is totally determined by the foreign interest rate. If all assumptions of UIP are fulfilled, then the domestic interest rate equals the foreign interest rate:

$$R_t = R_t^*. \tag{5}$$

If deviations between domestic and foreign interest rates occur, this may be an indication of the existence of risk premia.

In a floating exchange rate system where, as is often empirically observed, exchange rates follow a random walk, UIP also implies a long-run equilibrium relation between nominal interest rates.

Purchasing power parity is one theoretical long-run relation determining exchange rates. In empirical work this relation is often used in its relative form

$$p_t - p_t^* = \alpha + e_t \tag{6}$$

with

- p_t: logarithm of domestic price index,
- p_t^*: logarithm of foreign price index,
- α: a constant scaling term.

Taking conditional expectations of (6) we get

$$E_t(p_{t+n}) - E_t(p_{t+n}^*) = \alpha + E_t(e_{t+n}), \tag{7}$$

and subtracting (6) from (7) leads to

$$E_t(p_{t+n}) - p_t - (E_t(p_{t+n}^*) - p_t^*) = E_t(e_{t+n}) - e_t. \tag{8'}$$

[5] See e.g. Kirchgässner and Wolters (1990) and the literature quoted there.
[6] See e.g. Cumby and Obstfeld (1984). We use the linearization $\ln(1 + x) \approx x$.

With π_t^e the n-period expected inflation rate we can write

$$\pi_t^e - \pi_t^{e*} = E_t(e_{t+n}) - e_t. \tag{8}$$

Substituting (8) into (4) gives the equalization of *ex ante* real interest rates

$$R_t - \pi_t^e = R_t{}^* - \pi_t^{e*} \tag{9}$$

If identical tax systems, no capital controls, no risk premia, and no realignment expectations exist in a fixed exchange rate system, then according to (5) it is expected that nominal interest rates are the same across all countries. If additionally relative purchasing power parity theory holds, then according to (9) also *ex ante* real interest rates are equalized across countries.

Since, as we have seen in section 3, there is clear evidence that nominal long-term bond rates and inflation rates are I(1)-processes, we formulate the relations in error-correction form. This allows testing and estimating co-integrating relations and to discriminating between short-run adjustment processes and long-run parity conditions.

The long-term rates which are chosen according to data availability and to their importance in the national policy discussion have different times to maturity. In the countries considered different tax systems exist. During our sample period capital controls existed, especially for Italy and France. Moreover, it is extremely difficult to model and to measure long-term inflation expectations in a correct manner. Here we employ annual inflation rates for period t and assume some kind of static expectations for the *ex ante* inflation rate. The prevailing rate is the predictor for the future rate. Due to all these reasons we do not impose the theoretical coefficients in the parity conditions but estimate these parameters.[7] Moreover, in the short run we also allow for the influence of national and German monetary policy by including corresponding changes of short-term interest rates. In the following, r (r^*) denotes the domestic (foreign) short-term nominal interest rate. Thus, we not only explain the development of long-term interest rates by currency substitution but also by impacts of monetary policy.

Our empirical approach is, in the sense of the Hendry methodology, a general to specific one. We start the process of estimation with the same general model for all countries:[8]

$$\begin{aligned}\Delta R_t = {} & a_0 + a_1 \Delta R_{t-1} + a_2 \Delta R_t{}^* + a_3 \Delta R_{t-1}{}^* + a_4 \Delta\pi_t + a_5 \Delta\pi_{t-1} \\ & + a_6 \Delta\pi_t{}^* + a_7 \Delta\pi_{t-1}{}^* + b_1 \Delta r_t + b_2 \Delta r_{t-1} + b_3 \Delta r_t{}^* + b_4 \Delta r_{t-1}{}^* \\ & + c_1 R_{t-1} + c_2 \pi_{t-1} + c_3 R_{t-1}{}^* + c_4 \pi_{t-1}{}^* + u_t\end{aligned} \tag{10}$$

with

$$c_1 < 0, c_2 \geq 0, c_3 > 0, c_4 \leq 0.$$

[7] See also Muscatelli *et al.* (1989), who develop models of risk-adjusted UIP which do not lead to a one-to-one relationship between nominal rates.

[8] The lag length chosen is general enough to empirically model the adjustment processes.

There is a general consensus that Germany plays a dominant role in the EMS. Therefore, we use the German interest and inflation rates as foreign variables. With the variables belonging to parameters a_1 to a_7 we measure adjustment processes and allow for contemporaneous correlations between the dependent and the explanatory variables.[9] The coefficients b_1 to b_4 and the corresponding variables comprehend the dynamic influence of monetary policy. The long-run relations are estimated through the parameters c_1 to c_4. In addition, the coefficient c_1 measures the reaction of the dependent variable to deviations from the long-run equilibrium which is given as

$$R_t = -\frac{a_0}{c_1} - \frac{c_2}{c_1}\pi_t - \frac{c_3}{c_1}R_t^* - \frac{c_4}{c_1}\pi_t^* .$$

This relation contains the parity conditions discussed above as special cases. We get nominal (uncovered) interest rate parity in its strict form with

$$a_0 = c_2 = c_4 = 0, c_3 = -c_1: R_t = R_t^*, \tag{12}$$

and in its weak form, allowing for risk premia, with

$$c_2 = c_4 = 0, c_3 = -c_1: R_t = -\frac{a_0}{c_1} + R_t^*. \tag{12'}$$

This corresponds to equation (5), whereas equation (9), determining real interest rate parity needs the following restrictions:

$$a_0 = 0, c_1 = -c_2 = -c_3 = c_4: \quad R_t - \pi_t = R_t^* - \pi_t^* \tag{13}$$

in its strong version, and

$$c_1 = -c_2 = -c_3 = c_4: \quad R_t - \pi_t = -\frac{a_0}{c_1} + R_t^* - \pi_t^* \tag{13'}$$

for its weak form.

5. EMPIRICAL RESULTS

Before estimating the error-correction model (10), we test whether co-integrating relations exist between European long-term interest and inflation rates and the corresponding German rates. We use two different test procedures: the multivariate approach by Johansen (1988) and the augmented Dickey–Fuller test as proposed by Engle and Granger (1987). With the Johansen approach we estimate the number of co-integrating vectors, **r**, in a vector autoregressive (VAR) model including the four variables: *XLR, INFX, GLR, INFG*, with *X* being *B, BG, D, F, I, IR*, or *N*, respectively. We choose a maximum lag length of four. The augmented Dickey–Fuller test is applied to the residuals of the following static regression equation:

$$XLR_t = \alpha + \beta_1 INFX_t + \beta_2 GLR_t + \beta_3 INFG_t + u_t, \tag{14}$$

[9] See e.g. Phillips and Loretan (1991).

estimated by OLS. If these variables are co-integrated, then the residuals follow a stationary process.[10]

The results of both tests are presented in Table 11.5. Although in some cases these two tests lead to different results, we find at least one co-integrating relation for all countries but Belgium. Thus, for these countries equation (10) provides an appropriate starting-point for further investigations.[11] To treat all countries in the same way, we use the same approach also for Belgium. Using the general-to-specific approach proposed by Hendry, we start in all cases with the full model and we reduce it successively due to insignificant *t*-statistics.

TABLE 11.5. *Test of co-integrating relations between XLR, INFX, GLR, INFG, X* ε {*B,BG,D,F,I,IR,N*}

	1981(1)–1991(12)		1983(1)–1991(12)	
	Johansen (4 lags)	ADF [(*k*)]	Johansen (4 lags)	ADF [(*k*)]
Belgium	$r = 0: 31.44$	–2.85	$r = 0: 27.33$	–3.77
	$r = 1: 17.04$	(2)	$r = 1: 13.43$	(0)
Denmark	$r = 0: 35.31$	–4.18(*)	$r = 0: 31.49$	–4.70*
	$r = 1: 19.72$	(0)	$r = 1: 15.42$	(0)
France	$r = 0: 57.65$**	–5.47**	$r = 0: 43.70$	–4.43*
	$r = 1: 24.61$	(3)	$r = 1: 19.25$	(3)
Italy	$r = 0: 53.60$*	–5.24**	$r = 0: 57.01$**	–5.68**
	$r = 1: 23.71$	(1)	$r = 1: 19.67$	(1)
Ireland	$r = 0: 42.88$	–4.92**	$r = 0: 56.74$**	–3.57
	$r = 1: 23.24$	(1)	$r = 1: 20.73$	(1)
Netherlands	$r = 0: 48.08$*	–4.11(*)	$r = 0: 53.42$*	–4.47*
	$r = 1: 27.65$	(1)	$r = 1: 29.78$*	(2)
United	$r = 0: 44.70$(*)	–3.14	$r = 0: 46.97$(*)	–4.71*
Kingdom	$r = 1: 21.82$	(0)	$r = 1: 17.10$	(1)

(*),*,**, The null hypothesis of no cointegration can be rejected at the 0.10, 0.05, or 0.01 level, respectively.
r: Number of cointegrating relations.
k: Number of lags used.

5.1 Results for The Netherlands

The Netherlands is the EMS country whose monetary policy is the most strongly linked to Germany: there has been no realignment between the German mark and the Dutch guilder since March 1983. As can be seen from the following estimates, this results in a very strong, nearly one-to-one relation between the nominal interest rates of these countries:[12]

[10] Computations are performed with Micro TSP 7.03. For the Johansen approach we used Reg-X.

[11] See Stock (1987).

[12] The numbers in parentheses are the absolute values of the *t*-statistics of the estimated parameters. Besides the standard error of regression (SEE), we use the following criteria for evaluating the estimated equations: the Lagrange-Multiplier test for autocorrelation of order one (LM(1))

$$\Delta NLR_t = -\underset{(0.7)}{0.052} + \underset{(2.4)}{0.190}\,\Delta NLR_{t-1} + \underset{(3.8)}{0.183}\,\Delta NSR_t + \underset{(8.4)}{0.715}\,\Delta GLR_t$$

$$-\underset{(2.8)}{0.273}\,\Delta GLR_{t-1} - \underset{(2.9)}{0.119}\,NLR_{t-1} + \underset{(2.9)}{0.130}\,GLR_{t-1} + \hat{u}_t, \qquad (15)$$

$\bar{R}_2 = 0.668,\quad SEE = 0.164,\quad ARCH(2) = 0.54,$
$LM(1) = 0.08,\quad LM(4) = 1.33,\quad Q(12) = 10.72,$
$SK = -0.61,\quad EK = 4.78,\quad BJ = 133.69^{***}.$

The period of estimation is from 1981 to 1991. We are unable to find any significant influence of inflation rates for the short- or the long-run. Besides a small short-run influence of domestic monetary policy the Dutch long-run interest rate seems to be solely determined by the German long-run rate. Looking at the residuals, we find no indication of significant autocorrelation, but due to the high excess kurtosis the estimated residuals are clearly non-normal.[13]

To test for long-run relative UIP of the nominal interest rates we have to check whether the coefficients of the lagged levels of the two interest rates sum up to zero. Using an *F*-test, we find a *p*-value of 0.28. Thus, the null hypothesis cannot be rejected. Keeping all other variables constant we calculate the cumulative impulse–response function describing the change in the Dutch long-term nominal interest rate given a unit change in the German long-term rate (see Fig. 11.3). Three-quarters of the total effect take place within the first month, but it takes about one year until the full effect is reached.

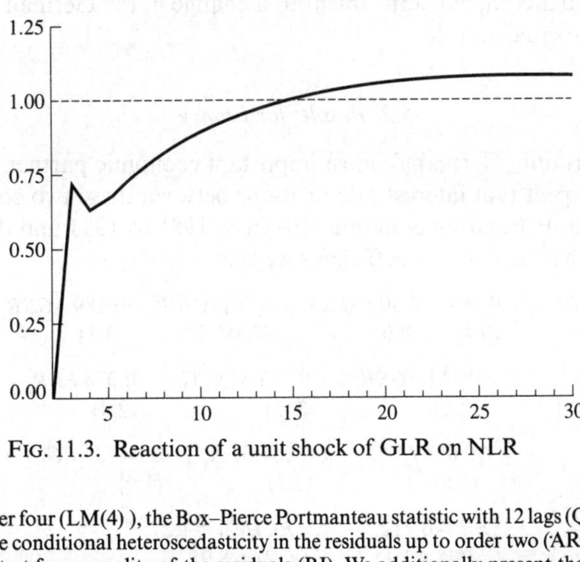

FIG. 11.3. Reaction of a unit shock of GLR on NLR

and up to order four (LM(4)), the Box–Pierce Portmanteau statistic with 12 lags (Q(12)), a test for autoregressive conditional heteroscedasticity in the residuals up to order two (ARCH(2)) and the Bera–Jarque test for normality of the residuals (BJ). We additionally present the skewness (SK) and the excess kurtosis (EK). –'(*)', '*', '**', or '***' show that the corresponding null hypothesis can be rejected at the 0.1, 0.05, 0.01, or 0.001 level, respectively.

[13] For all countries recursive coefficient estimates for all level variables are performed. In most cases they show a rather stable development.

The development of the interest rate differential shown in Fig. 11.1 indicates that the relation between the two interest rates which had already been rather strong before 1988 has been even stronger since then. If we check this by a Chow break-point test dated at January 1988 we get an F-statistic of 1.86 which indicates significance at the 10 per cent level. Re-estimating the above equation for the period from 1988 to 1991, we get:

$$\Delta NLR_t = \underset{(0.7)}{0.139} + \underset{(18.7)}{0.988}\,\Delta GLR_t - \underset{(5.0)}{0.615}\,NLR_{t-1} + \underset{(5.0)}{0.600}\,GLR_{t-1} + \hat{u}_t, \qquad (15')$$

$\bar{R}^2 = 0.883$, $SEE = 0.069$, $ARCH(2) = 0.12$,
$LM(1) = 0.16$, $LM(4) = 0.35$, $Q(12) = 7.67$,
$SK = -0.10$, $EK = 1.62$, $BJ = 5.32(*)$.

According to this equation, there is no other influence on the Dutch long-run rate but the German rate. Moreover, a change in the German rate is totally absorbed in the same month. Skewness and excess kurtosis are much smaller in comparison with the estimates in equation (15).

Equation (15′) can be rewritten in the following way:

$$NLR_t = 0.23 + 0.99\,GLR_t + \hat{u}_t,$$
$$\hat{u}_t = 0.39\hat{u}_{t-1} + v_t. \qquad (15'')$$

This shows that complete adjustment to a change in the German rate is performed in the same month.

5.2 *Results for France*

France is certainly Germany's most important economic partner. Therefore, one might expect that interest rate relations between these two countries are rather strong. Estimating equation (10) from 1981 to 1991 and deleting the variables with insignificant coefficients we get:

$$\Delta FLR_t = \underset{(0.4)}{0.098} + \underset{(8.0)}{0.300}\,\Delta FSR_t + \underset{(7.3)}{0.761}\,\Delta GLR_t - \underset{(3.1)}{0.189}\,\Delta GSR_t$$
$$- \underset{(2.3)}{0.113}\,\Delta GSR_{t-1} + \underset{(2.2)}{0.133}\,\Delta INFG_{t-1} - \underset{(2.4)}{0.074}\,FLR_{t-1}$$
$$+ \underset{(2.6)}{0.054}\,INFF_{t-1} + \underset{(2.3)}{0.064}\,GLR_{t-1} - \underset{(1.9)}{0.047}\,INFG_{t-1} + \hat{u}_t,$$

$\bar{R}^2 = 0.601$, $SEE = 0.212$, $ARCH(2) = 1.27$,
$LM(1) = 0.83$, $LM(4) = 1.15$, $Q(12) = 8.05$,
$SK = 0.34$, $= 0.60$, $BJ = 4.48$.

As in the Dutch case, we find a rather strong contemporaneous influence of the German long-term rate. The cumulative impulse–response function in Fig. 11.4

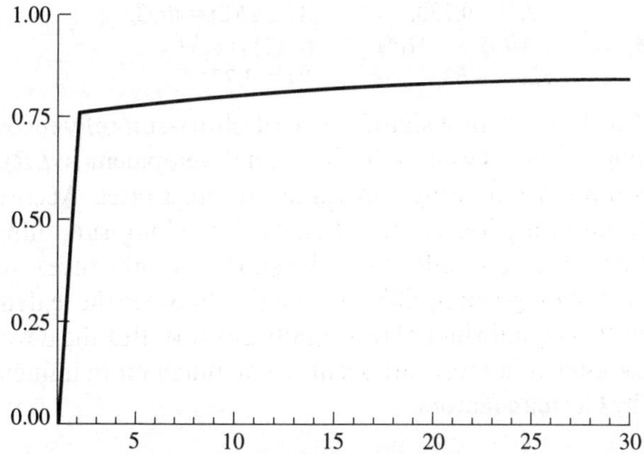

FIG. 11.4. Reaction of a unit shock of GLR on FLR

shows that almost the whole adjustment takes place in the same month. However, the long-run relation between the two countries occurs in real instead of nominal interest rates. The hypothesis of real interest rate parity between France and Germany cannot be rejected on any conventional significance level. Moreover, we find direct influences of French and German short-term interest rate changes with nearly the same size, but opposite signs. This shows that differences of monetary policies between both countries have an additional influence on the French long-run rate.

The properties of the residuals are, from a statistical viewpoint, rather satisfying. None of the tests gives any indication of deviations from the traditional assumptions. A Chow break-point test dated at the last realignment between the two currencies in January 1987 is insignificant even on the 10 per cent level.

5.3 *Results for Italy*

Due to frequent realignments during the first years of the EMS, reasonable results for Italy are only available for the period from 1983 to 1991. With the Engle–Granger two-step procedure we get:[14]

$$\begin{aligned}\Delta ILR_t = {} & \underset{(4.6)}{0.338}\,\Delta ILR_{t-1} + \underset{(5.6)}{0.294}\,\Delta ISR_t + \underset{(3.6)}{0.389}\,\Delta GLR_t \\ & - \underset{(4.3)}{0.199}\,(ILR_{t-1} - 5.125 - 0.804\,INFI_{t-1} - 0.242\,GLR_{t-1} \\ & + 0.247\,INFG_{t-1}) + \hat{u}_t,\end{aligned}$$

14 Italy is the only case where using the one-step procedure by Stock (1987) we could not find any significant and economically plausible long-run relation with Germany, whereas the two-step Engle–Granger procedure indicates such a relation. Therefore, we show the results of the two-step instead of those of the one-step procedure.

$\bar{R}^2 = 0.528$, $SEE = 0.230$, $ARCH(2) = 0.93$,
$LM(1) = 0.88$, $LM(4) = 2.27(*)$, $Q(12) = 8.32$,
$SK = -0.29$, $EK = 0.63$, $BJ = 3.27$.

This equation shows strong significance of short-run influences: domestic monetary policy (*ISR*) as well as the German development (*GLR*) have an instantaneous influence on long-run Italian interest rates. According to the impulse–response function given in Fig. 11.5, the long-run influence of the German interest rate is smaller than the short-run influence. Nevertheless, there seems to be a long-run equilibrium relation between the real rates, and deviations from this equilibrium play a significant role. But the development of the Italian long-term interest rate seems to be much more influenced by domestic than by German factors.

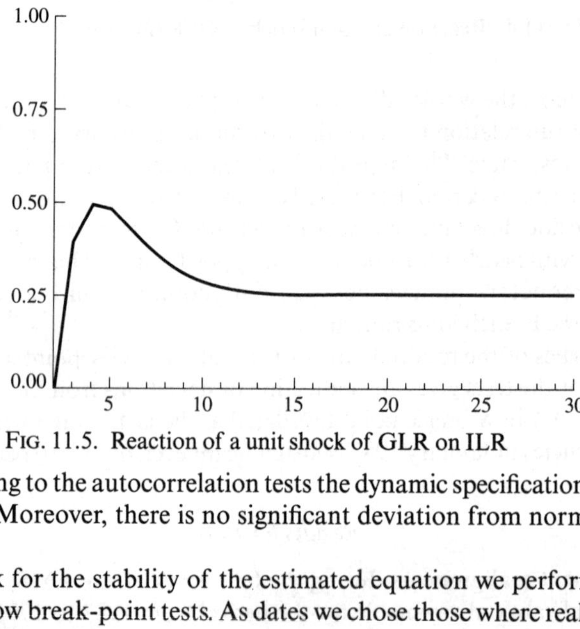

FIG. 11.5. Reaction of a unit shock of GLR on ILR

According to the autocorrelation tests the dynamic specification seems to be adequate. Moreover, there is no significant deviation from normality of the residuals.

To check for the stability of the estimated equation we performed the following Chow break-point tests. As dates we chose those where realignments of the Italian lira took place.

Sample breakpoint	85(7)	86(4)	87(1)	90(1)
F-Statistic	0.81	0.36	1.45	0.67
p-value	0.54	0.88	0.21	0.67

According to these results there is no indication of a structural break.

5.4 *Results for Belgium*

As with Italy, reasonable results for Belgium are only available for the period from 1983 onwards, due to frequent realignments during the first years of the EMS. Thus, we get:

$$\Delta BGLR_t = \underset{(2.4)}{0.763} + \underset{(5.6)}{0.318}\,\Delta BGSR_t + \underset{(3.5)}{0.416}\,\Delta GLR_t - \underset{(1.4)}{0.166}\,\Delta GLR_{t-1}$$

$$+ \underset{(2.2)}{0.140}\Delta INFBG_t - \underset{(3.4)}{0.172}\,BGLR_{t-1} + \underset{(3.3)}{0.119}\,INFBG_{t-1}$$

$$+ \underset{(2.1)}{0.075}\,GLR_{t-1} - \underset{(1.8)}{0.058}\,INFG_{t-1} + \hat{u}_t, \qquad (18)$$

$\bar{R} = 0.418$, $SEE = 0.226$, $ARCH(2) = 2.37(^*)$,
$LM(1) = 0.00$, $LM(4) = 1.14$, $Q(12) = 14.75$,
$SK = -0.27$, $EK = 0.33$, $BJ = 1.83$.

The tests for the residuals give no indication of misspecification. Though we do not find a significant co-integrating relation with the Johansen and the Engle and Granger procedures, the influence of the level variables in (18) is significant. As Fig. 11.6 shows, changes in the German bond rate are transmitted to Belgium rather rapidly, but only to about 50 per cent. We find a long-run relation between both interest and inflation rates, but if we check whether Belgium real rates are important, i.e. whether the sum of the coefficients of the Belgium variables is zero, this is rejected with very high significance, whereas the same hypothesis cannot be rejected for Germany. Thus, we do not find a stable long-run relation between the real rates. Using the Chow test there is no indication of a significant break in January 1987.

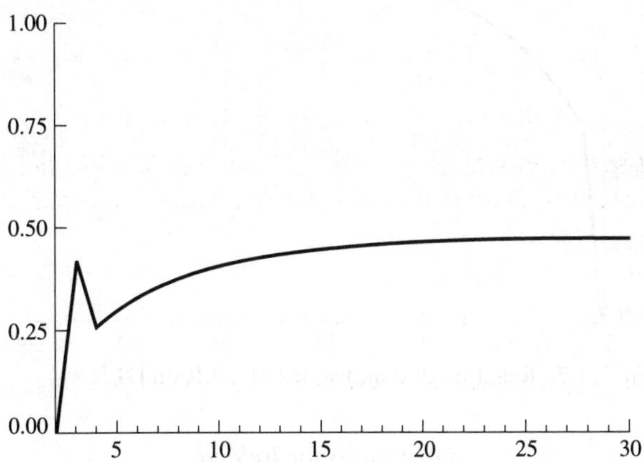

FIG. 11.6. Reaction of a unit shock of GLR on BGLR

5.5 Results for Denmark

Denmark witnessed a change from a social democratic to a liberal-conservative government in autumn 1982. The new government introduced a stabilization programme, which resulted in a decline in the long-term interest rate by about

8 percentage points from October 1982 to May 1983.[15] Therefore, we performed our estimations only from June 1983 onwards. We got the following results:

$$\Delta DLR_t = \underset{(0.2)}{0.078} + \underset{(3.1)}{0.601}\,\Delta GLR_t - \underset{(4.4)}{0.194}\,DLR_{t-1} + \underset{(4.4)}{0.221}\,INFD_{t-1} \qquad (19)$$

$$+ \underset{(3.0)}{0.209}\,GLR_{t-1} - \underset{(3.4)}{0.209}\,INFG_{t-1} + \hat{u}_t,$$

$\bar{R}^2 = 0.213$, $SEE = 0.392$, $ARCH(2) = 0.40$,
$LM(1) = 0.91$, $LM(4) = 2.75^*$, $Q(12) = 33.02^{**}$,
$SK = -0.07$, $EK = 0.41$, $BJ = 0.81$.

As Fig. 11.7 shows, there is a strong instantaneous effect of more than 50 per cent. After this first shock, additional adjustment works only through deviations from the long-run equilibrium, and within less than one year changes of German bond rates are fully transmitted to Denmark. The estimated error-correction term shows strong parity in real rates: the corresponding null hypothesis could be rejected only at a significance level of 82 per cent. Employing the Chow test we cannot find significant breaks. The only drawback for this equation is significant higher-order autocorrelation of the residuals.

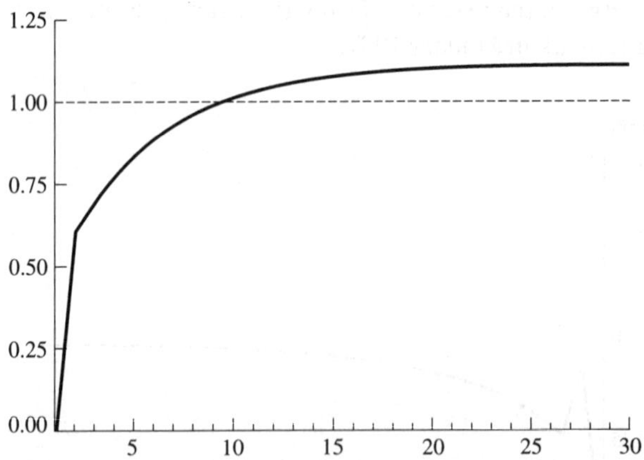

FIG. 11.7. Reaction of a unit shock of GLR on DLR

5.6 *Results for Ireland*

Estimating equation (10) over the whole period from 1981 to 1991 and deleting variables with insignificant coefficients we get:

[15] See Andersen and Risager (1988). Denmark is an exception, in so far as long-term (government bond) interest rates are directly influenced by the monetary authorities; for a long time there was no money interbank market of any importance. Therefore, we did not include Danish short-term interest rates in our investigation.

$$\Delta IRLR_t = \underset{(1.0)}{0.422} + \underset{(6.4)}{0.309}\,\Delta IRSR_t + \underset{(4.1)}{0.709}\,\Delta GLR_t - \underset{(2.8)}{0.495}\,\Delta GLR_{t-1}$$

$$- \underset{(2.6)}{0.100}\,\Delta INFIRt_{-1} - \underset{(4.0)}{0.130}\,IRLR_{t-1} + \underset{(3.9)}{0.084}\,INFIR_{t-1}$$

$$+ \underset{(2.3)}{0.129}\,GLR_{t-1} - \underset{(3.2)}{0.182}\,INFG_{t-1} + \hat{u}_t,$$

$\bar{R}^2 = 0.360$, $SEE = 0.421$, $ARCH(2) = 1.62$,
$LM(1) = 0.41$, $LM(4) = 2.51^*$, $Q(12) = 19.65(^*)$,
$SK = -0.09$, $EK = 2.13$, $BJ = 25.16^{***}$.

The impulse–response function presented in Fig. 11.8 shows rather strange behaviour: a strong positive reaction in the first period is followed by a negative reaction in the second period, before a monotone convergence to the long-run level starts, which lasts about two years. There is no easy explanation for such behaviour. It might be only a spurious statistical result. However, this short-run 'bang-bang' influence of the German bond rate is highly significant, and this behaviour of the model cannot be adequately represented by an ARMA-model for the error term.

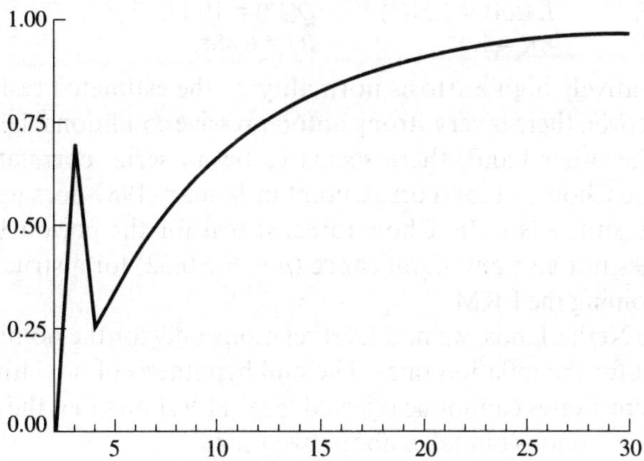

FIG. 11.8. Reaction of a unit shock of GLR on IRLR

The long-run relationship implies a one-to-one correspondence between German and Irish nominal bond rates. Besides this, inflation rates of both countries play a significant role, but equalization of real interest rates does not exist.

Looking at the test results, we find some significant autocorrelation of higher order and a strong deviation from normality due to fat tails. A Chow test with January 1987 as break point gives no significant result. One could argue that the above equation is mis-specified since no British influence is included. Including the contemporaneous change of the British long-term rate improves the test statistics. Especially, there is no longer indication of fourth-order autocorrelation and deviation from normality. With respect to the levels relation, an additional inclusion of *BLR* and *INFB* did not lead to meaningful results. We get meaningful and statistically satisfactory results, however, when we substitute GLR_{t-1} and $INFG_{t-1}$ by BLR_{t-1} and $INFB_{t-1}$. But then we leave the general frame we supposed for this investigation.

5.7 *Results for the United Kingdom*

The United Kingdom is the only country in this study which did not participate in the exchange rate mechanism of the EMS for nearly the whole observation period from 1981 onwards: Britain joined the ERM as late as October 1990. Nevertheless, we estimated the British model also over the whole period. Thus, we get:

$$\begin{aligned} \Delta BLR_t = {} & \underset{(2.1)}{0.521} + \underset{(5.8)}{0.270}\, \Delta BSR_t - \underset{(3.6)}{0.191}\, \Delta BSR_{t-1} + \underset{(1.7)}{0.201}\, \Delta GLR_t \\ & + \underset{(2.4)}{0.149}\, \Delta INFB_t - \underset{(3.1)}{0.128}\, BLR_{t-1} + \underset{(2.9)}{0.103}\, GLR_{t-1} + \hat{u}_t, \end{aligned}$$

$\bar{R}^2 = 0.309$,	$SEE = 0.310$,	$ARCH(2) = 11.20^{***}$,
$LM(1) = 1.55$,	$LM(4) = 2.21^{(*)}$,	$Q(12) = 10.18$,
$SK = 0.18$,	$EK = 1.02$,	$BJ = 6.48^{*}$.

Due to a relatively high kurtosis normality of the estimated residuals is rejected. Moreover, there is very strong autoregressive conditional heteroscedasticity. On the other hand, there seems to be no serial correlation of the residuals. The Chow test for a break point in January 1987 does not provide a significant result. Also, the Chow forecast test for the period 1990(10) to 1991(12) does not give any significance (*p*-value 0.62) for a structural break implied by joining the ERM.

As for the Netherlands, we find level relations only for the nominal interest rates but not for the inflation rates. The null hypothesis of a relative parity of nominal interest rates cannot be rejected. Fig. 11.9 shows that the adjustment process is monotonous but takes about two years.

The high dependence of British long-term rates on German rates might seem surprising, given the non-adherence of the UK to the ERM. Therefore we additionally included US long-term interest rates in the above equation. We find some significant influence of US long-term interest rate changes, but in no case was the level of the US long-term rate significant.

6. COMPARISON OF LONG-RUN RELATIONS

To get the long-run relationship (11) from the error-correction models we re-estimated equations (15) to (21), except for Italy, by non-linear least squares (NLS). For the long-run relations, this leads to equations like (14),

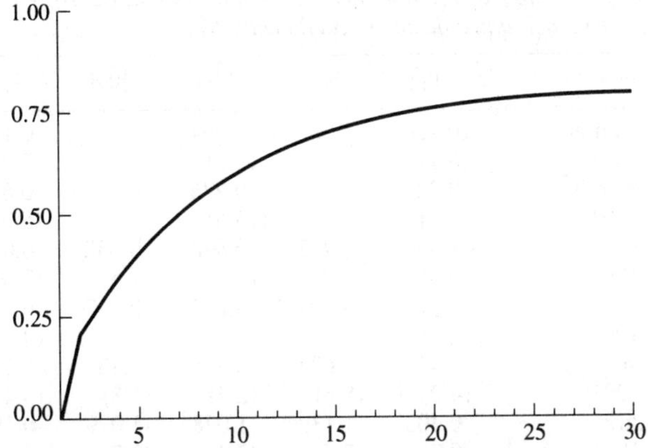

FIG. 11.9. Reaction of a unit shock of GLR on BLR

$$XLR_t = \beta_0 + \beta_1\, INFX_t + \beta_2\, GLR_t + \beta_3\, INFG_t + u_t. \tag{14}$$

The results are presented in Table 11.6.[16] For the Netherlands and the United Kingdom we get nominal interest rate parity. For both countries the coefficients of the German bond rate are not significantly different from 1.0, even though the point estimate for the United Kingdom is less than the one for the Netherlands. However, the main difference between the two relations is reflected by the constant term. For the Netherlands it is insignificant,[17] indicating absolute UIP, whereas it is significantly positive for the United Kingdom, which implies that between Germany and Britain only relative UIP holds. Thus, compared with the German mark, assets denominated in British pounds contain a risk premium.

In all other cases the long-run relations also contain the inflation rates. For France and Denmark absolute uncovered parity for real interest rates cannot be rejected. However, the absolute values of the slope coefficients are further away from 1.0 and less significantly different from zero in the French than in the Danish case. For Belgium, Italy, and Ireland the German real interest rate has a significant long-run influence, but for Belgium and Italy the coefficients are rather low. Additionally, in all three cases the coefficients of the domestic inflation rates are significantly less than 1.0 and the constant terms are comparably high, but only for Belgium and Italy the latter ones are significantly positive.

16 If the adjustment coefficient γ (last column) is significantly less than zero, this gives additional evidence for the existence of level relations (co-integration). According to the critical values in Banerjee *et al.* (1992, Table 4) we find that γ is less than zero in the least at the 10% level with the exception of France. But for France we found with the Johansen and with the Engle–Granger approach a co-integrating relation (see Table 11.5). On the other hand these tests did not indicate a significant long-term relation for Belgium, but the error-correction approach given in Table 11.6 does.

17 If we look at the period from 1988 to 1991, the constant term is significantly positive for the Netherlands. However, if we test jointly whether the constant term is zero and the slope parameter is 1.0, the null hypothesis cannot be rejected at the 5% level.

TABLE 11.6. *Long-run relations derived from the estimated error-correction models and adjustment coefficients* (γ)

	$[\hat{\beta}_0]$	$[\hat{\beta}_1]$	$[\hat{\beta}_2]$	$[\hat{\beta}_3]$	$[\gamma_4]$
Netherlands	–0.436	—	1.094	—	–0.119
1981–1991	(0.7)		(13.5)		(2.9)
Netherlands	0.226	—	0.976	—	–0.615
1988–1991	(2.2)		(73.6)		(5.0)
France	1.324	0.733	0.868	–0.632	–0.074
1981–1991	(0.4)	(6.0)	(1.8)	(1.5)	(2.4)
Italy	5.125	0.804	0.242	–0.247	–0.199
1983–1991	(42.6)				(4.3)
Belgium	4.430	0.693	0.438	–0.337	–0.172
1983–1991	(4.0)	(8.6)	(2.4)	(1.8)	(3.4)
Denmark	0.403	1.139	1.078	–1.079	–0.194
1983–1991	(0.2)	(7.5)	(3.4)	(3.7)	(4.4)
Ireland	3.245	0.642	0.990	–1.395	–0.130
1981–1991	(1.2)	(7.9)	(2.2)	(3.4)	(4.0)
United Kingdom	4.064	—	0.805	—	–0.128
1981–1991	(3.5)		(5.5)		(3.1)

Taking all results together, we find rather strong relations from Germany to the Netherlands, France, and Denmark. This might be due to the fact that the monetary policies of these countries were tightly connected with the policy of the German Bundesbank. For Ireland there also seems to be a close connection in the long run. It is not astonishing that the linkages with Italy and the United Kingdom are less pronounced: Italy had wider exchange rate bands until January 1990, and the United Kingdom was not a member of the ERM until October 1990. Moreover, this different behaviour of Italy which is more or less the same for Belgium (see also Figs. 11.5 and 11.6) may be a hint that due to high government debts in these countries the international linkages alone are not able to explain completely the development of long-term nominal interest rates for government bonds.

7. SIMULATIONS FOR 1992

The econometric results explaining the development of long-term interest rates are relatively stable for all countries in our sample. We now ask for the stability of these relations outside the sample period. If it is true that convergence of long-term interest rates has been more or less achieved and the system as a whole is credible and stays on this convergent path, we should be able to forecast the future development of long-term interest rates relatively precisely with our estimated equations. Therefore, we perform for January 1992 until November 1992 one to eleven periods ahead dynamic *ex post* forecasts for all long-term interest rates. By dynamic forecasts, is meant that for all lagged dependent variables the predicted values are used, whereas all other explanatory variables are set equal to their observed values. Clearly, these are not real forecasts, but this procedure gives us a measure for judging the stability and credibility of the system. Our simulation period includes September 1992 where, especially for Italy and the United Kingdom, major disturbances in the exchange market took place.

Global measures for root mean squared errors, mean absolute errors, and Theil's inequality coefficients are given in Table 11.7. Looking at the global forecast measures in Table 11.7 we find two different groups of countries. The Netherlands, Belgium, and France form one group. Here we observe a maximum mean absolute forecast error of about 0.3 percentage points. The other measures are also very small. Italy, Denmark, Ireland, and the United Kingdom belong to the other group. Here the mean absolute errors for Italy, Ireland, and the United Kingdom amount to about 0.8 percentage points and the one for Denmark to 1.1 percentage points. For Ireland the global measures can be improved using the equation where the German level influence is replaced by British long-term interest and inflation rates. The observed and predicted values together with the two-standard error bands are given for the second group of countries in Figs. 11.10 to 11.13.

TABLE 11.7. *Forecast evaluation 1992(1)–1992(11)*

	Root mean squared error	Mean absolute error	Theil's Inequality Coefficient
Netherlands	0.144	0.118	0.0088
France	0.363	0.315	0.0215
Italy	1.089	0.783	0.0473
Belgium	0.264	0.224	0.0153
Denmark	1.265	1.115	0.0756
Ireland	0.985	0.781	0.0567
United Kingdom	0.867	0.791	0.0454

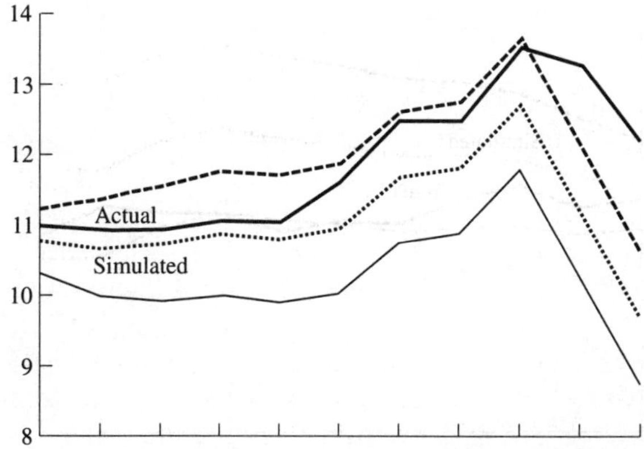

FIG. 11.10. Italy: Long-term Interest rate levels, 1992

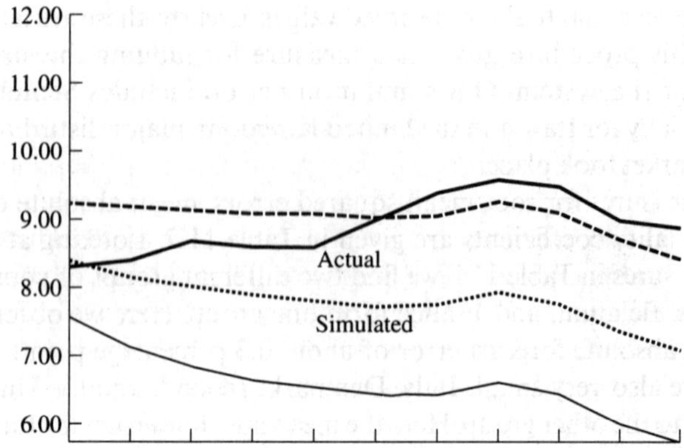

FIG. 11.11. Denmark: Long-term Interest rate levels, 1992

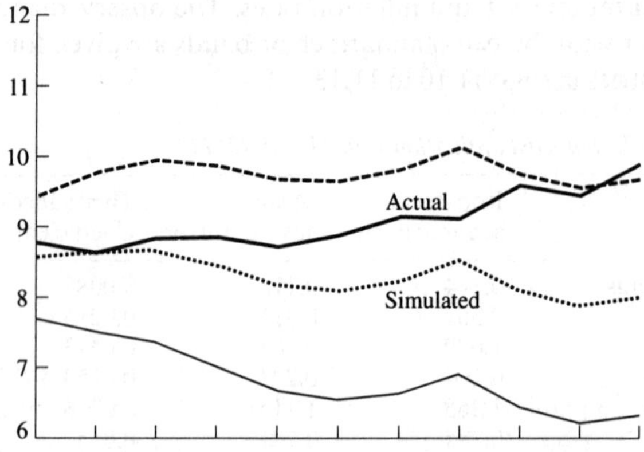

FIG. 11.12. Ireland: Long-term Interest rate levels, 1992

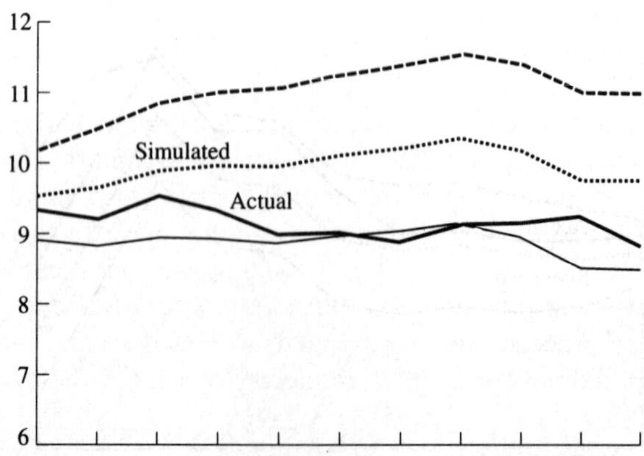

FIG. 11.13. UK: Long-term Interest rate levels, 1992

The first group comprises countries with strong economic relations with Germany. Looking at the observed and simulated values (which are not shown here for the countries in this first group in order to save space) we see that they are very close together for the whole forecast period.[18] These developments are hardly affected by the exchange market perturbations of September 1992. These results may be interpreted as evidence for a convergence *vis-à-vis* Germany. According to Blanchard (1984) it seems that these relations are not subject to the Lucas critique (1976) since the formation of expectations does not appear to have changed in 1992. The good prediction results for Belgium are somewhat astonishing given that the estimated relation presented above and used for these predictions is relatively unstable. For Italy the simulated and the actual values in Fig. 11.10 are relatively close together for the period from January to May 1992. But for the rest of the year the simulated and observed values diverge more and more. The actual development is systematically under-predicted. The change in direction in September 1992 is well captured. For Denmark and Ireland (see Figs. 11.11 and 11.12) we find an increasing under-prediction of the actual development for the whole period. The simulation experiment for the United Kingdom (see Fig. 11.13) results in a systematic overprediction of the observed development of the British long-term interest rate. Thus for these countries expectations seem to have changed and our estimated relations appear to be subject to the Lucas critique.

8. CONCLUDING REMARKS

We did not find significant structural breaks during the estimation period, not even at dates when realignments took place. On a first view, this might seem to be astonishing as fixed exchange rate systems with narrow bands of fluctuations suffer from speculative movements. However, at least before 1992 the bands implemented in the exchange rate mechanism of the EMS eliminated (most of) those destructive speculative movements,[19] since for the realignments the changes of the central rates where lower than the bandwidths. This, especially, holds for Italy with its larger bandwidths.

On the other hand, when looking at the forecast period we find rather strong deviations between actual and predicted values for Denmark, Ireland, Italy, and the United Kingdom. The first three countries are those which at the beginning of the 1980s had the highest inflation and interest differentials with respect to German rates and, therefore, showed the strongest convergence to German development during our observation period. Since we uniformly underpredict their interest rate developments for 1992, we may infer that the market probably did not consider the monetary policies of these countries as

[18] The figures are available from the authors upon request.

[19] See e.g. De Grauwe (1992, pp. 104–7)

really credible in the long run. Therefore, it is not astonishing that these countries had to adjust their exchange rates once perturbations in the exchange market occurred. From this point of view, the Maastricht referendum in France just released forces which had accumulated earlier in 1992. In addition, one has to take into account that the final convergence of interest and inflation rates between Germany and Ireland, and Germany and the United Kingdom which took place since 1990 did occur because German rates increased, which was—at least partly—a consequence of the German (monetary) unification.

Another question is how much the decrease of European interest and inflation rates during the 1980s really depended on the creation and working of the European Monetary System. During this period, inflation and interest rates decreased (and converged) also outside this system. One has to take into account the possible US influence on the European rates. On the other hand, the fact that European interest rates did not follow the strong decrease of American rates after 1989 shows some independence of the European from the American development at least for the most recent period.

Taking all these together, despite the convergence which took place during the 1980s, it seems questionable whether more than a very few countries will meet the Maastricht criteria for joining a European Monetary Union at the end of this decade.

APPENDIX: *Definition of Variables*

Belgium

Short-term interest rate
BGSR: 3-month Treasury certificates
Source: Main Economic Indicators

Long-term interest rate
BGLR*: Central government bonds (more than 5 years)*
Source: Main Economic Indicators

Inflation rate

$$INFBG = \frac{BGCP - BGCP_{-12}}{BGCP_{-12}} . 100$$

BGCP: Consumer prices (not seasonally adjusted); 1985 = 100
Source: Main Economic Indicators

Denmark

Long-term interest rate
DLR*: Central government bonds (10 years)*
Source: Main Economic Indicators

Inflation rate

$$INFD = \frac{DCP - DCP_{-12}}{DCP_{-12}} \cdot 100$$

DCP: Consumer prices (not seasonally adjusted); 1985 = 100
Source: Main Economic Indicators

France

Short-term interest rate
FSR*: 3-month PIBOR*
Source: Main Economic Indicators

Long-term interest rate
FLR*: average rate of government bonds*
Source: Banque de France

Inflation rate

$$INFF = \frac{FCP - FCP_{-12}}{FCP_{-12}} \times 100$$

FCP: Consumer prices (not seasonally adjusted); 1985 = 100
Source: Main Economic Indicators

Germany

Short-term interest rate
GSR: *3-month FIBOR*
Source: Monatsberichte der Deutschen Bundesbank

Long-term interest rate
GLR: *Umlaufsrenditen festverzinslicher Wertpapiere insgesamt*
Source: Monatsberichte der Deutschen Bundesbank

Inflation rate

$$\text{INFG} = \frac{GCP - GCP_{-12}}{GCP_{-12}} \cdot 100$$

GCP: Consumer prices (not seasonally adjusted); 1985 = 100
Source: Main Economic Indicators

Ireland

Short-term interest rate
IRSR: *3-month Treasury bills*
Source: Main Economic Indicators

Long-term interest rate
IRLR: *15-year government bonds*
Source: Main Economic Indicators

Inflation rate

$$\text{INFIR} = \frac{IRCP - IRCP_{-12}}{IRCP_{-12}} \cdot 100$$

IRCP: Consumer prices (not seasonally adjusted); 1985 = 100
Source: Main Economic Indicators

Italy

Short-term interest rate
ISR: *Treasury bill rate*
Source: International Financial Statistics

Long-term interest rate
ILR: *Treasury bonds*
Source: Main Economic Indicators

Inflation rate

$$\mathrm{INFI} = \frac{ICP - ICP_{-12}}{ICP_{-12}} \cdot 100$$

ICP: Consumer prices (not seasonally adjusted); 1985 = 100
Source: Main Economic Indicators

The Netherlands

Short-term interest rate
NSR: *3-month AIBOR*
Source: Monatsberichte der Deutschen Bundesbank

Long-term interest rate
NLR: *5 longest-running issues of central government bonds*
Source: Main Economic Indicators

Inflation rate

$$\mathrm{INFN} = \frac{NCP - NCP_{-12}}{NCP_{-12}} \cdot 100$$

NCP: Consumer prices (not seasonally adjusted); 1985 = 100
Source: Main Economic Indicators

United Kingdom

Short-term interest rate
BSR: *3-month Treasury bills*
Source: Monatsberichte der Deutschen Bundesbank

Long-term interest rate
BLR: *20-year government bonds*
Source: Main Economic Indicators

Inflation rate

$$\mathrm{INFB} = \frac{BCP - BCP_{-12}}{BCP_{-12}} \cdot 100$$

BCP: Consumer prices (not seasonally adjusted); 1985 = 100
Source: Main Economic Indicators

REFERENCES

Andersen, T. M., and O. Risager (1988), 'Stabilization Policies Credibility, and Interest Rate Determination in a Small Open Economy', *European Economic Review*, 32: 669–79.

Artus, P., S. Avouyi-Dovi, E. Bleuze, and F. Lecointre (1991), 'Transmission of US Monetary Policy to Europe and Asymmetry in the European Monetary System', *European Economic Review*, 35: 1369–84.

Banerjee, A., J. J. Dolado, and R. Mestre (1992), 'On Simple Tests for Cointegration: The Cost of Simplicity', mimeo.

Blanchard, O. J. (1984), 'The Lucas Critique and the Volcker Deflation', *American Economic Review*, 74: 211–15.

Bruneau, C., and J. P. Nicolai (1991), 'Monetary Policy, Term Structure, and Cointegrated VAR Models: The Contribution of the Dynamics of Deviations from Equilibrium to the Study of US, French and German Interest Rates', mimeo.

Campbell, J. Y., and R. J. Shiller (1987), 'Cointegration and Tests of Present Value Models', *Journal of Political Economy*, 95: 1062–88.

Cumby, E. R., and M. Obstfeld (1984), 'International Interest Rate and Price Level Linkages under Flexible Exchange Rates: A Review of Recent Evidence', in J. F. O. Bilson and R. C. Marston (eds.), *Exchange Rate Theory and Practice*, Chicago: 121–51.

Currie, D. P. Levine, and J. Pearlman (1992), 'European Monetary Union or Hard EMS?', *European Economic Review*, 36: 1185–204.

De Grauwe, P. (1992), *The Economics of Monetary Integration*, Oxford.

Dickey, D. A., W. R. Bell, and R. B. Miller (1986), 'Unit Roots in Time Series Models: Tests and Implications', *American Statistician*, 40: 12–26.

Engle, R. F., and C. W. J. Granger (1987), 'Co-integration and Error Correction: Representation, Estimation and Testing', *Econometrica*, 55: 251–76.

Johansen, S. (1988), 'Statistical Analysis of Cointegration Vectors', *Journal of Economic Dynamics and Control*, 12: 231–54.

—— —— (1993), 'Does the DM Dominate the Euro Market?, An Empirical Investigation', *Review of Economics and Statistics*, 75: 773–8.

Kirchgässner, G., and J. Wolters (1990), 'Uncovered Interest Parity, Interest Rate Linkage, or Independence? Empirical Results for 1961–1987', *Jahrbuch für Sozialwissenschaft*, 41: 289–311.

Kneeshaw, J. T., and P. Van den Bergh (1985), 'International Interest Rate Relationships: Policy Choices and Constraints', BIS Economic Papers, 13 (Jan.).

Lucas, R. E. Jr. (1976), Econometric Policy Evaluation: A Critique, in K. Brunner and A. Meltzer (eds.), The Phillips Curve and Labor Markets, Carnegie-Rochester Conferences on Public Policy, Amsterdam, *Journal of Monetary Economics*, Suppl. 1: 19–46.

Modiglinani, F., and R. Sutch (1966), 'Innovations in Interest Rate Policy', *American Economic Review, Papers and Proceedings*, 56: 178–97.

Muscatelli, V. A., A. Stevenson, and D. Vines (1989), 'Uncovered Interest Parity, Exchange Rate Risk and Exchange Rate Dynamics', in R. MacDonald and M. P. Taylor (eds.), *Exchange Rates and Open Economy Macroeconomics*, Blackwell, 159–77.

Perron, P. (1988), 'Trends and Random Walks in Macroeconomic Time Series. Further

Evidence from a New Approach', *Journal of Economic Dynamics and Control*, 12: 297–332.
Phillips, P. C. B., and P. Perron (1988), 'Testing for a Unit Root in Time Series Regression', *Biometrika*, 75: 335–46.
—— and M. Loretan (1991), 'Estimating Long-run Economic Equilibria', *Review of Economic Studies*, 58: 407–36.
Schwert, G. W. (1989), 'Tests for Unit Roots: A Monte Carlo Investigation', *Journal of Business and Economic Statistics*, 7: 147–59.
Stock, J. H. (1987), 'Asymptotic Properties of Least Squares Estimators of Cointegrating Vectors', *Econometrica*, 55: 1035–056.

12

The Demand for Money Functions in Europe and in Germany before and after the Fall of the Berlin Wall

GIUSEPPE TULLIO
ERIC DE SOUZA
PAOLA GIUCCA

INTRODUCTION

With the aim of stabilizing inflationary expectations and keeping monetary expansion in the medium term consistent with price stability, a crucial role has been attributed to the setting of monetary targets in implementing and monitoring monetary policies in stage one of EMU. Mainly as a result of this development, growing efforts in the field of applied research have been devoted since the end of the last decade to the empirical estimate of aggregate money-demand functions for the countries participating in the Exchange Rate Mechanism (ERM) of the European Monetary System (EMS). In particular, recent studies (see Bekx and Tullio, 1989; Kremers and Lane, 1990; Monticelli and Strauss-Kahn, 1992*a*, 1992*b*; Artis *et al.*, 1992; Monticelli, 1993) have provided evidence that demand for money equations estimated for the aggregate European (ERM) area offer advantages with respect to those estimated at the individual country level in terms of stability, predictability, and more plausible reaction to discrepancies between actual and desired money balances. Currency substitution is often invoked as one of the factors explaining the greater stability of the ERM-wide money demand.

As it has been stressed in Lane and Poloz (1992), if the above results should be confirmed by further research, they would have several important policy implications: first, they would strengthen the case for EMU, suggesting that a European central bank might be able to implement monetary control more effectively than the individual national central banks (see Russo and Tullio, 1988; Kremers and Lane, 1992); second, they could provide a basis on which the European Monetary Institute (established on 1 February 1994) could already use an ERM-wide money supply target or indicator as a means to enhance co-ordination of monetary policy during the transition to EMU.

The views expressed in this chapter are personal and do not involve the institutions to which we belong. It has been written for the SPES Project CT 91–0053 on 'The Control of Inflation in the Transition to Monetary Union', financed by the European Commission. We would like to thank Paul De Grauwe and Stefano Micossi for useful comments on an earlier draft.

This chapter looks at the aggregate European (ERM) demand for money function during the EMS period and before, using different definitions of the money stock (M1 and M3). Co-integration is used in order to isolate a long-run money-demand function, and the short-run dynamics are studied using the error-correction model (EMC), as has become customary in studies on this subject in recent years.

In order to study the contribution of large countries' money-demand functions to the stability of the aggregate European money demand we first remove from the ERM-wide money demand the three largest countries (Germany, France, and Italy) one by one, following Artis *et al.* (1992), then we look at the stability of money-demand functions in each of the three countries. Given the importance attributed to currency substitution in explaining the stability of the aggregate ERM-money demand, we explore the role of substitution with the US dollar in the European demand function and of currency substitution within Europe and with the US dollar in the national studies.

Our sample period ends in the second quarter of 1989, about five months before the fall of the Berlin Wall (November 1989). During these five months, particularly the German economy was influenced by the immigration from the East and the expectation of major political changes there; therefore it was thought preferable to leave the months preceding the fall of the Wall outside of the sample period.

For Germany, however, given the importance attributed by German monetary authorities to monetary targeting and the overshooting of monetary aggregates with respect to the previously set targets in 1990–2, we extend the estimation to the third quarter of 1992 (the last available observation at the time of writing) in order to study the stability of the demand for money function also beyond the fall of the Berlin Wall and the German economic and monetary union of 1 July 1990. We find that the problem of instability of the German demand-for-money function increases substantially after the second quarter of 1989; this makes the Bundesbank's policy based on monetary targeting somewhat shaky after 1989, although one should not forget that it followed monetary targets with flexibility during the period.

The chapter is divided as follows. Section 1 contains the quarterly estimates of ERM-wide money-demand functions, separately for the pre-EMS period 1972(1) to 1979(1) and for the EMS period 1979(2) to 1989(2), and for the aggregates of narrow money (M1) and broad money (M3). Appendix 1 contains the estimates for the EMS period of the demand function for extended M3 which includes some cross-border deposits. In line with previous studies we find that a very stable aggregate ERM-wide demand function for money exists during the EMS period both for M1 and M3. Before the inception of the EMS the demand function for money was less well behaved.

Section 2 analyses the contribution of each of the three largest countries (Germany, France, and Italy) to the stability of ERM-wide money demand. We present estimates of the ERM-wide money-demand functions excluding

Germany, then excluding France, and finally excluding Italy. Intra-European currency substitution is considered explicitly in this section by introducing into the function the average discount of the ERM-currencies included in the aggregate with respect to the excluded currency. We find that it is the exclusion of Germany which creates problems for the stability of the ERM-wide money demand, contrary to the finding of Artis *et al.* (1992) who conclude that it is the exclusion of France which causes problems.

Section 3 contains the estimates of the demand for narrow and broad money for Germany, France, and Italy from 1979(2) to 1989(2). Currency substitution with the US dollar is significant for all three countries, while the evidence is not so strong for the intra-European currency substitution: very weak for Italy, probably because of extensive capital controls for most of the EMS period, somewhat stronger but still not crucial for the stability of the function in France and Germany.

Section 4 extends the estimates of the demand functions for M1 and M3 for Germany to the third quarter of 1992. After the fall of the Berlin Wall and the German economic and monetary union the demand function for German M3 became very unstable, even including the currency substitution terms. The same holds for extended M3, whose estimates are presented in Appendix 3. The demand for M1 withstood the shock of the fall of the Wall and the unification shock somewhat better.

The problem with the estimates for Germany beyond 1990(2) relates to the construction of the price and real GDP data for the whole of Germany. The Bundesbank publishes data for the money stocks for the whole of Germany. The monetary targets set by the Bundesbank are based on the national aggregate. The exchange rates and interest rates also refer to the whole of Germany, while data on the price level and real GDP are published separately and those referring to the East with much greater delays. We constructed quarterly price and real GDP series for the whole of Germany to be able to update the estimates of the overall money-demand functions. The behaviour of these variables will be discussed and an estimate of the initial monetary overhang created will be presented in this section.

We frequently read during 1991–3 in the German and international press that the Bundesbank had to increase interest rates because M3 was growing above target or that it could not reduce interest rates or reduce them further because M3 was growing above target. If one of the main conclusions of this chapter is correct that the demand-for-money function in Germany became unstable after the fall of the Wall, the justification of nominal supply targeting and of the interest rate policy based on it is lost. After the fall of the Berlin Wall, in addition to the further increase in the openness of capital markets and the related increased importance of currency substitution, there were important unification shocks to the German money-demand function which have made it more unstable than before. The tests presented in this chapter suggest that after 1989 the demand function for M1 remained relatively more stable than the demand function for M3. An interest rate policy based on M1 would therefore have been preferable.

Section 5 contains concluding comments.

1. THE ERM-WIDE MONEY-DEMAND FUNCTION BEFORE AND AFTER THE INCEPTION OF THE EMS

The long-run demand for money is specified in real terms, assuming unitary elasticity of nominal money demand with respect to the price level. The ERM-wide aggregates have been constructed using fixed weights as in Bekx and Tullio (1989) and Artis *et al.* (1992). The use of current exchange rates has been avoided because it causes jumps in the aggregate series in the quarters in which a realignment occurs, while purchasing power parity weights are as arbitrary as the use of fixed weights as there are many ways to measure the exchange rate corresponding to purchasing power parity (PPP). The UK and Spain are excluded from our area-wide aggregation as their currencies joined the system after the end of our estimation period. The demand for money is expressed as a positive function of real GDP and a negative function of the short-term interest rate and of the deviation of the average dollar exchange rate of the currencies belonging to the exchange rate mechanism (ERM) from the level predicted by purchasing power parity; the latter variable is assumed to reflect currency substitution with the US dollar.

Several variables have been used in empirical studies of the demand for money to reflect currency substitution: the foreign interest rate, the forward discount (or premium), the deviation of the official and black market exchange rate, the rate of change of the nominal exchange rate and the nominal exchange rate. The last variable has generally given the best results in previous studies on the ERM-wide money demand. However, it is not easy to justify theoretically the introduction of the nominal exchange rate *level* as an indicator of currency substitution, even though it appears to dominate on empirical grounds. Our choice of the deviation of the nominal exchange rate from PPP is based on two considerations: (i) on the one hand, it is closely correlated with the nominal exchange rate; and (ii) on the other hand, considering that in the 1980s there were long-lasting deviations (up to 3 to 5 years) of the dollar exchange rate *vis-à-vis* European currencies from the level predicted by PPP, it reflects best the long periods during which dollar bank deposits were 'in' (early 1980s) and during which they were not 'in' (after 1985). It is consistent with this view that the coefficient of deviations of the dollar exchange rate from PPP turned out to be significantly different from zero (and negative, as expected) only in the cointegrating (long-run) equations and not in the dynamic (error-correction) equations.

The 1985 (current) exchange rate has been used to convert the money stock and real GDP of each member country into DM. For the other variables the

ERM averages have been defined using 1985 GDP weights. The money stocks and real GDP are expressed in logs, interest rates, and the currency substitution terms in natural numbers. The ERM-wide aggregates exclude Spain and the UK. For a more detailed description of the sources of the data used and of the method used for the construction of the ERM series see Appendix 4. Since the national money stocks have been converted into DM at the average 1985 exchange rate, the weight of the money stock of the high-inflation countries in the ERM average increases after 1985. In addition, to the extent that the 1985 exchange rate of the high-inflation currencies was overvalued with respect to 1979, the weight of their money stock tends to be biased upwards already before 1985. These biases are likely to involve mainly Italy. However, particularly the first one is likely to be quite small since there were very few realignments after 1985 and inflation had to a large extent already converged.

Table 12.1 contains the empirical results of the co-integrating equation for M1 from 1972(1) to 1979(1) and from 1979(2) to 1989(2) and for M3 for the latter period. M3 could not be estimated for the pre-EMS period because the data on M3 are missing for some countries.

The DF and ADF tests at the bottom of the table indicate that all three equations are cointegrated at the 1 per cent or 5 per cent level. For the EMS period the income elasticity of M1 is not significantly different from 1 and significantly lower than for M3. The semi-elasticity with respect to the interest rate is significantly higher for M1, as was to be expected since the fraction of the M1 stock yielding an interest is much lower than for M3. The coefficient of the

TABLE 12.1. *ERM countries co-integrating equations for M1 and M3* (pre-EMS and EMS; OLS, quarterly data)

	M1 1972(1)–1979(1)	M1 1979(2)–1989(2)	M3 1979(2)–1989(2)
Regression	(1)	(2)	(3)
Explanatory variables:			
Constant	–1.32(–0.92)	–0.56(–0.66)	–0.99(–3.40)
LY	1.19(5.72)	1.08(9.47)	1.26(31.87)
RS	–0.99(–3.51)	–1.16(–3.97)	–0.68(–6.69)
dPPP	0.04(0.47)	–0.13(–3.88)	–0.09(–7.66)
*D*78(1)	0.08(4.01)	—	—
R^2	0.93	0.93	0.99
SER	0.025	0.027	0.009
DW	2.97	2.84	1.35
DF	–8.94**	–8.82**	–4.02**
ADF	–6.05**	–3.22*	–3.86**

* Co-integrated at the 5 per cent level.
** Co-integrated at the 1 per cent level.

Notes: D 78 (1) is a dummy variable which assumes the value of +1 in 1978 (1) and zero otherwise; it reflects a jump in the money stock series for France. *t*-statistics are indicated in parentheses.

term reflecting currency substitution with the US dollar is very close to zero during the pre-EMS period; conversely it appears to be quite large for both monetary aggregates after 1979, presumably reflecting the much higher degree of capital mobility during the EMS period.

All coefficients are more precisely estimated for M3. The explanatory power of the regression is also higher for M3 than for M1.

Table 12.2 contains the dynamic (ECM) models corresponding to the three co-integrating equations previously shown in Table 12.1. The dynamic (ECM) version of the demand function can be estimated in one stage or in two stages, the latter implying the substitution into the ECM of the residuals of the OLS estimates of the co-integrating equation. In Appendix 2 we show first that the two-stage estimation leads to inferior results confirming the recent theoretical work which suggests that the estimates in one stage are superior (see Banerjee *et al.*, 1993, ch. 6). Then we perform a Wald F-test on the null hypothesis that the parameters of the co-integrating variables in the ECM model estimated in one stage are all the same as implied by the two-stage estimation. The Wald tests indicate that the hypothesis that they are all the same must be rejected as suggested by theory. We use therefore the one-stage procedure. *D* stands for the first difference operator and *DDLP* is the acceleration of inflation. *LMP* is the logarithm of the real money stock and *RS* the short-term interest rate.

TABLE 12.2. *ERM countries, EC-model for M1 and M3* (pre-EMS and EMS, OLS, quarterly data)

	M1 1972(1)–1979(1)	M1 1979(2)–1989(2)	M3 (1979(2)–1989(2)
Regression	(4)	(5)	(6)
Explanatory variables:			
Constant	–0.21(0.56)	–0.07(0.39)	–0.20(–1.74)
DRS	–0.51(–3.83)	–0.48(–3.08)	–0.26(–2.92)
DDLP	0.002(0.005)	–0.69(–1.67)	–0.39(–1.99)
LMP–1	–0.89(–11.47)	–0.47(–5.09)	–0.25(–3.86)
LY–1	0.93(9.11)	0.49(4.84)	0.31(3.94)
RS–1	–1.27(–11.96)	–0.89(–7.15)	–0.40(–6.68)
dPPP–1	–0.011(–0.46)	–0.033(–2.47)	–0.015(–2.02)
R^2	0.985	0.987	0.839
SER	0.0059	0.0060	0.0035
DW	2.62	2.10	2.28
AR-CHI2 (3)	11.59	4.86	1.23
AR-F	3.30(0.052)	1.21(0.33)	0.30(0.83)
ARCH-CHI2 (3)	0.88	5.31	7.26
ARCH-F	0.13(0.94)	1.30(0.30)	2.05(0.13)
N-CHI2 (2)	0.18	0.02	1.57
RESET-F	0.75(0.40)	0.13(0.72)	0.88(0.35)

Notes: The following dummies have been added: D78 (1) in regr.(4) and D84 (2) in regr.(5) and D80(1) and D80(2) in regr.(6). *t*-statistics or probability of rejection of the null hypothesis when the latter is true, in parentheses.

For the pre-EMS period the residuals of the dynamic M1 regression (regr. (5)) show evidence of autocorrelation. In addition several parameters show instability starting towards the end of 1977. For the EMS period the residuals of the estimates of the dynamic M1 and M3 real-money-demand functions are instead very well behaved: there is no evidence of autocorrelation and the residuals are normally distributed and homoscedastic. The speed of adjustment of actual to desired balances is higher for M1 (about two quarters) than for M3 (about four quarters); the short-run effect of interest rate changes on M1 is much stronger than on M3. Currency substitution with the US dollar is more significant for M1 than for M3. When we remove from the dynamic model the deviation of the average ERM dollar exchange rate from PPP, the residuals of both regressions continue to be well behaved (results are not shown here for the sake of brevity).

Appendix 1 presents the estimates of the aggregate ERM demand function for extended M3 for the EMS period. Extended M3 includes European residents' holdings of national currency deposits at banks located abroad and excludes foreign currency deposits at domestic banks. As for the ERM-wide demand functions for M1 and M3, the relationship is co-integrated and the dynamic version has well-behaved residuals and parameters. In addition the currency-substitution term is larger and more significant, as expected.

The main conclusions stemming from the analysis made in this section and in Appendix 1 are in line with the results of previous studies on the subject: first during the EMS period, which for us ends in 1989(2), there were satisfactory and well-behaved demand functions for ERM-wide M1, M3, and extended M3, in contrast with the evidence observed for the demand for M1 in the 1970s. Second, during the EMS period currency substitution with the US dollar is very significant, reflecting probably increased integration of world capital markets; its removal from the function, however, does not represent a cause of instability.

2. THE CONTRIBUTION OF THE THREE LARGEST PARTICIPANTS IN THE ERM TO THE STABILITY OF THE AREA-WIDE MONEY-DEMAND FUNCTION

Following Artis *et al.* (1992) we estimate in this section the co-integrating relationships presented in Table 12.1 excluding in turn Germany, France, and Italy from the ERM aggregate (Table 12.3). We then estimate the dynamic EC model specified as in Table 12.2 excluding again in turn each of the three countries (Table 12.4).

Table 12.3 shows that the long-run ERM-wide demand function for M3 becomes partly unstable and that the equation is not co-integrated only in the case in which Germany is the excluded country (regr. 8). The long-run demand for M1 continues to be stable and the relationship to co-integrate irrespective

TABLE 12.3. *ERM countries excluding Germany, France, and Italy, co-integrating equation* (EMS period 1972(2)–1989(2))

	M1[c]	M3[c]	M1[d]	M3[d]	M1[e]	M3[e]
Regression	(7)	(8)	(9)	(10)	(11)	(12)
Explanatory variables:						
Constant	3.55(4.66)	2.29(5.77)	−3.68(−4.15)	−1.26(−3.98)	−2.29(−3.09)	−4.32(−12.73)
LY	0.51(4.71)	0.81(14.37)	1.53(12.22)	1.31(29.04)	1.31(12.60)	1.75(36.60)
RS	−1.33(−4.63)	−0.99(−6.64)	−1.31(−4.18)	−0.79(−7.02)	−1.21(−4.81)	−0.61(−5.27)
dPPP	−0.13(−3.54)	−0.11(−5.63)	−0.14(−4.52)	−0.09(−8.12)	−0.14(−5.56)	−0.07(−5.99)
R^2	0.867	0.967	0.944	0.988	0.945	0.99
SER	0.028	0.015	0.029	0.010	0.023	0.010
DW	2.59	0.65	2.85	1.28	3.08	1.55
DF(a)	−8.09**	−2.48	−8.73**	−3.99**	−10.34**	−4.9**
ADF(a)	−3.37*	—	−4.56**	−4.07**	−2.98*	—
Joint instability test(b)	0.39	1.96**	0.35	1.03	0.28	0.94

a * null hypothesis of a unit root rejected at the 5% significance level.
** null hypothesis rejected at the 1% significance level.
b ** unstable at the 1% significance level.
c Excluding Germany
d Excluding France
e Excluding Italy

Note: *t*-statistics in parentheses.

to the excluded country. This partly contradicts the quite surprising result obtained by Artis *et al.* (1992), who conclude that the exclusion of the French demand for M1 and M2 causes the greatest problems with the ERM-wide money-demand functions.[1]

The dynamic equations for the ERM-wide money stocks excluding in turn each of the three largest countries do in part confirm the fact that the exclusion of Germany causes the biggest problems to the residuals of the function. The results are presented in Table 12.4. The only change in specification with respect to the previous section is the addition of the first difference of the forward discount of the currencies in the ERM-wide aggregate with respect to the excluded ERM currency (DFD). Without Germany, the ERM-wide demand for M1 has autocorrelated residuals. The fit (measured by the *R2*) worsens considerably (by between 7 and 18 per cent) depending on which country one excludes. The change in the forward discount has the right sign in all but one case but is generally not statistically significant.

3. INDIVIDUAL COUNTRY'S MONEY DEMANDS: GERMANY, FRANCE, AND ITALY

Looking at the long-run demand functions the results are roughly similar for France and Germany (Table 12.5). For the aggregate M1 both relationships are co-integrated at the 1 per cent per level (D–F test) and jointly stable. For the aggregate M3 they are co-integrated only at the 5 per cent level and do not pass the joint stability test. The long-run income elasticities are much higher for Germany than for France. The coefficient of the dollar substitution term is particularly high for German M1. For Italy there is evidence of money illusion in the long run, as a 1 per cent increase in the price level tends to cause only a 0.78 per cent increase in the nominal money demand. *LP* is the log of the price level—see regr. (23) and (24).

However, taking into account the presence of money illusion, both relationships are co-integrated and pass the joint stability test. The coefficient of the dollar substitution term is either close to zero or it has the wrong sign, probably reflecting the tighter degree of Italian capital controls and the less developed Italian financial markets during the sample period.

Table 12.6 contains the ECM estimates of the real demands for M1 and M3 for Germany and Italy. Results for France are not shown since we were unable to estimate satisfactory dynamic versions of the demand functions for this country. By far the most satisfactory regression is the one for M1 for Germany (regr. 25). The residuals are extremely well behaved, the null hypothesis of

[1] The difference between our and Artis's results may be due to the different sample period, the different weights used for aggregation, the different definition of broad money, and different variables used (we use the short-term rate while they use the long-term one; we use the deviation of the exchange rate from PPP, while they use the exchange rate itself).

TABLE 12.4. *ERM countries, excluding Germany, France, and Italy, EC-model (EMS period)*

	M1[a]	M3[a]	M1[b]	M3[b]	M1[c]	M3[c]
Regression	(13)	(14)	(15)	(16)	(17)	(18)
Explanatory variables:						
Constant	1.57(4.14)	0.29(1.45)	−1.01(−2.73)	−0.08(−0.54)	−0.70(−2.07)	−0.90(−2.50)
DRS	−0.43(−2.11)	−0.11(−0.86)	−1.10(−5.26)	−0.65(−4.71)	−0.53(−2.59)	−0.35(−2.78)
DDLP	—	—	—	—	−1.32(−2.55)	—
DFD	0.08(1.09)	−0.02(−0.38)	−0.07(−1.27)	−0.05(−1.54)	−0.14(−2.19)	−0.004(−0.10)
LMP–1	−0.43(−4.78)	−0.19(−3.24)	0.43(−4.53)	−0.24(−3.05)	−0.47(−4.12)	−0.21(−2.50)
LY–1	0.22(4.12)	0.19(3.73)	0.60(−4.17)	0.28(2.88)	0.57(3.86)	0.37(2.58)
RS–1	−0.83(−5.97)	−0.40(−4.97)	−1.03(−6.66)	−0.47(−5.46)	−0.94(−5.48)	−0.34(−4.09)
dPPP–1	−0.02(−1.49)	0.0007(0.08)	−0.05(−3.05)	−0.02(−2.31)	−0.05(−2.50)	−0.02(−1.62)
R^2	0.977	0.782	0.984	0.759	0.970	0.678
SER	0.008	0.005	0.007	0.004	0.008	0.005
DW	2.53	2.11	1.93	1.94	1.94	2.74
AR-CHI2(3)	11.38	7.00	7.58	1.00	0.68	8.26
AR-F	3.46(0.03)*	1.99(0.14)	2.04(0.13)	0.24(0.87)	0.14(0.93)	2.44(0.08)
ARCH-CHI2	3.13	2.59	3.59	1.02	0.28	1.53
ARCH-F	0.72(0.55)	0.63(0.60)	0.83(0.49)	0.24(0.87)	0.06(0.98)	0.37(0.78)
N-CHI2(2)	1.15	0.96	0.02	0.28	0.11	1.31
RESET-F	0.63(0.43)	3.05(0.09)	0.008(0.93)	0.02(0.89)	0.28(0.60)	0.58(0.45)

[a] Excluding Germany
[b] Excluding France
[c] Excluding Italy

Notes: The following dummy variables have been added: in regr. (13), (15) and (17) D84 (2); in regr. (14), (16) and (18) D80 (1) and D80 (2) (see also Table 12.2); One asterisk indicates rejection of the null hypothesis at the 5% level, two at the 1% level. *t*- statistics or probability of rejection of the null hypothesis when the latter is true, in parentheses.

TABLE 12.5. *Money demand functions for Germany, France, and Italy, co-integrating equations* (EMS period, 1979(2)–1989(2))

	Germany		France		Italy	
	M1	M3	M1	M3	M1	M3
Regression	(19)	(20)	(21)	(22)	(23)	(24)
Explanatory variables:						
Constant	6.81(8.62)	–4.35(–7.51)	4.92(6.54)	–1.22(–3.04)	–0.92(0.26)	–4.71(–3.62)
LY	2.05(16.05)	1.83(19.60)	0.33(3.13)	1.17(21.12)	1.11(3.96)	0.94(8.88)
LP	—	—	—	—	–0.22(–4.87)	–0.22(–10.64)
RS	–0.92(–3.17)	–0.67(–3.15)	–1.11(–4.50)	–0.91(–6.90)	–1.27(–3.78)	–1.47(–15.24)
dPPP	–0.24(–7.19)	–0.08(–3.09)	–0.07(–2.09)	–0.07(–4.28)	—	0.06(2.45)
R^2	0.95	0.96	0.73	0.97	0.72	0.97
SER	0.031	0.023	0.030	0.016	0.042	0.011
DW	2.48	0.74	2.25	0.87	2.43	1.35
DF	–7.27**	–3.62*	–6.55**	–3.18*	–7.28**	–4.20**
ADF	–2.92	–3.12*	–3.27*	—	–3.93**	–3.95**
Joint instab. test	0.76	2.73**	0.66	1.81*	0.31	1.24

Note: One asterisk indicates rejection of the null hypothesis at the 5% level, two at the 1% level; *t*-statistics in parentheses.

TABLE 12.6. *Money demand functions for Germany and Italy, EC-model* (EMS period: 1979(2)–1989(2))

	Germany		Italy	
	M1	M3	M1	M3
Regression	(25)	(26)	(27)	(28)
Explanatory variables:				
Constant	−3.62(−6.06)	−1.47(−2.95)	1.97(1.93)	−0.95(−0.79)
DLY	0.82(5.03)	0.38(2.40)	—	—
DRS	−1.38(−5.29)	−0.64(−2.41)	−0.53(−2.06)	−0.93(−5.55)
DRS–1	—	−0.59(−2.59)	—	—
DDLP–2	—	—	−0.67(−2.03)	—
DDLP–3	—	—	−0.91(−2.86)	—
FD	−0.17(−1.95)	−0.05(−0.62)	—	—
FD–4	—	—	−0.14(−1.39)	—
LMP–1	−0.48(−5.81)	−0.25(−3.02)	−0.60(−3.92)	−0.54(−4.40)
LY–1	1.05(6.20)	0.53(3.12)	0.48(2.59)	0.38(2.67)
RS–1	−0.83(−7.26)	−0.27(−2.79)	−1.07(−4.91)	−1.05(−5.48)
dPPP–1	−0.14(−6.09)	−0.03(−2.44)	—	0.04(2.01)
LP–1	—	—	−0.10(−2.63)	−0.09(−2.84)
R^2	0.979	0.502	0.980	0.730
SER	0.009	0.008	0.011	0.008
DW	1.98	2.09	1.80	2.02
AR-CHI2(3)	0.85	2.70	3.30	2.35
AR-F	0.18(0.91)	0.68(0.57)	0.76(0.53)	0.63(0.60)
ARCH-CHI2(3)	1.19	2.57	3.72	4.51
ARCH-F	0.25(0.86)	0.63(0.60)	0.83(0.49)	1.26(0.30)
N-CHI2(2)	0.98	1.20	0.70	1.57
RESET-F	0.23(0.64)	6.44(0.02)*	0.77(0.39)	3.74(0.06)

Notes: The following dummy variable has been added: D87(4) in regr.(25); one asterisk indicates rejection of the null hypothesis at the 5% level, two at the 1% level; *t*- statistics or probability of rejection of the null hypothesis when the latter is true in parentheses.

misspecification of the functional form (Reset-*F* test) is strongly rejected, the explanatory power very high and the parameters are all very precisely estimated except for the forward discount with respect to other ERM currencies (*FD*), measuring intra-European currency substitution. For German M3 the results are not equally satisfactory: the null hypothesis of no functional form misspecification cannot be rejected at the 5 per cent confidence level (Reset-*F* test), the hypothesis that the residuals are not well behaved can be rejected, but at a much lower confidence level than for M1 and the parameters less precisely estimated.

For Italy, apart from the problem of long-run money illusion already mentioned in connection with the co-integrating equation (Table 12.5), there is some evidence of functional form misspecification for M3 in equation (28); in addition both for M1 and M3 the residuals are less well behaved than for German M1.

We shall see in the next section that this relative robustness of the demand function for German M1 extends beyond 1989(2).

4. THE STABILITY OF THE DEMAND FOR MONEY IN GERMANY BEFORE AND AFTER THE FALL OF THE BERLIN WALL

We have seen in the previous section that the dynamic demand function for real M1 in Germany was relatively well behaved during the EMS period, 1979(2)–1989(2), while we cannot say the same thing for real M3. In this section we first look at the stability of the two dynamic demand equations for M1 and M3 during the EMS period presented in Table 12.6 when we remove the currency substitution terms; then we extend the estimation beyond 1989(2) to analyse whether the fall of the Berlin Wall and German economic and monetary union had significant consequences for the stability of the German demand for money functions.

Appendix 3 completes the analysis by looking at the demand function for German extended M3, which includes cross-border deposits held by German residents and excludes residents' holdings of foreign currencies with domestic banks.

We first present in Table 12.7 the Wald tests carried out for the exclusion of each currency-substitution term and for the exclusion of the pair of them.

The first column suggests that the hypothesis of a zero restriction on the coefficient of the DM–US dollar substitution term in the demand function for real M1 is rejected at the 1 per cent confidence level. The same is true for the hypothesis of a zero restriction on the coefficients of both currency substitution terms. The hypothesis of a zero restriction on the coefficient of the intra-ERM currency substitution term is rejected only at the 10 per cent confidence level. As to the real demand for M3 the hypothesis of a zero restriction on the coefficient of the DM–US dollar substitution term is rejected at the 5 per cent level, and the joint restriction is rejected at the 10 per cent level. These results indicate that currency substitution cannot be neglected in the demand for

TABLE 12.7. *Germany: Wald tests for exclusion of currency substitution terms* (see regr.(25) and (26) of Table 12.6, sample period 1979(2)–1989(2))

	M1	M3	Ext. M3
Regression	(25)	(26)	(26-Ext.)
Zero restriction on: intra-ERM curr. subst. (*FD*)	$F(1,29) = 3.81$ (0.06)	$F(1,32) = 0.39$ (0.54)	$F(1,32) = 0.87$ (0.36)
Zero restriction on: US $ curr. subst. (*dPPP*-1)	$F(1,29) = 37.03$ (0.00)**	$F(1,32) = 5.97$ (0.02)*	$F(1,32) = 7.47$ (0.01)**
Zero restriction on: *FD* and *dPPP*-1	$F(2,29) = 19.55$ (0.00)**	$F(2,32) = 2.99$ (0.06)	$F(2,32) = 3.85$ (0.03)*

* rejection of the null hypothesis at the 5% confidence level;
** rejection of the null hypothesis of the 1% confidence level.
Probability of rejection of the null hypothesis when the latter is true, in parentheses;

Germany money function, especially as far as M1 is concerned. Of the two forms of substitution, the one with the US dollar is much more relevant.

Table 12.8 contains the dynamic demand functions for real M1 and real M3 in which the currency substitution terms have been eliminated in two successive steps: first the less important intra-ERM one, then the more important DM–dollar term. Regr.(25) and (26) of Table 12.6 have been reported here in order to faciliate the comparison of coefficients, *t*-statistics, and standard tests on the residuals.

Taking the demand for real M1 first, the elimination of the intra-ERM currency substitution term causes little change in the coefficients and *t*-statistics (regr. 29). However, the normality test on the residuals, *N-CHI2(2)*, indicates that the hypothesis that they are not normally distributed cannot be rejected at the 10 per cent confidence level and comes close to being rejected at the 5 per cent confidence level (the critical value of the *CHI2(2)* at the 10 per cent confidence level is 4.61 and at the 5 per cent confidence level it is 5.99). When we remove the DM–US dollar currency substitution term the error-correction model breaks down, as all variables except the interest rate become insignificantly different from zero.

As to the real demand for M3, it should be recalled that there was already some evidence of functional form misspecification when all currency substitution terms were included. When we remove the intra-ERM currency substit tion term the confidence level with which the hypothesis of functional form misspecification increases from 98 to 99.4 per cent (regr. (31)) and when both terms are excluded all parameters lose most of their significance, and the error-correction model almost breaks down. In fact comparing the results of Table 12.8 with those of Section 2 and 3 it seems safe to say that currency substitution with the US dollar is very important for Germany and more important than for France and Italy, as has to be expected for a reserve currency country with developed and open financial markets. In addition it seems safe to say that the importance of this term in the ERM-wide money-demand functions of Section 1 comes most of all from its importance in the German demand function.

The next step consists in extending the estimation of the dynamic EC-model of the demand function for real M1 and M3, (regr.(25) and (26)) to 1992(3), the last available observation in our data bank at the time of writing. A problem in updating the series beyond the third quarter of 1992 arises because the series for the East of Germany become available with substantially greater delays than for the West of the country. Until the second quarter of 1990 our data refer to the West of Germany, from the third quarter of 1990 onwards to the whole of Germany. Jumps in the series occurred for nominal money, real GDP, and prices. The jump in M1 anticipated the one in M3 by about six months. In 1990 M1 increased by about 27 per cent; in the twelve months ending in June 1991 M1 increased by about 12 per cent and M3 by about 20 per cent. Real GDP increased by 11 per cent in the third quarter of 1990 with respect to the second quarter of the same year mostly owing to the addition of East German

TABLE 12.8. *Germany: EC-model with and without currency substitution terms* (EMS period)

	M1	M1	M1	M3	M3	M3
Regression	(25)	(29)	(30)	(26)	(31)	(32)
Explanatory variables:						
Constant	−3.62(−6.06)	−3.29(−5.49)	−0.59(−1.14)	−1.47(−2.95)	−1.33(−3.01)	−0.70(−1.85)
DLY	0.82(5.03)	0.79(4.68)	0.39(1.80)	0.38(2.40)	0.36(2.34)	0.22(1.45)
DRS	−1.38(−5.29)	−1.62(−6.83)	−1.53(−4.54)	−0.64(−2.41)	−0.70(−2.81)	−0.39(−1.72)
DRS–1	—	—	—	−0.59(−2.59)	−0.59(−2.61)	−0.40(−1.78)
FD	−0.17(−1.95)	—	—	−0.05(−0.62)	—	—
LMP–1	−0.48(−5.81)	−0.47(−5.49)	−0.04(−0.71)	−0.25(−3.02)	−0.24(−2.98)	−0.10(−1.71)
LY–1	1.05(6.20)	0.99(5.69)	0.15(1.14)	0.53(3.12)	0.49(3.11)	0.23(1.89)
RS–1	−0.83(−7.26)	−0.81(−6.78)	−0.38(−2.90)	−0.27(−2.79)	−0.25(−2.75)	−0.16(−1.83)
dPPP–1	−0.14(−6.09)	−0.14(−5.68)	—	−0.03(−2.44)	−0.03(−2.39)	—
D 87(4)	−0.03(−2.79)	−0.03(−2.58)	−0.02(−1.62)	—	—	—
R^2	0.979	0.976	0.950	0.502	0.496	0.409
SER	0.009	0.009	0.013	0.008	0.008	0.008
DW	1.98	2.01	1.75	2.09	2.15	1.99
AR-CHI2(3)	0.85	0.79	3.36	2.70	3.35	3.20
AR-F	0.18(0.91)	0.18(0.91)	0.83(0.49)	0.68(0.67)	0.89(0.45)	0.88(0.46)
ARCH-CHI2	1.19	1.63	2.08	2.57	5.01	6.70
ARCH-F	0.25(0.86)	0.35(0.78)	0.48(0.70)	0.63(0.60)	1.37(0.27)	2.00(0.14)
N-CHI2(2)	0.98	5.38	0.17	1.20	1.21	1.16
RESET-F	0.23(0.64)	0.65(0.43)	2.00(0.17)	6.44(0.02)*	8.71(0.006)**	6.16(0.02)*

Notes: One asterisk indicates rejection of the null hypothesis at the 5% level, two at the 1% level; *t*-statistics or probability of rejection of the null hypothesis when the latter is true, in parentheses.

output to the West German one (West German GDP increased by only 1.7 per cent in the quarter). The price level for the whole of Germany fell by about 7 per cent in the third quarter of 1990 with respect to the previous quarter (not annualized), as the East German price level was substantially lower than in the West. It should be pointed out, however, that this figure is a crude estimate whose validity depends largely on the accuracy of the comparison of pre-unification purchasing power of the two currencies reported by Sinn and Sinn (1991). According to our calculations, it took almost two years for the overall German price level to return to the pre-unification West German level of the second quarter of 1990. In 1990 the nominal M1 to nominal GDP ratio increased by 19 percentage points and in the 12 months from June 1990 to June 1991 the M3 to GDP ratio increased by 12 percentage points. These numbers understimate the excess supply of money created in the aftermath of the economic and monetary union, which entered into force on 1 July 1990, since the excess money creation must have influenced prices and GDP positively during the twelve months.

Fig. 12.1 shows the real stock of M3. A large increase occurred in real M3 during 1990 and the first semester of 1991.

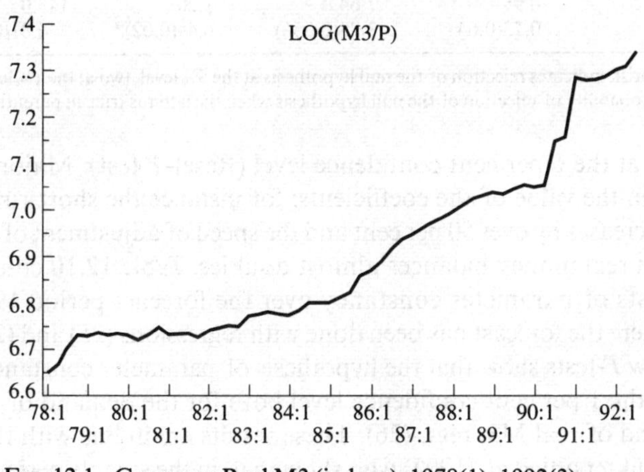

FIG. 12.1. Germany: Real M3 (in logs), 1978(1)–1992(3)

Table 12.9 shows the dynamic real demand for money functions estimated up to the third quarter of 1992. The specification is the one of Tables 12.6 and 12.8 (including the currency substitution terms). Regressions (25) and (26) of Table 12.6 are reproduced in Table 12.9 to make the comparison in the coefficients and in the standard diagnostic tests easier in the two estimation periods.

Overall the EC model of the demand for real M1 resists much better to the shock of unification than the EC model of the demand for real M3. As to the demand equation for real M1 (regr. (33)), the hypothesis that the residuals are not normally distributed cannot be rejected at the 2.5 per cent confidence level, *N-CHI2(2)*, and the hypothesis of no functional form misspecification cannot

TABLE 12.9. *Germany: EC-model for M1 and M3 estimated up to 1992(3)*

	M1 1979(2)–1989(2)	M1 1979(2)–1992(3)	M3 1979(2)–1989(2)	M3 1979(2)–1992(3)
Regression	(25)	(33)	(26)	(34)
Explanatory variables:				
Constant	−3.62(−6.06)	−5.75(−6.83)	−1.47(−2.95)	−1.69(−4.83)
DLY	0.82(5.03)	1.34(8.21)	0.38(2.40)	0.56(4.12)
DRS	−1.38(−5.29)	−1.26(−2.59)	−0.64(−2.41)	−0.58(−1.16)
DRS–1	—	—	−0.59(−2.59)	−0.73(−1.75)
FD	−0.17(−1.95)	−0.14(−0.85)	−0.05(−0.62)	−0.13(−0.83)
LMP–1	−0.48(−5.81)	−0.82(−6.86)	−0.25(−3.02)	−0.37(−4.70)
LY–1	1.05(6.20)	1.71(6.86)	0.53(3.12)	0.69(5.12)
RS–1	−0.83(−7.26)	−1.15(−6.83)	−0.27(−2.79)	−0.44(−3.06)
dPPP–1	−0.14(−6.09)	−0.22(−6.28)	−0.03(−2.44)	−0.05(−2.34)
D 87 (4)	−0.03(−2.79)	−0.03(−1.82)	—	—
R^2	0.979	0.933	0.502	0.535
SER	0.009	0.017	0.008	0.016
DW	1.98	1.85	2.09	2.69
AR-CHI2	0.85	2.10	2.70	11.20
AR-F	0.18(0.91)	0.39(0.82)	0.68(0.57)	2.68(0.045)*
ARCH-CHI2	1.19	5.95	2.57	9.76
ARCH-F	0.25(0.86)	1.15(0.35)	0.63(0.60)	2.24(0.083)
N-CHI2	0.98	7.64	1.20	143.05
RESET-F	0.23(0.64)	3.88(0.056)	6.44(0.02)*	4.81(0.034)*

Notes: One asterisk indicates rejection of the null hypothesis at the 5% level, two at the 1% level; *t*-statistics or probability of rejection of the null hypothesis when the latter is true, in parentheses.

be rejected at the 6 per cent confidence level (Reset-*F* test). Major changes occur also in the value of the coefficients; for instance the short-run income elasticity increases by over 50 per cent and the speed of adjustment of actual to equilibrium real money balances almost doubles. Table 12.10 contains the Chow *F*-tests of parameter constancy over the forecast period 1989(3) to 1992(3), where the forecast has been done with regressions (25) and (26).

The Chow *F*-tests show that the hypothesis of parameter constancy can be rejected at the 1 per cent confidence level both for the demand of real M1, regr.(25), and of real M3, regr. (26). These results are in line with those presented by Lüktepohl *et al.* (1994) who show that, in the sample period 1960(1) to 1990(4), the coefficients of the demand function for real M1 are unstable in Germany.

As to the real demand for M3 (regr. 34), major problems arise with the behaviour of the residuals. They are strongly autocorrelated, heteroscedastic, and not normally distributed. The hypothesis of no functional-form misspecification

TABLE 12.10. *Chow F-tests of parameter constancy over 1989(3) to 1992(3)*

Definition of money	M1	M3
Forecast done with regression number	(25)	(26)
Chow *F*-test	$F(13.29) = 10.07$**	$F(13.32) = 11.91$**

** indicates that the hypothesis of parameter constancy is rejected at the 1% confidence level.

cannot be rejected at the 5 per cent confidence level. Again there is large instability in the parameters (see for instance the short-run income elasticity and the speed of adjustment). The hypothesis of parameter constancy is strongly rejected (see Table 12.10). Fig. 12.2 shows the fitted and actual values from regr. (26). Fig. 12.3 shows the one-step out of sample forecast performed with regr. (26). It suggests that monetary policy turned to be very restrictive in 1991 and 1992, as indicated by the fact that during this period the model systematically overpredicts the actual money stock.

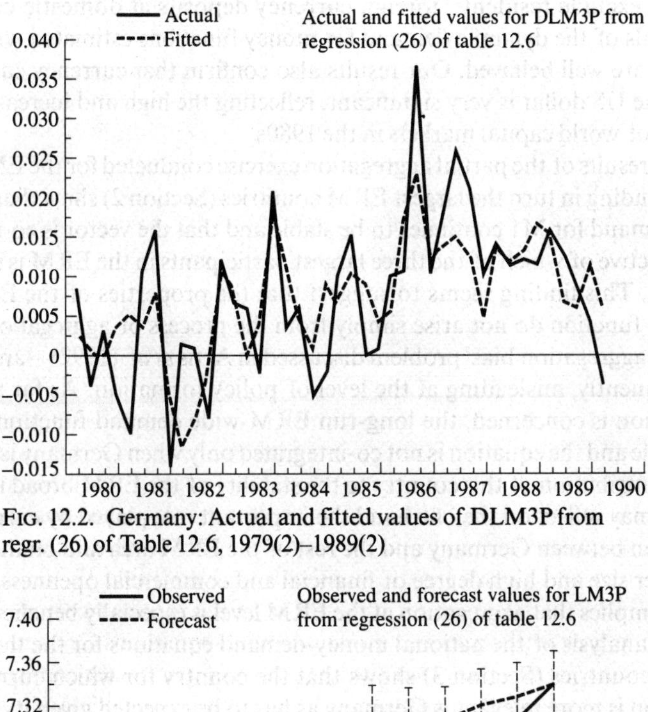

FIG. 12.2. Germany: Actual and fitted values of DLM3P from regr. (26) of Table 12.6, 1979(2)–1989(2)

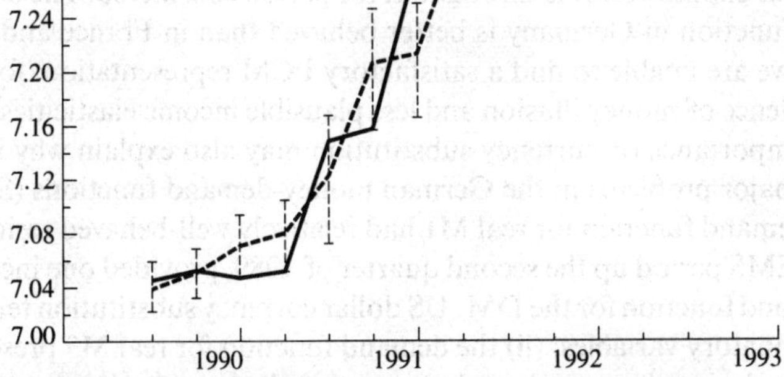

FIG. 12.3. Germany: Forecast vs observed values of LM3P. (Estimation period: 1979(2)–1992(3))

5. CONCLUSIONS

In line with the most recent literature on the ERM-wide real demand for money function, we found that during the EMS period prior to the fall of the Berlin Wall the demand for money behaved better at the European level than at the individual country level (Sections 1–3). This holds not only for the M1 and M3 definitions but also for the M3 extended aggregate; the latter is defined to include residents' holdings of national currency deposits at banks located abroad and to exclude residents' foreign currency deposits at domestic banks. The residuals of the dynamic demand for money functions estimated with the EC model are well behaved. Our results also confirm that currency substitution with the US dollar is very significant, reflecting the high and increasing integration of world capital markets in the 1980s.

The results of the partial aggregation exercise conducted for the EMS period by excluding in turn the largest ERM countries (Section 2) show that the long-run demand for M1 continues to be stable and that the vector is co-integrated irrespective of which of the three largest participants in the ERM is in turn excluded. This finding seems to suggest that the properties of the ERM-wide money function do not arise simply from the process of aggregation—the so called 'aggregation bias' problem discussed in Artis *et al.* (1992)—and it is not, consequently, misleading at the level of policy formation. As far as the M3 definition is concerned, the long-run ERM-wide demand function becomes unstable and the equation is not co-integrated only when Germany is excluded. The contribution of this country to the stability of the ERM broad money demand may reflect on the one hand the important role played by currency substitution between Germany and the rest of the ERM area and on the other by its sheer size and high degree of financial and commercial openness. Also this result implies that aggregation at the ERM level is especially beneficial.

The analysis of the national money-demand equations for the three largest ERM countries (Section 3) shows that the country for which currency substitution is more relevant is Germany as has to be expected given its role of reserve country and its more developed financial markets also owing to the absence of capital controls throughout the period considered. The demand for money function in Germany is better behaved than in France and Italy: for France we are unable to find a satisfactory ECM representation, for Italy we find evidence of money illusion and less plausible income elasticities.

The importance of currency substitution may also explain why its neglect causes major problems in the German money-demand functions (Section 4): (i) the demand function for real M1 had relatively well-behaved residuals during the EMS period up the second quarter of 1989, provided one includes into the demand function for the DM–US dollar currency substitution term among the explanatory variables; (ii) the demand function for real M3 presents some problems during the period, in the sense that the hypothesis of no functional form misspecification cannot be rejected at the 5 per cent confidence level, even if we include the currency substitution terms; if the latter are removed, the problems increase substantially. These outurns suggest that the presence of currency substitution (both with the US dollar and with other ERM currencies) invalidates the theoretical framework of Bundesbank monetary policy, namely monetary targeting based on M3, and provides some support for the transfer of the legitimacy of such targeting to an ERM aggregate level.

After the shock caused by the fall of the Berlin Wall and the unification, the demand function for real M3 becomes highly unstable, while the demand for real M1 resists these shocks somewhat more effectively. In a more recent study focusing only on the German demand for money function we update the estimates to the fourth quarter of 1993, we introduce the own rate of return on M3 and the long-term interest rate among the explanatory variables; we also introduce dummies for the reunification shock and we try with the German–US interest rate differential as an alternative variable reflecting currency substitution (Boero and Tullio, 1996). The results found in the present chapter concerning the instability of the German demand for money function are confirmed. From both studies we conclude that monetary policy was much too expansionary during 1990, while in 1991 and 1992 the Bundesbank tried to absorb the initial monetary overhang, thus tilting monetary policy towards a too restrictive stance. Bundesbank monetary policy contributed to the September 1992 breakdown of the ERM.

If our results about the area-wide money-demand function and about the importance of intra-European currency substitution are correct, it follows that once the ripples caused by German unification are over and provided there is the political will to continue the process towards European monetary union, it will make a lot of sense to base European interest rate policy on an ERM-wide aggregate rather than on German M3 as at present.

APPENDIX 1.

Demand Function for EMS-Wide extended M3

In this Appendix we estimate a dynamic demand function for ERM-wide extended M3 using the error-correction model. The explanatory variables are exactly the same as for regr. 6 of Table 12.2 relating to the ECM estimate of ERM-wide M3 with which we want to compare it. The sample period is 1979(2) to 1989(2). Extended M3, real GDP, the rate of interest, and the deviation from PPP of the ERM currencies with the US dollar are co-integrated (results not shown to save space).

The traditional definition of M3 typically includes residents' holdings of national and foreign currency deposits at domestically located banks (see Giucca and Levy, 1992). On grounds of logical consistency, an extended monetary aggregate based on a national money concept should include residents' and non-residents' worldwide holdings in national currency. However, non-residents' holdings of national money can be ignored because they are less influenced by national fundamentals. Hence, in order to obtain an extended measure of M3 comprising only ERM currency deposits we added to the ERM-wide M3 traditional money stock residents' holdings of national currency deposits at banks located abroad and subtracting foreign currency deposits of domestic residents at domestic banks.

Table A1.1 shows the estimated EC equation. We reproduce regr. 6 from Table 12.2 to facilitate the comparison. The dynamic demand function for extended M3 is better behaved than for M3. The residuals are not heteroscedastic and the coefficient of the explanatory variables are all more precisely estimated except the one of the acceleration of inflation. It is worth noting that the coefficient of the currency substitution term is about 25 per cent larger in absolute value and statistically significantly different from the one in regr. (6). This may be explained by the fact that extended M3 only contains ERM currency and no dollar deposits, and by the fact that deposits located at foreign banks are more rapidly transformed into dollar deposits and at lower transaction costs.

The speed of adjustment of extended M3 is slightly higher, but not significantly so. Also the long-run income elasticity is fractionally higher.

TABLE A1.1. *ERM countries, EC-model for extended M3* (EMS period 1979(2)–1989(2))

	M3	Ext-M3
Regression	(6)	(6-Ext)
Explanatory variables:		
Constant	–0.20(–1.74)	–0.26(–2.12)
DRS	–0.26(–2.92)	–0.30(–3.18)
DDLP	–0.39(–1.99)	–0.38(–1.82)
LMP–1	–0.25(–3.86)	–0.28(–4.36)
LY–1	0.31(3.94)	0.36(4.42)
RS–1	–0.40(–6.68)	–0.46(–7.15)
dDPPP–1	–0.015(–2.02)	–0.021(–2.42)
R^2	0.839	0.840
SER	0.0035	0.0037
DW	2.28	2.09
AR-CHI2(3)	1.23	0.66
AR-F(3.29)	0.30(0.83)	0.16(0.92)
ARCH-CHI2(3)	7.26	0.22
ARCH-F(3.26)	2.05(0.13)	0.05(0.99)
N-CHI2(2)	1.57	1.10
RESET-F(1.31)	0.88(0.35)	0.03(0.87)

Note: D80(1) and D80(2) have been added in regr. (6) and (6-Ext); *t*-statistics or probability of rejection of the null hypothesis when the latter is true, in parentheses.

APPENDIX 2.

Two-Step Estimation of Dynamic EC-Model of ERM-Wide Money Demand: Comparison with One-Step Estimation of Section 1

In Table A2.1 we present estimates of the EC model performed in two stages: by estimating first the co-integrating equation (see Table 12.1) and then substituting the residuals into the EC formulation. This is done for M1 in regression (5-2ST) and for M3 in regr. (6-2ST). '2ST' stands for '2 stages' and the numbers of the regressions are the same as those in Table 12.2 with which they have to be compared.

The sample period is the EMS period up to 1989(2). We also reproduce from Table 12.2 all the statistics and diagnostic tests of regrs. (5) and (6) to facilitate the comparison. The standard errors of the regressions estimated by two stages are 50 per cent higher for M1 and almost double for M3. In addition the residuals of the regressions estimated in two stages are highly autocorrelated as shown both by the *CHI2* and the *F* tests while the hypothesis of no autocorrelation could be rejected for the one-stage estimates.

As an additional piece of evidence we report the results of a Wald test for the linear restriction that all coefficients of the EC terms in regrs. (5) and (6) are the same. The

TABLE A2.1. *Two step estimation of EC-model of ERM-wide money demand* EMS period 1979(2)–(1989(2))

	M1	M1	M3	M3
Regression	(5–2ST)	(5)	(6–2ST)	(6)
Explanatory variables:				
Constant	0.06(14.93)		0.007(7.26)	
DLRS	–0.48(–2.29)		–0.15(–1.11)	
DDLP	–0.53(–0.90)		–0.12(–0.35)	
RES–1	–0.49(–3.49)		–0.34(–2.88)	
*D*84(2)	–0.01(–1.18)		—	
*D*80(1)	—		–0.02(–2.61)	
*D*80(2)	—		–0.02(–3.02)	
R^2	0.967	0.987	0.490	0.839
SER	0.0090	0.0060	0.0060	0.0035
DW	0.848	2.10	0.80	2.28
AR-CHI2(3)	17.93	4.86	21.51	1.23
AR-F	7.85(0.0006)**	1.21(0.33)	12.02(0.00)**	0.30(0.83)
ARCH-CHI2	1.73	5.31	3.28	7.26
ARCH-F	0.42(0.74)	1.30(0.30)	0.91(0.45)	2.05(0.13)
N-CHI2(2)	1.12	0.02	1.36	1.57
RESET-F	0.16(0.69)	0.13(0.72)	2.05(0.16)	0.88(0.35)

Notes: RES stands for the residuals from the cointegrating regression; *t*-statistics or probability of rejection of the null hypothesis when the latter is true, in parentheses.

TABLE A2.2. *Wald F-test for linear restriction on coefficients of EC-variables in regr. (5) and (6) of Table 12.2*

Regression	(5)	(6)
Definition of money	M1	M3
F-tests	*F*(4,30) = 12.64	*F*(4,32) = 19.67
	(0.00)**	(0.00)**

** indicates rejection of the null hypothesis at the 1% confidence level.

Note: Probability of rejecting the null hypothesis that all coefficients of the EC-variables are the same, when the hypothesis is true

restriction is strongly rejected at the 1 per cent significance level for both definitions of money (Table A2.2).

APPENDIX 3.

Germany: Estimation of Long-Run and Dynamic EC-Model of Demand for Extended M3

In this Appendix we replicate the estimates of the German real demand for M3 performed in Section 4 for the extended M3 aggregate. We are particularly interested in comparing the performance of the real demand function for this extended aggregate with the real demand function for M3 both before and after the fall of the Berlin Wall and the economic and monetary union of 1 July 1990. We are also interested in whether the currency substitution terms are as relevant for extended M3 as they are for M3 and M1.

Extended M3 started growing faster than M3 in the mid-1980s, in line with the sustained growth observed for residents' holding of deposits with banks located abroad (see Giucca and Levy, 1992). We have defined extended M3 by adding to the traditional definition of M3 residents' holdings of domestic currency deposits at banks located abroad and subtracting foreign currency deposits of domestic residents at domestic banks.

The co-integrating equation is given in Table A3.1 where also the co-integrating equation for the real demand for M3 is reproduced from Table 12.5 of Section 3 to facilitate the comparison. The relationship is co-integrated at the 5 per cent significance level as for M3. In addition, as has to be expected from the behaviour of extended M3 with respect to M3, the long-run income elasticity is significantly larger (20 per cent). Also the elasticity of the real demand for extended M3 with respect to the DM–US dollar substitution term is larger than for M3 (25 per cent). This is probably explained by the

TABLE A3.1. *Germany: money demand functions for M3 and extended M3 aggregate* (1979(2)–1989(2))

	M3	Ext. M3
Regression	(20)	(20-Ext.)
Explanatory variables:		
Constant	–4.35(–7.51)	–6.49(–9.13)
LY	1.83(19.60)	2.18(19.05)
RS	–0.67(–3.15)	–0.66(–2.55)
dPPP	–0.08(–3.09)	–0.10(–3.28)
R^2	0.96	0.96
SER	0.023	0.028
DW	0.74	0.72
DF	–3.62*	–3.54*
ADF	–3.12*	–3.35*
Joint instability test	2.73**	2.69**

Notes: One asterisk indicates rejection of the null hypothesis at the 5% level, two at the 1% level; *t*-statistics in parentheses.

fact that extended M3 does not include foreign currency deposits of domestic residents held at domestic banks and by the fact that DM deposits of domestic residents with banks located abroad can be substituted with foreign currency deposits, if the need should arise, faster and at lower transaction costs.

Table A3.2 contains the dynamic demand function for extended M3 estimated for the periods 1979(2) to 1989(2) and 1979(2) to 1992(3), using the EC model. They have to be compared with regrs. (26) and (34) of Table 12.9, Section 4.

For the period up to 1989(2) the dynamic model for the extended M3 demand function is slightly more satisfactory than for the national aggregate M3 in terms of explanatory power of the regression and precision of the estimated parameters. However, the problem with the specification of the functional form found for M3 does not disappear. The extension of the sample period to 1992(3) leads to instability in the parameters and non-normality of the residuals, exactly as with the extension of the estimation of the dynamic model for the aggregate M3. However, for the extended M3 the residuals are not autocorrelated and much less heteroscedastic. So it seems that among the three candidates for monetary targeting M1, M3, and extended M3, the Bundesbank used in recent years the one for which the demand function was the least stable.

The out-of-sample forecast of extended M3 performed from 1989(3) to 1992(3) with regr. (26-Ext.) of Table A3.2 yields a path and differences with actual values which are very similar to the ones shown for M3 in Fig. 12.3 (the figures are not reproduced here to save space).

TABLE A3.2. *Germany: ECM model for extended M3*

	1979(2)–1989(2)	1979(2)–1992(3)
Regression	(26-Ext.)	(34-Ext.)
Explanatory variables:		
Constant	–2.11(–3.97)	–2.16(–5.00)
DLY	0.36(2.36)	0.63(4.53)
DRS	–0.50(–1.87)	–0.63(–1.24)
DRS–1	–0.76(–3.41)	–0.76(–1.79)
FD	–0.07(–0.933)	–0.11(–0.67)
LMP–1	–0.23(–3.51)	–0.33(–4.58)
LY–1	0.61(3.89)	0.72(5.02)
RS–1	–0.24(–2.65)	–0.45(–3.15)
dPPP–1	–0.04(–2:73)	–0.06(–2.52)
R^2	0.58	0.54
SER	0.008	0.017
DW	1.71	2.49
AR-CHI2	4.93	4.66
AR-F	1.32(0.29)	0.97(0.44)
ARCH-CHI2	0.55	5.62
ARCH-F	0.13(0.94)	1.17(0.34)
N-CHI2(2)	0.43	162.64
RESET-F	5.12(0.03)*	6.47(0.015)*

Notes: One asterisk indicates rejection of the null hypothesis at the 5% level, two at the 1% level; *t*-statistics or probability of rejection of the null hypothesis when the latter is true, in parentheses.

APPENDIX 4.

Data Sources

Money (M1):	*International Financial Statistics* (IFS) of the IMF: line 34
Money (M3):	National sources
Cross-border holdings (for extended definition of M3):	Data published by the BIS
Prices (Consumer Price Index, base year 1985):	IFS data bank: line 64
Real GDP (quarterly, base year 1985):	National sources for France and Italy
Real GDP (annual, base year 1985):	*OECD National Accounts* for Belgium, Denmark, Germany, Ireland, and the Netherlands.
Industrial production	IFS data bank: line 66 b or c (used for quarterly interpolation of GDP for Belgium, Denmark, Germany, Ireland, and the Netherlands).
Interest rate:	IFS data bank: line 60b (call money rates)
Spot and forward exchange rates:	IFS data bank

ERM Aggregates

National money and real GDP are converted into DM at average 1985 spot exchange rates, then aggregated.

Prices, interest rates, and the forward discount rates are weighted by GDP shares in 1985. Weights are adjusted when a country is excluded from the aggregate.

Deviations from *PPP* (*dPPP*) are defined as (*E-PPP*)/*PPP*, where *E* is the weighted exchange rate of the currencies of the ERM group of countries with respect to the US dollar and *PPP*, the purchasing power parity level, is defined as the ratio of the ERM price aggregate (base 1985) to the US consumer price index (base 1985), scaled to equal the average exchange rate with respect to the US dollar during 1985. For the other countries or groups of countries *dPPP* is defined in a similar way.

REFERENCES

Angeloni, I., and P. Giucca (1991), 'The Role of Monetary Aggregates in the Coordination of Monetary Policies in the EEC', *Quaderni di Ricerca*, LUISS University, Rome.

—— C. Cottarelli, and A. Levy (1992), 'Cross-Border Deposits and Monetary Aggregates in the Transition to EMU', *Temi di discussione*, Bank of Italy.

Artis, M. J., R. C. Bladen-Hovell, and W. Zhang (1992), 'A European Money Demand Function', mimeo, University of Manchester.

Barnett, W. A. (1980), 'Economic Monetary Aggregates: An Application of Index Number and Aggregation Theory', *Journal of Econometrics*, 14: 11–48.

Bayoumi, T., and P. Kenen (1992), 'Using an EC-Wide Monetary Aggregate in Stage Two of EMU', mimeo, Bank of England.

Bekx, P. and G. Tullio (1989), 'A Note on the European Monetary System and the Determination of the DM–Dollar Exchange Rate', *Cahiers Economiques de Bruxelles*, 123 (3rd quarter): 329–43.

Benerjee, A., J. Dolado, J. W. Galbraith, and D. F. Hendry (1993), *Co-integration, Error-correction, and the Econometric Analysis of Non-Stationary Data*, Oxford University Press, Oxford.

Boero, Gianna, and Tullio Giuseppe (1995), 'Currency Substitution and the Stability of the German Demand for Money Function before and after the Fall of the Berlin Wall', Discussion Papers of the Department of Economics, University of Brescia, repr. in Paul Mizen and Eric Pentecost (eds.), *The Macroeconomics of International Currencies: Theory, Policy, and Evidence*, Edward Elgar, Aldershot (1996).

Boughton, J. M. (1991), 'Long-Run Money Demand in Large Industrial Countries', *IMF Staff Papers*, 38 (Mar.): 1–32.

Committee of Governors (1992), *Annual Report* (July 1990–Dec. 1991).

Giucca, P., and A. Levy (1992), 'Monetary Aggregates and Monetary Policy Coordination on the Way to Economic and Monetary Union: the Role of Cross-Border Deposits', *Temi di Discussione*, Bank of Italy.

Goodhart, C. (1990), 'International Financial Linkages', *LSE Working Papers*, 21.

Kremers, J. J. M., and T. D. Lane (1990), 'Economic and Monetary Integration and the Aggregate Demand for Money in the EMS', *IMF Staff Papers*, 37 4: 777–805.

—— —— (1992), 'European Monetary Union Raises Questions about Policy Targets and Indicators', *IMF Survey*, 21 (Apr.) 27: 136–9.

Lane, T. D., and Poloz, S. S. (1992), 'Currency Substitution and Cross-Border Monetary Aggregation: Evidence from the G-7', *IMF Working Paper*, 81 (Oct.).

Lüktepohl, Helmut, Moryson Martin, and Wolters Jürgen (1994), 'Stabilitätsanalyse der bundesdeutschen Geldnachfrage anhand alternativer Ansätze zur Modellierung variierender Regressionskoeffizienten', mimeo, Humboldt-Universität of Berlin.

Monticelli, Carlo (1993), 'All the Money in Europe? An Investigation of the Economic Properties of EC-Wide Extended Monetary Aggregates', *Working Paper*, 19, BIS, Basle.

—— M. O. Strauss-Kahn (1992*a*), 'European Integration and the Demand for Broad Money', Basle. *Working Paper*, 18, BIS.

—— —— (1992*b*), 'Broad Monetary Aggregates and Money Demand in European Countries. Where do we Stand?', mimeo, BIS, Basle.

Russo, Massimo, and Tullio Giuseppe (1988), 'Monetary Policy Coordination within the EMS: Is There a Rule?', in F. Giavazzi, S. Micossi, and M. Miller (eds.), *The European Monetary System*, Cambridge University Press.

Sinn, Gerlinde, and Sinn Hans-Werner (1991), *Kaltstart: volkswirtschaftliche Aspekte der deutschen Vereinigung*, J. C. B. Mohr (Paul Siebeck), Tübingen.

Tullio, Giuseppe, Alfred Steinherr, and Herbert Buscher (1996), 'German Wage and Price Inflation before and after Unification', Ch. 1 this volume.

Van Riet, A. G. (1993), 'Studies of EC money demand: survey and assessement', *De Nederlandische Bank Quarterly Bulletin*: 63–75.

098

INDEX